THE JEWISH REVOLUTION IN BELORUSSIA

THE MODERN JEWISH EXPERIENCE

Deborah Dash Moore and Marsha L. Rozenblit, editors
Paula Hyman, founding coeditor

A Helen B. Schwartz Book

Published with the support of the Helen B. Schwartz Fund for New Scholarship in Jewish Studies of the Robert A. and Sandra B. Borns Jewish Studies Program, Indiana University

THE JEWISH REVOLUTION IN BELORUSSIA

Economy, Race, and Bolshevik Power

Andrew Sloin

Indiana University Press
Bloomington and Indianapolis

This book is a publication of

Indiana University Press
Office of Scholarly Publishing
Herman B Wells Library 350
1320 East 10th Street
Bloomington, Indiana 47405 USA

iupress.indiana.edu

© 2017 by Andrew Sloin

Manufactured in the United States of America

Library of Congress Cataloging-in-Publication Data

Names: Sloin, Andrew, author.
Title: The Jewish revolution in Belorussia : economy, race, and Bolshevik
power / Andrew Sloin.
Description: Bloomington ; Indianapolis : Indiana University Press, [2017] |
Series: The modern Jewish experience | Revised version of the author's
thesis (Ph. D., University of Chicago, Department of History, 2009). |
Includes bibliographical references and index.
Identifiers: LCCN 2016045764 (print) | LCCN 2016046922 (ebook) | ISBN
9780253024510 (cloth : alk. paper) | ISBN 9780253024664 (pbk. : alk.
paper) | ISBN 9780253024633 (e-book)
Subjects: LCSH: Jews—Belarus—History—20th century. | Jews—Belarus—Social
conditions—20th century. | Jews—Belarus—Economic conditions—20th
century. | Jewish communists—Belarus—Biography. | Nationalism and
communism—Belarus. | Belarus—Ethnic relations.
Classification: LCC DS135.B38 S59 2017 (print) | LCC DS135.B38 (ebook) | DDC
947.8/004924009041—dc23
LC record available at https://lccn.loc.gov/2016045764

1 2 3 4 5 22 21 20 19 18 17

CONTENTS

ACKNOWLEDGMENTS

WHILE WRITING IS a solitary process, books are the fruits of collaboration. This work has benefitted since its inception from the support, critiques, assistance, and guidance of colleagues, friends, family, and institutions.

I owe a tremendous debt of gratitude, first and foremost, to my phenomenal dissertation committee at the University of Chicago—Leora Auslander, Sheila Fitzpatrick, Moishe Postone, and the late Richard Hellie—who guided the original version of this project through numerous twists and turns. Each generously offered their time, knowledge, and remarkable intellectual insights. Not only did they devote their considerable talents to this project, they treated me with great personal warmth and collegiality from the outset, for which I am eternally grateful. Their voices, ideas, and lingering questions remained with me through the process of revising that work into the present book. Collectively, they taught me how to read, think, and argue like a critical historian.

Numerous institutions and foundations have provided generous support to this project. I would like to thank the Fulbright-Hayes Program, the CUNY-PSC Research Foundation, the Committee on Jewish Studies at the University of Chicago, the Fuerstenberg Fellowship founders, the Erich Cochrane Research Fellowship, the Foreign Language and Area Studies program of the Department of Education, and the Nevzlin Foundation for support for various stages of this project. I am particularly thankful to the Frankel Institute for Advanced Judaic Studies at the University of Michigan, which provided a fellowship and an inspiring intellectual atmosphere during the early stages of revisions. I am likewise deeply grateful to Indiana University Press and to Deborah Dash Moore, Marsha Rozenblit, and Dee Mortensen for their enthusiastic support of this project from the start. Their guidance and suggestions, as well as feedback from Jeffrey Veidlinger and an anonymous reader, made this work significantly stronger. I am also thankful for the generous support provided by the Borns Jewish Studies Program and the Helen B. Schwartz Fund at Indiana University during the final stages of book preparation.

I had the good fortune to have been a member of two supportive history departments while writing this book. I am thankful for kind support from department conveners at Earlham College, including Carol Hunter, Tom Hamm, and Randall and Alice Shrock, as well as for the friendship of colleagues, including Elana Passman, Joanna Swanger, Joann Martin, Jonathan Diskin, Joann Quinones, Vincent Punzo, and Jennifer Seely. I am likewise grateful to Katherine Pence and Thomas Desch-Obi, my department chairs, and the entire Baruch College History Department for their support and feedback during the final stages of writing.

This work is a testament to the intellectual vigor of many brilliant teachers I have encountered along the way, including Paul Mendes-Flohr, Wiliam Sewell, Peter Novick, Menachem Brinker, Michael Geyer, Ronald Suny, Anna Lisa Crone, Francis Randall, Jefferson Adams, and Elizabeth Boles. I owe particularly hardy thanks for the patience and guidance of numerous language teachers, especially Howard Aronson, who first sparked my interest in Yiddish, and also Gerald Frakes, Dov Ber Kerler, Avrom Lichtenbaum, Valentina Pichugin, Radislav Lapushin, and Rebekka Egger.

The ideas presented here have been tested, refined, and sharpened through ongoing conversations with comrades from the Social Theory Workshop at Chicago. While I learned a tremendous amount in the classroom, most of what I understand about what I learned came from long, rigorous, sometimes heated, and always productive conversations with Jason Dawsey, Mark Loeffler, Spencer Leonard, Timothy "Mac" James, Andrew Sartori, Robert Stern, Aaron Hill, Parker Everett, Tom Dodman, Venus Bivar, and Elizabeth Heath. I am also grateful for critiques and conversations shared with friends in the Russian and Soviet, Modern European, and Modern Jewish Studies Workshops, including Oscar Sanchez—who pushed me to think more deeply about the structure of Soviet economy—Ke-chin Hsia, Ben Zaijcek, Alan Barenberg, Brian LaPierre, Kristy Ironside, Julia Fein, Andrey Shlyakhter, Andrew Janco, Ari Joskowicz, Kati Vorros, Melissa Weininger, and Benjamin Sax.

My ideas about Russian, Soviet, and Jewish history benefited from conversations with and feedback from numerous scholars, including the late Jonathan Frankel, Zvi Gitelman, Israel Bartal, Jonathan Dekel-Chen, Steven Zipperstein, Nancy Sinkoff, Jeffrey Veidlinger, Geoff Eley, Mikhail Krutikov,

Kiril Tomoff, Brian Horowitz, Anna Krylova, Tara Zahra, Elissa Bemporad, Simon Rabinovitch, Steven Maddox, Brigid O'Keefe, Benjamin Lazier, Benjamin Loring, Marcie Cowley, Zohar Weiman-Kelman, Brendan McGeever, Michael Schlie, Dmitrii Belkin, and Boris Tarnopolsky. The editors of *Kritika: Explorations in Russian and Eurasian History*, and two anonymous readers, provided thoughtful feedback on the article that became chapter six of this book, and I am grateful for their kind permission to republish a revised version here. Sam Johnson and the editors of *East European Jewish Affairs* offered excellent feedback on chapter two and have also allowed for republication. Michael Hickey, Golfo Alexopoulos, Kate Brown, Deborah Yalen, Michael Schlie, and Roger Haydon provided tremendously useful feedback on conference versions or early iterations of several chapters. A special thanks is also due to the librarians and archivists of the National Archive of the Republic of Belarus, the State Archive of the Minsk Oblast, the National Library of Belarus, the National Library of Russia in St. Petersburg, the YIVO Institute for Jewish Research, and the National Library of Israel for kind assistance. I am likewise grateful to the Belarusian State University in Minsk for helping to arrange my research visa, and to Inna Gerasimova and the Jewish Museum in Minsk for kind help at the outset of my research.

At moments when this project seemed insurmountable, friends and family helped me through with emotional support, laughter, and love. Kevin Burnham, Damian Hickey, Youngho Sohn, and Wyeth Friday kept me grounded throughout. Jason Dawsey, Mark Loeffler, and Brendan McGeever read versions of multiple chapters, and their critical insights helped shape many ideas in these pages. I am thankful for the continuing love and support from Charlie and Peggy Sloin, Allen and Sam Hadelman, Jordan, Debbie, Spencer, and Ben Hadelman, Shira and David Zimbeck, and Martha and Cathy Heath. My sisters Hilary and Felicia Sloin, and my nephew Elijah, have been rocks of strength and encouragement.

While completing this project, I lost three individuals of great importance to me. Richard Hellie, my original cochair, passed away during the final stages of my dissertation; he was the first professor at Chicago to show confidence in my abilities, and he offered continual encouragement, support, and insight during many long conversations in his notoriously cluttered office. My father-in-law, Robert Heath, passed unexpectedly during the writing of the book; I miss his warmth, wisdom, and good humor. My mother, Susan Sloin, who was always my biggest fan and whose sacrifices made my life of intellectual pursuits a possibility, died in 2011 following a lengthy battle with cancer. She would have been thrilled—and probably a bit shocked—to see this book in print. It is to her memory that this work is dedicated.

Finally, my wife, Elizabeth, has been an endless source of happiness, warmth, support, love, and humor. She has read every page of this book more times than either of us care to remember. At each difficult moment, she helped me find the way forward. Every part of this book—and my life—has been made better and stronger as a result of her attention, care, intelligence, and love. It is to her that I owe the deepest, most heartfelt thanks and appreciation.

NOTES ON TRANSLITERATION, TRANSLATION, AND NAMES

For Russian and Belarusian transliterations, I have used a revised version of the Library of Congress system. This system leaves out all diacritic marks, save for the apostrophe used to designate the soft sign (*miagkii znak*) in Russian. For Yiddish transliterations, I have used the YIVO system. Insofar as Yiddish remained a notoriously nonstandardized language throughout the period, variations of spelling and orthography exist. I have rendered these in standard Yiddish transliteration throughout. I would like to thank Ben Sadock for his generous assistance in reviewing these transliterations and for his insightful feedback regarding questions of Yiddish translation. For the transliteration of names, I have generally striven to use the most common form of names when the individuals or concepts are well known; consequently, I use the spelling of Trotsky, Agursky, and Bolshevik, as opposed to the "correct" transliterations of Trotskii, Agurskii, and Bol'shevik. For individuals who are known only from archival documents, I have transliterated all names based upon the language of the original document. In many instances, lesser known individuals encountered are identified only by surname in documents; where full names cannot be identified through additional sources—an issue complicated by the absence of *lichnye dela*, or personal files in the National Archives of Belarus'—they are identified in the index with a short descriptor. Unless otherwise noted, all translations are my own, as are any remaining mistakes in transliteration, translation, or interpretation.

THE JEWISH REVOLUTION IN BELORUSSIA

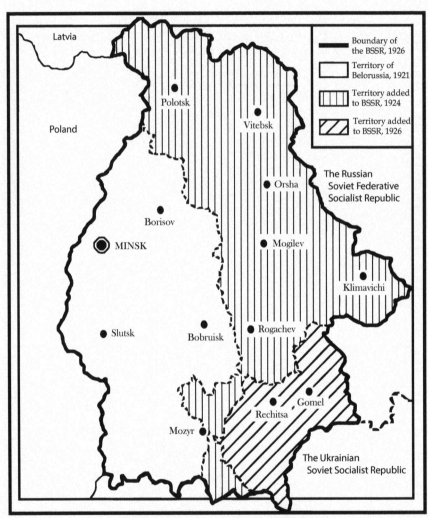

The Belorussian Soviet Socialist Republic (BSSR), 1921-1926

INTRODUCTION

THE BOLSHEVIK REVOLUTION of 1917 initiated the last great project for Jewish emancipation in modern European history. Made in the name of international socialism and proletarian rule, the Bolshevik Revolution offered the Jews of the Soviet lands a new form of emancipation that would transcend the type of "bourgeois" liberal emancipation that proliferated across Europe in the wake of the French Revolution of 1789.[1] Having seized power in October 1917, the Bolsheviks rejected the system of Jewish emancipation granted by the February Revolution, which ended tsarist legal discrimination and opened paths for full Jewish integration into an envisioned liberal order.[2] In place of formal legal equality, the Bolshevik regime promised a qualitatively new model of Jewish emancipation that would transcend the mere "negative" logic of liberal emancipation by engaging in an activist, positive program for the total economic, social, and cultural transformation and integration of Soviet Jewry within a postcapitalist order devoted to social and national equality.

In the eyes of the new Bolshevik leadership, the project of transforming Jews into integrated Soviet citizens was bound inextricably to labor.[3] Having made revolution in the name of the working class and under the banner of Marxian socialism, the Bolsheviks asserted that human emancipation depended upon a doubled understanding of labor. Labor, as a noun, constituted the collective agent of revolutionary change that toppled the monarchy, overturned the "bourgeois" provisional government and its "Capitalist Ministers," and would transform the Russian lands into an enlightened, radiant, socialist order. Labor, as a verb, referred to the practices of creative human production through which the totality of socialist society would be constructed. Viewed through this double-sided concept of labor, Jewish emancipation, as a subset of human emancipation, necessitated the full proletarianization of

1

Jewish social life. To labor and to become labor became the basic entry ticket to active citizenship under the workers' state.[4]

The Bolshevik fusion of labor, citizenship, and political power necessarily led to a complete overturning of the prerevolutionary order for Jewish communities across the former Pale of Settlement, the western region of the tsarist empire where the vast bulk of Jews had been legally bound to reside. Throughout the Pale, the Bolshevik Revolution unleashed a Jewish Revolution, empowering Jewish artisans and workers while simultaneously casting aside the rabbinate, cantors, wealthy communal leaders, merchants, industrialists, religious educators, and secular non-Bolshevik intellectuals as archaic and politically dubious vestiges of an eradicated order.[5] The revolution deposed old elites, old meanings, old languages, old prayers, and old politics.[6] In their place, the revolution promised the permanent rule of the working class, thereby drawing to its flag Jewish artisans, workers, day laborers, apprentices, and white-collar workers. Some entered its service as reluctant members of deposed Jewish political parties; others sought tactical social mobility; still others joined as fervent believers in the promise of social reconstruction through and by labor. Once pulled into the orbit of the revolution, formerly outcast and recently politicized Jews utilized the new revolutionary space to push for the reconstruction of Jewish society and culture.

Nowhere was the intertwined nature of the Bolshevik and Jewish Revolutions more evident than in Belorussia. The Bolshevik Revolution transformed Belorussia from a peripheral region in the Jewish geographic imaginary into a center of the revolutionary project to transform Jewry through statist means. Carved from the northeastern provinces of the Pale of Settlement, the Soviet Republic of Belorussia constituted part of the historic homeland of Eastern European Jewry.[7] At the time of the Soviet census in 1926, the 407,000 Jews living in Belorussia constituted 8.2 percent of the republic's population of roughly 5 million people.[8] Jews constituted half of the republic's urban population and formed majorities or pluralities in virtually all major cities, including Minsk, Vitebsk, Bobruisk, and Gomel.[9] Jews likewise made up majorities in many of the ubiquitous small towns, or *shtetlekh*, that spotted the Belorussian countryside. Most significantly, from the standpoint of a regime that ruled in the name of the working class, Jews accounted for roughly three-quarters of the prerevolutionary artisanate in the Belorussian *gubernii*, constituting the closest approximation of an urban proletariat in an overwhelmingly agrarian region.[10] Jews formed a similar percentage of merchants, traders, and itinerant peddlers who mediated the circulation of goods throughout the region.[11] In Belorussia, the Promethean struggle between proletarian and capital, fundamental to Bolshevik narratives of redemption, fused inseparably with the Jewish Revolution.

While historians and other social scientists can never expect the type of control group requisite for investigations in the "hard" sciences, Belorussia offers the nearest approximation for examining the trajectory and turns of Soviet nationalities policy during the 1920s. Given the region's relatively benign history of intranational relations, the Soviet Socialist Republic of Belorussia (BSSR) constitutes a unique geopolitical space in which to investigate root causes of intranational conflict that erupted anew across the western Soviet Union at the end of that decade.[12] Compared to the neighboring territories of Russia and Ukraine, which were marked by pronounced histories of official and popular antisemitism, the Belorussian territories, historically speaking, constituted one of the most tolerant settings for Jewish life in the lands of the former Russian Empire.[13] No period demonstrated this relative acceptance more clearly than the period of the Russian Civil War, 1918–1921; while the Jewish communities of Belorussia experienced devastating violence at the hands of competing armies, instances of organized, mass pogroms remained limited when compared to the mass anti-Jewish violence that blazed across the Ukrainian territories and claimed tens of thousands of lives.[14] In Belorussia, by contrast, the concentration and political organization of the Jewish working class seemed to offer a unique opportunity to build a higher social order that would "solve," once and for all, the so-called Jewish question through radical, unique, and progressive means.

Despite this initial revolutionary promise, the project of constructing a new form of integrated socialist state based upon the principles of equality and free autonomy between "peoples" failed. Over the course of the 1920s, the goal of constructing a postracial state of intranational cooperation repeatedly ran into the headwinds of political and economic crisis. The spirit of intranational cooperation that prevailed in the initial years of the revolutionary project faded. By the last years of the 1920s, Belorussia witnessed a surge in intranational animosity, as the promise of equality between national groups gave way to intense factional fighting driven by ethnic hostility and growing racial antagonism. Outbreaks of popular antisemitism, fierce internal tensions between Belorussians and Jews (as well as among the republic's Polish, Ukrainian, Russian, and Latvian populations), erupted, seemingly overnight, across the republic. Antagonisms became so intense that the central Soviet government in Moscow—under the newly consolidated leadership of Joseph Stalin—intervened directly, launching a mass purge of proponents of "national" antipathy, cracking down on minority groups, and abruptly ending programs to promote national autonomy. By the end of the 1920s, Belorussia, once a paragon of the Soviet project of national liberation and equality, was transformed into one of the first "Stalinist" states, as the principle of local national autonomy was displaced by an overarching structure of nationalities bound together under the universalizing, centralizing, and increasingly russifiying metropole of Moscow.

The Jewish Revolution in Belorussia examines the promise and ultimate failure of national reconstruction in Belorussia, seeking to explain how a revolutionary project devoted to radical equality between nations ended up producing resurgent ethnic and racial animosity. Insofar as prerevolutionary national antagonisms and nationalist politics in general proved comparatively muted (for Belorussians and Jews alike), the abrupt surge of "national" animosity presents a unique opportunity to conceptualize and isolate causes of resurgent antagonism in the Soviet context. In the absence of "eternal" or "age-old hatreds," (which are, critical historians of nationalities stress, never eternal and rarely age-old) the Belorussian case requires deeper analysis that transcends commonplace explanations based upon the "inevitability" of national conflict.[15] Rather than treating the resurgence of intranational and ethnic conflict as a result of the failure of Soviet nationality policy alone or the unintended consequences of Soviet efforts to implement national "affirmative action," this work locates the eruption of such hostilities in the realm of political economy.[16] In doing so, I argue that resurgent ethnic and racialized animosity in Belorussia emerged from social tensions generated by the recurrent economic crises of the postrevolutionary Soviet economy, which were in turn structured by the onset of the global crisis of the late 1920s.

Economy and the Jewish Revolution

This work interrogates the intertwined fates of the Jewish and Bolshevik Revolutions in Belorussia until the onset of the Stalin Revolution of 1928–1929 from the standpoint of labor, economy, and political culture. It explores the transformation of Jewish life from the "ground up" by focusing upon the actors who populated the front lines of the revolutionary struggle, with particular attention paid to those Jews who joined the Bolshevik movement. Unlike many previous treatments, this history does not approach these questions from the standpoint of "high" politics, whether that term is taken to refer to the politics of the Communist Party, its Jewish Sections (*evsektsii*), or the platforms of oppositional political parties.[17] Rather, it focuses on how the policies of "high" politics were enacted in the factories and workshops, in the workers' clubs and union meetings, and on the Jewish streets of White Russia. The protagonists are not, for the most part, the usual suspects in the historiography of Eastern European Jewry. They are, broadly speaking, not writers, artists, intellectuals, or leading politicians. Most are drawn from the ranks of ordinary and anonymous Jewish actors who were swept up, willingly or otherwise, in the Bolshevik project.

They are shoemakers and speculators, glassmakers and peddlers, leatherworkers and militiamen, needleworkers, Red Army soldiers, trade unionists, local
party operatives, students, Bundists, Bolsheviks, and Zionists. All were Jewish by designated nationality, many by conviction as well. All participated
in the revolutionary process; some embraced it fully from the outset, others
opposed it with equally ardent vigor, but nearly all struggled with its multifarious contradictions.[18]

From this ground-level perspective, it becomes clear that the Bolshevik
Revolution opened unprecedented opportunities for previously marginalized sectors of Jewish society—most notably, the Jewish working class and
artisanate—to push for the radical political, economic, social, and cultural
reconstitution of Jewish society. Yet, as I will show, these opportunities and
the larger project of Jewish renewal and political integration were bound from
the outset by broader constraints of the Soviet economy. Far from being a
purely autonomous process of national self-creation, the attempt to constitute
new forms of Soviet Jewish cultural and social life consistently ran up against
the limits of the Soviet economy. Specifically, attempts to construct "autonomous" Jewish identity were persistently constricted by the repeated waves of
economic crisis that characterized the period of the New Economic Policy
(NEP) of 1921 to 1928. Even as Soviet and Bolshevik actors stressed the need
to reform Jewish life in toto, successive crises led to the implementation of
policies that reconstituted Jewish actors in "traditional" undesirable economic
roles, thereby reinscribing them as detrimental social anomalies. In sum, economic crisis repeatedly threw into question the legitimacy and place of Jewish
participation in postrevolutionary society.

Ultimately, this work argues that fundamental contradictions implicit in
the double-sided concept of labor employed by the Bolsheviks delimited the
fate of the Jewish Revolution in Belorussia (and, implicitly, the entire Bolshevik revolutionary project). On one side, the Bolsheviks proclaimed the political emancipation of labor as the key to universal human emancipation in a
postcapitalist social order. On the other side, the Bolshevik regime insisted
pragmatically that the construction of postrevolutionary socialist society
required the reconstitution of "free" labor (which is to say wage labor) as the
fundamental structuring and mediating principle of social organization. Bolshevik efforts to construct "socialism" consequently intensified contradictions
between labor as a political category and labor as a social action. Efforts to build
socialism through the intensification of productivity and the rationalization of
labor led to heightened conflict between the party and Jewish labor. Heavily
concentrated in light consumer industries that faced the most direct pressures
for increased productivity, Jewish workers repeatedly found themselves in the

front lines of Soviet programs to intensify labor output; unsurprisingly, then, they emerged at the forefront of movements opposed to these policies within the Belorussian working class. The party responded to economistic opposition by inscribing recalcitrant workers as politically and, ultimately, ethnically dubious members of the Soviet body politic. Economy and labor consequently delineated possibilities of national, ethnic, and racial belonging.

By stressing the fundamental relationship between economy and identity formation, this book offers a new understanding of the fate of the so-called Jewish question after the Bolshevik Revolution. It shows how, following the revolution, the Bolshevik party officially outlawed antisemitic speech and action as part of a broader campaign to eliminate international animosity and racial hatred globally. From the standpoint of the party, Jewish integration and the eradication of antisemitism remained intrinsically bound to the overcoming of capitalist social relations and the establishment of socialism. Yet insofar as the postrevolutionary system of production maintained the underlying structure and logic of capitalist social production—the production of value through the application of alienated labor—it necessarily replicated the social conditions under which modern antisemitism flourished across modern Europe.[19] Competition, economic anxiety, anger at limited social mobility, struggles over resources, and growing disparities of wealth and power contributed to the intensification of intranational animus generally, and the resurgence of antisemitic tendencies specifically.[20] As antisemitism became an unspeakable offense, discussions about the place of Jews in Soviet society came to be suppressed in official party discussions.[21] Bolshevik policies, in short, sought to eradicate through political and administrative means the logics of race and intranational animosity produced socially by contradictions within the Soviet economy. Yet the attempted suppression of antisemitism ultimately had the effect of infusing the entire Soviet language system with anxieties about Jews. In the context of suppressed antisemitism, virtually all categories of Soviet political discussion in Belorussia during the 1920s—including such ostensibly "social" categories as labor, proletarians, the bourgeoisie, and so forth—came to be inflected with language of nationality, ethnicity, and race.

The Historical Setting

Unleashed national, ethnic, and racial animosities would, ultimately, transform the region of Belorussia into the "bloodlands" of Europe, a center of ideological warfare and genocidal barbarism during the Second World War.[22] Yet for most of its historical existence, the geographic space that would become Belorussia was distinguished, paradoxically, for its legacy of tolerance. Called *Belaia Rus'*, or "White Russia" in Old Slavonic, *Belorussia* in Russian, *Belarus'* in Belorussian, and *Raysn* or *Vaysrusland* ("Rus," or "White Russia") in Yiddish, the region existed for much of its modern history as an amorphous and heterogeneously populated space that defied easy categorization for projects of national imagining.[23] Until the end of the eighteenth century, White Russia formed the eastern part of the Polish-Lithuanian Commonwealth, the remarkably tolerant early-modern state forcibly dismembered by absolutist Prussian, Austrian, and Russian neighbors during the Partitions of Poland.[24] The Russian Empire swallowed most of what would later become Soviet Belorussia—including the provinces (gubernii) of Vitebsk, Polotsk, Mogilev, and Minsk—during the First (1772) and Second (1793) Partitions of Poland. For the Jews residing in the Belorussian lands, absorption into the Russian Empire and the establishment of the Pale of Settlement in 1835 brought explicit legal restrictions on rights of residence, occupation, and movement. Yet in general terms, Jewish everyday life within the Belorussian territories remained largely autonomous and mostly free of the recurrent popular violence that ripped through the neighboring Ukrainian lands beginning with the Odessa Pogroms of 1871.[25]

Throughout the nineteenth century, Jews constituted a major demographic presence throughout the Belorussian gubernii, particularly in the urban enclaves that dotted the countryside. Yet Vaysrusland remained a discernibly peripheral region of the Eastern European Jewish cultural-geographic imagination. Although renowned for learned rabbis and *yeshivot* (rabbinical seminaries), including famed yeshivot in Minsk, Mir, and Volozhin, the religious legacy of White Russia remained overshadowed by Vilna, the so-called Jerusalem of Lithuania (*Yerushalayim d'Lite*). Similarly, while cities like Minsk and Shklov became early centers of the nineteenth-century movement for secular learning known as the Jewish Enlightenment (*Haskalah*), they were dwarfed by Vilna, L'vov, Odessa, or, for that matter, the imperial capital of St. Petersburg.[26] If anything made Vaysrusland distinct, it was the fact that it became an early northern outpost of the pietist *Hasidic* movement, which engulfed much of Eastern European Jewry during the nineteenth century. This fact won the region no great esteem in areas dominated by the defenders of rabbinic scholarship (the *Mitnagdim*) or the Haskalah, which invariably associated the Hasidim with obscurantism, superstition, and backwardness. Located, in sum, between the Russian capitals of St. Petersburg and Moscow and the Polish metropolis of Warsaw, between the great centers of Jewish learning, between Hasidim and Mitnagdim, between Haskalah and "traditional" religious learning, Belorussia was perpetually betwixt.[27]

The ubiquitous Jewish centers of White Russia were "betwixt" in a second sense; as points of exchange, they played a critical social role within the

Imperial Russian economy. Outside of urban centers, the shtetlekh served as mediating points between the mostly Belorussian peasant countryside and the multiethnic urban centers. Jewish social life was predicated upon varying forms of mediation: mediation between countryside and town, between the peasantry and the urban economy, between regions, and between states. Jewish communal institutions, self-financed as they were, depended directly upon trade and local industry, particularly the small-producer handiwork industry that proliferated throughout the Pale. In the late nineteenth century, the expansion of the railway and small industry remade many cities and shtetlekh of White Russia into bustling points of exchange in times of plenty.[28] Yet the onrush of industrial modernity rendered Jewish social existence increasingly precarious, as the modernizing Russian economy and centralizing state began to break down all forms of social mediation following the Great Reforms of the 1860s.[29]

By the turn of the nineteenth century, economic restructuring and forced modernization unleashed violent social paroxysms across the Empire, signaled by the outbreak of anti-Jewish pogroms in the 1870s and 1880s.[30] While such violence remained comparatively rare in White Russia, social dislocations engendered by rapid industrialization and an economic slump stirred new forms of political activism and unrest. In the autumn of 1897, shortly after the founding of the General League of Jewish Workingmen in Lithuania, Poland, and Russia, or the Jewish "Bund," in Vilna, Jewish workers and intellectuals in Minsk formed the second branch of the organization.[31] The following year, a group of mostly Bundist socialists in Minsk organized the founding congress of the general Russian Social Democratic Workers' Party (RSDWP)—the group that would eventually split into Bolshevik and Menshevik factions.[32] In the ensuing years, support for the Bund grew sharply, particularly in the party's strongholds of Minsk, Bobruisk, Gomel, and Vitebsk. Belorussian cities and towns also became fertile ground for all shades of Zionist politics. One of the earliest chapters of the Socialist Zionist movement *Poalei Tsion* (literally, Workers of Zion) formed in Minsk during the late 1890s, and the city served as the locale for a conference designed to unite disparate left Zionist factions into a single party in 1901.[33] Minsk and other cities became important centers of the general Zionist movement as well as the legal "Independent" Jewish labor movement formed under the auspices of the state with the expressed intention of leading Jews away from revolutionary politics and toward a purely economistic labor struggle.[34]

The intense concentration of Jewish socialist politics, as well as the close interactions between Jewish and general political parties, made the towns of Belorussia centers of revolutionary activity throughout the late nineteenth century.[35] The Bund, in particular, emerged as one of the most important socialist parties in the region, due to the movement's ability to mediate between Russian, Jewish, and European socialist movements. Bundists likewise played critical roles as organizers, helping to establish extensive underground presses and networks for smuggling illegal revolutionary materials across the borderlands of the Russian Empire.[36] Most critically, the party's embrace of Yiddish as its principle language of activism allowed it to mobilize the broad, but previously isolated, Jewish popular classes into a sizable, active, revolutionary constituency. By the first years of the twentieth century, the Bund claimed some thirty thousand members, ranking it among the largest socialist parties in the entire Russian Empire.[37]

The Bund's rapid rise to prominence made it a primary target of rival socialist movements, from both outside and within the Jewish milieu. Despite its formative role in helping to create the RSDWP and fostering the socialist movement in the Pale, the Bund found itself isolated within the Social Democratic movement because of its increasingly vocal call for Jewish national autonomy within the socialist movement. During the 1903 second congress, the RSDWP's central leadership, led by the young radicals Vladimir Lenin, Leon Trotsky, and Iulii Martov, fiercely rejected the Bund's claim to be recognized as the sole representative of the Jewish working class within the RSDWP, leading Bund representatives to walk out of the congress and break from the party.[38] The party's claim to be the primary voice of the Jewish working class was likewise challenged within the Jewish communities of Belorussia by rival Zionist socialist parties. Like the Bund, the Poalei Tsion movement garnered strong support in Minsk and beyond, due in large part to its emphasis on Yiddish-language agitation to mobilize mass political support from the Jewish artisanate and working class. Unlike the Bund, which focused primarily on local politics and revolutionary class struggle within the Diaspora, Poalei Tsion followed its founding ideologist, Ber Borochov, in combining a traditional Marxian emphasis on class struggle with an overarching commitment to the eventual establishment of a Jewish homeland in Palestine.[39]

The fierce rivalry between these disparate movements culminated in the acute politicization that burst forward with the outbreak of revolution in 1905. When shockwaves of political revolt ripped through the Belorussian lands, Jewish parties, and the Bund in particular, played key roles in organizing revolutionary activity in Minsk, Vitebsk, Grodno, Bobruisk, and beyond. Mass demonstrations broke out in Minsk upon the arrival of news of the Manifesto of October 17, wherein Nicholas II, under pressure from the uprising, promised to implement liberalizing reforms. Yet while revolution bloomed in the imperial center, tsarist troops wasted no time in putting down revolt in the periphery. On October 18–19, they opened fire on a demonstration in the central Station Square in Minsk, killing some one hundred civilian demonstrators, almost all Jewish. A subsequent outbreak of anti-Jewish pogroms played a crucial role in the intensification and diversification of Jewish political action throughout Belorussia.[40] The reactionary post-1905 interregnum brought a brief semblance of stability, but this would be blown apart when the Great War once again turned White Russia into a battlefield and cauldron of revolutionary turmoil.[41]

As it did across the empire, the First World War served as the catalyst for revolutionary transformation in Belorussia, but to an even greater extent. Following Central Power advances in 1915, the Belorussian provinces became the fault line of the Eastern Front and the site of garrisons for the increasingly war-weary Imperial Russian army. Over the course of 1917, armies in and around Minsk became incubators of revolutionary ferment and, increasingly, Bolshevik support.[42] In the Constituent Assembly elections of November 1917, the Belorussian provinces became one of the few regions of the Russian Empire to return a majority for the Bolsheviks.[43] Despite that fact, the Bolshevik Revolution came piecemeal to the lands of White Russia. Unlike in Petrograd, where Bolshevik power became an established fact in October 1917, local resistance from rival socialist parties in Minsk, including the Bund, temporarily blocked the Bolshevik seizure of power. By early 1918, the region was plunged back into gruesome world war and civil war. The Germans, the Red Army, and the army of Józef Piłsudski's newly reestablished Polish Republic successively overran Belorussia before the Bolsheviks retook the region in 1920. Years of internecine warfare left the population starved and decimated in some places, impoverished and homeless in many others. Once again, social upheaval brought mass anti-Jewish violence, as anti-Bolshevik irregular armies mounted pogroms across the chaotic borderlands of the collapsed empire.[44]

Having finally succeeded in reconquering the borderlands, the Bolsheviks established as a primary goal the task of eradicating the national and social tensions that drove the fratricidal violence of the Great War and Civil War. Against the postwar trend of nationalizing revolutions seen across Central and Eastern Europe, the Bolsheviks established the Soviet Republic of Belorussia as a deliberately multinational and multiethnic state. In place of a singular national identity and monolithic national culture, the state recognized four national languages—Russian, Belorussian, Polish, and Yiddish. State and party activists constructed schools, newspapers, worker clubs, and administrative institutions to promote the cultural autonomy of the republic's constitutive nationalities. In theory, this logic of multinationality and the promotion of autonomous national institutions pervaded the totality of the early Soviet state.[45] Yet few locations saw this vision of overcoming ethnic, linguistic, and national tensions through the promotion of autonomous national culture pursued as vigorously as Belorussia, the provincial capital of the western borderlands of the reconstituted Soviet empire.

Far from being incidental, the social integration of Jewry into postrevolutionary society constituted an explicit aim of the Bolshevik regime from its inception. Given the mass anti-Jewish violence of the civil war period, as well as the upsurge of right-wing political movements across Europe that conflated Bolshevism and Jewry, the Bolsheviks viewed antisemitism as a particularly insidious form of national hatred. Following Lenin, the party officially denounced antisemitism as a particular ideology of capitalist society and bourgeois political domination that sought to divert the attention of workers from their true class enemies by attributing exploitation to the Jews.[46] Yet even as the party stressed the need to combat antisemitism unflinchingly, the Bolsheviks likewise tied the resolution of the Jewish question to the full reconstitution of Jewish social and economic life on the basis of labor. Only the total reconstruction of Jewish social and economic life would transform Jews from allegedly dubious economic agents into integral participants in the Soviet body politic.

In stressing the need for the total social, economic, and cultural reconstitution of Jewry, the Bolsheviks opened the gates for radical reform that had been building in Jewish society over the previous century. Under Bolshevik auspices, a Jewish Revolution erupted on the streets of Belorussia. This Jewish Revolution restructured social relations, transforming previous social and cultural "outsiders" into insiders. Jewish activists performed linguistic insurrection, dethroning Hebrew, the language of old prayer and old fathers, for the "mother's tongue" of Yiddish. Jewish revolutionaries established Yiddish schools, theaters, lecture halls, and worker clubs, institutes to reexamine the Jewish past, and Yiddish journals to propagate new theories of Jewish being in the world. The Bolshevik Revolution signaled the start of the Jewish Revolution in Belorussia from without. But this revolution was driven from within and from below, by individuals who harbored their own, distinct visions of revolution.

Economy, Culture, and Histories of the Soviet Jewish Question

The first histories of the Jewish experience in the Soviet lands—many of which were penned by émigrés who participated in the revolution as members of anti-Bolshevik parties—generally stressed narratives of decline and the top-down repression of Soviet Jewish life and culture under the Bolsheviks.[47] Beginning with the publication of Zvi Gitelman's study of the Jewish Section (*evsektsiia*) of the Communist Party, a successive wave of historians and political scientists reconsidered the role of Jewish political elites in the building of new forms of Jewish life under the auspices of the Communist Party.[48] Yet in seeking to reform radically Jewish social and cultural life, Gitelman argued that these Bolshevized elites became unwitting agents of Sovietization, modernization, and centralization on the "Jewish Street," contributing—inadvertently or otherwise—to the suppression of ostensibly authentic Jewish national and cultural life.

The fall of the Soviet Union and the opening of Soviet archives led to a renaissance in the writing of Soviet Jewish history. In the broadest terms, this new historiography challenged older paradigms by emphasizing the constructive building of new forms of distinctly Soviet Jewish culture that occurred in the aftermath of revolution. Jeffrey Veidlinger, David Shneer, and Anna Shternshis, in particular, explored how cultural activists and everyday Jews formed new, meaningful, and surprisingly autonomous forms of cultural production, despite official pressures toward conformity.[49] Other studies, most notably Elissa Bemporad's work on postrevolutionary Minsk, emphasized the degree to which many Jews struggled to maintain "traditional" Jewish cultural practices, even as they accommodated themselves outwardly to new institutions of the Bolshevik regime.[50] Collectively, these findings challenge older narratives of cultural decline, as well as claims that Jews entered the revolution for the sake of waging spiritual revolt against Jewish culture and escaping the stigma of Jewishness.[51]

While the present work also engages with questions of Jewish culture, it departs from these earlier studies in three critical ways. First, while the new Jewish cultural history has stressed the importance of sites of culture and the public performance of culture through revolutionary festivals, plays, show trials, and the like, this study defines culture in an anthropological sense to mean the ever-contested and ever-changing system of language, signs, and symbols employed to make meaning of the world.[52] Following this concept, I maintain that "culture" extended far beyond the Yiddish theaters, newspapers, poetry circles, schools, or any other normative sites of "authentic" culture; rather, Jewish culture was made in the language of production, criminality, labor, and commerce as assuredly as in the language of poetry, prose, or prayer. For these reasons, the first half of the book pushes beyond the boundaries of the Jewish public sphere to examine how ostensibly abstract and universal categories central to the revolutionary project—namely labor, capital, trade, and economy— became inflected with anxieties about questions of Jews and Jewishness. This work shows how anxieties about Jews continued to operate within the collective unconscious of postrevolutionary society even though postrevolutionary political language stressed the need for workers and citizens to eradicate racial logics from their revolutionary consciousness.

Second, unlike Bemporad's excellent study of Minsk Jewry, which highlights the efforts of local Jews to maintain Jewish identity in the face of revolutionary change, this book focuses on those Jews who threw their lot in with the Bolshevik movement. The processes of making Jews "Bolshevik," as opposed to the making of "Soviet" Jewry, forms the focus of part 1 of this book, "Revolution." At the same time, this work emphasizes persistent ambivalences about Jewish participation in the revolutionary project. In doing so, this work treats Jewish identity not simply as a self-defined concept to be embraced or discarded by individuals, but also as an ascribed category that became increasingly imposed from without. The concepts of Jews and Jewishness are treated not simply as forms of reified identity, but also as tropes within postrevolutionary Jewish and Bolshevik *political* culture, by which I mean not only the practices of political action in which Jews engaged, but also the ways in which Jews and non-Jewish actors made sense of Jewish participation, action, and purported deviation within the Bolshevik party. For this reason, the second half of the book focuses extensively on successive campaigns to purge the party of alleged deviations, including agitation campaigns against Bundism, Trotskyism, and antisemitism—all of which focused directly on questions of Jewish political life. By deconstructing these successive campaigns against deviation, this study explores the shifting place of Jews and Jewishness in postrevolutionary political consciousness and the persistence of the Jewish question—or, perhaps, more accurately, Jewish questions—in early Soviet society. In doing so, this work throws into relief the limits of Soviet Jewish cultural reconstruction.

Third and most significantly, this study argues that throughout the postrevolutionary period, the factors limiting the full integration of Jewish actors into Soviet society were fundamentally economic and social in nature; yet over the course of the 1920s, and with the Stalin Revolution in particular, party activists increasingly attributed deviation to the national, political, or ethnocultural peculiarities of the Jews. Economy consequently established the parameters within which Soviet Jewish culture and identity could be reconstituted. As emphasized in part 2, "Capital and Labor," discourses about Jews, integration, and emancipation, as well as intrinsic conceptions of Jewish culture, developed in a context of perpetual economic crisis. Jewish social and political integration remained bounded by the limits of socioeconomic structure. In moments of economic crisis, Jewish actors became disgorged from the structures of Soviet society; displaced Jews once again became reinscribed as politically or culturally unassimilable. Crisis, however, also opened up possibilities for new and deeper forms of social integration, which became realizable only at the moment in which the market-oriented strictures of the New Economic Policy (NEP) era were torn asunder in the period known as the Great Break of 1928–1929. Yet the promise of social integration opened by the Great Break and the Stalin Revolution coincided with the erosion of space for fully autonomous cultural production. In this context, social emancipation and social mobility trumped the project of Jewish cultural renewal. The story of this work is, consequently, as much the story of the turn from the economic structure of the NEP to that of the Great Break as it is about the contradictory fate of White Russian Jewry caught in this epochal process of social restructuring.[53]

Nationality, Ethnicity, and Race

In stressing the relationship between economy, culture, and identity, this work critically engages recent studies of Soviet nationality policy, as well as the treatment of Jews within these studies. While questions of Bolshevik policies concerning nationality and culture run through the entire work, they form the core of part 3, "Political Culture and Nationality." Despite sharp disagreements, works on nationality have stressed the primary role of statist agendas, imperial logics of civilizing missions, state agencies and bureaucracies, and Marxian evolutionary ideologies of development to explain the relationship between the Soviet regime and its multitude of subject nationalities. Indeed, as Ronald Suny, Terry Martin, Francine Hirsch, and others have demonstrated, Soviet and Bolshevik policy makers developed vast networks of policies and institutions to categorize, classify, organize, civilize, discipline, nationalize, and ultimately rule disparate subject nationalities.[54] In Francine Hirsch's terms, Soviet specialists developed sophisticated systems of "ethnographic knowledge" and entire language systems to classify subject populations by *narodnost'*, *natsional'nost'*, and *natsiia*.[55] Within this context, Jews have generally been treated as one nationality (technically, a subnational *narodnost'* or multiple *narodnosti*) within a constellation of nationalities governed by the changing whims of Soviet nationality policy.[56] Recent histories of Soviet Jewry have largely followed this framework, viewing Jews as a minority nationality subject to policies of "affirmative action" and "indigenization" (*korenizatsiia*) designed to promote the interests of minority nationalities throughout the Soviet Union.[57]

While deeply indebted to these studies of Soviet nationality, this work challenges such works by taking as axiomatic the idea that the official language and stated programs of Soviet nationality policy alone cannot adequately account for the permutations of Jewish identity within postrevolutionary society. Rather, I argue that the project of transforming postrevolutionary Jewish nationality was bound by the reconstitution of distinctions based upon ethnicity and race that operated alongside official policies of nationality. Part 4, "The Politics of Crisis," in particular, focuses upon the relationship between economic and social change, and the simultaneous reconfigurations of ascribed Jewish identity. Through an examination of the continued reconstruction of Jewish identity in the midst of economic crisis, this work intervenes in contemporary debates concerning the importance concepts of race played in shaping Soviet understandings of nationality.[58]

In order to understand the changing relationships of nationality, ethnicity, and race, it is imperative to disentangle and disambiguate these frequently overlapping concepts. In this work, I use the term "nationality" to refer specifically to official concepts and discourses about Jews that self-consciously accepted the approved, official language of nationality (whether *natsional'nosti* or *narodnost'*).[59] I employ the term "ethnicity" to refer to the specific concept, drawn from Max Weber and the historian Anthony Smith, of a form of constructed, affective group identity that is understood to be grounded in shared cultural traits, practices, and beliefs, and a subjective belief in common descent. Following this definition, I understand ethnicity to imply a degree of subjective self-definition, as opposed to being a purely ascribed identity.[60] Race, as examined more fully below, constitutes the most elusive and controversial of these concepts. As utilized in this study, race refers specifically to constructed, ascribed forms of identity that attribute to group actors uniformity of thought, action, and belief based upon purported inherent or essential qualities.[61] Race, to be clear, is not used in the sense of an actually existing biological group, but rather as a socially constructed form of difference made "real" through rhetorical, legal, and social practices.[62]

According to official utterances, the Bolshevik party and Soviet government categorically rejected the language and logics of race as a basis of policy. The state and party persistently denounced race as a "zoological" theory positing false distinctions between humans based on pseudoscientific ideas of biologically grounded difference.[63] The logic and language of race, moreover, was understood to be a particular manifestation of the degraded nature of thought in the capitalist lands and the "West," reaching its depths in the morally and scientifically debased context of the Nazi racial state. As a result, the Soviet state not only denounced the very foundation of racial thought, but also actively pursued politics of antiracism from the outset, going so far as to criminalize expressions of racial animosity in the form of antisemitism.[64]

Despite official pronouncements, recent works have raised substantial questions concerning the underlying racial logics that structured Soviet nationality practices. Most forcefully, Eric Weitz argued that over the course of the Stalin era, Soviet practices exhibited a pronounced "slide from nationality to race," as the state targeted and punished specific national groups for ostensible political offenses that increasingly came to be interpreted as manifestations of naturalized and essentialized characteristics of targeted groups.[65] The racialization of Soviet nationalities politics reached its nadir, he argued, during the 1937–1953 period, as the Stalinist state carried out mass deportations of targeted national groups, including Koreans, Chechens, Germans, and Poles, among others.[66] Francine Hirsch sharply criticized this argument, rejoining that while the Stalin regime did draw increasingly sharp lines between friend and enemy nations, those lines were absolutely political in nature and rejected the biological racism that defined policies and practices in Nazi Germany. Far from practicing racial policies in absence of a theory of race (as Weitz contended), the Soviet Union understood such theories of race explicitly and rejected them absolutely.[67]

Notwithstanding their sharp disagreement, Weitz and Hirsch each employed rather extreme measures in determining the degree to which race persisted in the Soviet context. For Weitz, racial logics became real only with the onset of mass deportations of national groups in 1937; for Hirsch, the presence or absence of racial logics should be measured against the eliminationist, genocidal, biologized racial policies of Nazi Germany. These maximalist measures constitute exceedingly high thresholds, ones that would exclude much scholarship on the everyday constructions of race in comparative national and imperial contexts.[68] This study, in turn, adopts an understanding of race gleaned from such comparative studies to explore changing reconstruction of Jewish identity in postrevolutionary society. For the sake of clarity, I am definitively not arguing that the Soviet Union embraced biological racism of the variety proffered in Nazi Germany or across interwar Europe, covertly or otherwise. Nor do I claim that Soviet political language simply masked or veiled underlying racialist agendas. What I am arguing is that despite the real and serious commitment to the politics of equality, antiracism, and internationalism, the social and economic policies embraced by the Soviet state served to reproduce the conditions and logics of race socially.

Rather than view the resurgence of racialized discourse as the inevitable reconstitution of "biopower" endemic to imperial regimes, this study stresses that race reemerged as a meaningful category at specific historical junctures structured by political economy.[69] Conceptions of Jewish nationality, ethnicity, and race gained new coherence in discreet moments of economic and structural crisis during the 1920s. At each phase of crisis, questions about Jews, Jewishness, and the possibility of integration returned forcefully to the Soviet discursive sphere. Such moments revealed a spectrum of available conceptions of Jewish identity, ranging from benign notions of nationality, to potentially problematic identities grounded in ethnicity, to increasingly racialized conceptions of Jews as unassimilable and inherently distinct populations. With the final breakdown of the NEP and the turn to the Stalinist planned economy in 1927–1928, discourses concerning Jews—as with all national groups—hardened. The eruption of grass roots antisemitism that accompanied the onset of the Stalin Revolution provided the clearest evidence of the resurgence of racial thought; yet even within the official language of the party, which rejected overtly biological racism, logics of race ascended with the final crisis of the NEP.[70] Far from a quasi-natural or inevitable process, I argue that the "slide from nationality to race" was structured, fundamentally, by economy. Moreover, this slide from national, to ethnic, to racial conceptions of Jewishness and Jewish identity was articulated in language about political deviation—such as deviations of "Bundism" and "Trotskyism"—that studiously avoided recourse to the concept of race.

Regardless of official Soviet policy and pronouncements, the eruption of postrevolutionary antisemitism necessarily challenged official insistence upon the fundamental normality of the Jews.[71] The high visibility of Jews in postrevolutionary party institutions, administrations of Soviet power, and sites of production appeared to affirm racial discourses about Jewish power, especially in Belorussia. Even in places and periods in which state and party organs held firmly to antiracist positions, race repeatedly returned to the language of politics at the grassroots level, influencing local debates and shaping local understandings of nationality. For outright antisemites, the Jews caused the revolution and pulled the strings of global Bolshevism. For ambivalent populations, Jews appeared as prime beneficiaries of Soviet rule, raised to positions of power unimaginable in the late imperial period. Finally, for the party leadership, the question of the Jews was always double sided. On one hand, Jewish support proved critical to the victory of the revolution and the establishment of Soviet power in Belorussia. On the other, Jewish support cast the legitimacy of the revolution in doubt insofar as it seemed to confirm conspiratorial narratives of Jewish power. The party responded by seeking to regulate, manage, and "normalize" national representation—which largely meant "normalizing" the numbers of Jews in political institutions—through purges, propaganda campaigns, and party reviews.

Ultimately, the reemergence of racialized forms of thought and practice in the Soviet context cannot be grasped by focusing simply on the internal story of Soviet politics and economy alone. Rather, this book stresses the need to conceptualize Soviet policy within a global environment structured economically by the onset of the global crisis of the late 1920s, and, politically, by the ascendancy of increasingly racialized, integral nationalist, and rightist politics across Europe. In this context, antisemitism emerged globally—with particular vehemence across Central and Eastern Europe—as a dominant form of racialized thought engendered by the global crisis. The contemporaneous eruption of antisemitism across Europe and the Soviet Union in the 1920s consequently underscores the degree to which the Soviet Union remained firmly embedded in structures of the capitalist global economy throughout the 1920s, despite claims of having made anticapitalist revolution.

As I show in the pages that follow, the interlinked global and domestic economic crisis fused nationality and race into new configurations of politics that threatened the viability and stability of postrevolutionary Belorussia as an integrationist society. The resurgence of antisemitism and racialized thought in the late 1920s triggered a total reversal of Soviet nationality policy, as the Soviet state and the Bolshevik party ultimately decided that the politics of integration mattered more than the politics of nationality. In this moment of crisis, the promise of full Jewish emancipation offered by the Bolshevik Revolution appeared to necessitate, however paradoxically, the radical suppression of nationality. Through an examination of the relationship between economy, politics, nationality, and race, this study seeks to explain why the Bolshevik revolution, which promised qualitatively new forms of Jewish emancipation, ultimately brought about the attempted suppression of Jewish—and all—national particularity for the sake of realizing the universalizing culture of Stalinism.

PART I

REVOLUTION

1

MAKING JEWS BOLSHEVIKS

ON DECEMBER 10, 1918, the Minsk Military Soviet posted an order announcing the evacuation of German forces and the seizure of Minsk by the Red Army. The decree, signed by Stanislaw Berson, the chairman of the Military Soviet, extended greetings on behalf of the "Workers' and Peasants' Government and its Red Army" to the "now liberated proletariat" of Minsk and called on all appointed individuals to remain in their posts and fulfill the orders of the new Soviet regime. Any attempts at sabotage, noncompliance with orders, or attacks on workers would be met, the decree warned, "in the most energetic manner," up to and including shooting.[1] The Bolshevik Revolution came to Belorussia on horseback and by railway; it consolidated power at the end of the bayonet and the machine gun.[2]

The military capture of Minsk created a new form of revolutionary state, envisioned from the outset as an explicit repudiation of the minimalist "bourgeois" liberal state. This postliberal state would regulate production, control the distribution and circulation of goods, provide necessary health and educational services, codify and enforce sanitation minimums, and ensure worker protection and social advancement. Above all else, the Soviet state would replace, in Vladimir Lenin's inimitable words, "the venal and rotten parliamentarianism of bourgeois society" with an active, participatory, primitive democracy.[3] This democracy was to be based not upon the "Rights of Man" or any such recipe of abstract individualism, but upon the direct political participation of laboring groups qua labor. True to this vision, the Constitution promulgated in 1918 tied political rights and representation to the function of labor.[4] Such a state—expansive, participatory, and vigorously interventionist—required far more than coercive military and police force. It required cadres, activists, technocrats, and bureaucrats.

The emancipation of labor, in the eyes of most Bolsheviks, meant the political self-rule of the proletariat—the landless, propertyless mass of workers divorced from the means of production through processes of primitive accumulation. As any good Bolshevik familiar with Marx's most basic writing knew, this army of laborers fell like chaff from the ever-grinding mills of capitalist production. Mechanization, the intensification of productive power, falling rates of profit—the fruits of crisis-prone capitalist production—generated ever-expanding masses of downwardly mobile proletarians. In the factories and Satanic mills of capitalist production, this dispossessed mass, squeezed from the ranks of the bourgeoisie and the petit bourgeoisie—from the artisans, craftsmen, and shopkeepers—was reformed into abstract, uniform labor. The Bolshevik project was to transform this mass of dispossessed labor into a machine of political control and social transformation.

The degree to which the schematic Marxist model did *not* match the actual social conditions in revolutionary Russia was glaringly evident to contemporary observers. A gaping chasm existed between Marxist theory and the social actuality of predominantly agrarian Russia. Faced with this reality, the Bolsheviks—especially Lenin and the ex-Menshevik Leon Trotsky—famously innovated. They asserted that worker revolution, *if* supported by peasant revolution at home and revolution in the advanced industrial world, would enable Russia to skip the capitalist stage of historical development and establish a socialist order. "Leninism," which posited the need for an alliance with the revolutionary peasantry (as opposed to the invariably treacherous bourgeoisie) for the purpose of solidifying proletarian rule, drew immediate scorn from contemporary critics. "Orthodox" Marxists, including the Mensheviks Iulii Martov and Pavel Aksel'rod, accused the Bolsheviks of forcing through a "premature" proletarian revolution—an attempt, Engels had argued, that would invariably lead to domination by a revolutionary minority.[5] From abroad, the sympathetic but critical Rosa Luxemburg chided the Bolsheviks from a different angle, accusing them of capitulating to the petty bourgeois peasantry by allowing the spontaneous partition of landed estates, and to reactionary nationalist elements by adopting the slogan of national self-determination. Such concessions, she insisted, violated Marxist principles for the sake of political expediency.[6] Moreover, the Bolshevik emphasis on the centrality on peasant revolution recapitulated strains of rejected *Narodnik* populism long rejected by Russian Marxists.

Against such appeals to ideological purity, the Bolsheviks forced, innovated, negotiated, and compromised their way to power in accordance with social realities on the ground. In Belorussia, the Bolshevik compromise depended unconditionally upon the support of the peasantry. It was, after all, the mass of peasants in arms, garrisoned along the Western Front running throughout Belorussia, that delivered majority support to the Bolshevik platform in the Constituent Assembly elections of 1917.[7] Likewise, it was this group—the newly "propertied" beneficiaries of the land seizures of the summer of 1917—that steadfastly defended their gains against the counter-revolutionary threat of the old landowning classes during the Russian Civil War.[8] When Bolsheviks in Belorussia, following Lenin, emphasized the need for a *smychka*, or union, between the countryside and the city, they explicitly acknowledged, however grudgingly, the enormous political weight wielded by the social group Marx once dismissively likened to sacks of potatoes.[9]

But with whom, precisely, was the peasantry to conclude this *smychka*? In the gigantic Putilov works of Petrograd, the steel mills of the Donbass-Dnepr Bend, the coalfields of the Donets Basin, or the oil fields of Baku, the presence of a mass industrial workforce rendered plausible the idea of a revolutionary union between an industrial proletariat and the peasantry. In Belorussia, this type of industrial proletariat was virtually nonexistent. In June of 1917 there existed a total of 126 trade unions representing an estimated thirty-five-thousand workers throughout the major Belorussian gubernii of Minsk, Mogilev, Vitebsk, and Smolensk.[10] By comparison, the Artillery Administration in Petrograd *alone* employed more than fifty-three-thousand workers.[11] The largest Petrograd factories, such as the massive pipe works (*trubochnyi zavod*) and cartridge works (*patronnyi zavod*) employed over ten thousand workers apiece; in Belorussia, only a handful of industrial undertakings had workforces exceeding five hundred workers.[12] Moreover, many of these—such as the Shereshevskii tobacco factory in Grodno (with some fourteen hundred workers in 1913) and the Progress-Vulkan matchstick factory in Pinsk—were located in imperial-era Belorussian gubernii captured by Polish forces during the Polish-Soviet War of 1919–1921.[13] By the end of the war, roughly half of Belorussia's forty-eight-thousand workers labored in shops with fewer than fifteen employees; of these, more than half employed, on average, 1.5 people, including the proprietor.[14]

The vast majority of "industrial" enterprises in revolutionary Belorussia were, in short, petty manufactories and small artisanal workshops. Most were owned and operated by individual artisans (*remeslenniki*) or cottage producers (*kustari*) employing little hired labor.[15] In other words, most enterprises engaged in what traditional Marxism regarded as nonproletarian or petit-bourgeois forms of production. Despite their dubious claims to "proletarian" status, *kustar'* producers and artisans were among the most active participants in the revolutionary transformation of Belorussia, mirroring the pattern that prevailed throughout industrializing Europe.[16] In urban areas—whether regional centers such as Minsk, Vitebsk, and Mogilev, or smaller townlets (*mestechki*, shtetlekh) that dotted the countryside—the "Workers' Revolution" was principally carried through by artisans and small craftsmen. The young Marx predicted that the industrial proletariat would inherit the postrevolutionary world. In White Russia, the postrevolutionary inheritance passed over to the shoemakers, the leather tanners, the soap boilers, and the tailors.

In Belorussia, this meant that the revolutionary mantle largely passed to the Jewish working class. According to the 1897 census, Jews constituted an overwhelming percentage of artisans and petty producers in the prerevolutionary Belorussian gubernii. Jewish artisans and kustari made up 71 percent of all such producers in Vitebsk *guberniia* (province), 75 percent in Minsk guberniia, and 80 percent in Mogilev guberniia.[17] In Minsk, artisans and cottage producers constituted roughly 42 percent of the total Jewish population of 47,561.[18] Jews, moreover, concentrated in those sectors of production—the sewing, shoemaking, leatherworking, wood-, food-, and tobacco-producing industries—that emerged as primary bastions of political radicalism following the 1917 revolutions. Revolution and Civil War transformed this mass of Jewish artisanal labor into a force for the radical transformation of Jewish political and social life from below. In doing so, these actors transformed the cities and shtetlekh of Belorussia into centers of Jewish experimentation while simultaneously playing a critical role in establishing institutions of Bolshevik rule and Soviet power throughout the region.

This chapter examines Jewish radicalization in Belorussia from 1917 to 1921. Drawing on records from the 1921 Belorussian Communist Party (KPB) purge of twenty-one party cells in Minsk, including information on roughly 297 Jews who joined the Bolsheviks, it examines processes of radicalization at the grassroots level.[19] These purge materials—including questionnaires in which party members retold their revolutionary biographies, as well as records of mass meetings in which the fates of party members were decided—provide unprecedented insight into the experiences, conflicts, and motivations that pulled and pushed Jews into the Bolshevik ranks. By focusing on voices drawn from the least literate and literary of the hundreds, and then thousands, of Jews who entered the party during this formative period, this chapter revises previous accounts that have taken the experience of atypical intellectuals—and frequently anti-Bolshevik, émigré intellectuals—as normative on the "Jewish Street." In doing so, it challenges apologetic attempts to marginalize Jewish participation in revolutionary politics while contesting the notion that Bolshevization took place primarily among so-called non-Jewish Jews, to use Isaac Deutscher's enduring phrase.[20]

Politics on Jewish Streets

Mordukh Zokorov Lipets, a self-described "Belorussian Jew," was born in Minsk in 1860. As a child he completed two classes of primary school before setting to work in a coppersmith workshop, beginning his lifelong career as a metalworker. In 1879, Lipets joined an underground Narodnik revolutionary circle, embarking on a second lifelong career as a revolutionary activist. Twice arrested for Narodnik revolutionary activity (in 1885 and 1887), Lipets eventually broke with his populist politics and, in 1893, joined a local self-education cell in Warsaw that followed the émigré Marxist circle of Georgii Plekhanov, Pavel Aksel'rod, Vera Zasulich, and others.[21] Two years later he returned to Minsk and began implementing the early Marxist program of agitation and labor organization, helping to found an underground metalworkers union. With the 1901 appearance of the journal *Iskra*, the mouthpiece of Plekhanov's Social Democrats edited by Vladimir Lenin and Iulii Martov, Lipets became an *Iskraist* and self-described Social Democrat. Following the 1903 Social Democratic party split between Lenin's Bolsheviks and Martov's Mensheviks, Lipets became a fervent Leninist. After a third arrest during the 1905 Revolution, Lipets returned to the railroad industry during the First World War and resumed his underground political agitation. When revolution broke out in Minsk in 1917, Lipets unsurprisingly became an enthusiastic Bolshevik; after the Bolshevik seizure of power in October, he joined the ranks of the revolutionary administration in the newly established Palace of Labor (*Dom Truda*). Mordukh Lipets was, in short, a Jew and an Old Bolshevik. As such, he was an extreme rarity in Minsk.[22]

Few Minsk Jews followed Mordukh Lipets's path into the Bolshevik party for one simple reason: prior to 1917, there were few Bolsheviks of *any* sort, Jewish or otherwise, in Minsk. One observer estimated that at the time of the February Revolution of 1917 there existed only ten to fifteen active Bolsheviks in the entire city, compared to two hundred or so supporters of their Menshevik rivals.[23] Support for the Bolsheviks remained marginal until July and August of 1917, when the collapse of a last-gasp military offensive and the threat of counterrevolution in Petrograd by General Kornilov sharply radicalized the political scene. Following the defeat of Kornilov's attempted coup (due largely to the actions of railroad workers in Belorussia) in late August, Bolshevik ranks grew rapidly, swelling to an estimated 9,190 members in mid-September and reaching 28,000 by early October. Of these, the vast majority were soldiers garrisoned across the military front.[24]

As was the case throughout the former Russian Empire, Jewish support for the Bolsheviks in Belorussia remained marginal through 1917.[25] In the aftermath of the February Revolution of 1917, Jewish voters in Minsk and across Belorussia largely threw their political support behind explicitly Jewish political parties.[26] Such support allowed Jewish political parties to win control of 27 out of 102 seats in midsummer elections for the Minsk City Soviet. Of these, the *klal yisroel* bloc, a coalition of the religious Orthodox *Agudas Yisroel* party and nonsocialist Zionists won sixteen seats, becoming the second largest bloc in the city soviet behind the Socialist Revolutionary (SR) party. The Jewish socialist Bund captured ten seats, making it the second largest socialist party, after the SRs but ahead of the Polish Socialists (eight seats), the Bolsheviks (six), the Mensheviks (six), and Poalei-Tsion (Labor Zionists; one).[27] In November elections for the Constituent Assembly, held in the aftermath of the Bolshevik seizure of power in October, Jewish parties again won considerable victories.[28] The klal yisroel bloc received some 65,046 votes throughout Minsk guberniia, against some 6,184 for Poalei Tsion and 4,880 for the Jewish Socialist Workers Party (SERP), a non-Marxist socialist party affiliated with the SRs. Additionally, there were some 16,277 votes for the Bund-Menshevik alliance, a number that undoubtedly included a significant percentage of Jewish votes.[29] Given that the total Jewish population in the city of Minsk alone had grown to some sixty-seven thousand people by 1917, and that newly enfranchised women voters likely swelled the number of Jewish voters throughout the guberniia, it is probable that significant numbers of Jews voted for All-Russian parties including the Constitutional Democrats, SRs, and Bolsheviks. Nevertheless, the vast majority of Jews cast their votes for explicitly Jewish parties.[30]

Historians have generally taken the Constituent Assembly elections as evidence of widespread and enduring grassroots opposition to the Bolsheviks (and socialists generally) on the "Jewish Street."[31] The tendency to read initial opposition as an indicator of future political action appears problematic, however, if the image provided by the 1917 election results is compared to a second snapshot of Jewish political life from 1921, following four years of revolution, Civil War, and Bolshevik consolidation. In the summer of 1921, Yankel Levin, the head of the Jewish Sections (evsektsii) of the Belorussian Communist Party (KPB), submitted a report on local conditions in Minsk to the Central Bureau of the party. His report underscored the central role Jewish actors had taken within the republic's main productive and administrative apparatuses. "In the cities and shtetlekh of Belorussia," Levin wrote, "the predominant majority of workers—with the exception of the railroad workers—are Jewish." An investigation of twenty-six leading industrial enterprises in Minsk indicated that Jewish workers accounted for 1,692 of the 2,630 employees, or 74 percent of the workforce; in thirteen of these enterprises, the workforce was exclusively Jewish. Of the 155 Communist Party members working in these enterprises, 93 (60 percent) were Jews. Jewish activists played a similarly preponderant role within the administrative apparatuses of Soviet power. Of the 1,390 white-collar workers (*sluzhashchii*) serving in eight administrations of Soviet power in Minsk, 1,035 (75 percent) were Jewish. Jews, likewise, accounted for

89 of the 105 (84 percent) Communist party members drawn from these ranks. "Approximately the exact same situation exists in the entirety of Belorussia," Levin concluded.[32]

As the head of the evsektsii, Levin undoubtedly had an interest in emphasizing Jewish support for the Soviet regime. Nevertheless, the Central Soviet of Trade Unions (*Sovprofbel*), the umbrella organization for all labor unions, corroborated Levin's analysis. According to a 1921 *Sovprofbel* report, Jewish workers constituted 36 percent (18,979 of 52,466) of unionized workers in Belorussia and 55 percent (7,367 of 13,633) of workers in the so-called productive unions—the metalworkers, woodworkers, needleworkers, food producers, leatherworkers, chemical workers, printers, and builders unions (table 1). Jewish representation in these unions was even higher in the Minsk *uezd*, where 9,983 Jewish union members constituted almost 42 percent of the entire unionized workforce of 23,871, made up a majority or plurality within thirteen of the seventeen trade unions in the *uezd*, and composed roughly 71 percent (3,648 of 5,122 total workers) of membership in the "productive" unions (table 2).[33]

Membership in trade unions and Soviet administrative institutions constituted objective support for the Soviet regime insofar as these institutions served as primary mechanisms for extending state control over the production process and the general implementation of Soviet social goals. But objective support did not *necessarily* correlate to subjective political support. Workers could become union—and even party—members while ostensibly rejecting many of the ideological presuppositions of the regime, most notably those relating to cultural issues and religious practices.[34] Moreover, party and union membership offered access to privileges, goods, and employment; large numbers of individuals undoubtedly joined these organizations for reasons that had little to do with ideological or political commitment. Finally, the presence of significant numbers of Jewish actors within the apparatuses of Soviet power by no means meant uniform support for the regime. Religious Jews, liberals, cultural elites, nonsocialist Zionists, and others remained vehemently opposed to the regime throughout the first decade of Soviet rule.[35]

Nevertheless, the pronounced presence of Jews in key productive and administrative institutions suggests a strong degree of political accommodation toward the Soviet regime in Minsk. Two conjoined processes drove the turn from widespread hostility toward the Bolsheviks in 1917 to increasing accommodation by 1921. The first was the completely unprecedented entry of Jewish commoners, drawn in particular from the ranks of young Jews and the large Jewish artisanate, into the structures of political rule. The second was the large-scale migration of former activists from specifically Jewish socialist parties—most importantly, former Bundists—into the ranks of the Bolshevik party.

Making Bundists Bolshevik—An Overture

Jewish working-class activism and political radicalism in Belorussia long pre-dated the revolutions in 1917. The outbreak of a Jewish locksmith strike in Minsk in 1887 marked the beginnings of a protracted period of labor unrest that had intensified sharply by the end of the century.[36] Rapid industrialization, crippling deflation, and wage stagnation during the last years of the nineteenth century sparked widespread worker unrest. Between 1894 and 1897, some fifty-four strikes by Jewish workers broke out in Minsk alone;[37] labor unrest spread throughout the "Jewish" industries of Belorussia: tobacco and matchstick production, garment manufacturing, leatherworking, and shoemaking.[38] Economic dislocation and widespread unemployment transformed the cities of Belorussia into incubators of new Jewish political movements devoted to amalgams of Marxism, Anarchism, and the amorphous concept of socialism. In 1897 followers of the iconoclastic Marxist-Zionist theorist Ber Borochov founded the first cell of the Poalei Tsion movement in Minsk.[39] Anarchism, rife among Jewish workers in nearby Bialystok, found support among Jewish artisans in the city.[40] Minsk also became a center of the "legal" trade union movement, or independents, organized by Police inspector Sergei Vasilevich Zubatov.[41]

Within socialist circles, Minsk was known above all as a Bundist city. Developing directly from the inchoate Social Democratic movement that gained Jewish followers (including Mordukh Lipets) in Warsaw, Bialystok, Vilna, and Minsk during the 1890s, the Bund (officially, the General Jewish Labor Bund of Russia and Poland) was established in Vilna in October 1897.[42] Shortly thereafter a second cell was founded in Minsk. Inspired by Plekhanov's exiled Social Democratic movement, the Bund embraced the group's Marxism, mass worker political mobilization, and rejection of the peasant-orientation and terrorist activism of the Russian Narodniki.[43] In opposition to the Plekhanov group, which stressed the absolute primacy of class struggle over national concerns, the Bund organized itself as a specifically Jewish socialist movement, arguing that the Jewish proletariat suffered from a doubled exploitation, simultaneously oppressed as Jews and as laborers. Plekhanov and his followers, most notably the young Lenin, rejected the Bund's nationalist "deviation" from the outset (Plekhanov dismissed the movement as "Zionists afraid of seasickness").[44] Yet it was the Bund, ironically, that brought Plekhanov's Social Democratic politics back from exile and into the heart of the Russian Empire. In 1898 the Bundists of Minsk organized the founding congress of the Russian

Social Democratic Workers Party in Minsk, effectively establishing the party that would eventually split into Bolshevik and Menshevik factions.[45]

By 1903 the Bund constituted one of the largest socialist parties in the Russian Empire, claiming a following of more than 30,000 workers, including some 1,200 adherents in Minsk.[46] The party found many of its earliest followers among tanners and leatherworkers, gaining broad support in the leather-producing centers of the empire, including Vilna, Minsk, Krinki, and Smorgon.[47] Shoemakers composed another primary constituency, providing the movement its first revolutionary "martyr" in the shoemaker Hirsh Lekert, hanged in Vilna in May of 1902 for attempting to assassinate the local governor.[48] Needleworkers, including tailors, seamstresses, milliners, and glove makers, formed another bastion of Bund support, along with carpenters, joiners, and the extremely volatile matchstick makers.[49] With the outbreak of revolution in 1905, the Bund played a leading role in organizing Jewish political activism and self-defense in Minsk, Bobruisk, Gomel, Vitebsk, and across Belorussia. When revolution returned to Minsk in 1917, the Bund remained among the strongest socialist parties in the city and the region, buoyed by a spike in membership following the February Revolution.[50] In June a Bund conference in Minsk drew some thirty-six delegates representing a total of 7,656 members from twenty-six cities and towns across Belorussia.[51]

With the Bolshevik seizure of power in October, the Bund demonstrated its political power on the streets of Minsk. In the days following the Bolshevik seizure of power in Petrograd, local Bolsheviks attempted to spread the revolution to Minsk through armed revolt, gaining effective control of the city on November 8 (according to the new-style calendar implemented by Bolsheviks). Minsk Bundists vigorously opposed the Bolshevik power grab, joining with local Mensheviks and SRs in an anti-Bolshevik alliance, the Committee to Save the Motherland and the Revolution. Unlike in Petrograd, the alliance of oppositionists proved strong enough to force the Bolsheviks to agree to a coalition government on November 10. This compromise lasted only briefly; the arrival of an armed train filled with pro-Bolshevik reinforcements from the Sixtieth Siberian Rifle Regiment reestablished Bolshevik control over the city on November 15–16.[52] Despite this defeat, Bundist opposition to the Bolshevik regime remained steadfast throughout February 1918, when the region came under control of the advancing German Army.

The Bolsheviks, backed by the newly reconstituted Red Army, reestablished political power across Belorussia in November and December 1918, following the collapse of the German Empire and capitulation of the German Army. After retaking Minsk on December 10, the Bolshevik regime encountered a dire political situation. Local organizational networks and cadres built up during 1917 had been completely suppressed by the German army. "Party work practically died away in Minsk during the period of the occupation," a report from the Central Bureau of the party observed in March of 1919. "As a result, all organizational work here has to begin all over again. Meanwhile, there is practically no one aside from members of the Central Bureau to do any of the work."[53] The Central Bureau warned against attempts to establish political control simply through military means and coercion, pointing to the morass created by the Bolshevik attempt to do so in nearby Vilna. Faced with widespread opposition from "petty bourgeois" parties in Vilna, most notably the Bund and Polish Socialists, the Bolsheviks sought to consolidate political control exclusively through small pockets of Russian workers and the broad application of coercive measures. The results proved disastrous. Party organizations remained almost nonexistent, the vast majority of workers were indifferent, and the party increasingly relied on the Cheka to bring about the "merciless crushing of the bourgeoisie." Cognizant of the failures in Vilna, the Central Bureau in Minsk focused on building support among the most potentially powerful political ally in the city: the Jewish working class. "From the first day of the entry of Soviet forces into Belorussia," the Central Committee stressed the need to "win . . . over the petty bourgeoisie and the leaders of its socialist parties, the 'Bund,' Poalei-Tsion, and the United Jewish Socialist Party."[54]

At the all-Soviet level, the task of drawing Jewish workers into the Bolshevik orbit fell to the evsektsii, Jewish sections of the party created in 1918 to propagate Bolshevik policy among the Jewish population. In Minsk, the local evsektsii remained extraordinarily weak due to lack of cadres, and the party turned directly to left-leaning members of the Bund to bolster support. On January 15 the party's Central Bureau convened negotiations with the Bundist Sverdlov, a representative of self-designated "Communist Bundists" in Minsk, to discuss tactics for drawing support for the regime among the city's Jewish workers.[55] Following prolonged debate, the Central Bureau agreed, over the objections of the evsektsii, to form a distinct Jewish Communist Party (EKP).[56] The willingness to compromise clearly reflected Bolshevik anxieties over support in the city. Yet the compromise also reflected growing anxieties and divisions within the ranks of the Bund. Addressing the Central Bureau, Sverdlov spoke of a "crisis in the present moment," caused by the fact that the "most revolutionary elements" were leaving the "dying Bund." This crisis, he argued, made it necessary for the Bund to enter into the Party, with the understanding that the Bolsheviks would respect its right to maintain "the principle of autonomy within national-cultural life."[57]

The EKP lasted for less than two months before dissolving in internal party squabbles. Members of the mainstream Bund dismissed the organization as little more than a thinly veiled and ineffectual Bolshevik front, an assessment largely shared in the subsequent historiography.[58] In actuality, the EKP appears to have had some success in organizing Jewish activists, particularly outside of Minsk.[59] Despite its weakness, the EKP constituted the start of a growing tendency among the Bolshevik leadership to seek accommodation with the numerically powerful Jewish working class. Simultaneously, the organization opened an avenue for Bundist sympathizers to distance themselves from the "dying Bund" and align with the "workers' revolution," without fully embracing the Bolsheviks. Regardless of the success or failure of the EKP, Sverdlov's dire prediction concerning the waning influence of the Bund seems to have been borne out on the streets. In elections for the Minsk Soviet of Workers and Red Army Deputies, held at the end of January 1919, the Bund collected only 26 seats, finishing well behind the Bolsheviks (who won 253 seats) and SRs (33 seats), and only narrowly edging out the Poalei Tsion (20 seats), who historically held a far smaller base in the city.[60]

In truth, the task of mobilizing Jewish support for the regime proved far too important to trust to any single organization, however closely aligned. Throughout the first half of 1919, the Bolsheviks mobilized all available resources to win Jews to the cause. To this end, they dispatched streams of instructors, lecturers, and proselytes to union meetings and remote locales in order to organize workers, establish local soviets, draw in cadres for the party, and (increasingly) recruit soldiers for the Red Army. More critically, party activists launched a broad agitation campaign to propagate the rhetorical image of a cresting wave of Jewish support. The Yiddish-language Bolshevik organ *Der Shtern*, which had begun publishing on a more or less daily basis by mid-January, brimmed with articles trumpeting successes in winning Jewish workers over to the Bolsheviks. On January 6, the newspaper reported a mass meeting in Dvinsk, attended (reportedly) by some one thousand Jewish workers and Jewish poor. The meeting concluded with the adoption of a resolution that extended a "fiery greeting to the Russian Soviet government," lamented the fact that the Jewish proletariat did not take part in the October Revolution due to the "false politics of the petit-bourgeois intelligentsia," and vowed to support the Soviet government and the Bolsheviks in the project of "emancipation that they bring to the entire world."[61] On January 16 *Der Shtern* reported on a meeting of Jewish shoemakers in Minsk who decided to form a Communist faction within their union.[62] Shortly thereafter, *Der Shtern* heralded the news of elections within the Minsk printers union that returned a new leadership council composed of six communists, three Bundists, and two nonparty members.[63] From mid-February through March, the paper carried several articles on a developing split within the Bund party in Bobruisk, resulting in the formation of a left Bund faction that went over to the Bolsheviks.[64] The text of the story on the split in the Bundist "citadel" of Bobruisk reiterated the recurring theme: "the party grows every day."[65] The subtext spoke of the role Jewish workers played in this process of social construction. If "print capitalism" and the rise of the commercial press, in Benedict Anderson's famous formulation, played the role of constructing the basis for modern nationalism, "print Bolshevism" self-consciously and deliberately sought to construct a new form of "imagined community" of petit-bourgeois Jewish producers becoming proletarians and Bundists becoming Bolsheviks.[66]

Stories of Jewish workers going over to the Bolshevik cause undoubtedly served a propagandistic purpose, yet the phenomenon was not entirely fictitious. Records of the 1921 purge suggest that the period from late 1918 to mid-1919 witnessed a significant influx of Jews into the ranks of the Communist party. Of the roughly 297 future Jewish Communists whose purge records are considered here, seventy-five (25 percent) claimed to have joined the Bolsheviks between 1918 and 1919, compared to eleven who had joined the party in 1917 and eight others who claimed to have joined the party at any point *before* 1917. At the same time, nearly half of these new Bolsheviks defected from other political organizations, including seventeen Bundists, nine Poalei Tsionists, five Socialist Revolutionaries, two Mensheviks, an Anarchist, and one former member of Karl Liebknecht and Rosa Luxemburg's Spartacist League in Germany.

Beyond their party affiliation, who were these earliest converts to the Bolshevik cause within the Jewish community? While the question of party composition is examined below in detail, some general observations are in order. They were, first and foremost, extremely young. Of the eighty-six or so Jewish individuals who joined the Bolsheviks between 1917 and 1919, all but ten were twenty-five years or younger in 1917; half were teenagers at the time of the revolution. For the twenty-four women in this group, the average age at the time of the revolution was just over twenty years old. The vast majority who answered the question concerning their prerevolutionary social origin (proiskhozhdenie—soslovie) acknowledged that they came from the *meschanstvo*—a term that literally meant the urban estate, but in Marxist language was used synonymously with petit-bourgeoisie.[67] Of the sixty-three who listed a basic occupation, fifteen could be considered intellectuals, including three bookkeepers, two teachers, a nurse, a dental hygienist, an accountant, an agronomist, a technical mathematician, two journalists, several students, and a musician. A dozen were clerks, shop assistants, or had no specific form of employment. The remaining thirty-six claimed to be workers of one variety or another, including five tailors, five woodworkers, four seamstresses, four laborers in unspecified factories, two hat makers, two bakers, a hairdresser, a textile worker, a glove maker, a matchstick maker, a tobacco worker, a shoemaker, a watchmaker, a bricklayer, a mechanic, a smith, three apprentices, and a hairdresser.[68] To place these miniscule figures into perspective, it should be noted that there were, by one estimate, only 344 party members and 97 candidates in the entire Minsk city organization on February 1, 1919.[69] By another, more telling estimate, this number fell to ninety-eight Communist party members and fifty-three candidates in July of 1920, when the Red Army once again recaptured Minsk after a devastating year of Polish occupation.[70]

The Polish-Soviet War

It is probable that no event did as much to foster an alliance between the Bolsheviks and sections of Belorussian Jewry as the Polish-Soviet War of 1919–1920. The expansive, fluid western front, where warfare on horseback brought rapid devastation to small, unprotected communities, introduced episodes of anti-Jewish violence that mirrored in force if not in scale the far more widespread violence wrought by White Armies and associated Cossack brigades in Ukraine. Polish forces dealt mercilessly with Jews suspected of collaborating with the Red Army in cities "liberated" across the Pale. One of the most notorious (but by no means isolated) events followed the seizure of Pinsk in April of 1919, when Polish forces broke up a meeting of thirty-five people, mostly Jews, suspected of collaborating with the Communists and summarily shot them.[71] Similar episodes occurred in Lemberg (L'vov), Lida, and Vilna.[72] Following the capture of Minsk on August 8, 1919, Polish soldiers rampaged through the city, murdered thirty-one Jews, beat and attacked countless more, looted some 377 Jewish owned shops, and ransacked many more private homes.[73]

Far more devastating than the violence perpetrated by "regular" Polish troops was the "irregular" warfare conducted throughout southern Belorussia by marauding bands nominally allied with Polish forces. The pogroms, which began during the early days of the Polish occupation, intensified in 1920 as the Red Army reclaimed territories but proved incapable of pacifying anti-Bolshevik partisans. Beginning in the summer of 1920, irregular armies commanded by the former Tsarist officer Stanislav Bulak-Balakhovich unleashed a series of pogroms that devastated Mozyr, Gomel, Bobruisk, and surrounding shtetlekh. In October 1920, thirty-one Jews were killed in the town of Turov. Thirty-two more were killed in a nine-day pogrom in Mozyr in November of that year. Pogromists killed seventy-two Jews in the shtetl of Gorodiatichi, forty-four more in the region of Kopatkevich, and so on and so forth.[74] Anti-Jewish pogroms became an acute reality wherever counterrevolution spread.[75] As with virtually every pogrom, murder was accompanied by widespread material destruction, extortion, and systematic rape.

In recounting their political autobiographies before the 1921 purge commissions, significant numbers of Jewish Bolsheviks recalled the role that arrest during the Polish occupation played in their political development.[76] Ber Leibov Oliker, a sixteen-year-old shopkeeper's assistant at the time of the February Revolution, cited his arrest under the Polish occupation as a formative moment. Like many of his peers, Oliker became politicized following the February Revolution. Having joined the Bund, Oliker gravitated toward the Bolsheviks when the Red Army recaptured Minsk in 1918. His experience of arrest under the Polish occupation cemented his political choice to join the Bolsheviks.[77] Similarly, the Polish occupying force arrested Abram Osipovich Gol'dberg, a former SERP member, for underground political activity in 1919. Following the Bolshevik recapture of Minsk, he joined the party and the Red Army, emerging from the experience of political repression as a staunch supporter of Bolshevik power.[78]

For others, it was not arrest, but the direct experience of anti-Jewish political violence that drove radicalization. Roza Yoktelevna Gutman, for example, was an eighteen-year-old needleworker in Mozyr when the Red Army recaptured Belorussia in 1918–1919. In February of 1919 she joined the komsomol, "still not yet knowing, but feeling, that this was *my* party, the party of the humiliated and the exploited." Whatever doubts she had were resolved unequivocally by the arrival of Petlura's Cossack army, which crossed the border from Ukraine to pogromize Mozyr in March 1919.[79] "[C]onvinced by the pillaging and animal acts of this band," Gutman officially joined the party and threw herself into underground work.[80] Stories like these proliferated throughout the occupied territories, suggesting the truism that violence and political repression often serve as the best propaganda for radical causes. It is likely that the experience of political repression under the Polish army did as much, if not far more, to drive young Jews into the Bolshevik camp than did the writings of Lenin, Trotsky, and all of the party pamphleteers combined.

The Polish-Soviet War also drew Jewish actors into the Bolshevik movement through repeated drives for military mobilization. Following the capture of Vilna in April 1919, the Central Bureau in Minsk ordered a general mobilization of all party members. An additional resolution called members of the Bund and Poalei Tsion to join existing armed regiments in Minsk preparing for armed the "defense of the revolution."[81] Poalei Tsion leaders, whose efforts to gain official recognition had been repeatedly rebuffed by the party, proved particularly eager to comply; the party recruited an entire division, the First Minsk Guards Battalion, which was subsequently annihilated in the fighting— a devastating blow from which the Minsk party never recovered.[82]

The second, far more concerted effort to mobilize Jewish activists into the Red Army began with the reconquest of Belorussia in July of 1920 and the Red Army push toward Warsaw in August. As the Red Army advanced, Soviet authorities again mobilized Bundists and other Jewish activists to serve as propagandists among the Jewish populations along the revolutionary road to Warsaw. One such activist, Bernard Emmanuilovich Balkov'skii, a well-educated son of "half-propertied" Jews from Bobruisk with no discernible occupation, entered the party as a twenty-two-year-old on June 12, 1920, as the Red Army was closing on Bobruisk. He proudly reported volunteering for the Red Army "on that very day," and was immediately mobilized into the political wing of the military apparatus.[83] Another such figure, Comrade Rashon, a stocking maker and Bundist, joined the Red Army as a political activist during the assault on Poland and became a Bolshevik shortly thereafter.[84]

While many Jewish activists were initially organized for political work, the regime also mobilized Jews into the fighting ranks of the Red Army. Mordukh Nakhimov Kazhdan, an unskilled laborer and Bundist from Borisov, was one of the many Bundists dispatched to active fighting brigades following the general Bund mobilization in 1919.[85] Grigorii Borisovich Fuks, a shoemaker who had joined the Bund in 1904 in Slutsk, joined the Revolutionary Brigades immediately following the October Revolution and was transferred to the front in the Bund call-up of 1919.[86] Efforts to recruit Bundists and other Jews into fighting brigades increased significantly after the Red Army assault on Poland came to a grinding halt at the edge of Warsaw in August. The Red Army's unexpected defeat during the "Miracle on the Vistula" (August 12–24, 1920) turned into a full-fledged rout at the hands of the Polish army. As the Red Army was thrown back toward the Belorussian border, the Central Bureau in Minsk frantically passed a series of resolutions to spur the recruitment of Jewish reinforcements. A party circular distributed in mid-September to all local evsektsii employed long-standing anti-Jewish narratives of Jews shirking military responsibilities to spur recruitment among Jewish workers:

> Esteemed Comrades! The Red Army has freed Belorussia from the yoke of the *pani* by means of arduous struggle. The Jewish working class did not take an active part in this struggle and did very little for the emancipation of Belorussia from the Polish occupation.

> The Red Army is carrying out a strenuous battle against the offensive of the Polish and International Counterrevolution, defending the freedom won by the proletariat of all nations.

> But on the front in the Red Army ranks there have been, to date, very few Jewish workers; the Jewish proletariat has still not fulfilled its debt before the socialist fatherland and the international proletariat revolution.[87]

The circular concluded by urging evsektsii operatives to fulfill this revolutionary "debt" by redoubling efforts to draw Jewish workers into the Red Army ranks.

Successive recruitment drives succeeded in drawing many new Jewish recruits into the Red Army ranks, and, through the army, into the ranks of the party and Soviet administration.[88] They were joined by streams of politicized Jewish refugees who evacuated to Minsk following the collapse of the Red Army offensive against Poland. When the Red Army advanced along the road to Warsaw in July and August of 1920, they established a local revolutionary committee (*revkom*) in each city and town taken. Anecdotal evidence suggests that Jewish actors played a prominent role in the formation of revkoms throughout these conquered territories, stirring anti-Jewish sentiment, to which Bolshevik and Red Army administrators were not immune. Julian Marchlewski, a leading Polish Socialist and old Bolshevik, earned a rebuke from the KPB Central Bureau for delivering a paper at a Red Army meeting on the Western Front in early 1921 in which he attributed the failure of the Red Army offensive to the high number of Jewish activists in the revkoms. Wherever the Red Army appeared, Marchlewski argued, they established a revkom, "in the front ranks of which stood the Jews." While acknowledging that many joined the revkom out of joy that the "arrival of the Red Army signified their liberation from pogroms and other filth," he condemned those Jewish "speculators and scoundrels" who entered the revkoms as technical workers "and were even prepared to use the revkom for their own ends."[89] Comrade A. Voitsekovskii, a Red Army officer in attendance, wrote to the Central Bureau, denouncing Marchlewski's outburst and dismissing his interpretation of events. "The Polish population saw perfectly well," he wrote, "that Soviet power mercilessly requisitioned stores and goods from the Jewish bourgeoisie and even shot them for speculation." The failure of the Warsaw offensive, he argued, resulted not from the overly Jewish "face" of the revolution in Poland, but from the "political immaturity of the Polish working class," which was incapable of recognizing "the difference between us—who brutally persecuted the Jewish bourgeoisie and defended the Jewish proletariat"—and the *pani*, who "organized pogroms of the Jewish poor and took the Jewish factory owners and wealthy traders under their wings."[90]

While Voitsekovskii forcefully criticized Marchlewski's interpretation of the facts, he did not challenge the facts themselves. In all likelihood, Jews did constitute a significant portion of revolutionary committees under Red Army control. When the military tide turned and the Red Army evacuated territories it had seized during the march on Warsaw, local Soviet activists across the front found themselves in an extremely precarious and isolated situation.

Many chose to evacuate with the Red Army, rather than face certain retribution at the hands of the Polish army.

Such was the case with Bronia Natanovna Vosk, one of the many Jewish actors who faced this difficult decision in the summer of 1920. Born in the shtetl of Vyshkov (Wyszkow), some forty versts northeast of Warsaw in 1902, Comrade Vosk's father worked as an unskilled laborer in a brick-making factory in Vyshkov—a fact she emphasized during her 1921 purge hearing to underscore her proletarian pedigree. As a child, she received no formal education and was apprenticed to a local artisan sewing workshop at the age of twelve. Two years later, she moved to Warsaw by herself and found work as a hired laborer in a sewing factory. Feeling herself to be "sufficiently exploited," Vosk sought escape through education and political activism. She attended night school and, like thousands of Jewish workers, became a Bundist, entering the *Yugend Bund*—the party's youth organization—in 1916. Following the Bolshevik Revolution, Vosk became increasingly critical of Bundist politics. While appreciating the exposure to Yiddish literature and culture she received in the Bund, she dutifully reported to the purge committee that she came to realize that "the only party that could emancipate the proletariat was the Communist Party." In 1918 she joined the Polish Communists and worked underground in the Warsaw organization.

When the Red Army launched its offensive on Warsaw, Comrade Vosk returned home to Soviet-occupied Vyshkov and became a member of the local Communist party presidium. As the Polish Army drove the Red Army from the outskirts of Warsaw and began its eastward drive, Comrade Vosk unsurprisingly threw her lot in with the revolution. She evacuated with the Red Army to Minsk, rather than wait for what would likely have been an unpleasant fate at the hands of the Polish military. Perhaps she believed that it was only a matter of time before the revolution would once again "liberate" Vyshkov and bring her back home. But the revolution was busy making new meanings of the old idea that the proletariat had no homeland—especially not for a proletarian who was both competent and eager to work for the workers' state. Upon her arrival in Minsk, she was immediately mobilized into the ranks of the party and assigned to the evsektsiia under the Central Bureau of the Communist Party.[91]

Making Bundists Bolsheviks—A Reprise

Comrade Vosk represented part of the last and most significant wave of radicalization that brought Jewish workers and activists into the ranks of the Bolshevik movement in Belorussia. Despite being a native "Polish" Jew and outsider stranded behind the Soviet line, Comrade Vosk gained her right to citizenship and active participation in the Soviet project through labor and service to the revolutionary movement. Her inclusion in the body politic rested upon class origins and political devotion, rather than upon claims of ethnic or national belonging. Far from being an anomaly, Comrade Vosk's story points to the remarkably progressive nature of Belorussian nationality policy. Against the prevailing winds of nationalism blowing from the west—a nationalism that increasingly asserted integral uniformity between geography, ethnicity, and language—the Belorussian Republic constituted a defiantly multinational experiment. In place of one national language, it recognized four: Belorussian, Russian, Polish, and Yiddish. While the republic excluded individuals on a social basis, it sought, in theory, to integrate all laboring peoples equally, regardless of nationality. Rendered a political and national outsider in her "own" country, Comrade Vosk found inclusivity in the remarkably intranational and antinationalist state.

What made Comrade Vosk unique within the postrevolutionary milieu of Minsk was that she represented the comparatively small group of workers "at the bench" who passed from Bundism to Bolshevism *prior* to the reestablishment of Soviet power in Belorussia in 1920. Woodworkers, in particular, formed a large contingent of early workers who rejected Bundist calls for moderate reformism in favor of Bolshevik international revolution.[92] The foremost of these radicalized woodworkers, Abram Grigor'evich Beilin, broke with the Bund long before 1917, joining the Bolsheviks in 1905 and rising slowly through the party ranks (punctuated by frequent prison sentences) to become the head of the Belorussian evsektsiia in mid-1926.[93] Individual tailors, seamstresses, tobacco workers, and other workers likewise migrated from the Bund to the Bolsheviks. Yet the overwhelming bulk of tailors, seamstresses, and tobacco workers—not to mention the exceedingly steadfast leatherworkers and shoemakers—remained fervently loyal to the Bund throughout the first years of the revolution. So too did the vast majority of Bundist intellectuals, many of whom carried their ardent anti-Bolshevism into exile. A small but extremely influential group went over to the Bolsheviks prior to 1920, including the party historian Samuil Agursky (who left the Bund for the Anarchists in 1905), the litterateur and newspaper editor Boris Mikhailovich Orshanskii, and Il'ia Peretsevich Osherovich, a future Central Committee member and editor of the Yiddish daily *Oktyabr*.[94] All three emerged as key members of the evsektsii during the 1920s.

Loyalty to the Bund remained difficult to maintain as the Bolsheviks consolidated political power across Belorussia in 1920. Faced with the prospect of political marginalization, oppositional voices within the Bund began to push for closer relations with the Bolsheviks. In April of 1920, internal divisions within the party resulted in a split at the Twelfth Party Congress in Gomel, with the left faction led by Esther Frumkin and Aron Isaakovich (Rakhmiel) Vainshtein supporting a platform favoring the Bolsheviks.[95] This Communist Bund (*Kombund*) retained a nebulous, semiautonomous status for much of the next year, as the Bund leadership and the Bolsheviks party negotiated terms for the entry of Bundists into the party. Finally, in April 1921, the Comintern in Moscow ordered the Bundists to enter directly into the party ranks, completing what both parties referred to as the merger (*sliianie*) between Bolsheviks and Bundists.[96]

Subsequent historiography has generally rejected the idea that the process of integrating Bundists into the ranks of the Bolsheviks constituted anything approximating a "merger." On the contrary, the process has usually been described as the capitulation of isolated Bundists in the face of overwhelming pressure from the Bolshevik authorities. The facts on the ground in Belorussia suggest the need to reconsider this interpretation. Both parties negotiated the merger from positions of political weakness. For the Bolsheviks, the logic motivating the sliianie was simple: they desperately needed cadres. At the time of the Third Party Congress of the KP(b)B held in November 1920, there were a mere seventeen hundred party members in the entirety of Belorussia. While this number nearly doubled to three thousand party members by the Fourth Party Congress in February 1921, the party remained precariously understaffed.[97] Moreover, negotiations with the Bund took place at the height of the Polish-Soviet War, when Bolshevik administrative capacities were stretched to the limit. During internal party debates on the issue in August 1920, hardliners—most notably Shepshel Shepshelevich Khodosh, the chairman of the Central Soviet of Trade Unions—urged the party to reject any cooperation with the Bund. The prevailing moderate faction, however, viewed reconciliation as an absolute necessity, arguing that an alliance would leave the Bolsheviks with a definite majority in the unions and provide a base of support within the broader Jewish community. Vil'gel'm Knorin, the chairman of the Central Bureau of the party, stressed the necessity of merger as a temporary measure. Rather than getting "carried away" and provoking an "open struggle with the Bund right now," Knorin urged the party leadership to come to an immediate compromise with the Bund leadership and then "swallow them up along with the unions." This course of action, approved by the Central Bureau, revealed clear manipulative intent; yet it simultaneously revealed the belief that the party had neither the means nor the power to defeat the Bund in a direct struggle.[98]

For the Bundist leadership, the motivation for pursuing the sliianie was also straightforward: the party was outflanked to the left by the Bolsheviks and pressed from below by an increasingly radicalized party rank and file. The purge records of 1921 provide ample evidence that the Bund was hemorrhaging party members, particularly young party members who were increasingly drawn into the Bolshevik orbit. The Bund likewise faced mounting challenges in recruiting new members to the party ranks. In the face of Bolshevik claims to universalizing revolutionary equality, the Bundist political program of political and cultural autonomy, forged in the period of tsarist segregation, appeared anachronistic. Ultimately, the left wing of the Bund leadership in Belorussia recognized that the Bund in isolation risked being rendered irrelevant.

The precise number of Bundists entering the Bolshevik party in Belorussia remained a subject of politicized debate throughout the 1920s. Samuil Agursky, a former Bundist turned Anarchist turned firebrand Bolshevik and evsektsiia activist, persistently downplayed the role of the Bund in the party. Writing in 1928, Agursky asserted that only 175 Bundists from Minsk joined the party with the merger, adding that "about 80 percent of the Bundist members came from the intelligentsia."[99] Yankel Levin offered a far more plausible estimate in his evsektsii report from 1921 (cited above) to the Central Bureau. Levin, writing two months after the final merger between the Bund and the Bolsheviks, noted that some 283 Bundists had entered the party in Minsk, along with 29 Bundists in Bobruisk, 78 in Mozyr, 39 in Slutsk, 22 in Borisov, and 8 in Igumensk, for a total of 459 former Bundists in the KP(b)B ranks.[100] Internal party lists of former Bundists who entered the party in Minsk in 1921 placed the number at 221, but excluded most Bundists who joined the party before 1921;[101] resultantly, of the 146 former Bundists who made their way into the ranks of the twenty-one party cells considered in this chapter, eighty-one do not appear on the list compiled by the party, suggesting that the party vastly undercounted former Bundists in its ranks.[102] In short, it is likely that the total number of former Bundists who entered the Bolshevik ranks in Minsk alone between 1917 and 1921 was closer to 400 or 450 members, or just under one-half of the estimated number of Bund members in the city in December of 1917. This, at a time when the total number of Jews in the entire KP(b)B party organization likely numbered less than a thousand members.[103]

More telling than the absolute number of Bundists in the party was the extremely high concentration of former Bundists within key party cells. To cite but a few examples, among the twenty-one Jewish members of the House of Labor party cell, eleven were former Bundists (who worked alongside seven former Poalei Tsion members). As were thirteen of the sixteen Jewish members of the United Consumers Society (*edinoe potrebitel'skoe obshchestvo*—EPO), one-third of the Jewish members in the TsB KP(b)B administrative cell, fourteen of the thirty-one Jewish members of the Commissariat of Enlightenment

(*Narkompros*) cell, and eight of eleven Jewish members in the Commissariat of Social Security Cell. The numbers of Bundists in party cells tied to production were similarly high, if not higher. Thus half of the Jewish members of the woodworkers union party cell were former Bundists, as were nine of the fifteen members of the Minsk "new" shoemakers workshop and over 65 percent of the twenty-four (exclusively Jewish) members of the party cell attached to a uniform, hatmaker, and tailors workshop run by the Cheka for provisioning the Red Army.[104]

While suggestive of the crucial role that Jewish party workers and former Bundists played in the establishment of early Soviet apparatuses in Minsk, such statistics reveal little about individual Jewish actors who composed these cells. Undoubtedly, each individual who entered the party ranks did so for their own reasons based upon hundreds of individual judgments and life experiences that defy any simple attempt to construct a composite "snapshot" of these actors. A full analysis of the factors and experiences that drove Jewish actors into the ranks of the party would require a far more exhaustive study than possible here. A glimpse of these motivations, however, as well as a suggestion of the broad array of individuals who entered the rank and file of Soviet power may be discerned through a closer examination of the purge proceedings in a single party cell.

Purging the Jewish Party School Cell

On September 15, 1921, some sixty members of the Jewish Party School (*evpartshkola*) in Minsk gathered together for a mass meeting to conduct a general purge of the Bolshevik party cell affiliated with the institution. In an opening address before the committee, Comrade Sh. Osherovich, a leading member of the party cell, spoke to a packed room of party and nonparty members about the factors leading to 1921 purge. The purge, Osherovich noted, dated back to the period of the party's underground existence, when it was used to weed "ideologically foreign elements" from the ranks. "But now," Osherovich observed, "the situation is different. The party is in power, it appears to be privileged and it therefore attracts elements who discredit" the party. "These weak, petit-bourgeois (*meshchanskie*) ... elements ... weaken our party," Osherovich argued.[105] Yet the purpose of the purge was not simply to eliminate opportunistic elements from the party. Rather, he explained, "we must purge ourselves from harmful elements in order to be perfectly understood by the *nonparty*" members of Soviet institutions. The purge was therefore carried out openly, "to bring the matter before the nonparty members for their consideration."[106]

While the term "purge" (*chistka*) is often associated with the most egregious periods of Stalinist state repression during the 1930s, the party purges of

1921 bore little resemblance to these later events. In 1921, purges took place in mass meetings where participation was open to all members of the union or productive enterprise represented by the party cell under investigation. Each party member was publicly reviewed on an individual basis. After presenting a short autobiography, the party member answered questions from the review committee, as well as questions, comments, and accusations posed by fellow party members and nonparty workers from the floor. The purge was a moment in which party members eagerly, enthusiastically, and publicly expressed support for the revolutionary project and proudly defended their roles as foot soldiers in the project of building socialism.

The purge records, of course, cannot be taken at face value as simple articulations of the "truth" of personal experience and history. Party members of course reinvented biographies to emphasize revolutionary and proletarian credentials. Yet the purge structure, at least in 1921, was designed to subject cadres to public scrutiny and expose falsifications of biographical detail. Inaccuracies, embellishment of revolutionary credentials, or attempts to ignore past "transgressions" frequently met with challenges from the floor. After voicing grievances, the entire assembly voted on the candidate's fate. Needless to say, this exercise in direct democracy at the party-cell level did not always work as intended. Yet the records of relatively "successful" purges, such as the one inaugurated within the evpartshkola cell, provide rare insight into the complex dynamics that developed as workers constructed their own revolutionary biographies and conceptions of what it meant to be acceptably Bolshevik in this early historical moment.

The Jewish Party School cell was obviously a unique cell. Made up of forty members (twenty-seven men and thirteen women), the cell was composed exclusively of Jewish party members. Cell members were either students or worked as instructors, administrators, or white-collar workers in the school, which was established by the party to provide technical training, political education, and literacy courses to Jewish workers in the city. The cell consequently brought together numerous cultural workers who either had moved or were in the process of moving into a rapidly forming Soviet intelligentsia. The level of debate, discussion, and introspection was, as a result, atypically high. The cell was also atypical insofar as it had a uniquely high concentration of individuals who previously belonged to other parties. Thirty of the forty cell members had belonged to another party, with twenty-seven former Bundists and three more former members of Poalei Tsion among the ranks.

What united the members of the party cell, above all, was their youth. The average age in the cell was just over twenty-three years. The exceptions were eight "Old Bundists" who had joined the Bund before World War One and eventually gravitated to the Bolsheviks. For many younger members, Bolshevization was a two-stage process: in 1917 they entered into the growing revolutionary tide by joining "Jewish" parties, either the Bund or Poalei Tsion. Of those cell members who reported entering *any* political party in 1917, nine joined the Bund, one joined Poalei Tsion, and one (a former Bundist) joined the Bolsheviks. Most remained in these parties until the merger of 1920–1921.[107] The remainder—generally the youngest members—came of age in the midst of the revolutions and entered directly into the Bolshevik party. For both groups, to be young, Jewish, and "proletarian" increasingly meant to be or to become Bolshevik.

If there was an "ideal type" among the party cell members, it was Comrade Leizer Isaakovich Pam. Born in Minsk around the turn of the century, Comrade Pam lost his mother at six and his father at fourteen, after which he was raised in a foster home. From his earliest years Comrade Pam had been driven by need into an apprenticeship in the shoe industry. He reported being religious until the age of thirteen, when he broke decisively with religion. Following the February Revolution, Comrade Pam joined the Bund and became an active member in Minsk. He was reported to have participated tirelessly in Bund party work in the city following the return of the Red Army in 1919; with the restoration of Soviet power in 1920 he entered into the Jewish Party School, read voraciously in Yiddish, and familiarized himself with all new political pronouncements. One fellow party member and classmate, Comrade Grudko, applauded Comrade Pam for his diligent studies, noting that he "took an active part in the party school, was accurate, disciplined, and one of the best and most interesting comrades." A nonparty worker, Comrade Vol'fson, eagerly seconded this assessment: "He's a typical proletarian, who has overcome all hardships." Comrade Pam brought together the most obvious characteristics of what, in the eyes of the party cell, made for a good Bolshevik. He was a poor, hard-working laborer who dedicated himself tirelessly to the tasks of self-improvement and education. *And* he had been a Bundist. Rather than serving as a mark *against* Comrade Pam, his previous party affiliation clearly won him support from the heavily Bundist cell.[108] The assembly unanimously approved his renewal (with two abstentions) as a party member.[109]

As a worker in the shoemaking industry, Comrade Pam was in good company among the party cell ranks. Despite the white-collar nature of the cell, the membership of the evpartshkola cell had a decidedly proletarian shading. The cell included eight former seamstresses, five tailors, three carpenters, three shop assistants, three apprentices, two unskilled laborers, a hatmaker, a shoemaker, a stocking maker, a metalworker, and a tobacco factory worker.[110] Only four members had nonproletarian jobs prior to the revolution, including two pharmacy workers, one clerk, and a bookkeeper. Like Comrade Pam, cell members were all part of a rapid process of upward mobilization out of the workshop and into the office. Yet for all, a proletarian background and a history of labor remained the primary political qualifications during the purge hearings.

Comrade Pam was one of nine cell members who lost one or both parents early in childhood. While psychologistic accounts of Jewish radicalism frequently explain the phenomenon as a form of Freudian rebellion against parental (and especially paternal) authority, the fairly large contingent of cell members from single-parent homes suggests an important corrective.[111] For these individuals, political radicalism stemmed not from antiparental rebellion but from a sense of solidarity with parents who had been forced into the workplace after the loss of a spouse, whether due to illness, death, or emigration.[112] Such was the case of Comrade Sukenik, a young party member whose mother joined the workforce after her father, a teacher, developed an incapacitating illness. Need pressed Sukenik into the labor force shortly thereafter; she moved to Warsaw to gain "qualifications," before returning to Minsk to work in a tobacco factory. There, she joined the Bund and, after the February Revolution, the Bolsheviks.[113]

While political opponents frequently caricatured Jewish Bolsheviks as being Russified, assimilated, and "inauthentic" Jews, the Jewish party school cell suggests a decidedly different reality. Of the party members, the vast majority was bilingual, speaking both Yiddish and Russian. Of the monolingual members, four spoke only Yiddish, while only one spoke Russian exclusively. Perhaps unsurprisingly, this last individual, Comrade Kazhdan, was one of the three party members purged from the cell during the proceedings. During her review, the party assembly pilloried Kazhdan for her "uncultured" monolingualism—and *Russian* monolingualism at that. Comrade Zamergrad, a steadfast Bundist-turned-Bolshevik, offered a harsh assessment: "The impression made [by Kazhdan] is one of physical and spiritual backwardness. She is of no use, and brings nothing to the party." Comrade Osherovich chimed in: "We must say the good and the bad. She is backward." The hostile treatment of Comrade Kazhdan drew a sharp rebuke from Comrade Zelikhman: "She is not social and you can't approach her, but we Communists must support her—not antagonize and laugh at her." Despite Zelikhman's appeal (and his probable solitary vote in her favor), the vote against Comrade Kazhdan was nearly unanimous.[114]

As the hostile treatment of the Russian-speaking Comrade Kazhdan suggests, these party workers were neither Russified intellectuals nor the products of Russifying state schools. The vast majority of cell members were either home-schooled by a *melamed* (Jewish religious teacher) or attended a *heder* (Jewish religious day school). Such an educational background was by no means grounds for expulsion. Comrade Kastovich, for example, a twenty-three-year-old seamstress at the time of the purge, received a religious education up until the eve of the February Revolution. Despite this fact, she joined the party in 1920 and was cited as being an "honest working girl."[115] Labor, in this case, trumped a questionable educational background and her membership was renewed by a comfortable margin.

A questionable educational background combined with other nonproletarian tendencies, however, placed party members in a precarious spot. Such was the case with Leiba Berkovich Fridman, a young shop assistant with a mixed past. An orphan whose father died when he was a child and whose mother left for America shortly thereafter, Fridman was sent to a heder and went to work at the children's canteen in the orphanage. By the time of the Revolutions of 1917, Fridman asserted, he had broken with his religious past. In 1918 he entered the Bund, attended night school, gradually moved toward the Bolsheviks, and joined the party with the 1921 merger. By his own self-styled autobiography, he should have been an ideal candidate for rapid advancement. Yet during his hearing, sharp objections derailed this path. Comrade Grudko labeled him a harmful element; Comrade Ol'shenbaum denounced him as a "little saboteur" (*sabotazhnik*) who once demanded a bribe from another party member. Comrade Shteinklaper delivered the final nail in Fridman's party coffin, alleging that he had sold copies of the party newspaper allotted to him for one thousand rubles apiece, rather than the two thousand rubles that he and his peers were supposed to charge. This entrepreneurial spirit of underselling the competition was cited, along with his heder upbringing, as evidence of a "petit-bourgeois psychology." Deemed a harmful but potentially reformable element, Fridman lost his party membership but was sent back to the komsomol to mature.[116]

The fact that Comrade Fridman was not expelled from the party altogether points to the rather lenient nature of the evpartshkola purge—a trend that did not necessarily hold across the rest of the city.[117] Not even a yeshiva background was a priori grounds for expulsion, although former yeshiva students, an extreme rarity, had a hard time convincing their peers of their qualifications as good Bolsheviks. One such rarity, Comrade Movshovich, faced a grilling before the purge assembly. Movshovich studied in a yeshiva until 1919, but was thrown out when he was discovered to have an unspecified "ideological conflict" with leaders of the yeshiva. Presumably, this meant he had begun to dabble in revolutionary politics. He found work as an unskilled laborer and then as a shop clerk, before joining the Bolsheviks in 1920. Despite his religious education,

Comrade Movshovich avowed that he decisively broke with religion after leaving the yeshiva, a claim that went uncontested by his numerous critics. These critics did, however, offer numerous other objections to Comrade Movshovich. Esfir' Freiberg, a former seamstress, chastised Movshovich for ruling despotically over a workers' circle to which he belonged. A tailor, Comrade Monchazh, criticized him for conducting noncomradely relations with other party members. One comrade charged him with being aloof; another called him an egoist. Several complained he was too preoccupied with "abstract" ideas. Comrade Tsygel'nitskii accused him of engaging in "private calculations" in relations with others; Comrade Zamergrad concurred: "He uses his consciousness to his benefit." Comrade Vol'fson attributed this tendency to operate according to "personal calculations" to his yeshiva upbringing, but felt compelled to add that Movshovich was a "conscious and devoted Communist."[118]

These comments suggest that Comrade Movshovich was viewed as a particularly cunning and not quite trustworthy party member; yet they also reveal a considerable degree of anti-intellectualism in the party ranks. Such strains are perhaps more understandable when one considers that only one of the other party cell members was educated beyond the first two to three years of heder. Yet the critique of Comrade Movshovich's preference for "abstract thought," his reliance on "personal calculation," and his willingness to leverage intelligence to unfair advantage suggest a far more complicated process of identity construction taking place. Most revealingly, the criticisms evoked common antisemitic tropes depicting Jews as being too clever, too given to abstract thought, and too preoccupied with "instrumental rationality" for personal gain. In the context of a purge of one Jewish party member by a room full of Jewish party members—all hesitant about what it meant to be proletarian and Bolshevik—one response was to deduce that to be Bolshevik meant to not to be too "Jewish," if being "Jewish" meant being too clever. Comrade Movshovich was, however, not only clever. He was also useful. Despite multiple objections from the floor, Comrade Osherovich directly endorsed party renewal, arguing that Comrade Movshovich held great influence within the local party apparatus. In the end, the assembly agreed—narrowly.[119]

One particularly salient criticism in a cell filled with former members of other parties was the accusation that a comrade had not broken sufficiently with previous political traditions. Comrade Elka Katsman, for example, was a twenty-two-year-old party member who had lost both her parents early in life and went to work in a pharmacy. After the February Revolution, she joined the printers union and the Bund. The frequently blurry distinction between the Bund and the Mensheviks seems to have been particularly acute in the Minsk printers union, a fact that rendered her credentials as a Bolshevik suspect.

"She is serious and disciplined," observed one nonparty worker, "but she has Menshevik tendencies." The accusation of Menshevism, which likely meant trade union organization, brought a flurry of responses from party members. Comrade Tsygel'nitskii jumped to her defense:

Comrade Tsygel'nitskii: "She's a Communist!"

Comrade Fainbukh: "She's a Menshevik!"

Comrade Levin: "She's not a Menshevik, she's a Communist! But she still has not been assimilated."[120]

Comrade Osherovich finally intervened to settle the matter. "It has been revealed that [Comrade Katsman] has still not yet come to consciousness; she therefore may have no place in the party." While Osherovich's interjection clearly sealed the fate of Comrade Katsman, who was expelled, the rank and file did not always follow suit on questions of alleged political deviation. Comrade Gel'man, a seamstress and former Bundist was, like Katsman, accused of harboring Menshevik sympathies as well as anarchistic proclivities and ties to the Workers' Opposition movement within the Bolshevik party. As a result, Comrade Osherovich and the purge commission pushed for her expulsion. Despite, or perhaps because of this, the rank and file rejected the bureau's urging, and she was approved by a vote of twenty-one to five, with seventeen abstentions.[121]

The cases of Comrades Katsman and Gel'man reveal a key tension within the party cell, and the Bolshevik party generally, over what it meant to be "proletarian." According to older meanings, "being proletarian" resulted directly from process of labor and (as those who had read their Marx knew) relations to the means of production. Under emerging Bolshevik meanings of "being proletarian," however, party activism counted as much as, if not more than, relations of production. Such tensions can be further deduced from the treatment of two other party members whose claims to proletarian status in the former sense were highly suspect. Comrade Esfir' Freiberg, a twenty-five-year-old seamstress, was the daughter of the owner of a wood-manufacturing business. Her introduction to socialism came through the reading of "belles-lettres and social-economic writings in socialist circles." She claimed to have become a needleworker after the revolution and to have been arrested during the war in 1915 for writing a critical political article in a newspaper.

In her own account, she broke with religion in 1916, joined the Bund, and took an active part in the Bund for the ensuing five years. Yet in the cross examination before the party cell, several peers began questioning Comrade Freiberg's credentials. Comrade Grudko accused her of possessing weak discipline and of missing many meetings, adding, "Psychologically, she is not a worker," seemingly a reference to her questionable background as the daughter of a wood industrialist. A nonparty worker by the name of Zoneishain chimed in that Freiberg had never actually joined the Bund, but had only worked in the library at the Bund workers' club. Comrade Monchazh continued the attack: "She comes from rich people. I know that her sister won't even allow her to come over because of her views." Comrade Osherovich, however, dismissed the allegations against Freiberg, stating that she did serious work in the party school and should be approved. Which she was, despite her thoroughly *meshchanie* background.[122]

Similarly, Comrade Rashon was, by her own admission, the daughter of "petit-bourgeois, religious" parents involved in trade. She claimed to have broken with religion in 1917, argued with her parents (upon whom she depended financially), and entered full-time work in the Yugend Bund. In 1920 she joined the Red Army, took part in political work in Poland, and later worked in the Red Army as an administrator before taking a position in the party school (where she apparently disliked the "Jewish atmosphere, due to the fact that they did not understand Russian"). As with Comrade Freiberg, she was accused by several workers—both party and nonparty—of having a "petty-bourgeois psychology." "Everyone says," Comrade Shteinklaper added, "that she really doesn't work in the factory out of need," but rather to maintain her political appearance. Comrade Sukenink put it even more bluntly: "She's a typical shop girl (*lavochnitsa*) who entered into the party out of calculation." Despite this opposition from certain workers, she gained support from the usually irascible Comrade Grudko, who praised her as being "serious, disciplined, and conscious." Others praised her service in the Red Army and party. She was retained by a vote of eighteen in favor, with three against and fifteen abstentions.[123] Service to the party again trumped dubious *meshchanie* origins and social position.

The cases of Comrades Katsman, Gel'man, and Rashon raise questions about the role that gender played in the construction of what it meant to be acceptably proletarian and Bolshevik in the evpartshkola cell. Two of the three members purged from the party cell—Comrades Kazhdan and Katsman—were women, and virtually all women members experienced particularly close scrutiny in the party cell. Of the thirteen women in the cell, seven received decidedly negative comments and responses from the ranks. Fellow party members chided half of them for being undisciplined, politically passive, and not serious enough. In addition, three others faced questions that demonstrated a high degree of ambivalence. Comrade Musia Katsman, praised for her seriousness and discipline, was criticized for being insufficiently "conscious" and harboring Bundist proclivities (which begged the question of what constituted Bundist proclivities in a room half-filled with Bundists). Another, Comrade Fel'dman, was praised by one member for her discipline ("she could not be more disciplined") and accused by another of being too "mechanical" in her discipline. As the cases of Comrades Rashon and Katsman suggest, women were among those most frequently accused of harboring a "petty-bourgeois psychology" or being politically unreliable.[124] Of the twenty-seven men in the evpartshkola cell, by contrast, twenty-two received generally positive reviews, with nineteen of these individuals being praised for being some combination of active, extremely active, disciplined, serious, conscious, comradely, and the like. Only three of the male candidates were described as being undisciplined by at least one member.[125]

The vast discrepancies in the language used to characterize the activities and dispositions of women and men members of the party points to the role gender played in the process of constructing "ideal" Bolshevik types within the party cell. If Bolshevism was about action, discipline, and consciousness, the tendency to deny these attributes to women in the party cell clearly served to "protect" the party cell as a domain in which power and authority would remain in the hands of working*men*. Individual women could and certainly did challenge this norm. Yet to do so required exemplary proletarian credentials and a long career of party and revolutionary activism. Such was the case with the outspoken Comrade Zamergrad. While only in her mid-thirties, Comrade Zamergrad had been a "party" member, by which she meant a member of the Bund, for sixteen years at the time of the purge. As a child she lost both parents. By the age of six or seven, she had begun working as a domestic servant and, by her own account, suffered much as a result. She made her way to Minsk in 1904, where she first encountered members of socialist circles who introduced her to *Iskra* and other socialist writings. During the 1905 Revolution, she recalled, "the domestic servants went on strike and I took an active part, met with representatives of the Bund, and entered into that organization." By 1907 she had worked her way into the Central Committee of the Bund and was dispatched by the party to Ekaterinoslav to help build the organizational chapter there. In 1913 Comrade Zamergrad was arrested in Ekaterinoslav for revolutionary work. After her release, she continued her work in the Bund apparatus and remained in the organization until the merger with the Bolsheviks. Comrade Zamergrad's impeccable revolutionary biography spoke for itself. She was an orphan, a worker, an organizer, an activist, a former political prisoner, a strike organizer, and an agitator. In short, she was an exemplary Bundist. And among the members of the evpartshkola cell, that made her an exemplary Bolshevik. She was renewed unanimously, with two abstentions.[126]

Conclusion

The establishment of Soviet power completely restructured the landscape of Jewish politics in White Russia. Each successive stage—from the outbreak of revolutionary upheaval in 1917, to the periods of occupation under German and Polish forces, to the piecemeal reestablishment of Bolshevik power under the auspices of the Red Army—brought new sites of conflict and pressures for reconciliation between Soviet power and the Jews of Belorussia. The revolutions and military struggles that brought the Bolsheviks to power had little to do with the actions of Jewish actors. Soviet power came to Belorussia through the actions of the Red Army and small cadres of mostly non-Jewish Bolsheviks. Most politicized Jews of the left entered the revolutionary process through political parties directly opposed to the Bolsheviks. The Bolsheviks, in turn, viewed distinctly Jewish political responses to the revolutionary outbreak with dismissive derision. Yet as revolution gave way to processes of political consolidation, the Bolsheviks had little choice but to seek accommodation with the numerically significant Jewish working class and their political parties.

In Minsk and the major cities of Belorussia, the process of consolidating Soviet power depended explicitly on winning Jewish actors to the Bolshevik cause. Multiple pressures, expectations, motivations, and dynamics drove a portion of the Jewish population into the ranks of primary support for the Bolshevik Revolution in White Russia. The process occurred piecemeal, haltingly, as the project of constructing a revolutionary society pulled in increasing numbers of actors. Some Jews moved hesitantly toward this project. Others rejected it. Still others drove forward with zeal and determination. The Jewish response to the advent of Soviet power was multivalent precisely because the Jewish communities themselves were rife with tensions, competing conceptions of politics and power, rival factions, varied interests, and overlapping claims to solidarity. Any attempt to reduce the fluidity of this experience to a single "authentic" response is to necessarily construct a one-sided history in place of existing multiplicities. Large portions of the Jewish population throughout the deposed Russian Empire adamantly opposed not only the politics of Bolshevism, but also any form of radical socialism or democracy. An even larger (and frequently overlapping) section supported the politics of Zionism in one form or another. Yet the oft repeated apologetic truism that most Jews were not socialists, and *certainly* not radical socialists or Bolsheviks, does little to explain the fact that there were sizable groups of the former in most locales in Eastern Europe, and more than a smattering of the latter as well. These Jews did not, as antisemitic logics insist, "make" Bolshevism or the revolution; rather, as stressed here, the revolution made Jews Bolsheviks.

The motivations that drove these actors were as varied as the personal experiences of the individual themselves. Examining the choices of some of these actors from the shop floor, the party cell, and the union hall helps to reconceptualize the processes of political radicalization from the "bottom up." From such a perspective, the binary frameworks frequently proffered to explain the process of Jewish radicalization in Eastern Europe—whether that of proletarian against bourgeois, "Russian" children against "Jewish" parents, non-Jewish Jewish youths against Jewishness, assimilated Jews against traditionalists—begin to break down. Analyses of the rank and file of radicalized Jewish cadres reveal a host of conflicting allegiances and layered identities. The fluid nature of their identities rendered them highly sympathetic to the Bolshevik vision of universal emancipation and potentially suspect in the eyes of the Bolsheviks. From the standpoint of the nationality, they overwhelmingly identified themselves as Jews. From the standpoint of religious proclivity, they were largely indifferent, if not opposed, to Judaism. From the standpoint of party politics, they were largely neophytes to Bolshevism, many with oppositional pasts. From the perspective of gender, they confronted and at times reaffirmed divisions and power structures of gendered authority that could be traced back to prerevolutionary guild and party systems. In their own eyes, they were ideal proletarians and the children of the proletariat. In the eyes of the Bolsheviks, they remained kustari and artisans, semiproletarians and unskilled laborers, apprentices and white-collar workers. By profession, they were tailors, shoemakers, joiners, and seamstresses. And they had just inherited a revolution.

PART II

CAPITAL AND LABOR

2

SPECULATORS, SWINDLERS, AND OTHER JEWS: REGULATING TRADE IN REVOLUTIONARY WHITE RUSSIA

SPECULATION [Latin. *Speculatio*—observation, finding out (*razvedyvanie*)] ...
The buying up and reselling of valuables (securities, goods, any kind of property,
and the like) in accordance with the fluctuating, non-uniform course of
prices, with the goal of quick and easy receipt of profits as a result of differences in
prices and rates of exchange. *Speculation by means of the stock market. Speculation on
foreign currency. Speculation on Brazilian coffee* ... || Such activity—made explicitly
illicit by the law or public opinion—that increases the price on something,
in particular by means of violating fixed prices ... *The speculation in objects of
broad consumption is strictly punished by Soviet law. Speculation in theater tickets.*

Explanatory Dictionary of the Russian Language, 1940[1]

He wants to be the banker of his province.
And so he begins with speculation in salt.

Pushkin (with respects to Voltaire)[2]

KRASNOARMEETS RUBIN MOVSHA Gershovich Fitershtein, a drayman and
son of a drayman from Minsk, joined the Red Army as a twenty-year-old in
1918 following the occupation of White Russia by the advancing German army.
During the Russian Civil War, Comrade Fitershtein fought with the 165th
Guard against Denikin's army on the Don. As the Civil War spilled over into
a war to spread proletarian revolution to Poland (or to restore imperial hegemony, depending on one's perspective), he transferred with his regiment to
the western front, where he served until the end of the war. In addition to his
own sacrifices, Fitershtein's family suffered extreme hardship under the Polish
occupation. Polish troops seized most of the family's valuables and all of their

livestock, killing one uncle who tried to protect the last of the family's horses.[3] To those who knew him at the end of the Civil War, *krasnoarmeets* Fitershtein likely appeared as a robust defender of Soviet power and a paragon of revolutionary propriety.

This public persona began to crumble on September 13, 1921, when agents from the railway transport division of the Cheka discovered seventy-five tsarist-era gold rubles in Fitershtein's possession during a train ride home from Gomel to Minsk. Under interrogation, Fitershtein admitted to traveling to Gomel on behalf of his landlord, one Nosom Abramov Gantman, a mill owner by profession. Gantman, Fitershtein testified, sent him to Gomel with two million paper rubles and an order to purchase gold at the bazaar. While acknowledging his purchase of the gold coins in question, Fitershtein insisted that he had "not personally engaged in speculation" but rather acquired the gold for Gantman without knowing the latter intended to profit from the transaction.[4] Cheka investigators and the district court dismissed this flimsy defense, rejected Fitershtein's appeal for clemency in light of his loyal service in the Red Army and family hardship, and sentenced him to six months in prison.[5] In a moment, Fitershtein's outward identity as a stalwart defender of Bolshevik power vanished; in the eyes of the state, he became a disloyal and potentially counterrevolutionary element, a speculator, and a class enemy.

Several months following Fitershtein's release, in an unrelated case, authorities from the Special Boundary Department under the administration of the Western Front arrested twenty-three-year-old Etna Iudelevna Zel'din. Prior to the First World War, Zel'din lived and worked as a domestic servant in Minsk. In 1918, having received word that her mother had fallen ill, she left her husband and returned home to Oran, a shtetl in the Vilensk guberniia to the west of Minsk. Shortly after her departure, Polish forces arrived in Minsk, cutting off her return. During preliminary interrogations, Zel'din stated that family circumstances compelled her to cross the border to search for the husband she had left behind four years earlier. She set out on the morning of May 19, 1922, carrying her *ketubah*, or wedding contract, attesting to her marriage to one Moisei Izraelevich Zel'din, presumably to support the stated reason for her journey.[6] Authorities apprehended her shortly after she crossed the border separating the newly created nation of Poland from the newly created Soviet Socialist Republic of Belorussia.

Following the arrest, comrade Leonov, an old acquaintance from Minsk and administrator in the Union of Soviet Workers, identified Zel'din as a politically loyal comrade. Based in part on his good word, the lead investigator from the Special Boundary Department agreed to release her from custody and turn the case over to the People's Court of the third municipal district in Minsk on the charge of illegal border crossing. The prosecutorial investigation, however, ultimately turned its attention to a much different violation. Under interrogation, Zel'din confessed to having deliberately crossed the border with five gold rubles, intending to sell them at terms more favorable than the official course set by the Central Bank (*Gosbank*). The court convicted Zel'din and fined her a sum of five million paper rubles (*sovznaki*) for intending to engage in the crime of speculation.[7]

Jews broke the law in revolutionary Belorussia. In a period of rapidly shifting economic and legal boundaries, it was perhaps the case that Jews— "Mercurian" boundary crossers par excellence—could not help but find themselves on both sides of the line demarcating ill-defined and ever-changing "revolutionary" legality.[8] Yet in a period of war, revolution, and more war, when economic collapse and the implosion of the Russian Empire gave way to multiple successor states that drew new boundaries, scar-like, through the heart of the former Pale of Settlement, boundary crossing, wandering, and lawbreaking became an inescapable reality for many Eastern European Jews, whether "Mercurian," transient, or otherwise by "nature."

In absolute terms, it is almost certain that Jews committed and were convicted of far fewer crimes in the republic as a whole during the revolutionary period than their non-Jewish neighbors, if only because—as a minority population constituting around 10 percent of the entire population of the republic— they were vastly outnumbered by non-Jewish potential lawbreakers.[9] Yet in urban areas such as Minsk, where Jews constituted over half of the city population at the time of the Bolshevik Revolution, Jewish lawbreakers were as likely to end up in court for legal violations as were their non-Jewish cohabitants. This was particularly so following the introduction of the New Economic Policy (NEP) in 1921, which ultimately transferred the regulation of all economic crimes from the jurisdiction of the "Extraordinary Commission" (*chrezvychainaia komissiia*), or Cheka, and the revolutionary tribunals to the People's Courts (*narodnye sudy*). The main difference in criminal behavior (or, more correctly, the prosecution of criminal behavior) between Jewish and non-Jewish inhabitants of revolutionary Minsk and other urban centers was one of quality, not quantity.[10] In general terms, non-Jews were far more likely than Jews to be tried for acts of simple battery, assault, murder, desertion from the Red Army, property theft, public drunkenness, illegal distilling, and banditry—a crime that invariably combined most or all of the above. At the same time, Jews were far more likely than their non-Jewish neighbors to be brought before the courts for specifically economic crimes, such as selling stolen goods, trucking illegally produced alcohol, running worker *arteli* (cooperatives) and artisan workshops without proper registration, trading in proscribed goods, or peddling goods that were, following the introduction of the NEP, placed under the state monopoly.[11]

No legal transgression, however, was as readily associated with Jewish economic practice as the crime of "speculation" (*spekuliatsiia*). As a legal category, speculation was without doubt the most amorphous of economic crimes. Attacked legally and rhetorically throughout the First World War, the campaign against speculation was unleashed in its full force during the period of War Communism, with the Cheka charged with the specific task of stamping out this crime.[12] Despite the partial legalization of trade after the Civil War, the specter of speculation hung as a constant possibility over the entirety of the nascent revolutionary society and lingered, ever visible, on the fringes of the NEP. The legal transaction of today could—and, invariably, *would*—become the speculative practice of tomorrow, and vice versa, lending to the category of speculation an aura of randomness and irrationality.[13]

The language of speculation and the apparent randomness of its application served to obscure quite discernible patterns of enforcement and prosecution. Speculation may well have been, like treason, a matter of dates, but the dates were far from arbitrary. Episodes of intense policing and discourse about speculation in White Russia coincided with formative and discreet moments of early Soviet societal formation—the implementation of War Communism following the advent of Soviet power in Minsk in 1918–1919, the turn to the NEP in mid-1921, the period surrounding the hyperinflationary crisis of 1923, and the shift from the NEP to the planned economy, which began at the macroeconomic level in 1925–1926. This periodization suggests a direct relationship between the intensification of politicized discourse about speculation and systemic structural crises in Soviet economy and society.

If the proletarianized Jewish laborer constituted the positive ideal Jew within emerging Bolshevik political culture, the speculator emerged as the antithesis. Episodes of structural crisis in the NEP economy provoked spates of popular discourse concerning speculation that in turn evoked questions of Jewish economic practice, at times stated explicitly, and at times implicitly. Under a regime that understood economic practices as the determining structural base that shaped the realms of ideology, culture, and the like, such discussion invariably constituted a discourse about Jewish identity in revolutionary Belorussia. Speculation, in the most general terms, denoted unkosher trade. Shifting, fleeting, elusive, and illusive, speculation was also, perhaps, the truest allegory of the liminal place Jews occupied within the emerging revolutionary society in the western borderlands. In a region where Jews constituted an estimated 90 percent of all private traders during the NEP, efforts to describe, define, and delineate speculation, or to police, denounce, or liquidate speculators, frequently ran up against the limits of official ideology, which rejected naturalized or racialized conceptions of economics as being a priori counterrevolutionary.[14] In a context in which social position frequently mapped onto national difference, economic crisis generated tensions that fundamentally challenged the revolutionary commitment to race-blind justice and national equality under the law.

Given the concentration of Jewish actors in the realm of circulation, each crisis-ridden NEP economy and outbreak of speculation triggered spates of popular discourse concerning the nature of Jewish economic practices. It would, however, be mistaken to view the antispeculation campaigns simply as a process of engineering or constructing desirable Soviet Jewish subjects from above. While the Soviet state and the Bolshevik party—and the evsektsii in particular—played a lead role in launching antispeculation campaigns and rhetorical offenses, the process of policing speculation was intensely local.[15] In most locales, Jewish writers, polemicists, party activists, and apparatchiks who embraced the Bolshevik project of revolutionary transformation drove forward campaigns against speculation. In the process of doing so, these actors pushed for the reconstruction of Jewish social life and economic practices from below. The attempt to wean Jewish actors from "traditional" Jewish economic practices constituted a primary aspect of the Jewish Revolution that broke out in the midst of the Russian revolution.

This chapter utilizes the crime of speculation as a lens through which to examine the relationship between Jews as economic actors and agents of Soviet power in Belorussia during the Civil War and the NEP era. I argue that discourses about speculation and practices of regulating economic crime exhibited a threefold logic in revolutionary Belorussia. First, at the level of social practice, the crime remained a fluid legal category deployed in specific moments of economic crisis to forcibly regulate economic processes and direct the circulation of goods. Second, in terms of general discourse, the language of speculation was utilized throughout the NEP period to explain economic crises. As such, the language of speculation served to obscure the structural origins of these crises and, instead, place the onus for crises on the malignant agents, which, in postrevolutionary Minsk, almost invariably meant placing the onus for economic crisis on Jewish actors. Third, with regard to the Jewish community itself, antispeculation thought and practice served a secondary function of punishing and deterring crime. The primary function was to regulate Jewish economic practice and to instruct Jewish law abiders how to act under the new Soviet economic regime.

Genealogies of "Speculation"

The Bolsheviks by no means invented the concept of speculation. Rather, the phenomena of apparently inexplicable price increases and falling purchasing power due to currency debasement or devaluation has existed as a destabilizing possibility in all monetized societies. Yet the specific concept of speculation, denoting practices of rapidly moving, aggressive, profit-seeking capital investment that had the potential to generate sudden price movements and pressures on basic market functions developed only with the emergence of the modern commercial economy. Appropriately enough, one of the earliest appearances of "speculation" in this specific form entered into common English usage with the publication of Adam Smith's *The Wealth of Nations* in 1776.[16] Along with the "regular, established, and well-known" method of amassing a fortune (i.e., "a long life of industry, frugality, and attention"), Smith noted an alternative, at that time still rare phenomenon of amassing "sudden fortunes . . . by what is called the trade of speculation."[17] Rather than devote himself to a particular trade or branch of business, the merchant cum speculator, Smith observed, sought to maximize profit by the rapid transfer of capital to potentially profitable sectors based on an estimation of future market performance. By seeking to maximize profits through the rapid and prescient movement of liquid capital, the speculative merchant amassed a great fortune by "two or three successful speculations, but [was] just as likely to lose one by two or three unsuccessful ones."[18] Speculation thus entered into modern usage with a still familiar valence, implying the potential for great reward and even greater ruin, but only for the "bold adventurer," or investor, as an individual.

This positive valence, emerging in step with the expansion of the British commercial-imperial economy, gave way to a decidedly different turn on "speculation" a decade later as financial collapse swept aside the Old Regime in France. Attacks on speculation, as a distinct form of exploitative trade practice tied to the related practice of hoarding, became a catalyst for radicalization during the French Revolution. Antimerchant sentiments, which were articulated en masse with the grain shortages and sharp increases in bread prices at the outset of the revolution, reached their pinnacle with the turn to Jacobin dictatorship in 1793.[19] In the midst of the upheavals of that year, the *Enragé* Jean Varlet urged his extreme-left followers to seize power from the merchant-dominated Girondists and implement the death penalty for hoarders and speculators.[20] Relentless pressure from the sansculottes, urging terror against "the merchants, bankers, speculators, and even the rich," pushed the Jacobins to implement the "Maximum Laws," controlling prices in order to undercut speculative practices.[21]

As with so much of Bolshevik political language, the heavy emphasis on antispeculation rhetoric undoubtedly drew from the script written during the French Revolution.[22] Indeed, one could, in theory, draw an intellectual line from the Jacobin attack on speculation to Bolshevik policies and discourse about trade. Such a line—stressing the perpetual suspicion of urbanites, traders, and hucksters—might pass through Fourier, through the writings of Proudhon, and into the realm of Russian politics through Mikhail Bakunin and his Narodnik disciples; it would likely stress the tendency of each of these writers to conflate practices of speculation specifically with "the Jews." Moreover, it is entirely plausible that the conflation of antispeculation discourses and anti-Jewish tendencies entered into Russian Marxism and Bolshevism directly through the writings of Karl Marx.[23] Yet if distinctly "Jacobinic" strains of antispeculation thought existed inchoate in Bolshevism—or at least in Lenin's variation of Bolshevism—they remained impeccably well hidden. Lenin's early writings contain many references to speculation (frequently translated as "profiteering"), but he initially used the term in the Smithian (and Marxian) sense, to designate large-scale capital in search of investment opportunity. Tellingly, Lenin did not pen his first missive against speculation in the Jacobinic sense until November of 1917; that is, until after the Bolsheviks seized power.[24]

Rhetorically, when Lenin did attack the practice of speculation in its Jacobinic sense, he consciously jettisoned the racialized language that accompanied earlier critiques of speculation. Although a relentless critic of Jewish "petit-bourgeois" national aspirations in the form of Zionism and Bundism, Lenin remained equally adamant in his repudiation of antisemitism as a barbarous manifestation of deformed capitalist society. On the question of Jewish integration into social and political life, Lenin was closer to the liberal universalism of the Kadet party than to the Mensheviks, who accepted rather late the Bundist and Austro-Marxist platform that decoupled nationality from territory. The Bolshevik party was, in rhetoric, the most consistently universalistic, and by consequence among the most consistently assimilationist parties when it came to the "Jewish question." Jews were to be given citizenship as proletarians or denied it as bourgeois elements; the Jewish proletariat was to be defended with one arm of the state and the Jewish capitalist expropriated with the other. All as class representatives, never as Jews.

As with many aspects of the Bolshevik Revolution, the rhetoric of universalizing assimilation, race-blind justice, and national equality under the law ran into complications as soon as they left the printed page and entered into calculations of implementing policy on the ground.[25] And few grounds proved murkier or more treacherous, particularly with regard to the so-called Jewish question, than the Western borderlands of the newly established Soviet state. In the towns and small cities that dotted the countryside, Bolshevik policy encountered complex ethnic, religious, and social stews of largely Jewish, Russian, or Polish urban populations enveloped in countrysides inhabited by Belorussians or Ukrainians. In Belorussia, where Jews constituted over half the urban population and an estimated 90 percent of private traders, the regulation of economic practices necessarily entailed the regulation of Jewish subjects.

Speculation in a Marketless World: Revolution and War Communism

The policies of stringent state control over trade and economic life, labeled in retrospect as War Communism, came to Belorussia with the Red Army.[26] Following the Red Army reconquest of Minsk in December 1918, the Minsk Military Soviet (*Minvoensovet*), established under the leadership of the Polish socialist Stanislav Berson, faced the immediate task of asserting control over the basic functions of life in Minsk. This meant, first and foremost, resolving the problem of how to provision the local population and the massive Red Army contingents garrisoned throughout the region. One of the *Minvoensovet*'s first actions was to reaffirm price controls inherited from the German occupation, which had inherited them from the provisional government, which had inherited them from the imperial government, which had implemented them in 1916.[27] On December 7, the revolutionary government asserted nominal control over market functions, ordering the Cheka to immediately shoot anyone found violating the ban on the trade of spirits, firearms, and weapons.[28] On December 12, two days after the Red Army took Minsk, the revolutionary committee for the Minsk guberniia sought to minimize market disruptions by decreeing that prices for all goods should not exceed those established under the German occupation.[29] Despite their willingness to implement broad price controls based on the previous German prices for most goods, both the Military Soviet and the Central Bureau of the Communist Party (Bolshevik) of Belorussia (TsB KP(b)B) wavered on whether to implement direct state control over the grain and bread market. In January of 1919 the TsK KP(b)B was forced by necessity to allow for the free trade in grain, but retained price controls on other basic goods.[30]

Price controls and free trade policies combined with escalating demands and shortages to ravage the wartime economy. Inflation wiped out the pre-revolutionary monetary system, which began to melt down as early as 1917 and reached a catastrophic state by late 1919. Acute financial crisis followed, as inflation itself became a mechanism of class warfare. This inflation-as-warfare spirit was epitomized by the radical Bolshevik Preobrazhenskii, who famously hailed the printing press as "that machine gun of the Commissariat of Finance that poured fire into the rear of the bourgeois system and made use of the laws of currency circulation of that regime for the purpose of destroying it."[31] The collapse of the ruble—combined with the implementation of price controls for all basic goods *except* grain—served to transform grain into one of the only stable values and a scarce commodity chased by increasingly worthless cash. This inflationary situation generated a classical and combustible response from the population: those who had grain held it as a counterinflationary measure; those who acquired surplus grain sold it at increasingly escalating prices in the hopes of remaining a step ahead of the inflationary tidal wave. To the former practice, the Bolsheviks affixed the label of hoarding; to the latter, speculation.

In an environment in which inflation became a revolutionary weapon, counterinflationary measures came to be read as de facto counterrevolution. Rising prices and shortages of goods spurred rancorous attacks by Bolsheviks against speculators. One young party member, a certain Comrade Shevkuna, sent to the *mestechko* (small town or shtetl) of Koidanov north of Minsk to gauge (and stir up) the mood of the population, showed little hesitation in assigning blame for the town's poisonous political atmosphere. The most pressing problem facing Koidanov, he reported, was that of sharply rising grain prices resulting from the "Bacchanalia of speculators" in the town. Wealthy peasants refused to sell food to state cooperatives at fixed prices and instead sold exclusively to speculators, who offered higher prices for this grain and, in turn, "raised the prices even higher" when they turned the produce back onto the market.[32] "The number of poor citizens in need of bread is great. They demand the introduction of emergency measures." In lieu of recording exactly which measures the citizenry "demanded," Shevkuna offered his own recipe to combat speculation: the party should outlaw the carrying of goods to the *volost* limits, fine those caught doing so, confiscate their goods, requisition any remaining grain from them, and distribute the bounty to the poor. Yet instead of taking decisive action, the party did nothing.[33] Even worse, they passed laws that benefited the enemy. "From the moment we received order No. 9, signed by Reingol'd and Botvinikov," he lamented, "such measures could not be brought into reality." Thanks to this order forbidding the requisitioning and redistribution of surpluses, "the speculators celebrated a victory."[34]

Comrade Shevkuna was no isolated voice railing against the ills of speculation. The situation in Minsk grew desperate, as stocks in shops dried up and hunger spread. In late January 1929, alongside stories of want and shortage, an anonymous writer in *Der Shtern*, the Yiddish Communist party daily, gave an old, well-known Yiddish jingle lamenting the starving life of the *yeshive bokher* a new spin for new times:

Sunday potatoes, Monday potatoes	*Zuntik bulbes, montik bulbes*
Tuesday, Wednesday, nothing at all	*Dinstik, mitvokh, on akhile*
For the fat ones—bread and muffins	*Far di zate—broyt un bulke*
For the paupers—air and prayer	*Far kaptsonim—luft un tfile.*
Babies languish, starve from hunger	*S'shmakhtn eyfelekh fun hunger*
Mamas cry out: "give us bread!"	*Mames veynen: broyt der iker!*
And the merchants become richer	*Un di kremer vern raykher*
And the bakers fatter, thicker	*Un di bekers zater, diker.*
Sugar? No! All we have's candy—	*Tsuker? Neyn! S'iz do konfetn*
Sold by the pood, a whole little sack.	*Khotsh a pud, a gantsn zekl*
Bread? You must be joking, Comrade—	*Broyt? Ir muzt es lakhn, khaver*
I swear, there's no crumb to be had.	*Kh'shver aykh, s'iz nito keyn brekl.*
And she pulls up close and whispers:	*Un ir sudyet a farklemter:*
"Mister, I will pay you dear . . ."	*feter, kh'vel batsoln tayer*
And the merchant rubs his hands,	*Un der kremer reynikt lapkes*
And his little eyes spit fire.	*Un di eyglekh shpritsn fayer.*
I have pity for you, Comrade	*Kh'hob af aykh rakhmones, khaver*
You understand . . . the price inflates	*Ir farshteyt dokh . . . s'geyt in mekekh*
Malke, give the Jew some crusts,	*Malke, git dem yidn lakhme*
Give no bread—here's plain old cakes!	*Git keyn broyt—s'iz poshet lekekh!*
Bread and cakes—not available	*Broyt vi lekekh—nit benimtse*
Swallow air and live on prayers	*Shling di luft un leb mit tfile*
Sunday potatoes, Monday potatoes	*Zuntik—bulbes, montik—bulbes*
Tuesday, Wednesday, nothing at all.	*Dinstik, mitvokh—on akhile.*[35]

Satirical jabs at merchants proffering sacks full of sweets and Antoinette-ish cakes to the revolutionary masses steadily yielded to more vigorous measures as prices rose, making goods prohibitively expensive where available. On February 10, Moisei Kalmanovich, a consistently radical voice in the early Bolshevik party administration in Minsk, called for the TsB KP(b) to abandon free trade and introduce a state monopoly. "Free trade gives us nothing," he argued, as "the peasants won't give us anything for money . . . and barter isn't possible, since there are no goods to trade." Despite vociferous objections from several members, the bureau ultimately agreed to implement a state monopoly on the grain market and accumulate stockpiles of grain in order to manipulate local prices.[36]

The turn toward state monopoly coincided with an intensified campaign against speculation in the pages of *Der Shtern*, the shrill vanguard of the new offensive.[37] While the ideologically fervent (and almost certainly non-Jewish) Comrade Shevkuna paid no attention to the nationality of the speculators he assailed in his report, the editors of *Der Shtern* laid the onus for speculation—with qualification, but unmistakably—on Jewish traders. On February 14, several days after the decision to implement administrative control over the market, Zalman Khaikin, a evsektsiia firebrand, published a commentary drawing a direct line between Jewish participation in speculation and the outbreak of anti-Jewish pogroms. "Pogrom agitation has taken on a threatening character in recent days," the article observed, noting that full-fledged pogroms had recently broken out in Kiev, Elizavetgrad, and numerous shtetlekh. Khaikin warned of brewing pogrom agitation in Minsk, which he attributed to the "insane" (*meshugedike*) and "terrible" (*shreklikhe*) speculation that gripped the city. Of course, Khaikin noted, since the revolution, the "previously obscurantist (*far-finstere*) Russian folk-masses gradually began to understand . . . that all Jews are not their enemies," but that the enemy was, rather, "in the economic catastrophe [and] wild speculation." While the "obscurantist folk-masses" may have located the cause of the situation in abstract "economic conditions" and depersonalized "speculation," Khaikin blamed more concrete targets: "We are not ashamed to say that the guilt for the pogrom agitation lies with the Minsk speculators . . . who are not ashamed to simply rob the poor Minsk population." "The sugar and salt speculators," he wrote, "are guilty for the terror in which the poor Jewish population now lives." In addition to fueling pogrom agitation, the speculators also served to explain the other inconvenient immediate reality of life under revolutionary rule: "We say equally to the Jewish and non-Jewish population: it is not Soviet power that is to blame for the fact that there is no bread and no sugar, no flour and no potatoes. No! The rich peasant and the speculator in the city are guilty." Rather than the cause, Khaikin declared Soviet power to be the only defense against the twin evils facing the city: "To the speculator—Jewish and non-Jewish—we say: No pogroms will come to us in Minsk. But we will also not allow hundreds of unemployed to die of hunger; it is better we should exterminate (*oysratn*) hundreds of speculators, Jewish and non-Jewish."[38]

In the days following the publication of Khaikin's article, the Cheka began to make good on this warning by turning to full "administrative" measures to combat speculation.[39] On February 19, *Der Shtern* announced the shooting of nine people accused of speculation in money, bread, and sugar; an unsigned editorial defended the turn to terror as a means to combat speculation. "We welcome, welcome from the bottom of our hearts the steps taken by the Cheka," the author (probably Khaikin) proclaimed. "We welcome them because no other measures proved capable against the speculators." While acknowledging that "democratic" opponents would reject the means employed by the Bolsheviks, the editorial insisted that all "democratic" methods tried by the regime had failed. "Previously the Cheka had not shot a single speculator. We had undertaken other measures. But a revolutionary state needs to be able to deal with bandit-speculators—And the best means is to exterminate, to shoot all the speculators." "In Nemiga and in the old market," the author concluded, "the Jews and non-Jews should know that we will shoot them, shoot them like wild animals."[40]

Though clearly vitriolic, the antispeculation campaign in *Der Shtern* exhibited a telling tension: on one side, the editors railed against speculators as a seemingly concrete, counterrevolutionary reality; on the other, in the pages of *Der Shtern*, these "concrete" speculators remained a purely undifferentiated, abstract antisocial swarm. By contrast, the far less frequent reports about speculation in the pages of the Russian-language party organ *Zvezda* took a less caustic, but also less abstract character. On March 6, for example, *Zvezda* published a matter-of-fact article, buried on page four, stating that Communist party member L. Levin, his nonparty wife Kh. Levin, and another citizen, one D. Livshits, had been arrested on charges of sugar speculation.[41] Three days later, the newspaper reported that a revolutionary tribunal found Levin, a "communist on paper only," and Livshits, a "recidivist speculator" who previously speculated in Vilna, Kovno, Minsk, and Moscow, guilty of speculation. The tribunal ordered both to be shot for "discrediting Soviet power." Levin's wife received a three-year prison sentence "on account of her age."[42] A follow-up article noting that the sentences had been carried out was published alongside the text of the entire tribunal decision in response to the negative "popular mood" generated in Minsk by the story.[43] *Der Shtern*, by contrast, carried no specific coverage of the Levin case, but did publish a sweeping editorial in response to the Bundist organ *Der Veker*, which had sharply criticized the sentences. Comrade Khaikin once again took the lead, defending the shooting of the abstract speculator who profited while the Red Army men and children died of hunger. "The city speculator has made a pact with the kulak," he wrote, to break the state goods monopoly. "We must," Khaikin demanded, "declare a life and death struggle with the speculators," making explicit the willingness of *Der Shtern*'s editors to fully defend the shooting of speculators as counterrevolutionary abstractions, if not quite as Levins and Livshitses.[44]

While the editors of *Der Shtern* emphasized the party's intention to eradicate all speculators regardless of nationality, most indications suggest that far more Jews than non-Jews faced revolutionary justice for speculation. Although no records exist indicating the number of Jews arrested or executed for speculation, sources suggest that the percentages likely remained exceedingly high.[45] This tendency became particularly pronounced in the aftermath of the Polish-Soviet War, when the Red Army retook Minsk and the surrounding environs in July of 1920. The regime change and return of the Red Army triggered price increases, which in turn triggered renewed antispeculation sweeps. Faced again with the problem of policing trade and controlling speculation, the Soviet state turned from a tactic of direct eradication to one of sequestration. On September 20, 1920, the TsB KP(b)B presented the city branch of the Commissariat for Labor with a record of all speculators in the city, with orders that they be rounded up and pressed into forced labor.[46] By early 1921 the party had established a full-fledged concentration camp for speculators and other (mostly) nonpolitical prisoners. The existent camp records indicate that nearly nine out of every ten people incarcerated on speculation charges were Jews.[47]

Clearly, not all speculators in revolutionary Minsk were Jews; but just as clear were the explicit facts of state violence and the rhetorical violence resonating from the pages of *Der Shtern*, which tainted all nonproletarian Jews with the stigma of possible speculation. The fact that the antispeculation campaign appeared almost exclusively in the Yiddish press provides a clear indication of the intended audience. So too did the repeated binary juxtaposition in the Yiddish press of the image of the poor Jewish masses against that of the Jewish speculator. In theory, policy targeted speculators abstractly; in practice, the policies targeted Jews discursively and concretely. Yet the rhetoric and practices of revolutionary violence, of course, cut both ways. While the Bolsheviks increasingly turned to "administrative" measures to regulate economic matters, they held no monopoly on the use of terror itself. This point was made explicit on the morning of May 20, 1919, when *Der Shtern* devoted much of its space to the short life of Zalman Khaikin himself, who had been captured by Polish legionnaires in Vilna and summarily shot.[48]

Trade Under the NEP—The Kosher and the *Treyf*

Speculators, Contrabandists	*Spekulantn, kontrabandistn*
Clergy Zionists	*Kley-koydesh tsienistn!*
Thrash them terribly	*Shmayst zey sakones*
Beat them pitilessly	*Shlogt on rakhmones*
See the throngs of poor,	*Zet di khevre-layt*
To sell and swindle[49] they set forth,	*Handlen mizrekhn forn vayt*
To grab a fatty little bone	*Tsu khapn a fetn beyndl*
They sharpen their little tooth.	*Sharfn zey a tseyndl*
To have a drink, a good meal	*Makhn a koyse, a gute akhile*
Is, for them, the best prayer.	*Iz bay zey di beste tfile*
They brought a *keter** from the Torah,	*Tsu handlen mit treyfe skhoyre*
To trade for *treyf* merchandise.	*Hobn zey a keser fun der toyre.*

Anonymous[50]

* *keter*—an ornamental crown, usually forged of silver, used to cover the top of the Torah scroll.

War Communism brought the state into a direct, unmediated relationship with all facets of circulation and distribution. As the state asserted its control over market functions through the Cheka and revolutionary tribunals, it necessarily emerged as a direct and present entity in the lives of peasants and traders throughout Soviet territories. Rebellion brewed. In the spring of 1921, the sailors of the Kronstadt garrison mutinied, calling in part for the end of the state monopoly on trade; in Tambov province, peasants revolted against grain requisitions. The New Economic Policy, introduced at the Tenth Party Congress in the spring of 1921, was intended to restore economic vitality following the Civil War and alleviate growing tensions generated by the unmediated relationship between Soviet state and society. By substituting a tax in kind for forced requisitioning and by allowing peasants to sell posttax surpluses on the market, the NEP announced a new toleration of markets and traders, and a partial restoration of "freer" trade relations.

Far from a unitary, smooth, or immediate transition, the NEP was introduced in piecemeal fashion and retained a spasmodic character throughout, as Alan Ball has demonstrated.[51] While the NEP period remains a quintessential moment of Soviet economic "normalcy" in contradistinction to the many "abnormal" periods of crisis (to use Julie Hessler's terms), "normalcy" by no means implied predictability or regularity.[52] Economic policies fluctuated throughout the 1920s, resulting in rapid, nearly constant oscillations between microbooms and microbusts. The NEP began to yield results only in the summer of 1921. By early 1923, however, monetary crisis and hyperinflation wrought disaster once again, bringing trade to a trickle by late summer. Currency instability sent Soviet trade into a chaotic spiral, leading to the introduction of a new, gold-backed currency, the *chervonets*, in late 1923–1924. The policing of speculation and discourses about the crime ebbed and flowed with these crises.

Confusion and consternation dominated a meeting of the Central Bureau of the Belorussian Communist party held on May 15, 1921, to discuss the implications of Lenin's "The Tax in Kind," which outlined the central tenets of the NEP.[53] The party leadership in Minsk responded to the abrupt turn in policy with underwhelming enthusiasm. While the debate in the Central Bureau touched upon implications for agriculture and industry, discussion repeatedly returned to questions of trade. "If the economy is no longer under our dictatorship," Comrade Iosif Abramovich Vainer noted rather presciently, "legal relations must change." This change demanded a complete reformulation of state policy toward speculators, whom Vainer could not yet bring himself to refer to by the new moniker of "private traders." Signaling what would become one shift in policy, he argued that the party "must struggle against speculators not because they trade, but because they evade registration."[54] In other words, while private trade was to be legalized, grudgingly, under the NEP, legalization was to entail strict regulation.

The legalization of trade under NEP prompted a discernible shift in tone within the pages of *Der Veker*, which had by then replaced *Der Shtern* as the official Yiddish party organ.[55] With the official endorsement of private trade, attacks on speculation became far more muted and qualified. An article reporting on the First Congress of Belorussian Trade Unionists in mid-May suggested a vague distinction between healthy trade, meaning *registered* trade, and speculation.[56] A similar theme appeared in an article honoring the convening of the Belorussian and All-Russian Conference of the Evsektsiia in July of 1921, in which the unidentified author drew a distinction between kosher trade and unkosher speculation. "The New Economic Policy," the author argued, "permits free trade, healthy and proper trade," while fighting against "unhealthy trade, against speculation."[57] As private trade became increasingly entrenched during the summer of 1921, speculation virtually disappeared from the pages of *Der Veker*.[58]

The fact that trade had been legalized and that missives against speculation ceased to fill the party organ did not mean that the practice formerly known as speculation ceased on the streets. In July, just as *Der Veker* extolled the development of "healthy and proper trade," Russian Communist Party member Iakov Shapiro painted a dramatically different picture of life in Minsk in a letter intended for a comrade back in Moscow. Shapiro, a Minsk native, described the good life he enjoyed after returning home to work for the People's Commissariat of Agriculture. After two weeks of "living on dry goods," he got his ration book, received a "stylish" and "well-lit" room decorated "with good bourgeois taste and a splendid couch" from the housing department, and spent his afternoons "drinking tea with his landlord, the 'bourgeois.'" Despite the newly acquired ration book, Shapiro got his goods the old-fashioned way. "In Minsk," he reported, "life approaches peaceful times; speculation is well-developed everywhere . . . as bread is accessible but very expensive. Black bread is 1,500 [rubles] a pound, and 2,500 for the better sort." In addition, the markets were filled with potatoes (600 rubles a piece), and, as a result of the bountiful 1921 harvest, "many fruits and good black cherries" could be had for 1,500 rubles a pound. "Whoever has fat pockets lives very well," he observed, "all except for the workers."[59]

While Shapiro still classified the phenomenon of sharply rising prices and the practice of selling dear as "speculation," it was no longer classified as such by the state. The process of delineating "healthy" and "unhealthy" trade meant that the state set specific, if constantly changing guidelines, as to how and where trade *could* be conducted. In the early summer of 1921, the Belorussian *Sovnarkom* (Soviet of People's Commissars) issued a series of instructions allowing trade to take place in shops and markets provided the traders were over sixteen years of age, had a requisite patent, only traded at designated times, and did not trade outside of specified areas. Most importantly, the Sovnarkom declared that it was "absolutely forbidden for private individuals to trade in goods under a government monopoly."[60] The violation of any of these provisions constituted one form or another of economic crime. Determining exactly which violation had been committed, however, remained something of an impossibility, as no established criminal law code existed for the Belorussian Republic until the government adopted the All-Soviet Criminal Code of 1922. Prior to the code's introduction, the courts simply labeled crimes by their "names." Yet while the meaning of "murder" may have been crystal clear, that of "speculation" remained anything but. The delineation of illegal trade necessarily involved the process of marking certain trade as *legal*, a process that required extended negotiation between law enforcement agencies and the courts.

The role of legal institutions in delineating legal and illegal trade was illustrated clearly in a case from early 1921 involving two sisters, Mera and Hinda As'man (twenty-seven and thirty years old, respectively), both accused of speculating in cloth and garments. On March 8, 1921, agents Gimel'shtein and Berenshtein from the city Criminal Investigation Department (*Ugolovnyi rozysk*) raided the As'man sisters' Zamkovyi street apartment on suspicion that they had engaged in the illegal sale of cloth and garments. The raid turned up a stockpile of women's clothes, garments, and linens, leading the officers to confiscate the goods on the grounds that they constituted commodities earmarked for illegal sale.

In contesting the charges against them, the As'man sisters forced a clarification of the fluid rules of the trading game. In July the sisters sent a letter to Comrade Krol', the head of criminal investigations in Minsk, complaining about the nature of the search and the confiscation of goods. The officers, the sisters wrote, searched the premises when no one was present except for the "completely illiterate" Hinda, who was not even able to speak Russian (but was, judging by the signature on her transcribed deposition, literate in Yiddish). The officers broke open their closet and, the complaint continued, proceeded to take away "all of our things from there." The items discovered by the officers were not for sale, the As'mans asserted, but rather were heirlooms collected over the course of fifteen years for their wedding dowries. Far from being speculators, the two sisters emphasized their ostensibly proletarian origins: "We, like our late parents, are tailors by profession and never had our own shop, but worked for others. All our lives we have been exploited by petty proprietors." After the death of their parents in 1919, they worked in various shops, but "now . . . are without work, without dowries, absolutely without bread and without any hope for the future. . . . We cannot believe that our workers' regime (*vlast'*) will take away from us workers the last good things."[61] In August the People's Court of the Third District upheld the charge of speculation and the confiscation of goods, despite the impassioned plea of proletarian distress. Four weeks later, however, the Soviet of the People's Courts of Belorussia reviewed the case and found that the Third District court had "mishandled the question of the confiscation," adding that it was necessary to "bring the changed trade policies" of the NEP to the attention of the Third District court.[62] The Third District court grudgingly ordered the return of the confiscated goods on the condition that the As'man sisters "would not sell the aforementioned manufactured goods." Apparently the court had still not internalized the idea that such trade would have been, in theory if not in fact, legal.[63]

Confusion over what constituted speculation continued in the following months. The legal designation of speculation increasingly focused on crimes that involved trade in staple goods specifically placed under state monopoly. Compared to the era of War Communism, when virtually all consumer goods fell under state monopoly, the NEP introduced considerable freedom of trade. The state, however, retained and vigorously defended a monopoly on basic commodity goods, including sugar, salt, saccharin, coffee, and tea. Trading in these staple goods—most frequently sugar and salt—constituted one major form of undesirable trading practice that came to be grouped under the redefined legal label of speculation.[64]

A second major subset of speculation cases involved the selling of contraband goods from abroad, which violated the state monopoly on foreign trade. In general, the line between speculation and contraband frequently blurred, particularly when the commodity in question was a nonmonetary good, such as leather, valued both for its usefulness and ready exchangeability. Given the preponderance of Jews in the leatherworking industry throughout Belorussia, it is hardly surprising that Jews played a primary (but by no means exclusive) role in the smuggling and distribution of this item. The Cheka, for example, arrested one Iakov Zendelev Rakovshchik in October of 1921 after discovering forty-eight pieces of good leather, four pairs of women's boots, and four pairs of shoes in Rakovshchik's belongings during a return trip from Kazan.[65] On another occasion, the Criminal Investigation Division raided the apartment of Khaiia Margolis and uncovered two sacks filled with shoe leather and pieces of box calf leather (*khromovaia kozha*). The agents seized the goods as contraband due to the fact that they lacked the necessary branding from the tax department indicating legal importation. The thirty-seven-year-old Margolis acknowledged in her deposition that she had engaged in petty trade from the time her husband was killed in the war. She likewise admitted to trading without a license due to the fact that she could not afford to purchase one. Despite admitting her intention to commit what amounted to speculation, she was charged with smuggling contraband (and ultimately acquitted).[66]

The adoption in the summer of 1922 of the newly promulgated Soviet Criminal Code should have put an end to the ongoing confusion of what, exactly, separated legal trade from speculation and speculation from contraband. Yet while article 97 of the Criminal Code of 1922 outlawed the trade in contraband, the legal code included no specific law concerning speculation.[67] More curiously, the one article that came closest in spirit to speculation— article 137 outlawing "the malicious increase of prices for goods, whether by means of buying up or of concealing such goods or withholding them from the market"—was used in practice on an *exceedingly* rare basis. The absence of a specific law prohibiting speculation did not mean that the practices previously defined as speculation became permissible; instead, the 1922 code divided these various practices between a series of legal infractions. Rather than solving the mystery of what constituted speculation once and for all, the new criminal code legislated the crime out of existence.

Driven by a desire to normalize and define legal trade, the absence of speculation as a legal category also reflected a fundamental shift in trade and taxation policy. The introduction of the new legal code coincided with the transition, over the course of 1922, from a system of trade based on state monopolies to one based on excise taxes. As such, the soviet regime reestablished indirect taxation on a variety of goods—including salt, sugar, candles, coffee, and tea—that had been abolished by the tsarist regime in 1881.[68] One significant form of speculation thus vanished with the state monopoly; on the flip side, yesterday's large pool of speculators trading in monopolized goods became tomorrow's large pool of tax evaders trading in (more or less) the same goods. Actions that previously constituted a large bulk of speculation cases now came to be policed, prosecuted, and punished as tax evasion under articles 79 and 139a of the new legal code.[69] While the logic of the law changed, patterns of prosecution did not. Jews figured heavily among those prosecuted for tax evasion, an unsurprising development given the large percentage of Jews involved in shop or kiosk trade in Minsk.[70]

While legal codes concerning tax evasion became one central means of regulating petty trade after the state monopoly had been partially lifted, not all commodities were freed from the monopoly. The possession of arms remained under state monopoly. The prohibition of alcohol, in place since the outbreak of the First World War, was abolished in 1923, but the production and distribution of alcohol and spirits once again came under state monopoly. The violation of this monopoly became punishable by up to three years in prison under article 140. Under the vague article 136, which punished "the infringement of statutes regulating the enforcement of State monopolies," the state likewise maintained a monopoly on select goods, including playing cards and binoculars.[71] Over the course of 1922–1923, however, this article was used almost exclusively to prosecute crimes involving the violation of the state monopoly in the trade of gold, other precious metals, and precious gems. Along with article 138, which prohibited the trade in *valiuta* (currency), article 136 became a primary means through which the soviet state reasserted hegemony over currency and media of exchange in post-Civil War society.

Golden Rules

The trade in gold, silver, precious stones, and various monies constituted the final major economic practice that fell under the rubric of speculation. The trade in money, which flourished in the environment of war and want, increasingly emerged as *the* quintessential form of speculation. As inflation wiped out the value of the Soviet currency beginning in 1919, a whole array of commodities moved in to fill the void; alongside the successively issued official Soviet paper currencies—the Reckoning Tokens (*raschetnye znaki*) and Soviet Tokens (sovznaki)—German marks, Polish marks, Polish zloty, American dollars, "Kerensky" rubles, and "Nikolai" rubles streamed across the border, from distant locales, or from local holdings into the Minsk marketplace. In this sea of coins and floating paper, some more or less worthless than others, individuals made calculated decisions about which currency retained value in the present and would continue to retain value in the future. But to hold or accept currency was more than a market calculation; it was potentially a political statement. Holding Nikolai (tsarist) or Kerensky-era rubles, in particular as paper currency, reflected some degree of confidence in the possibility of the defeat of the revolution. It was, anachronistically speaking, "shorting" Soviet power. Yet holding tsarist currency, particularly gold coins, made rational economic sense from the standpoint of hedging against inflation and political vagaries. White victory or Red victory, gold remained gold, and a Nikolai ruble could always be restruck to accommodate new visages, emblems, or symbols of power.

Despite isolated voices that hailed the moneyless economy of War Communism, the Bolshevik leadership increasingly demanded the restoration of monetary hegemony following the war. Even Evgenii Preobrazhenskii, who lauded the printing press for its inflationary service to the revolution, declared before the Tenth Party Congress that it was "impossible to trade with a ruble rate which fluctuates on the market not only in the course of days, but in the course of hours."[72] The turn from war to the construction of a new, revolutionary society demanded a restoration of basic state functions, including the restoration of state control over finance, credit, and money. "When we conquer on a world scale," Lenin famously observed in a speech in November of 1921, "we will make public latrines out of gold on the streets of some of the world's biggest cities."[73] Until that time, the state sought to build gold reserves to stabilize the currency with single-minded determination. Building gold and foreign currency reserves became even more imperative in 1922, when the Bolshevik regime initiated currency reform to return Soviet power to that most nineteenth-century of institutions, the gold standard.[74]

While the Cheka targeted monetary and gold speculation throughout the period of War Communism, the struggle against speculation in gold, precious metals, gems, and foreign currency assumed a renewed sense of urgency in the era of the New Economic Policy. The crackdown showed signs of developing in the summer of 1921, as arrests for speculation of all forms, which ebbed following the introduction of the NEP, began to reappear. In June of 1921, for example, members of the Cheka arrested thirty-nine-year-old Il'ia and thirty-one-year-old Mariia Shul'man for holding tsarist-era currency, gold, and sugar. The Fourth District court sentenced Il'ia Shul'man to a year of forced labor but freed his wife so she could look after their newborn baby, despite the fact that she was a recidivist speculator.[75] On August 15, members of the Cheka's railroad division arrested seventeen-year-old Roshel' Fainshtein and eighteen-year-old Aron Moisevich Bravyi near the Minsk train station for possession of American dollars, gold, and tsarist money; both were released, but authorities confiscated their gold and currency.[76] The next week train security arrested the thirty-year-old Miron Markovich Frenkin, a trade agent who worked for *Glavproduktsiia* in Moscow, for carrying several thousand German marks, fifteen dollars, and thirty tsarist rubles. Frenkin was arrested along with the non-Jewish Mikhail Aleksandrovich S'egnikov, a fifty-nine-year-old employee for the People's Commissariat of Finance (*Narkomfin*), who was holding twenty-five thousand tsarist rubles. The latter was eventually exonerated; the former found guilty of speculation and subject to confiscation.[77] The following week train security arrested twenty-five-year-old Isaac Borisovich Kaplan, a former Red Army soldier, originally from Vilensk province, for holding about eight thousand Nikolai-era rubles; under interrogation he confessed that he had received the bulk of the money from twenty-nine-year-old Hirsh Gordon, a member of the third division of the Minsk city militia, who was himself promptly arrested for speculation.[78]

As these cases, as well as that of *Krasnoarmeets* Fitershtein, which opened this chapter, suggest, trains and train stations were one major site for arrests of potential speculators. Fitershtein was himself arrested, it will be recalled, on a return trip from Gomel in mid-September of 1921, just as the crackdown on the speculation in gold mounted. On September 28, several weeks after the arrest of Fitershtein, Cheka agents apprehended four passengers on an inbound train from Moscow. One forty-seven-year-old passenger, a member of the Kharkov United Consumer Society (*edinoe potrebitel'skoe obshchestva*, or EPO) by the name of Lev Moiseevich Gitler, had in his possession a diamond-studded gold brooch. The search of Vol'f Birger, a former Red Army soldier who served in the central militia in Minsk since his demobilization, turned up 145 gold rubles and a golden diamond ring. Mariia Genfer, an actress in the Yiddish Theater in Moscow, was discovered holding twenty gold rubles and a golden brooch. Nikolai Romashev, a Russian, carried ten gold rubles. Under interrogation, Citizen Gitler stated that he intended to sell his wife's brooch to buy warm clothes for sick family members living in Minsk. Citizen Birger claimed that he had held the tsarist coins since 1916 and planned to sell them legally at *Narkomfin* (Commissariat of Finance) upon his arrival in Minsk. Citizen Genfer insisted that the gold brooch was the only remaining object of value she retained from her home in Ukraine, which had been destroyed by Denikin's Cossacks; as for the twenty gold coins, she carried them to Minsk with the intention of having false teeth made of them. Romashev claimed that he had received the coins as a wedding gift many years earlier. After interrogations, the Cheka released all but citizen Birger who, on account of the large number of coins in his possession, was charged with intention to speculate.[79]

The crackdown on monetary and gold speculation reached a fever pitch in the days after the arrests of citizens Gitler, Birger, Genfer, and Romashev. In early October 1921 police rounded up several dozen gold and currency speculators in the environs of the Minsk train station, most for holding small amounts of gold or currency.[80] One twenty-two-year-old Leiba Pozniak was grabbed for holding eighteen rubles in silver.[81] The Cheka pulled in the twenty-year-old Lyubvi Katsenbogen for holding forty-five gold rubles.[82] Mordukh Shapiro was hauled in for possessing ten rubles and two pieces of lamp glass.[83] Of course, not all speculators apprehended in this sweep were Jews.[84] But most were.

Not all cases labeled as speculation involved small-time petty trade or nominal amounts of cash or gold; Minsk was a town big enough for speculators of all sizes. Some traders handled sizable amounts of currency through dubious means. Thus, for example, authorities arrested one rather enterprising fifty-one-year-old man after pogrom refugees complained that he had been buying up tsarist-era currency from them. Upon his arrest, the Cheka found

1,700 tsarist-era gold coins in his possessions.[85] The police nabbed another large-scale operator, a watchmaker named Levin who moonlighted as a diamond appraiser, on the evening of October 14. On that night, the Cheka raided Levin's apartment on Sobornyi Ploshchad' and rounded up twelve individuals holding varying quantities of gold, silver, and diamonds. The arrested, the Cheka tribunal determined, formed part of a diamond buying and smuggling operation that originated in Moscow and was responsible for moving stones to Poland. Nearly all of the accused claimed that they visited Levin's apartment to have their goods appraised.[86] One of the arrested went so far as to write a letter to the Cheka complaining that he arrived at Levin's apartment with less than the legal limit of three carats in diamonds; as for the six thousand German marks found in his possession, they had been given "by [his] deceased father to his son before his death," and consequently retained great sentimental value for him. Shockingly, the Cheka rejected this moving appeal to familial loyalty.[87]

While the campaign against speculation in money and gold decreased discernibly after this high point in the autumn of 1921, policing continued even after the state, technically speaking, lifted the monopoly on the private trade in gold, silver, and precious stones in April of 1922.[88] It continued despite the fact that the legal code passed that year deliberately included no article outlawing speculation. Under the newly formed, vague articles 136 and 138, the campaign against speculation continued without being labeled as such, picking up steam during the harvest months of 1922. And throughout this period, the antispeculation campaign continued with little more than passing reference in the pages of the party organs. Without fanfare, the state continued its campaign against speculation driven, in part, by the single-minded intention to assert control over the ruble. No centralized socialist state hegemony could be asserted when tsarist coins and paper money filled markets from the Baltic to the Pacific, when Polish and German marks facilitated trade in the Western borderlands, or when the Japanese yen and Chinese silver coins did the same in the Far East. From late 1921 through 1923, the policing of speculation focused almost exclusively on the money, gold, precious metal, and precious stone trade because controlling these trades was imperative for eliminating competing mediums of exchange and building critically needed reserves with which to back the intended introduction of the chervonets. The policing of speculation became, in part, a rather direct means of primitive accumulation of gold and currency reserves.

Yet the campaign against speculation was about more than bald state accumulation. Speculation had been, and remained, a crime of exchange. Or more precisely, a crime of *intended* exchange. Authorities rarely apprehended speculators mid-transaction, but rather targeted individuals who *held* something with the apparent intent to sell. Yet from the opposite end of the looking glass, holding something with the intent to sell is simultaneously holding something with refusal to buy. In late 1921 the "something" being held was, increasingly, money or some proximity thereof, in contrast to contraband, a category reserved for proscribed nonmonetary commodities intended for sale. It became easier to distinguish speculation from contraband only after the economy became sufficiently remonetized following the Civil War, as two parts of one exchange became split and separately criminalized. The disappearance of "speculation" as a specific statute in the 1922 criminal code was in many ways a result of the splitting of moments of exchange into different, separable, potentially criminal parts.

The separate criminalization of specific moments of exchange became, therefore, most evident in those rare cases when authorities *did* interrupt a crime of speculation in action. Such an arrest occurred on the night of October 21, 1921, when the Cheka, having received a tip, broke into the apartment of Tsalia Rivo on Politseiskaia and found the occupant buying unspecified contraband goods from Sofiia Savel'eva in exchange for gold. Little debate was needed to charge Rivo, the holder of gold, with speculation and Savel'evna, the holder of goods, with contraband. Both (non-Jewish) actors were sent to the courts on separate charges.[89] Yet the cases were not always so clear. Thus, for example, the Cheka received a tip that the forty-six-year-old Keilu Itskovna Ginzburg had stashed contraband in a false wall located in her attic. They raided the house and discovered the double wall, but found no contraband goods inside. Instead they discovered twenty rubles in gold and an assortment of paper rubles and Polish marks. A suspected contrabandist became, after presumably liquidating her stock, a speculator.[90]

When the NEP market functioned "properly," as it did, briefly, from late 1921 to early 1923, these two parts of exchange—buying and selling—remained united in fairly unproblematic fashion. Yet when the market seized up, as it began to do in early 1923, these parts of the exchange process became separated. While the roots of the 1923 crisis have most often been attributed to discrepancies between the costs of manufactured and agricultural goods, monetary instability undoubtedly played a primary role.[91] The unchecked expansion of credit and the slow introduction of the gold-backed chervonets in late 1922 exerted tremendous hyperinflationary pressure on the sovznak.[92] The new, extremely scarce, gold-backed chervonets generated intense demand, and the state once again turned to the printing press to fill consumer demand for currency. From early 1923 until mid-1924, the sovznak was essentially printed out of existence as the state bled every ounce of value from it before discarding it, permanently, in April of 1924 in favor of the new chervonets.[93] Meanwhile, market prices for consumer goods, valued in the sovznak, sky-rocketed. By the summer of 1923, as hyperinflation ripped apart the German mark, the sovznak followed suit. In the midst of the inflationary crisis, the separation of sale and purchase, or the refusal of holders of goods to sell them for increasingly devalued money, became catastrophic. Official discourse labeled this breakdown in exchange as the "scissors crisis"—referring to the sharp separation of prices between high-priced commodities and low-priced grain, resulting in market paralysis.[94]

By early 1923, as the crisis set in, the administrative campaign against speculation picked up dramatically, but with a renewed, familiar twist. In the first days of April, as the value of the sovznak began its free fall and prices climbed, *Der Veker* published a series of articles exposing a widespread nest of corruption, graft, malfeasance, and speculation in the shtetl Koidanov. Throughout April, *Der Veker* continued to carry full-page updates about the machinations of the shtetl's financial administration (*Zagat kantor*) and bread production (*Khlebprodukt*) division. A group of 114 people, including the hierarchies of both the Zagat Kantor and *Khlebprodukt*, had engaged, the articles claimed, in widespread tax evasion by selling false receipts stating that payment had been received for taxes that had never been paid. On May 8, 1923, *Der Veker* announced that the leading members of the departments—Aron Tshernov, Abram Goldberg, Vladislaw Kozerski, and Makei Osip—had been sentenced to death. In addition, the court sentenced four traders allegedly involved in the scandal—Leyzer Fraynt, Moishe Bernshteyn, Sakhne Bernshteyn, and Peysakh Dikshteyn—to death for speculation.[95]

As the crisis unfolded throughout the summer of 1923, arrests for speculation on money and goods soared in the Nemiga district.[96] The campaign against speculation returned full throttle in the Yiddish press. Under a regime driven by "orthodox" fiscal policy, rising prices, overextended credit, and the dangerous increase of emission would have, in theory, triggered a market-driven credit crunch. Such a tightening of credit, by forcing liquidation of stock, would have resulted in the forcible restoration of the temporal unity between sale and purchase. Such measures would have also intensified already widespread unemployment, a politically untenable prospect. Voices in favor of this approach dominated the fiscally conservative Narkomfin; but for the summer of 1923, at least, the revolutionary radicalism seemed to gain the upper hand over financial orthodoxy. The antispeculation campaign offered a means to assert administrative pressure on the market that did not entail cutting available credit, or the further shedding of labor force, to shore up the collapsing currency. Police administration and strident propaganda became the tools by which the state attempted, and ultimately failed, to force the moments of purchase and sale back together.

Rather than confront the structural factors contributing to economic crisis, the state very publicly attributed that breakdown to the malfeasance of mostly Jewish agents.

Gold and *Gvald*: Imagining Jewish Speculators

As the sampling of examined speculation cases suggests, an extremely broad cross section of Jewish actors was swept up in the various and periodic campaigns against speculation. The crime, as it emerged in the courts, was a hypermodern crime tied to train transport, movement, definitive urban spaces, markets, and access to goods. From court records, speculation appeared as a "Jewish" crime, to be certain. But it was a crime committed by the most variegated cross section of Minsk Jewry. The old, the young and younger, men and women, drifters, Red Army men, Soviet *apparatchiki*, militiamen, and party members committed the crime of speculation. "Speculation" drew in a broad cross section of actors precisely because it was, in short, another name for trade; or rather, it was the name given to trade when trade malfunctioned.

The press campaigns that occurred alongside the legal crackdowns of 1923–1924, however, increasingly presented a far different archetype of speculators for Jewish readers. In the Yiddish press, the abstract treatment of speculators as a vague asocial category gave way to a different form of abstraction. While "speculation" remained a daily occurrence regulated on the streets of Minsk, "speculation" as a discursive trope was increasingly relegated to the countryside and the shtetl, as the sensational coverage of corruption in Koidanov suggests. Koidanov itself became a near synonym for "center of speculation," described, variously, as a town where the streets were "paved with gold" and as a "nest of speculators and contrabandists." Insofar as speculation was a crime about trade, which meant that it was, fundamentally, a crime about the movement of goods over space, the shtetl increasingly came to be discursively constructed as a space lying beyond the boundaries of an apparently functioning, urban, *Soviet* economy.

"Speculators," likewise, became discursively reconstructed into a new form of abstraction. In place of the Red Army soldiers, militiamen, and everyday urban Jews who filled the police blotters, the image of the speculator increasingly took the form of one-sided depictions of "archaic" cultural types—in particular, the shtetl dweller, the rabbi, and the cantor. While a whole range of variations on the theme made their way into the discursive sphere, several examples must suffice, atypical only in style and élan. The first—a missive penned by one Adam Krasnapelski, a member of the Minsk needleworkers union—appeared in *Der Veker* in early February of 1923, at the start of the hyperinflationary crisis:

The *shul* keeps the watch,	*Di shul untervakhn,*
Locked up and shut tight,	*Farshlosn, farmakht,*
The Rabbi and Cantor	*Der rov un der khazn*
They swindle 'til night.	*Zey shvindlen biz nakht.*
The NEP is here!	*Der NEP iz farnumen!*
But not in the *shul*,	*Er geyt nit in shul,*
From huckstering and noodles	*Fun knep un fun lokshn*
Its head has grown dull.	*Di kop iz im dul.*
The NEP is here!	*Der NEP iz farnumen!*
It is not a sin,	*Es iz nit keyn khet,*
If each *shabes* the kugel	*Abi shabes der kugl*
Is kosher and fat!	*Iz kosher un fet!*
If every *aliyah*	*Abi di aliye*
Is paid for with gold,	*Mit gold iz batsolt,*
Bribery's the key—	*Der geshefter boyrer*
The arbiter of all.	*Khabar hot gants kolt.*
It judges the guilty,	*Er teylt di mekhile*
to the right and the left,	*Af links un af rekhts,*
In the center—the ruble	*Far a tsenter—mezumen*
What's good becomes *shlekht*.	*Vert gut, vos iz shlekht.*[97]

Krasnapelski's poem captured an underlying abstraction that began to develop around trade in the early Soviet era. The poem, like the accompanying archetype of the shtetl as a site of archaic social relations, rested on an underlying logic that implicitly linked the ostensibly archaic social form of trade, or "merchant capital" in Marxian terms, with archaic social forms associated with archaic Jewish cultural types. Krasnapelski's doggerel constituted a particularly clever, but by no means atypical, example of the rhetorical notes that developed in the Yiddish press.

Indeed, the conflation of archaic Jewish cultural forms and forbidden economic practices became a repeated trope in the pages of *Der Veker*. An anonymous feuilleton published just before Lenin's 1924 death captured this equation of archaic Jewry and speculation. The piece depicted a fictitious encounter in the market section of Minsk, the Nemiga:

A crash . . .

The treacherous Barukh rolls along, rolls along toward the *shul* off the Nemiga.

The Nepmen gather around him in the market, and he begins to burst (*platsn zikh*).

"Have you heard? Eh? The Communists, they are quarreling. There's a sharp argument in the party. The *goyish* Communists are fighting with the Jewish [ones] . . .

"*Nu*? What's he talking about?"

"Uh-huh, uh-huh . . . soon we'll hear the *shoyfer* of the Messiah . . ."

"*Nu!*"

"What's the problem? Trotsky can say to them: *naplevat' mne na vas* (I don't give a damn about you . . .)

"To whom?!? I don't get any of this . . ."

"What do you mean, to whom? To the *goyish* Communists.

"And what did the little uncircumcised bums answer?"

"They said to him, to Trotsky, that he shouldn't mix in their *Russian* lot . . ."

"Oy, oy, oy . . . we should run and tell our guys!"

"To do what?"

"To negotiate . . . We can jack up the price of lemonade to three rubles . . ."

"A blessing, that I am a Jew . . ."

"You also have a head, just like the Narkomfin agent."[98]

As with Krasnapelski's speculating rabbis, the anonymous feuilleton concerning the Jewish (which is to say reactionary) speculators reaffirmed a close association between economic practice, cultural nonassimilability, and obscurantism. The nature of these discourses suggests an underlying function of antispeculation rhetoric and practice within the Jewish milieu. Clearly, the targeted audience of such poems and feuilletons was not the Jew as imagined in the imaginary marketplaces and holy dens of speculation. Rather, these tropes, appearing as they did in the Yiddish dailies, were aimed at a Jewish audience deeply embedded in the process of Soviet cultural- and self-reconstruction. Far from being intended to convince opponents of the debased nature of Jewish economic practices, such sentiments were an intrinsic part of the project of creating new, modern, Bolshevizing "cultural" types within the Jewish milieu. Through such practices, proponents of Bolshevik programs of Jewish self-reconstruction delineated for fellow travelers what it meant to be "modern" negatively—that is, in opposition to what it meant to be "archaic." The construction of Bolshevik Jewish identity rested, at its core, on the premise of negating old forms of Jewish social and economic life.

Conclusion

The antispeculation campaigns in general suggest a twofold logic. On one level, the campaigns were supposed to affect a specific economic result: namely, the lowering of prices and the restabilization of "normal" trade in moments of crisis. Yet, on another level, the legal and rhetorical campaigns against Jewish economic crime undeniably played a different, equally important role. As Emile Durkheim long ago argued, the primary function of policing and punishing crime is not to eradicate or to deter criminal activity; rather, the function of punishment is to instruct law abiders of how to behave within coherent cultural systems.[99] Campaigns against speculation thus delineated a system of economic practices purportedly bound to pre- or counterrevolutionary vestiges within the Jewish community. Yet if ethnicity is understood to be a system of group identity constituted, in part, through shared cultural traits and practices, the rhetorical campaigns against speculation simultaneously articulated a need for Jews to wean themselves from dubious "ethnic" practices for the sake of national renewal and the full integration into Soviet society.

Insofar as these debates took place in the Yiddish press, they simultaneously constituted moments of specifically inter-Jewish dialogue about the nature of trade and the proper attributes of being a healthy Soviet citizen. Taken as a whole, the intense focus on Jewish tropes in the press, as well as the rather bald targeting of Jews as suspects, suggests a persistent tendency inherent in the Soviet project from the outset to conflate Jewish economic practices with the workings of "merchant capital" and problematically ascribe to Jewish actors a certain immutable agency over basic economic functions. Ultimately, these practices and rhetorics point to a more provocative claim: if, in contemporaneous European right-wing discourse, race frequently served as a mechanism for discussing economy, in the "left-wing" discourse of the Soviet Union during the 1920s, economy increasingly came to serve as a mechanism for discussing race.

3

JEWISH PROLETARIANS AND PROLETARIAN JEWS: THE EMANCIPATION OF LABOR IN NEP SOCIETY

In order to live, men must produce.

Ber Borochov "The National Question and the Class Struggle"

To be a productive laborer is . . . not a piece of luck, but a misfortune.

Karl Marx *Capital, Volume 1*

ON OCTOBER 20, 1918, one year after the Bolshevik seizure of power, sixty-four leading Jewish activists of the short-lived Central Jewish Commissariat and members of the Jewish Sections of the Communist Party (evsektsii) gathered for the opening of the First Jewish Communist Conference in Moscow. The weeklong conference brought together party and nonparty cultural activists from across the Soviet lands to discuss the project of transforming Jewish cultural and social life in postrevolutionary society.[1] Following an opening address by Semen Dimanshtein, the head of the Commissariat for Jewish Affairs, the floor passed to Iulius Shimeliovich, a young former Bundist turned Bolshevik militant, who surveyed the political situation on the "Jewish Street." Shimeliovich opened his comments by bemoaning the fact that "Jewish workers, who fought so heroically against Tsarism and took an important place in the history of the Russian revolutionary movement until the February Revolution" of 1917, greeted the Bolshevik Revolution of October with complete passivity. On the political front, the primary task was to draw Jewish workers "away from their false leaders and from the intelligentsia, who did not want the working class to become the master (*balebos*) of Russia," and to fight against those Jewish parties, most notably the Bund and the *"klal-yisroel* front," who had thrown their lot in with counterrevolutionary forces.[2] Yet political struggle alone, Shimeliovich stressed, could not bring revolutionary transformation to the Jewish street. In concluding remarks, he turned his attention instead to the underlying economic challenge confronting the activists. "We have before us one great task: we must apply all of our strength to help our *'luftmentshn,'* who now occupy themselves with speculation, so that they should become honest and useful (*erlekhe un nutslekhe*) citizens of our Soviet republic. We must bring to bear all means to provide them with work."[3]

The vision of integrating Jews into Soviet society through labor long outlived Iulius Shimeliovich. Following the Moscow conference, Shimeliovich returned to Vilna, where, in December, he became the leader of the newly proclaimed Vilna Soviet. On January 2, 1919, as the Red Army advanced toward Vilna in an attempt to spread revolution, anti-Bolshevik Polish legionnaires laid siege to the Vilna Soviet. Rather than surrender, Shimeliovich and other leading members of the Soviet chose suicide, ending their lives three days before the Red Army took the city.[4] Two months later, members of the Bolshevik-backed Jewish Communist Party (EKP) opened their first (and only) conference in Minsk with a moment of remembrance for Shimeliovich, "who fell in the battle with the counterrevolution."[5] Samuil Agursky addressed the assembly in terms that echoed Shimeliovich's call to assimilate Jews through productive labor. Historical circumstances, Agursky argued, transformed Jews into "petty shopkeepers and speculators," who were left "hanging in the air" following the Bolshevik Revolution. Arguing that the social condition of Jews constituted "our sorrow and our shame," Agursky urged the party to implement policies to "draw Jews into productive work."[6] Only productive labor, he stressed, echoing Shimeliovich, would transform rootless, mercantile, petty-bourgeois Jewish *luftmentshn* into healthy, productive Soviet citizens.

The Bolshevik project of Jewish emancipation, which began with efforts to determinately negate "Jewry" in the form of merchant capital, set as its positive objective the task of integrating and "productivizing" Jewish populations through labor. Steeped in the productivist logic of dominant Bolshevik interpretations of Marxism, the Bolsheviks viewed labor as the fundamental basis for inclusion in the general body politic of the postrevolutionary "workers' state." Legally, the Constitution of 1918 made citizenship and political participation contingent upon labor. Ideologically, labor, as a collective noun, came to be universally understood within the Bolshevik party as the historically chosen agent of revolutionary transformation. In theory, the integration of Jews as active citizens and participants in Soviet society necessitated the "proletarianization" of Jewish subjects. According to this logic, the integration of Jews through productive labor would effectively overcome the "archaic," traditional "overrepresentation" of Jews among the ranks of traders, middlemen, and nonproletarian elements. Labor would, in short, transform Jews into "useful," socially unmarked members of Soviet society.

Like the war against speculation, the campaign to productivize Jewish populations through labor constituted a central thrust of Bolshevik efforts to reform and reconstitute Jewish economic practice. Yet while the language of speculation drew discursive lines between the regime and its purported enemies, discourses about labor opened possibilities for Jewish integration into proletarian society. For Jewish laborers, becoming proletarian involved more than simply working as hired labor in an industrial enterprise. Rather, as with "speculation," the process of simply defining who or what constituted the mythologized proletariat became an ongoing struggle with real political implications. Given their frequently precarious status on the legal and definitional boundaries of soviet industrial relations, Jewish laborers—particularly the ubiquitous Jewish cottage producers, or *kustari*—found themselves locked in an ongoing discursive struggle with the state and party to assert their claims as proletarians in the proletarian state. In fighting to be recognized as proletarians, Jewish laborers likewise asserted new forms of subjectivity that emphasized belonging in the project of socialist construction.

While considerable attention has focused on questions of creating new, productive Soviet Jewish subjects through agricultural settlements, little attention has been paid to Jews within the core constituency of Soviet power—the working class.[7] This chapter examines the ever-complicated intersection between politics, labor, production, and nationality in revolutionary Belorussia from the standpoint of Jewish labor. While the Soviet state and Bolshevik party—particularly the evsektsiia—played an undeniable role in promoting the "productivization" of Jews, this chapter challenges the idea that the process of "making Jews proletarian" can be reduced to state or party hegemony over passive Jewish laborers.[8] On the contrary, the valorization of labor constituted a formative part of Jewish political discourses from below, as Jewish workers, union members, artisans, and intellectuals vigorously championed proletarianization as a means to social and political integration. In doing so, they sought to reconstitute labor as the essential basis of a positively reformed Jewish identity—a conception fundamentally divorced from, and formed in opposition to, purportedly traditional Jewish petty-bourgeois economic practices, as well as Judaism as archaic belief.

At the same time, the chapter argues that despite the ostensibly uniform character of "labor" as a concept deployed in official and popular discourse, the various gradations of Jewish laborers acted in anything but a unified manner.

Rather than facing a simple dichotomous choice between "horizontal" allegiances based on class and "vertical" allegiances based on nationality, Jewish laborers confronted a far less coherent reality in revolutionary Belorussia.[9] Taking as primary examples the case of the leather and sewing industries, this chapter argues that the project of reconstructing Jewish identity ultimately ran up against the structural limitations imposed with the New Economic Policy (NEP) in 1921, which reestablished limited market relations throughout the Soviet economy. In the midst of restructuring under the NEP, both horizontal and vertical allegiances broke down as Jewish artisans competed with non-Jewish labor, and also Jewish trade unionists, in asserting claims to privilege and social hegemony. Jewish trade unionists in turn faced challenges to their newly won political status from predominantly Jewish kustari, who proliferated during the NEP. The story of Jewish labor in Belorussia was beset by factional discord and sharp division.[10] Ultimately, this chapter concludes that the recurring systemic crises of the NEP economy undermined the ability of the Soviet state to match the integrative zeal of Jewish voices from below.

Productivity and the Multiplicities of Jewish Working Classes

Given the centrality of labor, proletarianness, and production within Bolshevik ideology, questions concerning the productivization of labor were inherently tied to all aspects of Soviet rule in Belorussia. To be productive and useful promised political representation, privilege, and position. Being "productive" in the literal sense of applying physical labor to nature to create objects for consumption did not, however, ensure inclusion in the coveted category of "the proletariat." In the categories of Marxian analysis, being proletarian involved considerably more than being a poor or pauperized producer. It entailed being a producer subsumed in a specific set of social relations: divorced from the means of production; reduced to a state of propertyless subservience to holders of capital; and existentially dependent upon the ability to sell one's last remaining "property"—labor power—in exchange for a wage. Marx himself emphasized wage labor as the minimal condition demarcating capitalist relations ("wage labor presupposes capital; capital presupposes wage labor").[11] In theory, proletarianization, which meant entering the ranks of those compelled to labor for wages, appeared as the entry ticket for inclusion among the collective revolutionary agents of world historical transformation.

Determining what, or rather who, constituted the "proletariat" within the complex social conditions of revolutionary Russia proved a far more complicated undertaking. Vladimir Lenin himself devoted much of his first major work, *The Development of Capitalism in Russia*, to teasing out distinctions between forms of production. Production in nonmechanized mills based upon handwork (*manufaktury*) fit plausibly under the rubric of capitalist production; the proletarianness of producers in small workshops (*masterskoi*) was less clear. Vaguer still was the distinction between artisans (*remeslenniki*) and kustari. The former theoretically produced goods on order for predetermined customers; the latter came to include all forms of cottage industry, outwork, and petty commodity manufacture for the market. Kustari, moreover, were more likely to be sufficiently divorced from the means of production, insofar as they received advances of raw materials (and wages) from private traders in exchange for finished goods.[12]

On the ground, the lines between artisan, kustar', and proletarian labor remained exceedingly murky.[13] At times, kustari worked for wages; at times they hired labor. Artisans, on the other hand, became drawn into "marketized" production long before the revolution.[14] Moreover, rapidly changing local economic conditions thwarted precise classification, as illustrated in a 1926 report by the then head of the Belorussian evsektsiia, Abram Grigor'evich Beilin, on the state of Jewish kustar' production in the shtetlekh. Lamenting the fact that a sharp downturn in the rural market, coupled with an oversupply of producers in the shtetlekh, had curtailed the demand for labor, Beilin noted that many producers had been forced to take on sporadic work commissioned for individual consumption. "In actuality," Beilin continued, local conditions served to "turn them [the kustari] into artisans."[15] Upheavals and stoppages in the NEP market, in other words, threatened to force the recategorization of labor.

In theory, the *kustarnichestvo* was a *social* category, used to delineate specific types of labor bound to specific social relations. Yet in the context of Belorussia, the kustarnichestvo was also unmistakably marked by nationality. Throughout the NEP era, Jews constituted roughly 90 percent of the republic's kustari.[16] Insofar as many officially designated peasants also engaged in forms of undocumented petty commodity production, the accuracy of this figure is debatable. Jewish producers, however, indisputably constituted an even *higher* percentage of those individuals who self-consciously identified as kustari, forming over 93 percent of all "organized" kustari who joined credit unions and kustar' producer societies.[17]

The concentration of Jewish workers in areas of nonagricultural production was by no means a novel, postrevolutionary phenomenon in White Russia. Prior to the revolution, Jews constituted between 70 and 80 percent of "artisanal" producers in Vitebsk, Minsk, and Mogilev gubernii; in the city of Minsk alone, over 40 percent of all Jews were involved in "industrial production," according to the 1897 census, which almost uniformly meant artisanal or petty production.[18] In general terms, Jewish labor was employed overwhelmingly in factories and workshops that operated on a manufactory basis. The

expansion of mechanized industrial production during the last prerevolutionary decades paradoxically intensified the concentration of Jewish labor in light
handwork industries, as mechanization tended to coincide with the displacement of skilled Jewish labor by unskilled, non-Jewish labor.[19] Thus, according
to a factory inspector report from 1903, there existed 377 "industrial" undertakings, employing 9,100 workers, in the Minsk guberniia. Of these, seventeen factories, with a total of 3,750 workers, employed exclusively Jewish labor
forces. Jewish workers made up 98.6 percent of the 533-person workforce at
the Progress-Vulkan matchstick factory in Pinsk, a similar percentage of the
275-member workforce at the Vitenberg matchstick factory in Belitse, and virtually the entire workforce in the large Kharlin, Ginzburg, and Tsukerman
tobacco factories in Minsk.[20] In addition to being demarcated by nationality,
many of these labor forces were also highly gendered. Jewish women constituted roughly 60 percent of all matchstick industry workers in prerevolutionary Minsk, and in general constituted large portions of handworkers in the
extensive tobacco and needlework industries.[21]

The demographic preponderance of Jewish labor in light industry continued
into the revolutionary period. According to a 1921 report by the All-Belorussian
Soviet of Trade Unions, Jews composed clear majorities of unionized needleworkers (97.9 percent) and leatherworkers (74.2 percent), and just under half of
all woodworkers.[22] The 4,200 Jewish members within these industrial unions
constituted a significant bulk of the unambiguous commodity producers
among the 18,979 Jewish trade union members. Their numbers swelled during the first years of the NEP, as economic imperatives increasingly focused on
the production of consumer goods: the total number of Jewish members in the
leatherworker union increased from 1,215 (of 1,636 total members, or 74.2 percent) in 1921 to 3,859 (of 5,324 members, or 72.05 percent) by early 1925; Jewish
representation in the needleworkers union climbed from 1,592 (97.9 percent) to
3,227 (94.09 percent) during the same period; the number of unionized Jewish
woodworkers grew from 1,405 (48 percent) to 2,333 (41.9 percent).[23]

Consumer goods industries proved particularly vulnerable to the extreme
economic volatility. Jewish laborers consequently faced an increasingly unstable existence in postrevolutionary society, as rapid changes in economic policy
and market conditions brought about perpetual class recategorization. In periods of economic expansion, Jewish workers experienced "proletarianization"
and "assimilation" into industrial labor pools; in moments of contraction, these
same workers faced the prospect of deproletarianization and dissimilation.
Economic crises, such as the ones that recurrently ripped through the Soviet
economy throughout the NEP period, drove Jewish workers from the ranks
of proletarian labor and into the margins of the productive economy. Loss of

position entailed more than diminished livelihood. Given the sharply politicized nature of production, the reclassification of status that accompanied changes in employment type entailed the simultaneous loss of political status and legitimacy. Deproletarianized proletarians became kustari; in the context of Belorussia, this meant that they once again became marked as "Jewish."

Political and cultural integration depended directly upon social integration, which reached a high-water mark with the turn to statist production, or "War Communism," during the Civil War of 1918–1921. Given their proximity to the frontlines, the regions of Belorussia were rapidly subsumed in the wartime economy. Full mobilization obliterated the market economy. The increase in state control over production was both cause and result of the collapse of the currency system and the suspension of market relations. Administered production, barter, and rationing replaced the market mechanism of wage payments and monetized exchange. The Soviet state, through the central Supreme Soviet of People's Economy (*Vysshii Sovet Narodnogo Khoziaistvo—VSNKh*) asserted growing control over industrial, transportation, financial, and economic activities to coordinate production for the war effort.[24] At the height of War Communism more than half of Belorussia's industrial enterprises came under the direct control of army production.[25] Particular attention was placed on the metalworking, sewing, leatherworking, and shoemaking industries in order to provision the Red Army. To meet productive goals, the state created large workshops to bring handworkers under direct supervision. A decree issued on November 29, 1920, finalized the full wartime mobilization by nationalizing all but the smallest workshops (including mechanized shops employing five or more workers and nonmechanized shops employing at least ten workers).[26] Jewish labor, mobilized into these workshops, played a decisive role on the Bolshevik home front.

Insofar as kustar' workshops rarely reached the threshold for nationalization, they effectively remained outside state supervision at the height of War Communism. Bolshevik hardliners, however, continued to view kustari as suspect, accusing them of exploiting hired workers and harboring ambiguous political allegiances. Moreover, while the petty production of kustar' goods remained legal, in theory, the state explicitly prohibited the private trade of many raw materials required for production. All goods of military importance, including leather and textiles, fell directly under state monopoly. Attempts to maintain the monopoly over vital wartime goods fueled suspicion that kustari speculated in contraband trade to acquire raw materials. Consequently, the process of becoming proletarian was necessarily linked, in the eyes of the state, with "bourgeois" Jewish malfeasance and lawbreaking. Concern about the political reliability of kustari and their ability to undermine state monopolies prompted the Bolsheviks to push for greater control over kustari by mobilizing them into state-directed production.

Given their high concentration throughout Belorussia, the task of mobilizing, organizing, and overseeing the Jewish kustari fell to the evsektsiia, making this the only area where the evsektsiia held administrative control over organs of economy and production. In early 1920 the Central Bureau of the evsektsiia in Moscow issued a circular to all local organs urging the adoption of immediate measures to mobilize Jewish kustari into soviet productive apparatuses. While the circular opened with a declarative call to "begin active work for the transformation of the economic situation of the Jewish masses," the language of ameliorating Jewish social conditions quickly fused with imperatives of state production. Given labor shortages throughout the republics, the circular proclaimed it necessary to draw the mass of Jewish laborers into the state productive process. The circular urged the local evsektsii to agitate in favor of transforming Jewish "kustar' undertakings into shock enterprises (*udarnye predpriiatiia*) for shock production," in order to prevent desertion from the labor front and meet military needs. To facilitate the "voluntary" transition from kustar' production to shock labor brigades, evsektsiia activists underscored the futility of resistance in the face of historical change. The inevitable expansion of large, mechanized production ensured the eventual eradication of older forms of production, the circular warned, insisting that "the social relations of kustar' and artisan production are only temporarily supportable." Attempts to avoid this inevitable transition by clinging to outmoded petty-productive relations would result in the economic ruination of these petty producers. More immediately, kustari who refused to join shock brigades would be denied any privileges afforded to those Jewish workers willing sacrifice their "present well-being" for the sake of general mobilization.[27]

The process of subsuming kustari into organized forms of commodity production necessitated more than the reorganization of productive methods and the reconstitution of Jewish social life. It necessitated a reconstitution of Jewish subjectivity. Resolutions from an all-Soviet evsektsii conference on Political-Enlightenment Work (*polit-prosvetitel'naia rabota*) held in Moscow in March of 1921 lucidly captured this imperative of psychic reconstruction. Despite the ostensibly antiessentialist logic of Bolshevik constructivism, the resolutions opened with a thoroughly essentialized review of the task at hand. Political work among Jewish workers, the resolution maintained, needed to begin by considering the "lifestyle peculiarity" of the Jewish laboring masses and the "residue of antiquated consciousness," which "strongly hinders the entry of the Jewish masses into the building of Communist life." The reconstitution of Jewish life required a two-fold campaign. On one hand, evsektsiia cells needed to carry out "productivist agitation" aimed at convincing Jews to "escape from the rut of the petit-bourgeois masses through new types of labor." Specifically, they were to conduct propaganda campaigns "against speculation and for the transition to productive labor." On the other hand, the resolution asserted the need to "rework the consciousness and psychology of the Jewish laboring masses to accommodate them to the requirements of the Communist reconstruction of economy and everyday life in the Soviet Republics." Implicit in the project of reconstituting the "consciousness and psychology" and the practices of the "Jewish laboring masses" was the assumption that the type of labor and psychology of the unreformed laborers was historically conditioned to be petty bourgeois, prone to speculation, and, hence, decidedly unproletarian.

The Politics of Productivity—NEP Practices

The system of War Communism collapsed under the weight of three years of full mobilization and uninterrupted war. Peasant revolts, coupled with the demoralizing Kronstadt mutiny, forced Bolshevik leaders to rescind the statist economic policies of the War Communism era. At Lenin's urging, the party legalized market relations in the countryside by introducing a tax in kind instead of direct grain requisitions. Yet the reintroduction of the grain trade constituted only part of the radical about-face of the New Economic Policy. Equally crucial, the NEP overturned the productive relations of War Communism by reaffirming the legality and centrality of petty commodity production as the basis for consumption throughout the Soviet lands.

Lenin justified the abrupt, seemingly complete reversal in economic policy by pointing to the need to overcome the plague of speculation. Rather than continue debilitating policies of controlling trade through the Cheka and coercive state violence, Lenin cajoled the party into accepting the restoration of market institutions, however reluctantly. To stamp out speculation and other economic lawlessness, and, implicitly, to fund the postwar state, the Bolsheviks had no choice but to legalize trade and *tax it*. Legalizing the grain trade necessitated creating viable trading partners flush with goods desired by the newly "freed" peasantry. Insofar as the production of sufficient consumer goods lay beyond the capacity of a war-ravaged industry, the state had few options but to encourage petty production to fill the hunger for goods. Recognition of this stark political reality by no means implied an end to skepticism about independent producers. Such a policy would once again allow the "million tentacles of the petit-bourgeois octopus [to] engulf . . . the workers"; yet the legalization of trade between these various tentacles constituted the only viable mechanism for undermining the "speculation [that] worms its way into every pore of our social and economic organism."[28]

The abrupt shift in policy generated immediate debate within the Central Bureau of the Belorussian Communist party. While the TsB KPB generally greeted Lenin's "The Tax in Kind," the foundational document of the NEP, with hesitancy due to concerns that liberalized trade would promote speculation, members of the party leadership proved far more sympathetic to Lenin's call for the liberalization of production.[29] Iosif Abramovich Vainer—a former tailor with an anarchist past—embraced the new policies and pushed to establish labor cooperatives to organize kustar' producers. Adol'f Getner, a Latvian-born, Old Bolshevik stalwart, likewise backed the new policy as a measure necessary to rebuild the postwar economy. The party, he argued, faced a dire shortage of workers, who had "disperse[d] to the villages," where they continued to work as kustar' producers during the war. It was vital to draw these workers back into the cities and productive work by *organizing* their production. "After the October Revolution," he observed, "we were Communist consumers, but not Communist producers." The NEP, he insisted, offered the possibility of organizing production through the market.

Other voices, however, expressed far less enthusiasm for integrating these nebulous producers into the weak Belorussian economy. Anton Karpeshin, a leading VSNKh official, explicitly questioned the political implications of the policy shift. "One thing isn't clear. If we, in the interest of increasing our manufacture, move toward the revival of the petite bourgeoisie, then we invite the petite bourgeoisie to get stronger." Under such circumstances, he argued, the petite bourgeoisie would not "remain impartial to the question of politics; it will obtain a part in power." The encouragement of petty production would also alienate "part of the large industrial proletariat," which would be "overwhelmed by petty undertakings." Despite these misgivings, Vil'gel'm Knorin, the Chairman of the Central Bureau KP(b)B argued that the party had no choice but to follow the line from Moscow—to "draw the petite bourgeoisie into the organization of production" while maintaining political power "entirely in the hands of the proletariat."[30]

Fiscal constraints introduced as part of the NEP severely compromised the possibility of simultaneously incorporating "nonproletarian" labor socially while retaining political control in the hands of the "proletariat." To reinvigorate production, the Belorussian state began to denationalize sectors of industry (primarily light industry) by turning smaller industrial undertakings over to private *arendators*, or leaseholders, in July 1921.[31] As part of the general effort to restore fiscal discipline and currency stability, the NEP introduced the concept of *khozraschet* (economic accountability) in August 1921. The principle of khozraschet directed all Soviet industry outside of the most vital sectors to operate on the principles of self-financing.[32] Industrial enterprises were to establish budgets, stick to them, and ideally generate surpluses that would accumulate not as profit but as revenue to be poured back into the grand project of building socialism. Despite the lofty rhetoric, the actuality of the khozraschet policy included numerous practices previously jettisoned by the workers' revolution into the dustbin of history, namely, pay differentials based upon performance, the reestablishment of individual factory management, and the reintroduction of piecework on a mass scale. In short, the state unleashed the motive of profitability on Soviet society, even as it denied the existence of profit in the sense of accumulation for private gain.

Most significantly, khozraschet reintroduced that most recognizable byproduct of "rationally" organized market production—mass unemployment. Military demobilization and new directives for economic accountability brought about the massive displacement of labor previously employed in state-directed enterprises. Within Belorussia, the streamlining and rationalizing of production generated mass unemployment, which disproportionately affected Jewish producers. In the Minsk oblast, postwar unemployment reached acute levels, particularly among Jewish tailors and shoemakers. Some 1,500 Jewish workers in the needle industry were thrown out of work across Belorussia. In one garment factory in Vitebsk alone, seven hundred out of twelve hundred Jewish tailors lost their jobs. Almost all of these displaced proletarians became kustari in the aftermath of the restructuring.[33] Unemployment resulted not only in the loss of livelihood but also in a direct diminution of political power, as formerly "proletarian" laborers were transformed overnight into kustari with dubious political claims. Social marginality and political marginality reinforced one another.

Surrounded by tenuous labor markets and growing unemployment, Jewish laborers found themselves embedded in a continuum of productivity created by the dynamics of the NEP. On one end of the spectrum were those Jewish workers who remained firmly grounded in the industrial economy as "factory" or large workshop laborers. These workers were, on the whole, more likely to be union members, party members, and unambiguously "proletarian" labor loyal to the project of building Soviet power. At the other extreme stood those Jewish producers on the fringes, bouncing from unsteady employment to unemployment, from city to town to shtetl, from industry to workshop to factory. They were far less likely to be party members or trade unionists, although the number of former trade unionists, former party members, and former Bundists purged in 1921 among their ranks was considerable. The claims of these laborers to "proletarian" status were, from the state's perspective, ambiguous at best. Far from being abstract, denationalized proletarians, they were viewed as discernibly Jewish and placed under the de facto jurisdiction of the evsektsiia. Yet many of these laborers forcefully pressed their claims to proletarian status, political representation, and the right to work. Relegated to the fringe of the NEP economy, they *urged* the state to productivize them, particularly in moments of recurrent economic crisis under the NEP. This intimate relationship between economy, productivity, and politics emerges most clearly in the example of two prototypical crisis-ridden "Jewish" industries that experienced sharp upheaval as a result of the NEP: leatherworking and shoemaking.

The Shoemakers Lament: The Paradoxes of Soviet Productivism

The leatherworking and shoemaking industries constituted a sizable share of light industrial production in prerevolutionary Belorussia. As rapid, state-driven industrialization in the last decades of the nineteenth century intensified demand for leather industrial and consumer goods throughout the Russian empire, the northern region of the Pale of Settlement became a primary location for leather production. Jewish industrialists, including Pinkhes Bereznitski in the shtetl Shislevich (Grodno guberniia) and Khayim Frenkel in the Lithuanian town of Shavel, established extensive networks of tanneries, transforming sleepy backwaters into centers of light industry employing largely Jewish labor forces.[34] By the end of the nineteenth century, Jewish entrepreneurs owned 287 of 530 tanneries throughout the Russian Empire, and some 70 percent of tanneries in the Pale of Settlement.[35] In the Belorussian territories, Jewish tanners made up an estimated 75 percent of all leatherworkers at the time of the 1917 revolutions.[36]

Jewish shoemakers likewise played a critical role in the production of shoes, boots, and finished leather goods for the rapidly developing consumer goods market in Belorussia. Unlike in Moscow, St. Petersburg, Warsaw, and Riga, where mechanized, largely foreign-owned factories introduced at the turn of the century had rapidly transformed the shoe industry, handwork remained the norm for footwear production in prerevolutionary Belorussia. Arthur Butman, an American commercial agent dispatched by the United States Department of Commerce and Labor to investigate commercial possibilities, stressed the predominantly manufactory nature of shoe production in the Belorussian cities. According to Butman, the largest shoemaking factory in Minsk, the Adler Russian-American Mechanized Shoe factory, produced an average of 239 pairs of shoes a day, compared to a daily output of more than 5,000 shoes at the massive St. Petersburg Gessellschaft fur Mechanische Schuhwarenfabrikation.[37]

In addition to constituting three-quarters of all laborers in the leather industry, Jewish leatherworkers and shoemakers formed one of the most organized sectors of the Jewish labor movement in the Pale. Workers from both industries played formative roles in the establishment of the Jewish socialist Bund, and tanners constituted one of only two mass labor unions (along with bristle makers) established under direct Bund auspices.[38] In the midst of the revolutions of 1917, leatherworkers, along with needleworkers, tobacco workers, and woodworkers emerged as leading activists in local soviets; yet leatherworkers remained reticent to abandon distinctly Jewish politics for the politics of Bolshevik rule. On the whole, they remained loyalists of the Bund. By 1920, however, increasing numbers migrated toward the Bolsheviks, and former Bundists continued to hold considerable sway in the leatherworkers union and Bolshevik party factory cells.[39]

Following a trend that prevailed across industrializing Europe, shoemakers proved particularly susceptible to political radicalization in the revolutionary period.[40] Although highly skilled, literate, and attuned to the intimacies of revolutionary political debate, shoemakers were generally viewed with thinly veiled derision in prerevolutionary Jewish society.[41] These factors combined to make them ideal candidates for upward mobilization into the ranks of the emerging revolutionary order. El'ia El'iashev Raichuk—a lifelong radical shoemaker who claimed to have joined the Bund in 1892 (*sic*) before joining the Bolsheviks in 1920—became a member of the Central Executive Committee of Belorussia and a leading member of the leatherworkers union.[42] Nakhim-Leib Kats—another former Bundist, self-described son of the working class, and proletarian laborer in a "*mechanized* shoe factory" in Minsk—served as a ranking member of the trade union while making his way up the rungs of the local party administration in Minsk.[43]

As the cases of Raichuk and Kats suggest, the Civil War opened avenues for the rapid political and social integration of Jewish workers into state and party apparatuses. The end of hostilities, however, brought renewed conflict between the state and labor unions over questions of factory control and production, culminating in the crushing of the so-called Workers' Opposition within the Bolshevik party in 1921.[44] As full employment and labor conscription gave way to demobilization and mass unemployment, newly Bolshevized trade union activists refocused their attention on securing labor rights in the face of renewed economic instability. In the context of NEP society, the defense of trade union interests in the "Jewish professions" meant protecting unionized workers from the encroachment of kustar' labor, rhetorically conjured as a direct threat to the social position of the Jewish "proletariat."

In May 1921, while the Bolshevik leadership debated the merits and demerits of the newly unveiled NEP program, the leatherworkers union pushed for a hard line on the labor front. Demands for the further nationalization of workshops in the leather industry dominated a conference of unionized workers and managers in the Belorussian leatherworking industry that convened in Minsk on May 5. Conference delegates applauded the fact that Minsk authorities had recently closed the small "first" and "second" leatherworking shops and turned their goods and inventories over to larger, nationalized workshops. They likewise praised the fact that the shoemaking industry had consolidated around the large mechanized shoe factory in Minsk (presumably the former Adler factory). Conversely, the delegates decried the slow pace of change in the provincial cities of Bobruisk, Borisov, and Slutsk, where small workshops predominated, and lamented the fact that large leatherworking factories in Slutsk and Mozyr had yet to be nationalized. In these regions, the conference noted, "there is the strong development of petty kustar' leather production, which we are taking measures to liquidate."[45]

Anti-kustar' sentiments remained the order of the day within the leatherworkers union, despite NEP reforms encouraging petty production. In addition to calling for the regulation of production outside of unionized, "proletarianized" factories, trade union protocols focused on the alleged infiltration of kustar' elements into the factory system itself. In June of 1921, Comrade Epshtein, a leading member of the leatherworkers union, reported on the dire state of the shoemaking industry in Borisov. Production in the Borisov shoemaking workshop had recently ground to a halt. Shoemakers in the workshop refused to work, deliberately damaged finished goods, went on strike, and "persistently demanded to be freed from the workshops" to which they had been assigned under War Communism and allowed to open their own shops (*lavochki*). Comrade Epshtein attributed the production abnormalities and seething tension to the social origin of the workers. Given that "there were very few proletarian shoemakers" at the height of civil war, the local soviets had no choice but to "mobilize all of the petty proprietor kustari; consequently, the Borisov workshop is composed entirely of this element."[46]

Attributing work stoppages and unrest to unhealthy kustar' social elements became a recurring theme used to explain away production abnormalities. Yet responses to Comrade Epshtein's report suggest that the problems in Borisov had more to do with systemic structural slowdowns generated by the NEP than with kustar' sabotage. One union member, Comrade Miller, blamed worker idleness and hostility on the fact that rations had been cut and the government had failed to provide the workshop with work orders. Given the state's inability to provide adequate funding, he recommended liquidating the workshop and allowing workers to become independent producers. Comrade Raichuk proposed an alternate plan of targeted layoffs, pressing the union to keep the workshop open while dismissing the "unhealthy elements and keep[ing] the very best." Ultimately, the union allowed workers to leave the Borisov workshop on a voluntary basis in exchange for payment of a tax in kind of three pairs of boots per week. Thus was the productive side of the NEP—the freedom to exchange, the freedom to labor, the freedom to provision oneself on the market—established among the shoemakers of Borisov.[47]

The freedom to produce, however, meant little without the ability to acquire raw materials. Free trade did not mean that all goods traded freely. Leather, in fact, remained one of the goods kept under the state monopoly due to its importance for military provisioning. The scarcity and portability of leather also made it a highly desired and valuable contraband good. To protect its monopoly, the state consolidated certain leather-processing industries under its control, rented out several factories on *arenda* to private investors,[48] and theoretically closed all small workshops and kustar' shops producing fewer than five hundred pieces of leather a month.[49] One result was that leather became a scarce and highly desired good. Rising demand and prices led to widespread shortages, which fueled a flourishing contraband trade throughout the republic.[50] Reports from the leather union complained of systemic shortages of leather and other raw materials, including wood bark, a primary tanning ingredient, throughout the summer and fall of 1921.[51]

The Belorussian leather industry administration (*Belkozha*) responded to supply shortages and lack of effective demand for leather goods by slashing productive forces. Over the summer of 1921, Belkozha instigated layoffs and closed workshop across Belorussia. Faced with the near complete breakdown of provisioning networks in April and May 1921, Belkozha contemplated closing most workshops, leaving only the main leather-provisioning factory in Minsk to refine leather for the entirety of Belorussia. While stopping short of this drastic measure, Belkozha ultimately pushed through policies based upon classical market principles with downright liberal aplomb. In June and July, they "freed" (*osvobodit'*) workers from workshop obligations throughout the republic and cut provisions for workers to reduce labor power. In July, the main shoemaking workshop in Minsk slashed its staff by two-thirds, from 178 to 54 people. Minsk's First Soviet Leather Factory (*Sovkozhzavod*) likewise cut its workforce from 240 workers to 145.[52] One Soviet estimate suggests that some fifty-one out of seventy leather undertakings throughout Belorussia closed, while the total workforce fell from 2,612 to 1,156 (56 percent) during the period of "industrial concentration" between 1921 and 1922.[53]

Rather than oppose layoffs, trade union members celebrated the measures, arguing that reduced labor forces "free us from those elements who receive rations but don't do anything." Leatherworker representatives to a July 1921 Conference of Trade Unions called for additional measures, including the reintroduction of pay differentials to reward skilled laborers and reinvigorate production.[54] While the return to pay differential and piecework have long been cited as the most egregious aspects of the Bolshevik "betrayal" of the working classes, they seem, in Minsk at least, to have been championed by rank-and-file producers—particularly the most skilled, unionized producers.

Concerns about the fate of the "freed" workers were dismissed in a predictable manner. Reports from the 1921 All-Belorussian Conference of Trade Unions described laid-off workers as "former proprietors and petty kustari, forcibly mobilized into work, who had waited for the hour when they would be able to escape from the workshop."[55] During a presidium meeting to discuss new layoffs in the Second Minsk Shoemakers Workshop in November 1921, Nakhim Kats emphatically reiterated this logic. The recent period had witnessed the reduction of labor power on an "all-Russian scale with the goal of being freed of nonproductive elements." Yet the logic behind layoffs at the Second Minsk Shoemakers Workshop, Kats insisted, took an "entirely different form—namely, the necessity of eliminating from the workshop the half-proletarian element which is not interested in raising the productiveness of state enterprises." The elimination of such elements was, in other words, not only necessary but also correct politically.[56] Reports on the workshop closings never considered the firing of "proletarian" labor. On the contrary, displaced laborers became retroactively deproletarianized.

Official proclamations stressed the voluntaristic nature of labor reductions, emphasizing the enthusiasm with which deproletarianized workers celebrated their renewed freedom. While such enthusiasm existed, it was by no means the rule. That layoffs and the shuttering of "underproductive" shops tended to provoke hostility, not gratitude, can be discerned from opposition voiced in union meetings. One proposal to close additional shoemaking workshops in the Minsk guberniia received a sharp rebuke from the Borisov representative to the leatherworkers union presidium during a closed-door meeting in August.[57] A separate report in November criticized the fact that raw materials from shuttered workshops in Mozyr had been systematically diverted to Minsk to support leather production in the capital.[58] Another report, in turn, blamed the Mozyr leather workshop closings on the "speculation in labor" undertaken by workers who manipulated the high demand for labor and "unfairly" drove up wages.[59] These reports suggest that productive concerns in the center trumped those of the republic's periphery. Yet opposition also surfaced within the ostensible "center" of Minsk. Within the capital's workshops, tensions simmered throughout 1921 due to nonpayment of wages, irregular work, and rising costs of goods, culminating in a shoemakers strike lasting from mid-September to late October. Striking shoemakers, the Cheka reported, called for workshop closures and the reprivatization of industry—demands read as evidence of "limited consciousness and petit-bourgeois psychology."[60] While enthusiasm for privatization and the closing of workshops emerged as one potential effect of work stoppages, shortages, and inflation, local authorities read such sentiments as proof of petty-bourgeois proclivities and the a priori causes of productive breakdown.

The leatherworkers trade union, like all trade unions, was thus caught in the position of simultaneously trying to enforce state policies of productivism while defending workers against the vagaries of a rather cruel NEP labor market. Their task became far easier beginning in mid-1921, when the state began to turn idle workshops and factories back over to private arendators, or leaseholders. Denationalization effectively restored a level of mediation (or the appearance of mediation) between workers and the state, allowing the trade unions to reclaim an activist, proworker agenda vis-à-vis arendators. Thus, following the denationalization of the leather mill and the main shoe- and boot-making workshops in Borisov, workers immediately refocused animosities onto the new arendators. One internal union report by Comrade Rodzinskii complained that the new private proprietors systematically ignored worker efforts to organize and refused to respect collectively bargained agreements. Proprietors, it was further reported, circumnavigated legal avenues for hiring workers by refusing to employ labor through the Borisov labor bourse, choosing instead to hire nonunion kustari on the sly. As a result, workers began to turn, once again, to the unions for representation, realizing that the unions remained the "defenders of their interests." With denationalization, class struggle returned, in part, with a workable, statist bent.[61]

Layoffs, workshop closings, and denationalization helped to reestablish functioning market relations in production in Belorussia. Labor force reductions seemed to coincide with a direct resurgence in productivity. Thus, while workers in the Minsk Leather Factory produced 2,236 pieces of finished leather in May of 1921, output increased to over 4,000 pieces of leather in July, despite the dismissal of some sixty workers.[62] In the summer of 1921, the state began hiring private traders, or "counter-agents" to secure raw materials for state-run workshops and to "correct" market prices in times of shortage by releasing leather onto the market.[63] Through such measures, the state restored profitability to beleaguered industries, as acute material shortages began to abate by the end of 1921. Such measures simultaneously enmeshed workers more deeply in relations of production that depended on the extraction of ever-greater quantities of value from ever-cheaper and more docile labor forces. Far from emancipating labor from unnecessary labor time, the emerging Soviet system of production became increasingly predicated on the continued intensification of labor productivity. To achieve these increases, industrial conglomerates allowed the markets to discipline workers, while the state repeatedly stressed the necessity of universal and perpetual labor in exchange for civic inclusion. At the same time, the system of production transformed thousands of former "proletarian" workers into unemployed or partially employed laborers, creating a vast mass of reserve labor to drag down wages and further discipline recalcitrant workers.

Productivizing the Kustarnichestvo

Given the newly rediscovered spirit of capitalism, unemployed workers could have, in theory, waited for the market to regulate itself. Yet waiting for the invisible hand of the market to "self-correct" was hardly a formula for long-term survival in a period of acute scarcity. As the labor market collapsed in 1921, displaced laborers reconstituted themselves as independent producers or wage laborers in sites of production outside of the state apparatuses. In other words, they became kustari. Reports from Mozyr in November 1921 warned of a palpable spike in unorganized kustar' leather production following the closing of state-run leather factories.[64] A mid-1922 report from Vitebsk (which had not yet been incorporated into the Belorussian Republic) noted an alarming growth of Jewish kustari, "particularly in the provinces," where they constituted the "very definition of the *meshchanskii* element with speculative inclinations."[65]

With the introduction of the NEP and subsequent disruption of productive relations, kustari and kustar' workshops sprouted up like proverbial mushrooms after the rain. Despite continued opposition from trade unionists, kustar' production continued to expand, outpacing the growth of the unionized workforce. According to one evsektsiia report from the Minsk oblast, kustari constituted 25,000 of the 71,000 "Jewish producers" in all of Belorussia by 1924, roughly equaling the reported number of 27,593 unionized Jewish "producers." The apparent equivalence in size of the kustar' population and the body of unionized Jewish labor was purely formal, given the fact that the category of unionized "Jewish producer" included both "proletarian" and "white-collar" (*sluzhashchii*) workers.[66] The kustari, on the other hand, were invariably commodity producers concentrated in the "so-called Jewish professions," working as "tailors, shoemakers, and pieceworkers."[67] The numbers of kustari continued to grow rapidly throughout the decade. By January 1926 the number of Jewish kustari had swelled to forty thousand, 40 percent of whom engaged in shoemaking or tailoring. Of these, twenty-five thousand lived in cities or shtetlekh, with fifteen thousand in villages.[68] The expansion of the kustarnichestvo showed few signs of ebbing. By late 1926, the total number of kustari in Belorussia reportedly climbed to more than fifty thousand, 90 percent of whom (forty-five thousand) were Jewish.[69] Reports from evsektsiia and other party organizations, as well as state apparatuses and unions, seem to confirm a general trend: throughout the mid-1920s, the total numbers of kustar' producers grew absolutely and relatively compared to unionized producers.

The rapid expansion of kustar' production created a social reality that party and state apparatuses could not ignore. More precisely, kustari refused to allow the party and the state to ignore them, agitating for increased representation and financial support. In December of 1922, groups of unemployed shoemakers in Minsk appealed to the leatherworkers union for permission to form an *artel'*, or worker collective, to support themselves. In response, the union agreed to provide the workers with credit and materials.[70] While kustari pressed for support through official avenues, they also advanced their claims for political representation by simply showing up at mass worker meetings and demonstrations, whether invited or otherwise. In 1923, kustar' producers appealed for and "were granted" permission to participate in the official Minsk demonstration commemorating the October Revolution; the demonstrators repaid this magnanimous benevolence by marching under banners with the pointed slogan, "The kustari still wait for October!"[71] The following spring, masses of kustari in the shtetl Cherven showed up as unregistered "guests" at a workers' conference held on the second night of Passover. In Mogilev, kustari crashed a conference and received permission to participate in a trade union event with "consultative rights."[72] In the shtetl Liozno, large numbers of kustari arrived, uninvited, to a worker meeting in early 1924 to hear a paper delivered by Samuil Agursky. Following his talk, Agursky complained, the kustari besieged him with questions about taxes, political representation, and credit policies for kustari, while completely ignoring the undoubtedly illuminating content of his lecture.[73] Through such tactics, the kustari pushed their way into the vision of the state and party.

As swelling ranks of agitated kustari became a growing concern, state and party apparatuses increasingly sought to placate and win over *some* of these producers. In mid-1923, kustari in various regions of Belorussia began to forge kustar' "societies" (*obshchestva*) to promote tax reform, financial support, and the "unformed rights of kustari as laborers."[74] Taxation figured prominently among their complaints, due to the strikingly nonuniform policies implemented by the state. While the state exempted from taxation kustari who lived in villages (*derevnii*) and did not employ hired labor, they simultaneously imposed heavy taxes on those living in cities and *shtelekh*. This illiberal taxation policy, which maintained the old tsarist legal institution of "privileges" (*l'goty*) in the "countryside" while denying them to the neighboring shtetl, directly affected Jewish producers, partly explaining the overwhelming pre-ponderance of Jewish kustari who joined these societies. By mid-1924, sixty-eight kustar' societies had been formed in Belorussia, with 6,693 members, of whom 6,204 were Jewish.[75]

Rather than oppose these kustar' societies, Bolshevik activists embraced them as a mechanism for organizing kustar' production. Evsektsiia and party activists likewise began to treat the kustar' societies as a means for extending cultural, political, and educational work among kustari. If the trade unions, in Lenin's phrase, were to serve as "schools of Communism" for the industrial-ized working class, the kustar' obshchestva was envisioned as playing a similar role among non-unionized kustari. During a meeting of the Moscow evsekt-siia in October 1923, the prominent activist Avrom Merezhin underscored the didactic role that kustar' societies should play as organs for cultural education and social reform. The organizers of such societies, he argued, should "set for themselves the goal . . . of educating the kustari in the Soviet spirit; kustari must be drawn into general Soviet life and into all Soviet campaigns." Activ-ists ought to encourage kustar' society members to view themselves as "par-ticipants in new detachments of the Soviet state."[76] To support these efforts, the party encouraged the formation of mutual aid credit associations—purely economic institutions (with pre-revolutionary links) intended to pool money for cooperative assistance and badly needed credit to kustar' producers.[77]

The softening of state policy by no means meant that either the state or the party apparatuses had completely lost their skepticism toward the kustsari. Even as he lauded their potentially virtuous and useful role, Merezhin empha-sized the need to closely supervise the kustar' societies to keep out private trad-ers, kulaks, and exploiters of labor.[78] He recommended utilizing the evsektsiia to carry out this policing, "in light of the fact that the most active elements of kustari in the city [Gomel] are Jewish." A similar directive sent by Comrade L'vovski of the All-Russian evsektsiia in April 1924 urged evsektsiia activists everywhere to prevent the infiltration of kustar' societies by SR-Menshevik, Kadet, or Zionist elements. L'vovski stressed the need to attract the poorest, most proletarian-like elements into the leadership of the societies. The kus-tari, he insisted, must not be allowed to "bind themselves into slavery with independent traders, speculators, and usurers (rostovshchiki)," demanding that those who did unite with speculators "be thrown out of these associations."[79]

Despite the deep suspicions that flowed through each evsektsiia missive, the Bolshevik position toward the kustari clearly turned from hostility toward tentative engagement. Multiple factors drove this turn. First, kustar' produc-tion remained crucial for fulfilling the "goods hunger" (tovarnyi golod) that plagued the country. Kustari, in short, produced goods—particularly shoes, garments, gloves, and hats—of vital importance for everyday exchange in the NEP economy.[80] Placating the kustari was deemed necessary for strengthening the smychka, or union, between the peasantry and the city.[81] Second, the party increasingly viewed the kustar' society as a means with which to combat unemployment. The promotion of kustar' societies, along with state workshops for unemployed kustari, became a primary mechanism for dealing with the swelling ranks of those driven out of work by the twin dynamics of khozraschet and demobilization.

The struggle against unemployment veiled a third, unstated impetus behind the change in policy. By providing avenues for the expansion of independent production, the kustari unmistakably rationalized *all* production by helping to hold wage inflation and worker opposition in check. By early 1923, as the crisis of unemployment swelled, the Belorussian state had established, in cooperation with the trade unions, a new series of artel' workshops for unemployed laborers in Minsk. A trade union report from early March detailed the success of such endeavors, including the story of one workshop that brought together eighteen unemployed rope makers for the sake of producing, suitably enough, rope.[82] The item produced, however, mattered less than the terms of production. In creating the workshop, the state provided these kustari with raw materials and state contracts for goods. They also provided "half-wages" and a promise to provide additional compensation once their products had been realized on the market. A similar arrangement was introduced at a workshop for unemployed shoemakers in Minsk. The shoemaker collective received a steady supply of raw materials, had a large order for "350 pairs of high boots (*sapogi*) from the state militia," and paid workers roughly half of union wages. Business was so brisk that the workshop considered expanding by transforming unemployed saddle makers into sandal makers to meet an order for 200 pairs of sandals from Moscow. Kustar' labor, suitably rationalized, fueled further expansion.[83]

While business boomed in these workshops, the very same trade union report included an ominous third item for discussion. Following the rosy reports concerning handicraft workshops, El'ia Raichuk informed the presidium of the dire conditions in the "mechanized department" of the Minsk Shoemaker Workshop. While the language of "crisis" was by this point exceedingly familiar to the assembled trade unionists, the nature of the disruption described by Raichuk was indisputably novel, in the Soviet context, at least. Rather than confronting *shortages* of goods, the mechanized workshop faced a new threat. In the recent period, the once-again whirring factory machines had created a stockpile of more than one thousand pairs of boots that found no buyers on the market. An intense debate over possible solutions followed. Comrade Raichuk recommended cutting production to raise consumer demand. Comrade Rodzinskii insisted that the only solution lay in realizing the goods "beyond the boundaries of Belorussia" by exporting them to Moscow or abroad. Comrade Rubenchik countered that export alone would not solve the crisis; the union needed to redeploy a portion of the workers from the mechanized factory back into the artel' workshop for unemployed shoemakers. Which is precisely what the union resolved to do.[84] And so it was that the Minsk shoemakers of the Socialist Republic of Belorussia dealt with their first encounter with a "new" crisis that dared not speak its old name—overaccumulation.

Shmates, Shmates Everywhere: Crises of Overaccumulation

Beginning in late 1922, the Belorussian economy, following the broader Soviet economy, experienced an acute crisis of market disequilibrium as the rate of circulation of goods fell precipitously and abruptly. While trade never ceased entirely, the realization of goods experienced a sharp downturn. The experience of the leather industry in March 1923 repeated itself in industries across Belorussia. Party observers, newspapers, state organs, and trade unions decried the onset of an unprecedented crisis. Across the republic, manufactured goods sat, without buyers, as stockpiles of unrealized goods built up. Within official Soviet discourse, the "scissors crisis" (as Trotsky dubbed it) resulted from an acute divergence of exceedingly low agricultural prices (the result of a bountiful harvest) coupled with rapidly rising prices for manufactured goods.[85]

While this price divergence theory has been more or less accepted as the prevailing explanation in the secondary literature, substantial evidence suggests a far more complex dynamic at work. To begin with, the grinding halt of exchange undoubtedly resulted in part from hyperinflationary pressure generated by the collapse of the *sovznak* currency over the summer of 1923. Throughout the summer, the Yiddish daily, *Der Veker*, ran story after story attempting to make sense of the staggering increase in commodity prices and the equally rapid collapse of the sovznak. In March, editors printed the first of many stories about the plan to introduce the new gold-backed currency, the chervonets, and hinted about the possible price instability in paper money that might result.[86] By the end of March, *Der Veker* began publishing criminal reports of individuals arrested for speculating in gold and destabilizing the currency.[87] In April *Der Veker* offered regular updates on the rate of the paper ruble against the prerevolutionary ruble and still largely fictitious gold chervonets.[88] A half-page article on the divergence of prices (replete with an illustration of a pair of giant, separating scissors) appeared in mid-May.[89] In June *Der Veker* started a catchy, if infrequent, "From the Black Market" byline, replete with the news of the illegal trade of the day.[90] By late June, the paper was regularly publishing lists of prices for basic commodity goods in Minsk, presumably in the hopes of curtailing price inflation.[91] On August 12 the paper reported on the ominous financial news from Germany, as the mark passed ten million to the dollar.[92] If the stories, editorials, witticisms, and feuilletons did not drive home the reality of hyperinflation to the Yiddish-reading populace, the price of the newspapers surely did. On January 1, 1923, a copy of the *Der Veker* sold for sixty kopecks; by November 21 the price had skyrocketed to forty-eight rubles.[93]

In conditions of runaway inflation, the seizing up of trade had as much to do with the fact that money was violently shedding value as it did with the divergence of prices. Rapid depreciation meant that money could not fulfill its primary role of mediating the exchange of goods in different locations over time. By the summer of 1923, the crisis had spread to the needlework industry, reigniting a myriad of simmering social tensions. Needleworkers showed signs of increasing militancy, due in part to the decision to switch the language of business from the little-understood Russian to Yiddish, which allowed for more effective organization. In July 1923 Shveiprom bowed to pressure from union workers and agreed to readjust wages four times per month in order to combat inflation.[94] Nevertheless, wages failed to keep pace with inflationary pressures. An internal report from the *Minshvei* sewing factory noted that a bitter mood had descended on small needlework workshops throughout Minsk, due largely to the fact that work orders and wage payments had dried up as the workshops proved unable to realize stock.[95]

The Belorussian market, moreover, was not alone in experiencing the upheaval of the NEP. Volatility in the "center" of Moscow undermined any long-term hope of overcoming the crisis by realizing goods on the internal Russian market. In December of 1923 Comrade Levit, a representative of the needleworkers union from Minshvei, traveled to Moscow in the hopes of selling stockpiles of hats and winning new contracts from the Soviet state for production orders. Moscow authorities abruptly dismissed his efforts, noting that they had six thousand unemployed needleworkers in Moscow desperate for work.[96] Levit's inability to realize the excess needlework goods in Moscow made explicit the degree to which the crisis drove each local market toward constricted isolation.[97]

In the face of an intractable and noncompliant market, all parties involved sought to solve the crisis by regulating the one ever-pliable market—the labor market. The constriction of the labor market manifested itself, first, at the fringes of the economy with the weakening of support for kustar' production. In January 1923 the leatherworkers union in Minsk denied a request by unemployed shoemakers in Bobruisk to form a collective workshop, citing lack of funds.[98] Demands to reduce shoe production brought clashes between unemployed laborers and unionized workers in Borisov in early 1924; yet the leatherworkers union again rejected appeals to organize arteli to ameliorate tensions due to lack of funds.[99] Members of Minshvei similarly sought to constrict the market by attempting to drive from the union crypto-kustari who secretly moonlighted as private contractors for "apartment work" in addition to producing in the workshops.[100] The evsektsiia reported a similar intensification of animosity toward kustari in the outlying cities. In April 1924, regional evsektsiia officials from Bobruisk reported that hundreds of children of suspect kustari had been thrown out of the local schools due to nonpayment of school fees; in October 1924 the Bobruisk kustar' society carried out a purge to eliminate "all undesirable elements from the society." The crisis, in short, begot various and multifaceted manifestations of intralabor strife.[101]

In theory, the scissors crisis resolved itself over the course of 1924, due largely to the introduction of the stable, gold-backed, and counterinflationary chervonets. Government efforts to force down the prices for industrial goods proved equally central to the "solution." In noneuphemistic terms, this involved the shedding of labor force. On October 1, 1924, Comrade Peigin reported to members of the Minshvei union presidium about a recent meeting with representatives from VSNKh to resolve the "abnormal" conditions plaguing Minshvei. In response to requests for a new infusion of state credit and materials to help Minshvei restart production, the representatives from VSNKh offered their counterproposal: cut production and the labor force at Minshvei by 35 percent. After listening to the expected objections from the Minshvei representatives, VSNKh representatives countered with an argument whose rationality and understanding of *raschet* was indisputable. The recently refurbished and expanded central sewing factory in Vitebsk had far greater productive capacity than Minshvei, due to recent mechanization. While VSNKh had no intention of closing Minshvei (ominous words of reassurance, in any environment), they demanded that Minshvei reorganize *rationally* by cutting production and focusing on the "local" Belorussian market, meaning the Minsk oblast.[102] In sum, cheap, mechanically produced commodities from Vitebsk brought about the forced rationalization of the sewing industry in Minsk. Where stockpiled goods accumulated, rationalization and unemployment followed, as productive relations eviscerated purported logics of "center" and "periphery."[103]

The labor policies of the NEP in general, and the productivization of kustar' labor in particular, formed a decisive component of the NEP regime of market-driven production that pushed for ever-more and ever-cheaper goods. This transformation went beyond merely producing greater quantities of "stuff." It entailed the development and intensification of a particular temporal logic of production—one that emphasized a historical dynamic in which the ends of the intensified production of values became the production of more value still. For all of the discussion of rationalized planning in the early Soviet period, the logic of productivity that developed during the 1920s had its closest parallels in the early epoch of industrialization in nineteenth-century Western Europe. The making of the NEP Soviet working class involved, in large part, the making of handworkers and artisanal producers that drove productiviza-tion from the fringes, reentered the industrialized workforce in moments of expansion, and faced expulsion and disintegration in moments of contraction spurred by overproduction. The capitalist business cycle was alive, well, and savagely kicking in postcapitalist Belorussia.

Politicizing the Kustarnichestvo

NEP solutions to successive crises of overproduction generated highly vola-tile swings in employment throughout Belorussia. Increased unemployment was by no means limited to the Jewish population, but levels of unemployment among Jews remained considerably higher than for other national groups. Jewish laborers, however, responded to unemployment in ways that differed significantly from their conationals. In the midst of urban or industrial unem-ployment, the "reserves" of the overwhelmingly peasant Belorussian popula-tion could sink back into the village economy, as producers or day laborers, biding their time until the revival of the industrial economy.[104] Few Jews, by contrast, had subsistence agriculture upon which to fall back.

With no peasantry to absorb them, these unemployed or semiemployed laborers accumulated at the boundaries of the industrial economy. Many reverted to the ranks of unemployed *luftmentshn*. A portion turned to trade on either the black or "legal" market. Many lived off other forms of illegal or semi-legal activity opened by the NEP economy, such as smuggling, trading contra-band goods, and so forth. Others found temporary legitimate work where they could. Some formerly urbanized Jews undoubtedly made their way back to the shtetl. Yet for most outcasts of the constricted labor market, the direction of migration was not backward, but out—to either larger cities like Minsk, or to the burgeoning and long-forbidden cities of central Russia.[105] Despite these safety valves, the shtetlekh teemed with unemployed, underemployed, or pau-perized Jews. Some lived on charity or family donations sent from America; many others remained without any discernible means and survived through semilegal or illegal endeavors. In the eyes of Marxist theorists, these pools of docile bodies constituted the reserve labor army that spurred productivization by filling demand for labor and dragging down industrial wages. When the eyes of the Marxist *practitioners* turned toward the shtetlekh—as they began to do with much greater frequency and alarm in 1924—they discovered a displaced population that looked less like a reserve labor army and more like festering pools of unemployed, displaced, and potentially radicalize-able paupers.

By the end of 1924, the NEP began to catch its second wind, prompted in large part by the "normalization" of market relations following the scissors crisis.[106] As a corollary to the party's new "Face to the Countryside" campaign, evsektsiia activists across the USSR inaugurated their own "Face to the Shtetl" campaign that gathered steam over the course of 1925.[107] Along with its courtship of the peasantry and the private trader, the Soviet state rededicated itself to the promotion of the kustari by encouraging the further expansion of kustar' societies and mutual aid credit associations.[108] On April 1, 1925, the "Face to the Shtetl" campaign began to bear tangible fruit, as the state announced broad reductions in taxation policies for shtetl- and city-dwelling kustari, suggesting that they, along with peasants and traders, should embrace Nikolai Bukharin's new, if short-lived, NEP mantra: "Enrich yourselves!"[109] The turn toward the countryside dovetailed precisely with the crucial problems facing the Jewish population of Belorussia—issues of the legality of trade, of displaced labor, of kustar' production, and, above all, of the isolated state of the shtetl. Moreover, from the standpoint of party and evsektsiia activists, the turn toward the shtetlekh addressed what came to be perceived as a growing problem: political deviation.

Opposition to Soviet policies and Bolshevism did not, of course, suddenly materialize in the Jewish communities of Belorussia in the middle of the 1920s. Political conflict had been an ever-present feature of prerevolutionary Jewish society and remained so after the revolution. Moreover, unlike in Russia and Ukraine, where the Bolsheviks outlawed almost every Jewish opposition party, the Belorussian Communist party allowed a number of Zionist groups, including Poalei Tsion, the left-wing Zionist organization *Hashomer hatzair*, and even the more right-wing agriculturalist *Hechalutz* to operate legally (in theory, if not always in practice) until the end of the 1920s—much to the consternation of evsektsiia activists. In this respect, fiercely critical, non-Bolshevik voices remained a part of the Jewish political landscape.

By early 1924 party records warned of the ratcheting up of political opposition of all variations throughout Belorussia. Evsektsiia reports from this period increasingly noted the existence of pockets of political deviation, which came to be associated with kustar' producers. In urban centers, evsektsiia activists branded labor recalcitrance among Jewish producers and artisans as "Bundist-Menshevik" deviation, a term most frequently used to disparage workers who engaged in unauthorized or wildcat strikes.[110] In the towns and shtetlekh that dotted the Belorussian countryside, however, kustar' producers came to be associated with the more troubling (from the standpoint of the evsektsiia) political deviation of Zionism.[111]

The problem of Zionism among the kustari garnered significant attention during a 1924 evsektsiia conference on the shtetlekh held in Minsk. During the proceedings the evsektsiia secretary from Borisov, Comrade Al'tman, noted that Zionist elements had infiltrated the kustar' society, but had been "swept out in the purge" of 1924.[112] Vul'f Abramovich Nodel', another former Bundist who rose to the Presidium of the Central Soviet of Trade Unions, emphasized the dark political mood in the shtetlekh. While singling out shopkeepers as the most adamantly anti-Bolshevik elements, Nodel' warned of lurking danger from the kustari, noting that anti-Bolshevik sentiments in general, and Zionism in particular, had grown among this group due to the state's failure to correctly implement kustar' policy. Rather than recognize kustari as distinct social groups, local *raion* administrators tended to "distinguish little between kustari and traders," treating them all as speculators and taxing them accordingly. Such policies, he argued, pushed kustari into the hands of the Zionists.[113] Comrade Livit, the evsektsiia secretary from Mozyr, likewise warned that a large underground Zionist movement in Mozyr "seeks to utilize and does utilize every mistake we make" concerning the kustari. Il'ia Osherovich, a ranking member of the Central Bureau of the Belorussian evsektsiia, added a franker assessment. "It should not be forgotten," Osherovich told the conference, that until recently "members of the trade unions were strictly opposed to the kustari. Now the situation has changed." Shifting policies now obligated the evsektsiia and the state to take an active role in protecting the kustari from purported political dangers. Osherovich's logic was simple: "The Zionists are a danger for us in Belorussia . . . We protect the workers. We must now also protect the kustari from anti-Soviet influences."[114]

Recurrent emphasis on deviationism in the shtetl undoubtedly served a discursive function that allowed Bolshevik activists to differentiate "unhealthy" from "healthy" Jewish labor. Yet ample evidence suggests the problems of kustar' labor in the shtetlekh were not merely discursive. Successive evsektsiia reports concerning the state of kustari across the republic emphasized the intense stratification that existed among kustari. Even excluding those kustari who employed hired labor (and were consequently forbidden from joining kustar' societies), the monthly income for kustari fluctuated wildly. The *upper* echelons of skilled kustari in Minsk could earn monthly incomes in the range of 180–200 rubles in mid-1925. The vast bulk of urban kustari earned between 50 and 80 rubles, while the poorest and least skilled received between 25 and 40 rubles a month. By comparison, the upper echelon of kustar' producers in the shtetlekh, earned, on average, 25–40 rubles a month;

a significant number of kustari—in particular "the shoemakers, the tailors, the glaziers (*stekol'shchiki*), and others"—received between 7 and 15 rubles. At the bottom of the shtetl social system existed the "nomadic" (*kochevye*) artisans, semiskilled workers who traveled with their tools, accepting odd jobs and temporary employment in exchange for "natural" pay—food and occasional shelter.[115] Among the most debased kustari, one report from Bobruisk underscored, were large numbers of former traders and shopkeepers dispossessed by the revolution.[116]

Insofar as the Bolsheviks tended to derive political deviation from social origin, reports frequently singled out the poorest strata of the shtetl kustarnichestvo as being most susceptible to Zionist agitation.[117] Such reports should be read skeptically in light of the absence of any quantifiable data, not to mention the undeniable tendency of those reporting on the population's political "mood" (*nastroennyie*) to make observations about what they believed *should* be occurring on the ground. Moreover, the reports suggest anything but uniform patterns of anti-Soviet agitation. Impoverished kustari constituted only one of the groups—along with young shtetl Jews (particularly the unemployed youth) and university students,[118] shopkeepers, traders, and speculators, and the Jewish clergy—identified as constituting bastions of support for Zionist groups.[119] Yet if the idea that the lower stratum of the kustari constituted a bastion of Zionist support in the shtetl was a fantasy, it was a fantasy shared by many of the Zionist organizations as well. Hence an underground newspaper produced by the militantly leftist Hashomer hatzair repeatedly claimed that the lowest fringes of the shtetl kustari constituted the *authentic* working class, locked in a battle for survival against the "petit-bourgeois" Jewish supporters of Soviet power: the privileged kustari who joined the kustar' societies; the privileged petit-bourgeois urban kustarnichestvo; and the most privileged of all, the evsektsiia activists. "We concede to the evsektsiia influence among the children of the bourgeoisie; we don't worry—the children of the laboring classes are with us."[120] Evsektsiia activists noted such propagandistic efforts with concern. "The Zionists represent themselves as defenders of the working class," one report lamented. Needless to say, the author of the evsektsiia report attributed Zionist support to the "more privileged elements" of the kustari, while conceding that underground Zionist cells received broad support from the youth, particularly the "unemployed" youth in the shtetlekh.[121]

While Zionists and their evsektsiia opponents struggled vehemently in the political realm, they shared a strikingly uniform conception of labor and social usefulness. Available examples of the underground press suggest a recurring cohesion between Soviet and Zionist aims in terms of social vision. The left-Zionist organizations that constituted the most active (and *legal*) Zionist groups in Belorussia promoted programs that aligned explicitly with Soviet social presuppositions: they championed labor as a desirable, necessary, life-affirming practice; they denounced speculation absolutely ("speculators and parasites have no place in the economy of Palestine");[122] they promoted direct democratic participation through local worker cells; they pushed for Jewish land settlement; they supported artisanal workshops; and they demanded the productivization of Jewish labor. Their grievances targeted neither the principles of Soviet socialism nor soviet economic policies, but the very instrumental question of whom, precisely, was to benefit from the implementation of these principles on the ground. Privileged Soviet "insiders"—the evsektsiia activists, the state employees (primarily school teachers), the members of the kustar' society—constituted the main target of wrath from political outsiders. Soviet "outsiders"—the fringe kustari, the dispossessed and disenfranchised traders, the unemployed *luftmentshn*, the religious—constituted the political opposition in the eyes of the state.

While the influence of the "Zionist *Idea*" remains the dominant thrust of historical research concerning the Zionist movement, within the context of Soviet Belorussia, ideas followed practices.[123] Rather than shaping facts on the ground, ideologies flowed and followed from this juxtaposition of insider-ness/outsider-ness, particularly in the shtetlekh. As the discrepancies of pay differentials, organized representation, and access to employment strongly suggest, insider-ness and outsider-ness were, above all else, socially constructed concepts. Yet these socially constructed concepts contributed to the formation of nonsocial identities—particularly identities of politics and nationality. Just as deproletarianized abstract laborers faced the strong likelihood of being marked as kustari, and, hence, Jewish, so too did deproductivized or pauperized kustari face the prospect of being marked among the politically unreliable outsiders, whether Zionist, clerical, or merely petty bourgeois.

When mapped onto the systemic problems of social integration and labor, the construction of political deviationism and outsider identities appear to have fluctuated with the ebb and flow of the NEP economy. Like the mythicized image of the speculator, who reemerged in moments of crisis to threaten the normal functioning of the Soviet economy, the political enemies that emerged as constructs of social and economic breakdown threatened to undermine the totality of the sociopolitical order. The contradiction between ideals of universalizing inclusion and a reality of constricted integration *created* political deviationists. Stated otherwise, political deviation was, like unemployment, one crucial by-product of the contradictions of NEP society.

Conclusion

According to the strict parameters of Soviet Marxian theory, the productivization of kustar' labor should have had no intrinsic relation to the question of productivizing Jewish labor. In theory, the kustari constituted a uniformly *social* group defined by archaic, outmoded forms of production and dubious political reliability. From the opposite perspective, the project of productivizing kustari had little overt relation to the questions frequently associated with Jewish history and politics in the Soviet Union. That the Soviet state "productivized" Jews has been taken as an axiomatic truism of Soviet Jewish history, reaffirming the general belief that states act and Jewish populations passively react. *Acting*, and certainly acting *as Jews*, has generally been a verb reserved to depict opposition to Soviet policies. "Jewish," as an adjective, tends to be conceptualized as such only when Jews acted for explicitly "Jewish" causes—in defense of language, national autonomy, and overtly Jewish politics.

In the context of Belorussia, such one-sided conceptualizations veil and obscure the complicated fusion of politics, production, and nationality that existed on the ground. The kustar' question was inseparable from the Jewish question, because Jews constituted the overwhelming bulk of the kustarnichestvo. The Jewish question became imbricated with the crisis of the kustarnichestvo because significant portions of the Jewish population were—or became—kustari. As labor policies unfolded, no fixed boundary existed between Jew and kustar.' Far from being forcibly productivized from above, kustari organized for greater representation, political access, and the equalization of economic privileges under the Soviet state. Kustari organized as *social* actors; there was nothing particularly "Jewish" about many of their concerns. Yet, in pressing for self-productivization, the kustari simultaneously drove the process of productivizing their "Jewish" selves from below.

Kustar' labor was overwhelmingly Jewish labor, but Jewish labor was not exclusively kustarnyi. Rather, Jewish kustari existed at one end of a continuum of possible labor relations and identities; at the other end existed the ideal labor form—proletarianized labor. Regardless of what Marxian theory held, the social category of proletarian labor came to be defined less by relations to the means of production and more by relations to state production apparatuses and state power. The closer Jewish laborers came to this ideal of proletarianized labor, the closer they came to the state and distanced from the taint of kustar'nost.' Likewise, the closer Jewish laborers came to this embodiment of pure labor in the abstract, the closer they came to integration into *Soviet* society in full. This fully integrated labor was never understood during the course of the 1920s as being un-Jewish or assimilated. Yet it was understood as being free of the stigma of problematic, petit-bourgeois, or archaic "Jewishness."

The central contradiction of the NEP existed in this continuum of productivity. Productivized, integrated, proletarianized labor in the abstract existed as the ideal of labor. Yet the systemic contradictions of the NEP economy repeatedly drove large sections of the Jewish laboring population back into the ranks of the kustarnichestvo. As the proclamations by the Jewish Bolshevik activists Iulius Shimeliovich and Samuil Agursky that opened this chapter make explicit, the rhetoric of the Soviet experiment offered Jewish integration through labor as an ideal. Yet the social reality of the NEP continually reconstituted large portions of Jewish actors as social anomalies on the borders of the Soviet economy and, in doing so, reinscribed them as being ethnically, and problematically, Jewish.

PART III

POLITICAL CULTURE AND NATIONALITY

4

FROM BOLSHEVIK *HASKOLE* TO CULTURAL REVOLUTION: ABRAM BEILIN AND THE JEWISH REVOLUTION

ON FEBRUARY 5, 1923, at precisely eight o'clock in the evening, a trial took place at the Grosser Club, the main Jewish workers' club in Minsk. By curtain time, some five hundred people, mostly workers, filled the auditorium, which had been transformed into a courthouse. The crowd, *Der Veker* reported, constituted the largest group ever assembled in the club for an event. As the hour of the trial arrived, lights rose upon a solitary figure sitting in the dock, awaiting judgment. An entirely comprehensible sense of anticipation filled the air. Every person gathered in the assembly hall *knew* the accused, his plight, and his failings long before the first words were uttered in "court." It was, after all, the second time Bontshe Shvayg, stood trial before the court of Jewish public opinion.[1]

Bontshe Shvayg, or Bontshe the Silent, was not a real criminal, at least in any normative sense of the word. A creation by the "father" of Yiddish literature, I. L. Peretz, Bontshe Shvayg ranked among the most famous fictitious Jews ever introduced to the Yiddish reading public. What self-respecting, educated Jew in the Pale did not know the story of the accused's sad life? All could recite the miserable details of Bontshe's life: the botched circumcision at birth; the death of his mother at a young age; his rotten childhood at the hands of an abusive drunk of a father; and his pathetic life as a cheated, spat upon, and ignored drayman. Following his death, Peretz's readers knew, Bontshe awoke to find himself in the dock of a light-bathed, majestic courthouse, surrounded by angels and the minions of the Heavenly Court. The angel cum defense attorney laid out the details, explaining how Bontshe had been "saved" by his "protector," who hired him as a coachman. In addition to a coachman's whip and poor wages, Bontshe's protector was kind enough to provide him a wife and, through her, a son. Told of abandonment by his adulterous wife and

117

abuse at the hands of his "son," the verdict was assured. Even the prosecutor refused to argue against Bontshe. The Heavenly Court welcomed him with open hearts and dancing lights. Offered any portion of the Heavenly Kingdom he desired, Bonthse made one sheepish request: that he should receive a hot, buttered roll for breakfast every day. "The court and the angels looked down, a little ashamed; the prosecutor laughed." Such had been Peretz's verdict on Bontshe's wasted paradise.[2]

More than simply a part of Eastern European Jewish popular discourse, Bontshe Shvayg, the *shlimazel* everyman, *was* Eastern European Jewry. Which was precisely the reason he found himself before the Bolshevik revolutionary tribunal. The retrial opened with a reading of the indictment. Bontshe Shvayg, as a "member of the proletarian family," faced charges that he "tore himself away from his own environment, failed to value his own worth, had not an ounce of proletarian pride, bowed down before the rich, and remained silent." Unlike in Peretz's version, only the prosecutor spoke in the Bolshevik trial— save for cries from the audience. One worker reportedly shouted from the gallery, "To which Trade Union did Bontshe Shvayg belong? Was he a tailor? A metalist? A leatherworker?" This anonymous voice represented the minority, *Der Veker* conceded; the entire crowd stood on the side of the accused. Nevertheless, the court ruled against Bontshe for failing to realize his proletarian nature and class identity. Of course, *Der Veker* stressed, the trial was not of the "real Bontshe" of Peretz's story. That Bontshe, after all, had lived many years beforehand, before the revolution, and was consequently exonerated. The actual defendant, the article continued, was "today's Bontshe, who lives in today's times but commits the same crimes as the real Bontshe."[3]

Transformed into Bolshevik theater of the didactic absurd, Peretz's iconic story served as a vehicle to illustrate unacceptable ways of being Jewish in a world swept clean by revolution. As revolutionary spectacle, the trial of Bontshe Shvayg constituted one fleeting, expressive episode in the campaign to create and perform new, revolutionary Jewish culture in postrevolutionary public spaces. In addition to being a cultural performance, the trial also marked a moment of struggle over "culture" in an anthropological sense. An iconic creation by one of the most beloved Yiddish writers, Bontshe Shvayg was a sign, symbol, and set of meanings about Jewish identity wrapped in one literary package. The trial of Bontshe Shvayg constituted an everyday attempt to invest an existing cultural symbol with new meaning and to transform a "traditional" Jewish cultural trope into a symbol of revolutionary significance.[4]

For the ranks of innumerable supporters from the Jewish streets of White Russia, the Bolshevik Revolution was also a Jewish Revolution, and hence a struggle over Jewish culture and identity. Over the course of the Civil War, the revolution attracted growing numbers of Jewish activists, drawn from every walk of social life, but particularly from marginal social groups on the fringes of "traditional" Jewish society. For these formerly marginal Jews, the revolution promised a reconstituted social order and the inauguration of the last great emancipatory struggle in the history of European Jewry. From the standpoint of its most zealous proponents, the revolution promised not simply the political and legal equality of "bourgeois" Jewish emancipation, but rather a qualitative leap from the shackles of tradition—from the realm of heders, rebbes, rabbis, and superstitious obscurantism—into the kingdom of enlightened freedom.

The struggle to remake culture entailed the production of new creative works and the transformation of infrastructures of everyday Jewish life, including schools, theaters, workers' clubs, and the press into sites of revolutionary collective being. At the same time, remaking culture involved a far more abstract process of contesting, challenging, and resignifying the signs, symbols, and meanings of Jewish experience in order to forge new ways of being Jewish in postrevolutionary society.[5] In this sense, the campaign to transform culture was new in orientation, but not in spirit. Radical cultural revolutionaries harkened back to the most powerful idea of the Jewish nineteenth century, framing their struggle as a quest for Jewish Enlightenment, even as they rejected the legacy of the historical Haskalah—the Hebraic Jewish Enlightenment movement for cultural rebirth that was tied irredeemably, socialist critics argued, to the politics of bourgeois emancipation. From the outset, Bolshevik Jewish enlighteners posited their mission as one of *haskole*—a distinctly *Yiddish* enlightenment driven from below, by the Jewish working class and intellectuals, in the name and the *language* of the outcast and dispossessed.[6]

The project of building a new, distinctly Soviet Jewish culture consistent with the spirit of the revolution was, of course, no one-way street. From the very inception of the revolution, the Bolshevik party had its own distinct ideas about cultural change. Or, more precisely, it had many conflicting ideas about cultural transformation.[7] Bolshevik hard-liners, particularly young, left-wing activists, viewed culture as a battleground of class warfare, arguing for the complete abolition of prewar, bourgeois cultural forms for the sake of building a new Proletarian culture.[8] Cultural soft-liners, most notably Anatolii Lunacharskii, insisted that the cultural front could not be taken by force. Only education, persuasion, and the force of ideas could build a lasting socialist culture.[9] The party fought simultaneously over the question of national cultures, dividing between hard-line Bolshevik cultural universalists and soft-line defenders of national cultural autonomy.[10]

Rather than a simple dichotomous relationship between "Jewish" and "Bolshevik" visions, the struggle to reconstruct Jewish culture was consequently multivalent, variegated, and conflicted. Within Jewish society, non-Bolshevik outsiders fought with or against Bolsheviks over questions of education, religion, art, language, and everyday life.[11] Jewish activists within the party were divided between proponents of the "Jewish Revolution" and those who viewed the revolution as an avenue for escape from Jewish culture altogether.[12] Generational conflict grafted onto the politics of culture, as young Jewish Bolsheviks in particular drifted increasingly into the orbit of Bolshevik cultural universalists. All the while, the struggle within Jewish society took place alongside and in tension with equally fractious debates in the Bolshevik party, as well as the many permutations of intranational cultural conflict in the western Soviet borderlands.

Given the centrality of culture to the essence of Jewish identity and Judaism, it is hardly surprising that the building of Soviet Jewish culture has received the lion's share of historical attention. This chapter departs from earlier works by focusing on the limits of Jewish cultural reconstruction. While recognizing the vitality of the cultural creativity that accompanied the revolution, this chapter examines the processes through which the Bolshevik Revolution ultimately outflanked, contained, and subsumed the Jewish Revolution. In doing so, this chapter argues that the entire project of Jewish cultural transformation was limited by the imperatives of economic and social reconstruction. As the trial of Bontshe Shvayg suggests, labor became the universal measure against which Jewish culture was judged, even in periods of strong party support.

The question of reforming Yiddish culture was never simply a question of creative will and choice. Throughout the postrevolutionary period, the task of reforming Jewish culture was bound to questions of economic structure. Yiddish cultural autonomy flourished in urban centers tied to the liberal, mercantile economy of the early NEP period. The turn against autonomous Yiddish culture and toward universalizing Bolshevik culture, as examined in the second half of this story, was likewise structured by imperatives stemming from the need to strengthen rural Jewish social networks during the high NEP period. Shifts in Bolshevik social and economic initiatives, such as occurred with the Great Break of the late 1920s, necessarily shifted and redrew the boundaries of acceptable Jewish cultural reconstruction. In this context, Jews remade culture, but, to paraphrase Marx, never exactly as they pleased.

The second half of this chapter examines the intertwined fates of the Jewish culture and economic restructuring through a short biographical analysis of one of the most enigmatic figures at the center of the fight over Jewish politics in Belorussia: Abram Grigor'evich Beilin. Originally a carpenter from the shtetl Mstislav, Beilin spent his entire early life in revolution. An Old Bolshevik whose political career began in the 1905 Revolution, he rose through party ranks to become the unlikely second head of the Belorussian evsektsii in 1926. As head of the evsektsii, Beilin participated zealously in the struggle over Jewish culture, prioritizing the fight against "clericalism," Zionisim, Bundism, and other deviations. At the same time, he arguably became the single most dedicated proponent of positive Jewish social reform in the entire Belorussian Bolshevik party apparatus. Balanced on the precipice between the Jewish and Bolshevik Revolutions, Beilin serves as a fitting metonym for the ambivalent revolution that would swallow this most ambivalent of revolutionaries.

Theorizing the Bolshevik Haskole

When the Russian Civil War and the Polish-Soviet War finally ended in early 1921, Bolshevik priorities shifted immediately from mobilization for total war to the reconstruction of war-torn society. The end of the Civil War and the introduction of the NEP necessitated a similar shift on the cultural front. Throughout the war, the Bolsheviks deployed the Red Army, Cheka, and coercive apparatuses against ideological foes, attacking and frequently killing non-Bolshevik intellectuals and clergymen of all varieties, shutting down churches, synagogues and religious institutions, closing rival parties, and the like. With the end of hostilities, Bolshevik cultural policy shifted from direct confrontation to the promotion of cultural change through reform, persuasion, education, and a more muted (but never absent) use of coercion.

In May 1921 the evsektsii announced the dawning of this cultural shift by launching *Unzer Kultur* (Our Culture), a short-lived journal to promote Bolshevik culture in the Jewish milieu. The task of editing the new journal fell to Il'ia Peretsevich Osherovich, the son of a Yiddish teacher, born in Minsk in 1879, who devoted most of his life to the cause of the Jewish Revolution. Having joined the Bund in 1904, he remained an active member and literary activist until 1919, when he entered Bund's Communist wing and, through that, the Bolshevik ranks in 1920. Like many Bolshevik neophytes, Osherovich became a fervent devotee to the new cause, becoming a leading evsektsii activist, propagandist, and editor. The victory of the Red Army and Bolshevik forces only intensified his vision of forging a new Yiddish culture compatible with the revolution and the Bolshevik party.[13]

"The old world is dead," Osherovich proclaimed in the journal's opening salvo, setting the tone of epochal break that reverberated through the entire Jewish cultural experiment; "the base has already been laid for the new Communist culture." With a strong hint of generational (and Freudian) rebellion, Osherovich attacked the bearers of the "old" Jewish culture—writers, preachers, cantors, poets, and sages—on charges that they dominated and enslaved the Jewish laboring population. Having wiped away this this defunct and decadent culture, Jewish revolutionary activists needed to build "a new culture," that would emancipate the Jewish laboring classes. Osherovich's vision left no place for the rabbi, melamed (religious teacher), *magid* (itinerant preacher), or any other "ideologist" of the old order. Nor did it envision a place for Jews who understood their commitment to "Jewishness" as being either religious or explicitly "national" in nature. From the outset, he articulated a self-conscious proletarian identity for the laboring Jewish masses—but never for all of the masses. Tellingly, he labeled this new culture a "culture of labor," while demanding a "haskole of the new rulers."[14]

In evoking the concept of haskole, a proletarian appropriation of the Jewish Enlightenment, Osherovich reiterated a primary refrain of the Jewish Revolution in Belorussia. At first glance, this appeared to be an ill-fitting model for explicitly Bolshevik Jewish cultural renewal. Having emerged hand in hand with the eighteenth-century European Enlightenment, the Haskalah affirmed much of what the Bolshevik Jewish experiment explicitly repudiated. Maks Erik, a literature professor and leading Bolshevik Jewish theorist in Belorussia, eventually attacked the entire Berlin Haskalah movement as the ideological manifestation of an ascendant Jewish bourgeoisie. Through the Haskalah, he argued, the Jewish bourgeoisie sought its own emancipation through integration into the European middle class, while establishing its ideological control over the Jewish laboring classes.[15] As envisioned by Moses Mendelssohn and his German followers, the Haskalah was, moreover, a program of renewal grounded in Hebrew, a language denounced by proponents of the Jewish Revolution as the language of clericalism and Zionism. The *maskilim* (proponents of Haskalah) argued for the religious reform of Judaism based upon rationally defensible principles; the Bolshevik Jewish revolutionaries sought to overcome religion altogether as archaic superstitions of the presocialist world.

Clearly, neither Osherovich nor any Jewish cultural revolutionary sought to return to the principles of bourgeois Enlightenment, Jewish or otherwise. Rather, in calling for a "haskole of the new rulers," Osherovich evoked a traditional Marxist critique of the classical Enlightenment: that the Enlightenment had failed to realize its own philosophical premises precisely because of its classed limits. Proponents of bourgeois Enlightenment accordingly stressed the inherent truth and universality of Enlightenment ideals, including the supposedly natural basis of equality and liberty, so long as those principles advanced the self-interest of the bourgeoisie. Once the working class began to embrace these principles for the sake of challenging bourgeois political and social rule, the bourgeoisie turned sharply against the ethos of the Enlightenment. Class rule consequently obstructed the realization of human emancipation, insofar as it denied the lower classes the very rights the bourgeoisie previously proclaimed to be natural, universal, and eternal when advancing its own emancipation. From the standpoint of Marxian critique, the international proletariat was the only class capable of fully realizing the universal claims of the Enlightenment, as labor itself had become the increasingly universal class of industrial society.[16]

Embracing this logic, Bolshevik maskilim insisted that only the Jewish proletariat could bring about true Jewish Enlightenment. Rejecting Hebraism as a remnant of bourgeois Enlightenment, the Bolshevik haskole promoted Yiddish as the authentic voice of the Jewish laboring classes.[17] Rather than promote religious reform, the Bolshevik haskole envisioned Judaism, like all religions, as an ideological instrument through which the Jewish bourgeoisie manipulated and controlled the proletariat via "their" ideological mediators, the rabbis and religious institutions. As such, "clericalism" obstructed the realization of true enlightenment and needed to be cast off.[18] Nationalist ideologies, most centrally Zionism, likewise prevented the realization of true Enlightenment, because they emphasized vertical national allegiances over the horizontal allegiances of class, preventing the full political emancipation of labor. Only by negating the Haskalah could the Bolshevik haskole fully realize the promise of Jewish emancipation.

The negation of the fundamental precepts of the Haskalah was nowhere more apparent than in the social question. Even as they departed radically in terms of vision, the Bolshevik haskole and classical Haskalah focused upon labor as the necessary curative for the social ills of Jewish populations. As David Sorkin argued, the eighteenth-century Berlin Haskalah was inextricably intertwined with Prussian statist policies intended to wean Jews from mercantile, monetary practices and promote "productive" labor.[19] Derek Penslar likewise demonstrated that numerous German maskilim shared this disdain for Jewish petty mercantile pursuits. Most notably, the radical *maskil* David Friedlander, himself a wealthy silk magnate, spearheaded numerous campaigns to restrict Jewish petty trade and remake Jews into "productive" laborers, artisans, and peasants.[20] The need to transform Jews into productive laborers likewise formed a pillar of the Russian Haskalah. Pioneering Russian-Jewish maskilim Nota Notkin and Hersh Peretz urged Alexander I to implement sweeping social reforms, including mass agricultural resettlement, for destitute Jews.[21] Jacob Posner, a textile magnate and maskil from Lithuania, established a labor colony for several hundred poor Jewish families to teach them the useful trade of cloth making. In exchange, colony members pledged "to use simple homespun for their apparel, black on holidays, gray on weekdays, not to indulge in the luxuries of city life, and to avoid trading of any sort."[22]

Both the classical Haskalah and the Bolshevik haskole valorized productive labor while denouncing trade as morally corrupting, unhealthy, and nonproductive. The critical difference, from the standpoint of the Bolsheviks, was the underlying class dynamic. Viewed through the Bolshevik Marxian lens, Haskalah social reform was promoted by elites for the sake of "improving" their benighted "traditional" brethren, while simultaneously binding them to ostensibly productive labor; such reforms thus asserted the domination of an emerging bourgeois order. Once again, the antinomies of class rule constricted visions of emancipation. Without the abolition of underlying social relations of production, the Haskalah visions of redemption through labor would result only in the further domination of Jews. For the Haskalah vision of social emancipation to be realized, the relations of capital themselves had to be negated.

Everywhere, the Bolshevik haskole was predicated on the principle of negation. In theory, the Bolshevik haskole depended upon the abolition of old cultural norms and practices, as well as the abolition of existing social relations. In actuality, as examined in the preceding chapters, social relations proved exceedingly resilient. Rather than overcome relations of capitalist production, the social policies of the NEP era seemed everywhere to exacerbate and intensify those relations. Nevertheless, the Bolshevik party pressed forward with programs to transform Jewish culture and to emancipate Jews from the perceived backwardness of traditional Jewishness. In workers clubs, schools, universities, and trade union meeting halls, activists in the struggle for the haskole carried out an unyielding campaign to displace the heritage of the old world and willfully build the new.

The task of directing and organizing the Bolshevik haskole fell to the evsektsii. Frequently depicted in the historiography as inadvertent agents of Bolshevization, the role of the evsektsii was far more ambiguous. Most leading early activists had been, like Osherovich, former Bundists with strong commitments to Jewish cultural reform, secularization, education, and the promotion of Yiddish. While decried by their enemies as the watchdogs of Bolshevik power on the Jewish street, the evsketsii had no official coercive power.[23] The Jewish sections were, rather, a classic example of what Sheila Fitzpatrick labeled the Bolshevik party's "soft" line on culture.[24] Exemplified by Narkompros (the Commissariat of Enlightenment) under Lunacharskii, the soft-line institutions emphasized the need to achieve victory through relentless persuasion, propaganda, and, above all, mass education.[25] Like their Narkompros contemporaries, the Bolshevik maskilim remained tied, at root, to the promise of abstractly defined Enlightenment as an intellectual, philosophical, and moral project. Figures like Osherovich, Max Litvinov, Ester Frumkin, Semen

Dimanshtein, and Yankel Levin, the initial head of the Belorussian evsektsiia, all embraced the gradualist, education-driven policies of the cultural soft line.[26]

While the evsektsii central organizations in Minsk, in close coordination with the party Central Committee, played a leading role in forming Jewish cultural policy, implementing reform was an intensely local affair. Chronically understaffed and underfunded, particularly in the countryside and smaller towns, the task of bringing evsektsii policies into reality relied on the initiative, energy, and fervor of local activists. Like the maskilim of the nineteenth-century Russian Haskalah, local activists, including above all young schoolteachers and local trade unionists, faced intense opposition from community elites who viewed Bolshevik Jewish policy with alarm or outright hostility. Local activists shared with their maskilic predecessors the faith that books, literacy, critical thought, reason, and, above all, education would set their benighted conationals free. Yet from the standpoint of many of those conationals, particularly religious Jews, the Bolshevik haskole appeared as yet another in a long line of policies intended to acculturate Jewish populations into the institutions of the "Russian" state and society.[27]

Unsurprisingly, a central issue facing the Bolshevik haskole from the outset of the revolution was the very same issue that animated the nineteenth-century Haskalah across the Russian Empire: education reform.[28] Obviously, the Bolshevik haskole vision for education reform differed markedly from the Haskalah. The point of Bolshevik education was not to produce Enlightened Jews, as had been the goal of Haskalah reformers dating back to the nineteenth-century reformer Max Lilienthal. Rather, it was to produce good Soviet citizens of the Jewish nationality, schooled in Yiddish and inculcated with a sense of Jewishness emptied of explicit religious content, learned from an acceptable, selectively read canon of authors, texts, and events, filtered through the lens of Marxism. Nevertheless, numerous activists quite self-consciously understood themselves as having adopted and superseded the liberal promise of Enlightenment embodied in the writings of Mendele Moykher-Sforim, whose fierce criticisms of "traditional" Jewish education prefigured the polemical tone of Bolshevik reformers.[29]

Despite the acute differences, Bolshevik maskilim shared with their nineteenth-century cousins a common enemy: the traditional Jewish religious school, or heder, and institutions of Jewish religious education generally.[30] A report on school reform, delivered by one Comrade Belinski to a room of one thousand cultural activists from across Belorussia who convened in Borisov in January 1922, captured this continuity with unparalleled clarity. Reporting on local efforts to shut the heder in Borisov, Comrade Belinski stressed not the novelty of this campaign but rather its deep historical roots. "The struggle against the heder has been going on for 100 years, since the time of the maskilim," Belinski argued. Yet the "bourgeois governments did not close the heder," he continued, "since that was not in their interests." Rather, the government did the bidding of the bourgeoisie and kept alive the heder, which "made the child into a golem, a sickly creature, and an idiot." Recognizing the *melamdim* to be completely "without culture," the bourgeoisie refused to send their own children to the heder, but insisted upon religious education for the poor. In shutting the heder, Belinski argued, the Bolshevik Revolution transformed the idea of secular, enlightened education from a class privilege into a rule for the new revolutionary society.[31]

Comrade Belinski's attack on the heder reiterated the underlying logic of the Bolshevik haskole. Through new, Yiddish-language Soviet schools, he reasoned, the proletarian state would break the fetters of class domination and democratize the Haskalah. Belinski's critique laid out the limitations of the "old" heder; a late-1923 pseudonymous poem in *Der Veker*, appropriately entitled "The New Heder," cleverly trumpeted the promise of new, emancipated, proletarianized education:[32]

Motl the shoemaker, Berl the tailor	*Motl shuster, Berl Shnayder*
Get dressed up in new clothes,	*Tuen onet naye kleyder*
Peaked hats, army coats	*Hitlekh shpitsike, shineln*
And they return to school.	*Un men geyt tsurik in kheyder*
The melamed is a locksmith	*Der melamed iz a shloser*
Knows the Torah without a hitch,	*Ken af oysveynik di toyre*
It doesn't harm him (one still fears him),	*Knelt on lokshn, on a kantshik,*
That he teaches without whip, or switch	*Nor es shadt nit—men hot moyre*
And it's lively and it's cheerful	*Un s'iz lebedik un freylekh*
Our Rebbe is all smiles	*Undzer rebe iz tsufridn*
Oy, what a dear melamed we have	*Oy, a tayerer melamed*
With neither a beard nor piles!	*On a bord un on meridn!*
That he teaches Blacksmith-style	*Un arum undz di lamed-vavim*
It's no shame, and no one minds,	*Angegreyt fun kolaminim.*
For he's forging all around us	*Nor es shadt nit, zol er kneln*
*Lamed-Vavim** of all kinds.	*Af zayn nayem kuznye-shteyger*
Comrade Cobblers, *shlogt kapores**	*Khevre shuster, shlogt kapores*
With the old rabbi's carcass,	*Mit dem altn rebns-peyger*
Hammer out a brand new heder	*Oysgeshmidt a naye kheyder*
Where we'll learn to build	*Dortn lernt men zikh shafn*
A whole new living order.	*Gor an ander lebns-seyder*

*The "*Lamed-Vavim*," which literally means the "thirty-six," refers to the thirty-six truly righteous men who will, according to Jewish tradition, secretly defend the world through their righteousness.
*To "*shlog kapores*," is a term derived from the Yom Kippur ritual practice of atonement, during which Jews traditionally cast their sins onto a chicken that was then ritually killed. The phrase is used humorously in modern Yiddish to mean "revile" or "abuse."

Known only by the pen name "Heris," the poet described a world—and school—transformed through revolution. In place of the old, abusive, hemorrhoidal, teacher of the heder stands the working class engaged in a process of self-emancipation through self-education. In this vision, locksmiths teaching "blacksmith style" hammer away the soul-crushing school of past unhappiness and forge new centers of proletarian optimism. At the same time, the poem transforms the rituals of archaic Judaism into new avenues for emancipation. In place of dead chickens, the new proletarian Bolshevik Jews swings the carcass of the dead rabbis to atone for old sins. The mystical Hasidic rebbe of yesteryear is transformed into the proletarian teacher, teaching without violence. Most importantly, instead of turning out "heretics" (as their opponents claimed), the new school turns out "Lamed-Vavim," the "thirty-six" humble and righteous men who, according to legend, defend the world through their goodness and from whose ranks the messiah will come.

Obviously, the self-proclaimed "heretic" who wrote this poem did not speak for the totality of Belorussian Jewry. Nor was the poem a work of propaganda intended to convince nonbelievers of the truth of the Bolshevik program. On the contrary, the poem affirmed the faith of convinced believers confronted by long odds. Indeed, the Bolshevik maskilim found obstacles and opposition to the new schools wherever they looked. Across the republic, schools lacked physical infrastructure and qualified teachers, while local religious leaders fought vigorously against the new "heretical" schools. Parents proved exceedingly ambivalent about sending their children to schools that professed critical views of Judaism. Other parents refused to send their children to Yiddish schools when the universities and prospects for real social mobility required knowledge of Russian.[33] Resistance to the schools of the new haskole, particularly on religious grounds, proved most acute outside of the major cities.[34]

The problems of Yiddish education reform, grave though they were, should not overshadow the considerable successes. Throughout the 1920s, new schools were in fact built and the number of qualified Yiddish teachers increased.[35] Between 1922 and 1932, the number of Yiddish schools in the Republic climbed from 106 to 334, while the student body increased from under eleven thousand to more than thirty-three thousand.[36] Most significantly, the percentage of Jewish students receiving a "modern" secular education of one form or another reached levels that far exceeded the wildest dreams of the nineteenth-century maskilim. Moreover, Yiddish primary schools constituted only one part of a broader campaign to bring "Enlightenment" to the Jewish population, however delineated. Alongside primary schools, the party and state also established institutions for adult education, particularly for workers. Already by 1924 Vitebsk boasted two Jewish night schools, five evening Party Schools, and more than one hundred "cells" for worker education, providing adult education to more than one thousand workers. Across Belorussia, nearly ten thousand workers—either adults or teenagers—attended evening schools for workers in 1924. The state established two worker universities, one in Minsk and a second in Borbruisk; both had Jewish sections and large numbers of Jewish students. Six explicitly Yiddish workers' clubs existed in Belorussia; nineteen other clubs offered Russian and Yiddish language programs; thirty additional clubs had been established for kustari, many of which operated in and offered educational programming in Yiddish. Bolshevik didacticism thus extended well beyond childhood. The goal was to bring enlightenment to all mobilizable and "enlightenable" pockets of the Jewish population.[37]

Practicing the Bolshevik Haskole

School reform, although critical, constituted only a part of the struggle to remake, recode, and reconstitute Jewish culture. A second crucial battleground formed around the religion and practices of Judaism itself. In a fashion that directly mirrored the broader antireligious activism of the Bolshevik *bezbozh-niki* (self-proclaimed "godless" activists), Jewish *apikorsim* (self-proclaimed heretics) carried the cultural struggle straight to the heart of religious practice through broad campaigns of revolutionary iconoclasm. Revolutionary icono-clasm, particularly in the earliest phases, was rarely simply destructive. Rather, each ceremony, lecture, or transfigured ritual constituted a process of revolutionary negation and a struggle to remake meaning in service to the revolution.

Thus, the ceremony of the "Red Bris" became, like the related "Red Baptism," an opportunity for dedicated proletarians to offer up their child not to the Abrahamic covenant with God, as the ideologists of the old world asserted, but to the revolutionary covenant with history. One such ceremony, captured in the pages of *Der Veker*, depicted the gravity of the transition with the subtlety of a hammer blow. The story opened with a dark, decrepit tale of one father who insisted on providing a traditional bris (circumcision ritual) for his son in the traditional manner, spending his "last kopek" on whiskey, a *moyel*, food, and a cantor for the ceremony surrounding the circumcision. Against this image of ritual obscurantism, *Der Veker* reported on the events that took place in the Spartak workers' club in April of 1924. The father of a boy, an unidentified worker, stood in the middle of the club, surrounded by workers and placards proclaiming the victory of "freedom and workers' power." The mother, despite being a nonparty worker, participated eagerly, reportedly "overjoyed that her child would become a member of the proletarian society." In place of the cantor, a workers' orchestra played in the background. In place of the moyel, a young worker took the newborn in his arms for the "christening," delivering a strictly kosher blessing: "From now and forever, you will be ours: a comrade, a member of the Spartak Club" and a proletarian. The child, of course, received the only name possible for such a momentous occasion: Vladimir. Needless to say, no sign of the covenant was made.[38]

The Jewish liturgical calendar likewise offered an unending cycle of opportunities for struggle over the meaning of identity. Indeed, the religious calendar structured the Bolshevik Jewish cultural year as methodically and predictably as it had structured the traditional year. The Bolshevik Jewish cultural year began piously at the start of Rosh Hashanah, the Jewish New Year, continued through Yom Kippur, the Jewish Day of Atonement, and ratcheted up again for the holiest of antireligion festivals on the Jewish Bolshevik calendar—Passover, or *Pesach*. These holidays usually occasioned lectures or "trials" at the local workers' club. The Grosser Club, for example, in 1922 heralded in the holiday of Yom Kippur with a trial of the Day of Judgment itself.[39] Local activists in the town of Cherven celebrated a full High Holiday schedule in the autumn of 1923: on Rosh Hashanah they staged a series of lectures for the youth of the Jewish working class on the theme of "The Bourgeois God and His Judgment over Man"; on Yom Kippur, Comrade Novogrudskii delivered a public lecture on "The Origins of Man and the World"; local activists followed with an antireligious festival for Sukkot, the festival of the tabernacles.[40] Meanwhile, in Minsk, local evsektsiia activists carried out an antireligious High Holiday season on the theme of constructing a new "way of life" (*byt'*) for workers. Members of the builders union organized a study night and lecture series to coincide with the start of Rosh Hashanah. On Yom Kippur, the Minsk members of the food producers union held a mass demonstration and orchestral performance outside the Choral Synagogue to drown out the holiday prayers. The evsektsiia main bureau capped off the holiday festivities with a gala "literary-humoristic" evening at the Minsk Palace of Culture, reportedly attended by some three thousand people.[41]

As local activists staged demonstrations and lectures, newspapers reinforced the assault on religious holidays. Articles, letters from workers, and editorials denouncing the religious practices surrounding Passover arrived with far greater punctuality than the Prophet Elijah ever did. The prelude to the Passover celebration in 1923—a particularly turbulent year on the religious front—witnessed a ceaseless flow of antireligious letters and stories in the pages of the Minsk press.[42] One shoemaker, a certain M. Botvinik, wrote to *Der Veker* to deride Jewish workers who continued to celebrate Passover. The October Revolution, he wrote, had exposed the fact that "the entire story of the Hagadah is a lie," since it proved that true emancipation for the worker came not from God but from "the worker alone."[43] A few days later, the paper published a letter from one Abrahm Krasnoselski, a needleworkers unionist, who blamed the perpetuation of the holiday on a familiar target: "The women cry in one voice: 'our fathers, our grandfathers and our grandfathers' grandfathers ate matzo, therefore I will eat matzo." In the face of such gendered obscurantism, Krasnoselski complained, the "working class" had little choice but to capitulate; as he put it, "Go argue with such women."[44] The following week, *Der Veker* ran a series of "scientific" articles debunking the story of the Exodus from Egypt on historical grounds, thereby challenging the historic basis of Passover.[45] *Der Veker* buried the short, concluding portion of this article beneath a spread commemorating the arrival of the *real* holiday on the early spring proletarian liturgical calendar: the anniversary of the Paris Commune.[46]

Such antireligious activities were populist, but by no means universally popular—a fact that did not escape the attention of Bolshevik policy makers.[47] As Zvi Gitelman and subsequent observers have pointed out, these activities generated widespread opposition on the so-called Jewish street.[48] Religious Jews or vaguely defined "traditional" Jews rallied to the defense of Jewish cultural institutions and holidays—not to mention signs, symbols, and language.[49] In the spring of 1922, for example, the Central Bureau of the evsektsii organized a mass Jewish cultural conference for workers in Minsk timed to coincide with the start of Passover. The planned festival involved lectures by evsektsii activists and performances by young party members to educate the population about the struggle against clericalism, religious education, and "Jewish reactionary communal organizations."[50] A similar event was held in nearby Slutsk. Rather than simply stand by, local leaders in Minsk and Slutsk staged counterdemonstrations denouncing the Bolshevik heretics. Speakers at underground meetings in Minsk denounced the closing of synagogues, the appropriation of synagogue valuables during the antireligious campaigns, and attempts to suppress religious practice by cutting off access to matzo for Passover.[51] These struggles reached a crescendo in the spring of 1923, when the Bolshevik leadership, in a fit of antireligious fervor, attempted to shut synagogues in Poltava, Gomel, Rechitsa, and Minsk (not to mention Kharkov, Odessa, Simferopol, and other locales), provoking protests across Belorussia and beyond.[52]

Archival records reveal numerous instances in which local organizers mobilized against aspects of the Bolshevik program for cultural reform.[53] Understandably, opposition to reform has received the primacy of place within the scholarship on Soviet Jewry. The failure of Bolshevik policy on the religious front, as well as Jewish resistance to such policies, undeniably captures an important part of the story of cultural transformation. Clearly, numerous groups remained more or less active in their opposition to Bolshevik visions of cultural reform. The Bolsheviks did not, after all, invent out of thin air the idea that many groups were ardently counterrevolutionary, provided that the counterrevolution would ensure the reestablishment of prerevolutionary social hierarchies and rituals within the Jewish community. Likewise, traditional religious patterns persisted even among Jews who were sympathetic to some or all of the revolution's political or social aims, including many who had entered the party ranks.[54]

While opposition from religious and political groups, as well as the continuity of traditional cultural practices within revolutionary society, constituted an important part of the story, it was only *part* of the story. While aggressive activism in the cultural sphere spurred protracted and forceful resistance from some quarters, it simultaneously elicited vigorous support in others. A reported three thousand workers and kustari participated in mass meetings held throughout Minsk in February of 1923 calling for the Choral Synagogue to be turned into a workers' club.[55] Workers and cultural activists maintained a steady barrage of letters to *Der Veker* demanding that the Synagogue and other community buildings be turned over to the working class for revolutionary, proletarian spaces.[56] Evsektsii activists frequently supported and organized such activities.[57] Yet such coordination did not necessarily mean that the goal lacked popular support. The evsektsiia in Bobruisk, for example, supported the transformation of the main synagogue into a cultural club, though apparently not as aggressively as groups of angry kustari, who wrote numerous letters denouncing the evsektsiia and government for failing to close down this nest of "speculators, Zionists, vile traders, and other dark elements."[58]

Viewing such processes of cultural struggle through binary terms (whether "Jewish" vs. "non-Jewish" or "traditional" vs. "modern") masks the complex fusions of identities and cultural practices that developed on the ground in revolutionary society. Jewish policy ebbed and flowed throughout the 1920s, as did Bolshevik policy toward religion in general. Efforts to suppress, ridicule, or eliminate religious practices emerged alongside or in competition with more accommodationist tendencies. In certain moments and locales, the relationship between Bolshevik power and traditional sites of Jewish power was indeed sharply contested. In other moments and locales, particularly outside the cities, necessity gave rise to fluid policies. The contest between Bolsheviks and believers over meaning did not necessarily result in the predictable pattern of opposition.

A 1926 report on conditions in the shtetl of Turov provides a revealing glimpse into the ways that struggles over the meaning of religious signs, symbols, and language resulted in a fluid transformation of culture writ local.

Much to the chagrin of Comrade Rakhazel'skii, the evsektsiia activist who filed the report, the outward social structures of everyday life in Turov had changed little since prerevolutionary times. Turov remained an extremely religious community. At the head of the local order stood a core "committee" composed of leading members of the Jewish community, including (according to Rakhazel'skii) one moneylender (*protsentnik*) and a usurer (*rostovshchik*). Keeping with the spirit of the revolution, the committee members, including the local rabbi and several property owners, decided to reconstitute themselves as a "soviet of synagogues" to govern local institutions. This soviet reportedly included the two usurers, one contractor, eight shopkeepers (four wealthy shopkeepers, and four middling), and eight kustari (four rich, four middling). The soviet of synagogues initially attempted to gain official recognition from the central Soviet, and, failing this, continued to operate unauthorized.[59]

From such a motley collection of overt class enemies (as the report made clear), one should have expected fervent and relentless opposition to Bolshevik policies. Yet the illegal soviet acted in an unpredictable manner. It formed a proletarian synagogue for the shtetl and encouraged the development of proletarian education and political development. Members of the soviet collected philanthropy from abroad to help the impoverished town's more than four hundred Jewish families. The local soviet formed a komsomol cell and encouraged political activism among the youth, but it made sure the komsomol'tsy married in religious weddings and circumcised their children. In addition, the soviet organized a constant flow of cultural events, including a series of lectures on the themes of "Religion and Capitalism," "Divinity," "The Torah and Socialism," "Torah and the New Way of Life (The Contemporary Woman)," "Palestine," and so forth. Lecturers, the report noted, stressed a variety of ideas that one would be hard pressed to find in the writings of Comrades Rambam, Rashi, or Nahmanides: that God opposed hierarchies based on wealth; that God opposed the accumulation of private property; that—through episodes such as the condemnation of the "Golden Calf" at the foot of Mount Sinai— God continually roused the Jewish population "against Capital," and so on. "It is only a fabrication," one lecturer emphasized, "that religion necessarily goes hand in hand with Capital." The Bolsheviks, the same lecturer continued, "do not consider those people who believe that the building of socialism in one country will fail without faith in God."[60]

Comrade Rakhazel'skii expressed alarm at the strange amalgams of God and Marx, study and revolution he found in Turov. His skepticism reflected the predominant view of cultural revolutionaries who encountered such peculiar local efforts to build socialism. As a "conscious" cultural combatant, Rahazel'skii viewed this unorthodox synthesis as the deception of class enemies. Yet the situation in Turov serves as a reminder that the stridency of published missives, memoirs, reflections, and memories of committed oppositionists did not reflect the totality of the situation. Turov was an extreme but by no means solitary site of cultural fusion and confusion in the Bolshevik experiment. Did such experiences constitute an anomaly in an otherwise uniform system? More crucially, did such examples really constitute the *continuity* of "tradition" in the revolutionary project? Was this an attempted reassertion of class domination by the undead bourgeoisie through revolutionary language? Or was this, in the eyes of the Turov radicals, a revolutionary project shot through with sparks of holiness?

Going to the Jewish People

For the Jews of Turov, as for many participants in the revolution, constructing postrevolutionary Jewish culture involved some commitment to blending Bolshevism and "traditional" Jewish life. Among the most forceful proponents of constructing an autonomous Bolshevik-Jewish fusion culture were those activists who entered the evsektsiia and worked directly and wholeheartedly on the project of cultural reconstruction. The leading proponents of the Bolshevik haskole were, by and large, older Jews who entered the Bolshevik party through radical Jewish political parties. Most, like Il'ia Oserovich, had been Bundists until the mergers of 1919–1921. Yankel Levin, the first head of the evsektsii, had been a Bund leader before joining the Communist Bund, and then the Bolsheviks, in 1919.[61] Ester Frumkin was a revered Yiddishist and Bundist leader long before she became one of the leading evsektsii figures in the USSR.[62] Aaron Isaakovich Vainshtein, a teacher from Vilna who studied in the city's famed Yiddish Pedagogical Institute, joined the Bund in 1901; after moving to Minsk in 1917, he became a leading Bundist in the City Soviet before joining the Bolsheviks in 1921.[63] Boris (Ber) Orshanskii joined the Bund in 1903 and remained active until 1918, when he became a Bolshevik and a leading evsektsii litterateur.[64] Former Bundists likewise dominated the second rank of evsektsii activists. Vulf Abramowicz Nodel' spent two years in prison for Bundist activism in Vilna and Dvinsk before joining the Bolsheviks with the party merger in 1921.[65] Rebekka Simhovna Melikhovitskaia, originally a seamstress from Odessa, joined the Bund in 1913 and remained active until becoming a Bolshevik and member of the evsektsii administration in Minsk in 1920.[66] No matter where one looked in the evsektsii ranks, one found old Bundists turned Bolsheviks.

Bundists constituted the driving force behind the Bolshevik haskole. As activists with firm commitments to constructing new forms of autonomous Jewish culture, however transformed, these actors have understandably received the most sustained attention from historians. In general, as Elissa Bemporad has stressed, Bundists, along with a smattering of former Poalei Tsionists, played the most prominent role in efforts to construct new Yiddish cultural institutions across the Belorussian republic.[67] That being said, former Bundists, proponents of the Bolshevik haskole, and defenders of Yiddish cultural renewal did not hold a monopoly on cultural policy in Belorussia. This was especially so after 1924, when party recruitment policies and purges began to dramatically reconfigure the composition of the Jewish ranks in the Bolshevik party.

The changing composition of the Jewish Bolshevik ranks resulted directly from the so-called Lenin Levy, a mass party membership drive aimed at expanding the party ranks and launched following the death of Lenin on January 21, 1924. While the primary thrust of this campaign was to recruit Belorussian peasants into the Bolshevik ranks, the party also actively recruited a new generation of Jewish activists. The party simultaneously thinned its ranks, excluding many older Jews, including former Bundists, through the Party Review of 1924.[68] In contrast to this older generation, whose politics sought to merge radical Yiddishist cultural policy with Bolshevik rule, many younger Jewish recruits were largely raised in Russian- or Belorussian-speaking environments; others were self-consciously fleeing Yiddish-speaking ones, had weaker attachments to Yiddish culture generally, and had few contacts to prerevolutionary politics. As such, they looked askance at the task of building Jewish cultural institutions, forging new Yiddish culture, or establishing distinctly Jewish politics within the party.[69]

Like the leaders of the Bolshevik haskole, most of these activists shared an intense belief in the power of education, propaganda, and community organization to effect fundamental change. They likewise took up the cause of cultural work among the Jews with a mixture of reforming zeal and remarkable sincerity. Yet unlike proponents of Bolshevik haskole, these activists sought to draw Jews into the broader Bolshevik vision of universalizing proletarian enlightenment. They appealed to Jews first and foremost as laborers, sought to educate them to become "conscious" members of the working class, and stressed the fundamental relationship between proletarian rule and enlightenment. As proponents of Bolshevik internationalism in Yiddish-speaking milieus, they challenged the vision of the Bolshevik haskole. Insofar as these actors eschewed specific Jewish cultural ends, they have frequently been omitted from the story of postrevolutionary Jewish life or denounced as assimilationists, betrayers, or worse. Yet in challenging programs of explicitly Jewish cultural construction, they played a critical role in shaping Jewish cultural history as it actually developed in the Soviet context.

This second form of enlightenment work espoused Bolshevik internationalism and the need for explicit *"political* enlightenment work" (*polit-
prosvetitel'naia rabota*), as opposed to the cultural enlightenment of the
Bolshevik haskole. As used in the sources, political enlightenment aimed to
cultivate and integrate workers into a Bolshevik vision of universal, proletarian-
led cultural reconstruction. Within the Jewish milieu, proponents of this universalizing Bolshevik vision insisted on the need to overcome obscurantist,
outdated, and archaic ways of being Jewish in the world.[70] Most (but by no
means all) of the frontline cultural reformers in this camp were young activists
who came of age after the revolution or entered the party with the Lenin Levy.
Older evsektsii members, particularly those committed to the program of
Bolshevik haskole, frequently complained that these workers, to cite one typical evsektsii report from 1924, had "no ties with Jewish workers and consider
Russian to be their cultural milieu." Yet the same evsektsii report grudgingly
acknowledged a spontaneous upsurge in activism among these young Jews,
particularly among university students. Acting "without our influence," young
university students, previously indifferent to the fate of the Jewish working
class, suddenly expressed a "desire to connect with the Jewish working class,"
particularly through local educational excursions to the countryside and the
shtetl.[71]

Over the course of 1924 this initial trickle of young Jewish activists to
the countryside turned into a broad stream. As part of broad, new shifts in
nationality policy, the party and evsektsiia encouraged eager masses of young
college-aged students to head to the shtetlekh and villages to observe and
instruct their benighted Jewish brethren. Across the republic, young Jews
headed to the countryside as teachers, observers, ethnographers, and propagandists, forging a new, Yiddishized "to the People" movement that evoked the
spirit of 1870s populism. Unlike the activists of the Bolshevik haskole, these
young Jews viewed Yiddish as a necessary linguistic means to socialist construction, not a goal in its own right.

Reports to the Central Bureau of the Minsk evsektsii from young activists deployed to remote cities and shtetlekh during academic breaks provide
glimpses into the self-understanding of these frontline reformers. One such
student, Comrade Kagan, delivered an extensive report in September of 1924,
detailing her efforts to bring emancipation to the town of Rogachev. Upon
her arrival, Comrade Kagan reportedly found an environment completely
untouched by the revolution. She expressed shock over the lack of educational
opportunities for Jewish workers. Despite the fact that she had no previous
background in "Jewish work," Kagan immediately established two educational
circles for Jewish women. One cell focused exclusively on literacy; the circle's

twenty women met regularly to read Russian newspaper articles and discuss them in Yiddish, acquiring political education and Russian literacy along the way. In the second, advanced cell, Comrade Kagan introduced a small group of dedicated workers to "more serious work," studying the causes of the "Imperialist War" (i.e., World War I), the geography and historical development of the belligerents, and the history of the First and Second Internationals. In her spare time, Kagan delivered lectures to the women workers of the sewing industry, visited kindergartens in order to create pioneer groups for young Jewish children, and organized meetings with men and women kustari on political themes.[72] Like maskilim and the populists of the late nineteenth century, Bolshevik universalists believed in the emancipating power of directed self-education.[73]

Comrade Bernshtein, another young activist, described a similar set of experiences in the Mogilev region. Having traveled to Mogilev for agitation work, Bernshtein discovered the dismal state of cultural work among Jewish workers. Despite the town's large numbers of Jewish needleworkers, leatherworkers, and carpenters, the party had carried out virtually no cultural work due to the absence of local party activists with sufficient knowledge of Yiddish. Despite his own proclivities for Russian, Comrade Bernshtein immediately set to work securing subscriptions of Yiddish newspapers for the local party cells, organizing worker meetings, establishing Yiddish-language komsomol cells and pioneer clubs for young Jews, and organizing two Yiddish-language self-education cells for local kustari, one focused on political questions and another on antireligious propaganda.[74]

Across the Republic, young Jewish activists followed the paths of Comrades Kagan and Bernshtein, fanning out to preach the gospel of the universalizing Bolshevik Revolution, in Yiddish, to the Jewish working class. In December 1924 the party committee of the Minsk *Okrug* region heard reports from young activists dispatched to shtetlekh in the region during the summer, each of whom detailed the uphill battle to spread the ethos of the revolution to the remote corners of the republic. Comrade Guterman described the rather typical conditions in Smilovich, where the local working class carried out little cultural work. He arrived in the town, established local worker and komsomol cells in Yiddish, taught workers to make wall newspapers, and organized a night school for thirty-five Jewish workers. Comrade Kanchik, who had been deployed to Bobruisk, helped local schoolteachers carry out cultural work among workers and organized multiple spectacles and public lectures. Komsomol member Gurevich similarly extolled his accomplishments in the shtetl Shatsk, where he organized a komsomol cell, carried out extensive antireligious propaganda, assisted in closing the local heder, and cajoled local authorities into bringing criminal charges against underground religious teachers. Other young komsomol and party members likewise described their work to establish worker clubs, komsomol cells, libraries, drama circles, schools, newspapers, and other institutions in remote locations across the republic.[75]

Young activists dispatched to the countryside likely exaggerated the degree of work carried out in these remote regions. Hoping to impress party leaders, they likely inflated their own actions. Nevertheless, these activists and countless others played a critical role in bringing the party face to face with the countryside and with Jews living in remote corners of the republic. As such, they formed an advanced guard in the party's campaign to turn its "face to the shtetl" and address the pressing problems of poverty and unemployment in the countryside. Unlike the activists of the Bolshevik haskole, this new generation cared little about the promotion of Jewish culture for its own sake. Generally speaking, they conducted party work in Yiddish out of necessity, driven by local conditions, not as an end in its own right. Most significantly, they focused their attention almost exclusively on efforts to improve social conditions for Jewish workers and to cultivate Bolshevik political consciousness among Jewish workers in remote locales. The end goal for these activists was not to establish Jewish cultural renewal but to promote the project of socialist construction among Jewish workers.

This second wave of Jewish cultural reformers, the Bolshevik universalists, differed dramatically from proponents of Bolshevik haskole not only in their goals but also in their conception of the meaning and fate of the revolution. Rather than celebrate ties to the Bund or other Jewish parties, Bolshevik universalists adhered to the Bolshevik party mainstream, particularly concerning the NEP. In addition to generational divides, the two camps also reflected deep social cleavages in the Jewish milieu. The proponents of Jewish cultural renewal and Bolshevik haskole drew the vast bulk of their support from the organized urban Jewish working class in the "traditional" Jewish industries. The proponents of the Bolshevik universalism, in turn, focused on shtetl Jews, rural producers, and, above all, the kustari and artisans of the small towns and shtetlekh.

This shift on the ground reflected larger shifts within the party. Between 1924 and the end of 1925, power within the evsektsii shifted decisively away from the proponents of Bolshevik haskole. The clearest indication of this shifting valence occurred at the end of 1925, when the party leadership removed Yankel Levin, the former Bundist turned Bolshevik maskil, as evsektsii head, replacing him with one of the more ambiguous Jewish cultural activists, the reliable "old Bolshevik," Abram Beilin. The change in evsektsii leadership coincided with a shift in party power relations, as the Bolshevik leadership decisively rewrote the terms of its political relationship with its erstwhile partner, the Bund. The decision to replace Levin, a proponent of Yiddish cultural autonomy, with Beilin, a proponent of Bolshevization, also reflected a change in cultural policy against the path of the Bolshevik haskole and in favor of the Bolshevik universalists. Yet Abram Beilin's story underscores the degree to which cultural policy in the Jewish milieu was bound inextricably to questions of the economy generally, and the fate of the NEP in particular. The immediate postrevolutionary chaos had provided the potential for great autonomous flexibility concerning cultural policy in the Soviet periphery. By 1926 the centralizing wind had begun to pull once again toward Moscow and the heart of the revolution. Abram Beilin came to power in the evsektsii as a NEP-era reformer sent to Minsk to redress grievances of the countryside concerning the power of the city in the Jewish idiom. He was, in turn, swept away by the same onrushing storm that would rip apart the NEP itself: the Stalin Revolution.

Abram Beilin and the End of the Jewish Revolution

Relatively little is known about Abram Grigor'evich Beilin, aside from what he told the party about himself. According to an autobiographical statement he wrote for his 1924 Party Review, Beilin was born in the shtetl Mstislavl' in 1886, making him thirty-eight years old at the time of the review. The son of workers, Beilin became a carpenter's apprentice at the age of fourteen. Five years later, as the fires of revolution smoldered, he joined the local *Iskra* group (e.g., followers of Lenin's newspaper). Three months later, on September 14, 1905, policemen arrested Beilin for agitating among soldiers brought to Mstislavl' from garrisons in Trakai to prevent agrarian disturbances. Sentenced to eight years of hard labor, Beilin's punishment was commuted to a mere prison term after three years; he bounced between prisons in Mogilev and Smolensk before being released in 1910.[76] Arrested and reimprisoned for revolutionary activity in Vilna in 1912, Beilin was conscripted to the front when war broke out in 1914. He served in the tsar's army throughout the "Imperialist war."

When the February Revolution broke, Beilin deserted the army, "set off" to Petrograd, and resurfaced in April as a Bolshevik organizer in the town of Nevel', just across the northeast Belorussian border. The October Revolution drew him back to Petrograd, where he joined the revolutionary crowd. In November 1917, the Bolsheviks again ordered Beilin to "the front," this time as the secretary of the Military Revolutionary Committee in Nevel'. He went willingly. His lifelong career as a party activist finally brought employment. Following the establishment of Bolshevik power in 1918, Beilin joined the Cheka in Nevel' and was promoted shortly thereafter to the Vitebsk Guberniia Cheka. From the Cheka, Beilin moved into political work, joining the

Vitebsk Guberniia Committee, and the Vitebsk Executive Committee. A tireless worker, Beilin kept rising, eventually winning promotion to the Polotsk Executive Committee.[77]

In early 1926, the party again promoted Beilin, this time to the relatively plum assignment of party work in Minsk, where he joined the Central Executive Committee. This position came with an unexpected twist, as the party also appointed him head of the Belorussian evsektsii, despite the fact that Beilin had shown no interest in Jewish affairs previously. Although a curious choice at first glance, a number of factors made Beilin a promising candidate. For one, he was a highly competent bureaucrat. As a native Yiddish speaker, Beilin also possessed the necessary linguistic skills. As a longstanding Bolshevik, Beilin had a reputation for trustworthiness and aggressive opposition to Bundism, Zionism, and clericalism. Unlike the old evsektsii leadership, which hailed overwhelmingly from Minsk, Beilin was a provincial outsider. Given his close Cheka ties, it is highly probable that the party sent Beilin to Minsk to clean house and sweep the vestiges of Bundism from the evsektsii. Finally, Beilin was a former carpenter and, consequently, a kustar'. His rise to prominence coincided with the period when the party and evsektsii shifted priorities and began to lean toward the kustari as a new base of support. In short, Beilin's personal fortunes epitomized the political rise of the kustari as a result of the NEP. After years of complaining of neglect in the party, the evsektsii, and the unions, the kustari finally had one of their own in charge.

Once in Minsk, Beilin threw himself into work as the head of the evsektsii with the same verve he applied to all of his party pursuits. A prolific, if ungifted, writer, he produced extensive protocols, reports, and plans to weaken and eradicate class enemies in the countryside while strengthening the position of the kustari. In these missives, Beilin returned repeatedly to the idea that cultural struggle within the Jewish milieu could only be won through social struggle. From his perspective, only the promotion and strengthening of "proletarian" elements—by which he meant Jewish agricultural colonists, cooperatives, and above all, the kustari—would reinforce support for the Bolshevik project on the Jewish streets of the republic. Unlike the old evsektsii leadership, which had focused on urban areas and the unionized (and frequently Bundist) Jewish labor force, Beilin placed his bets on the countryside, the nascent cooperative producer economy, and the petty producers.

These themes underscored Beilin's June 1927 report outlining the "tasks" for party work among the kustari.[78] The kustar', Beilin argued, constituted the only true bulwark of proletarian rule and the guard against entrenched class enemies outside of the major towns. He therefore emphasized the need to bolster the lowest strata of the kustari, those suspended between artisanal and factory production, impoverished and exploited by wealthy kustar' producers, local kulaks, and private traders. To improve the conditions of these vital elements, Beilin suggested lowering taxes on small producers and providing them with the credit necessary to grow their business. Beilin's pro-kustar' stance replicated Nikolai Bukharin's appeal for the peasants to "enrich themselves." Through trade, markets, and exchange, society would, in theory, evolve toward socialism.[79] By strengthening the social position of the most proletarianized elements, the party would augment political support throughout the countryside.

In a nod to goals laid out by the Plenum of the Central Committee, Beilin also stressed that his proposal would help restore equilibrium to the NEP market and national economy as a whole. Bringing these kustari into producer cooperatives and onto the "rails of socialist construction," he claimed, would lead to higher production of consumer goods, thereby enticing peasant grain back onto the market, as well as provide necessary components for advanced industry.[80] In Beilin's vision, the kustari served as a point of political and economic mediation not only for the countryside but also for the entire socialist economy of the Belorussia republic.[81] In sum, Beilin stressed that the entire smychka, or union, between the countryside and city upon which the NEP rested depended fundamentally upon the success of the kustari. In doing so, he marked himself as a quintessential NEP politician.

Under Beilin's watch, the evsektsii did not simply provide rhetorical support but also undertook concrete measures to strengthen the kustari. By pressing for tax reductions as well as credits and resources for kustar' cooperatives, Beilin genuinely devoted the evsektsii to the social and economic improvement of the rural Jewish laboring population. During his tenure, the evsektsii oversaw the creation of collective farms, collectives, and local national soviets intended to integrate the countryside more seamlessly into the Soviet project. At the same time, Beilin rhetorically stressed the need for relentless struggle against clericalism, Zionism, the yeshiva, and heder. His office produced a series of missives outlining the danger posed by each of these forms of opposition. "The Rabbi, as usual," one of Beilin's circulars lamented, "appears to hold great authority, even among the shtetl laborers." Through soup kitchens, local networks, support groups, and the like, the evsektsii provided for local indigents, itinerant workers, and the plain old poor, particularly among the elderly.[82] At other moments, Beilin denounced rabbis, butchers, and religious leaders for the implementation of taxes such as the korobka (the tax on meat), the monopoly over candle taxes, the tax on Passover flour, and so on, to exploit the laboring population.[83] The Zionists, he stressed, attempted to garner support among the kustari by defending their rights as laborers. Despite his sharp rhetoric, Beilin as a politician oversaw a sharp scaling down of antagonism toward these purported enemies. In practice, Bolshevik harassment and persecution of the religious and Zionists in the shtetl declined during his tenure, again as part of the party's efforts to improve relations with the countryside.

Rather than strengthen support for the party, the "face to the shtetl" turn appeared to embolden and revive "undesirable" elements and groups in the shtetlekh. A widely circulated anonymous 1926 evsektsii report on clericalism, possibly written by Beilin himself, typically warned of an alarming "growth of religious activity in the Jewish milieu." The report attributed this increase to the changed economic system of the 1920s. The NEP, the report claimed, had revived trade and wealth, but with the unintended accoutrements of clericalism and Zionism. Bourgeois ideologies reemerged to lead the petit-bourgeois elements away from the revolution and back toward religious obscurantism.[84] The report warned, moreover, of "secret enemies" among the local eksektsii activists in the countryside, who organized lectures and public discussions that stoked rather than suppressed religious sentiments. These "this-worldly preachers" (magidim) posed as defenders of the Bolshevik regime but delivered lectures on themes like "socialism and Torah" and "Religion against Capital," thereby smuggling religious worldviews back into the public sphere.[85] Rather than suppressing clericalism, such efforts created retrenched enemies and underground institutions that fought against the party. In Petrikov, Shatsk, Cherven, Liady, and numerous other small towns, authorities located scores of underground hederim, yeshivot, and religious study circles. In the shtetl Koidanov, underground religious schools reportedly sent students to the party school to play and sing outside, "to draw students away from the Soviet schools."[86]

A second widely circulated anonymous report from 1926, also likely written by Beilin, stressed the economic and social conditions that gave rise to clericalism.[87] As the one "legal form of non-Soviet consciousness" allowed by the state, clericalism flourished due to the support of local bourgeois enemies and foreign capitalists, who used their ideological influence to win over the local Jewish petite bourgeoisie. Clericalism, moreover, gave the anti-Soviet intelligentsia in the shtetl a cover through which to organize their activities. These groups, in turn, infiltrated the kustari ranks by organizing secret "kulak groups" that were, in actuality, "merchant-capitalist elements masquerading under the screen of the kustari." These secret elements drew young potential supporters of the Bolsheviks away from party work. Indeed, the report lamented, young Jews, communist and otherwise, continued to go to synagogue to hear renowned guest cantors. Rather than declining, the report warned of the general "strengthening of the influence of clericalism" in the Jewish milieu.[88]

The evsektsii's tendency to read the persistence of Jewish religious practice as a conspiracy on the part of class enemies points to a growing sense of paranoia as well as a deeper paradox generated by the policies of the NEP. Socially and economically, the NEP was necessary to save the socialist revolution from economic collapse. Politically, however, the NEP's "enrichment" of the countryside appeared to give newfound courage to the regime's rural enemies. For Beilin, a pragmatic bureaucrat, the economic need far outweighed the ideological danger. The only viable solution was to continue to build support among the shtetl youth. On one hand, this entailed sending more young Jews to the countryside to form worker circles among young workers, educate kustari about the dangers of clericalism, carry out propaganda specifically targeting workers, and slowly build bastions of political support. On the other, the party redoubled its efforts to inoculate schoolchildren from the dangers of clericalism by ensuring that local party schools continued to teach students the "natural-scientific disciplines" in order to allow them to resist religious education. Given the overall tenor of the NEP era, the soft line of persuasion, as opposed to coercion and administrative measures, carried the day.

Despite his rhetorical bluster, Beilin was a relatively conciliatory moderate in the Bolshevik ranks.[89] As a proponent of reconciliation with the countryside and rural elements, his fate was fundamentally tied to the policies of the NEP system. As long as the NEP continued to function, Beilin and his associates played the unenviable role of attempting to balance the twin charges of the evsetksii: to shape, promote, and monitor Jewish life, and to administrate and defend the interests of the kustari. By late 1926 and 1927, however, the NEP economy displayed discernible signs of slowing. Cryptoinflation, coupled with falling trade revenues due to depressed global agricultural prices, monetary instability, and industrial underinvestment began to wreak havoc on the NEP's market institutions. In late 1927, goods began to disappear from shelves in stores, and the moribund NEP economy spiraled into full-blown crisis.

The collapse of the NEP simultaneously sunk the smychka that Bolshevik moderates attempted to build throughout the NEP era. The NEP crisis transformed the countryside overnight from a territory to be won over to the Bolshevik cause through persuasion into a purported bastion of counterrevolution. Wherever the party looked, it began to see enemies in the countryside. Peasants holding grain in response to inflationary monetary policies became "hoarders" and "kulaks." Private traders, barely tolerated in the heyday of the NEP, were derided first as "Nepmen" who made profits through mediating trade between town and country, and then, once again, as "speculators." Faced with the structural crisis of the NEP, the party began to interpret all signs of economic malfunction as the work of malignant counterrevolutionary agents.

In the face of purported class war from its enemies, who cut off bread supplies to the city, the Bolshevik party returned to the discourse and practices of the revolutionary era and declared open war against its ideological enemies. Over the course of 1928, the party unleashed a full political, social, and economic onslaught, which would come to be known as the Stalin Revolution or the Great Break. The turn to the Stalin Revolution was accompanied by an outburst of revolutionary fervor from below, driven by young Bolsheviks who hoped to return the party to its revolutionary origins by launching a new Cultural Revolution, or class war in the field of culture, against the multifarious, hidden enemies of the state.[90]

The twinned ruptures of the Cultural Revolution and the Stalin Revolution overran the evsektsii in general and Beilin in particular. Renewed assaults against speculation and the introduction of draconian taxation for private traders combined to devastate Jewish communities economically throughout the former Pale of Settlement.[91] No longer bound by the NEP principles of union between peasants and small producers, which was in turn delimited by the conservative fiscal policies of the NEP, the Stalinist party leadership devoted itself to massive and rapid industrialization. Kustar' production, vital to the functioning of the NEP economy, played a far more ancillary role in the emerging planned economy. Rather than promote the types of light industries necessitated by the NEP, the party leadership turned decisively toward heavy industry, implicitly relegating the kustari to a secondary concern. The decline of the social importance of the kustari followed the stark reversal in general policies toward the countryside.

As the Stalin Revolution unfolded, young communists in particular took to the standard of Cultural Revolution, returning to the highly aggressive anticlericalism of the Civil War era. Rejecting the conciliatory policies of Beilin's evsektsii, proponents of the Cultural Revolution reasserted the need for aggressive class warfare on the cultural front. Across the Soviet Union, organizations such as the League for the Militant Godless organized "shock" workers to renew aggressive assaults against religion.[92] By 1928–1929, the party renewed the confiscation and conversion of synagogues into workers clubs across the Russian, Belorussian, and Ukrainian Republics, leading to conflicts between Soviet authorities, Jewish worker groups, and local religious communities. In April 1929 *Bezbozhnik*, the newspaper of the League of the Militant Godless, reported that some two hundred synagogues had been converted to workers clubs in Belorussia and Ukraine since 1927.[93] Finally, in mid-1929 the party abruptly disbanded the evsektsii.

As the fundamental terms of social and political life turned on their head, the ground beneath Abram Beilin turned to quicksand. The collapse of the

NEP and the disbanding of the evsektsii ruined Beilin's political career. Insofar as the countryside appeared to be reverting into festering dens of counterrevolution, Beilin himself was held personally accountable for the failures of social and cultural policy. In the context of the emerging Stalinist state, failure could no longer be attributed to extenuating factors; rather, failure transformed Beilin into an enemy. At the end of 1929, the Presidium of the Central Control Commission of the KPB filed formal complaints against Beilin, leading to a full purge trial in 1930 and his dismissal from the party ranks in August 1930.

The charges against Beilin stemmed, in principle, from his policies toward the kustari. According to the formal complaint, Beilin and Comrade Mariasin, the head of the main kustar' union, violated party policy by supposedly advocating for the inclusion of "former people," (*byvshikh liudei*) and consequently "non-laboring elements," "speculators," and "merchant-manufacturers," into the ranks of the kustari.[94] The key evidence in the purge proceeding came in the form of an April 1928 thesis submitted by Beilin to the evsektsii bureau calling for a series of measures to improve the condition of kustari in the shtetlekh. Beilin's thesis stressed the need to pull the ranks of the unemployed, and particularly the unemployed in the shtetl, into the ranks of kustar' production. The thesis called for the building of new *arteli* across Belorussia that would employ eight hundred previously unemployed Jews in brickmaking factories, sewing industries, leather production, metalworking, and the like. It also demanded the expansion of government orders and resources to support these new arteli, as well as existing productive sites. The underlying logic was a familiar one: to productivize Jews, fight unemployment, and increase the production of kustar' goods for the market.[95]

In short, the Control Commission accused Beilin of doing exactly what he had been appointed to do: promote kustar' production in the shtetl. Viewed through the looking glass of the Stalin Revolution, however, his basic competency became a criminal act. By encouraging the incorporation of nonlaboring elements into kustar' cooperatives, Beilin purportedly promoted the interests of class enemies and strengthened their position. By appealing specifically to Jewish workers, the Control Commission charged, Beilin in fact stoked the flames of national and intranational animosity in Belorussia. As the investigation unfolded, other allegations came to light, questioning the very essence of Beilin's political soul. In particular, during their investigations the Control Commission produced a letter written by Beilin to the Bundist newspaper *Der Veker* in 1919. Beilin's letter attacked the Bund and forcefully defended Bolshevik policies concerning the suspension of freedom of the press, campaigns against speculation, and the like. While completely orthodox in its orientation, the letter also mentioned what was, at the time of its writing, a seemingly minor detail of Beilin's biographical past: he had, in 1905, been a member of the Bund before seeing the light and joining the Bolsheviks.[96] That Beilin clearly understood the significance of suppressing this youthful Bundist flirtation, however short-lived, was made plain by the fact that he omitted this detail from his previous party reviews.

This revelation from his deep political past instantaneously undermined Beilin's Bolshevik credentials. The purge unmasked a self-styled "Old Bolshevik" as being, in fact, an old Bundist. The fact that Beilin had been among the most aggressive of anti-Bundist activists in the party mattered little before the institutions of party purification. As the spirit of paranoia characteristic of Stalinist society spread, the revelation of a hidden past or earlier political transgression proved ruinous. The Control Commission voted unanimously against him, expelling Beilin from the party ranks for "national opportunism." His "crime," it might be suggested, was having been a steadfast advocate of the policies of the NEP, for which he was ultimately swept away as a "Right" deviationist and follower of Nikolai Bukharin. With the Stalin Revolution, the ex post facto criminalization of previous party policy was becoming the norm of justice. Yet the smoking gun evidence leveled against him was the charge of hidden "Bundism."

Conclusion

As a driving force behind the evsektsii during the waning days of the NEP, Abram Beilin rose politically in the Bolshevik party ranks as a proponent of Bolshevik universalism against the proponents of the Bolshevik haskole in the party ranks. On one level, Beilin's approach to the Jewish question was thoroughly negative in its orientation. As a proponent of Bolshevism, he saw little use in promoting specifically Jewish culture, autonomous or otherwise, and in fact aggressively campaigned against all manifestations of Jewish particularity. In this sense, he completely repudiated the promise of both the Haskalah and the haskole for Jewish cultural and spiritual renewal. At the same time, Beilin emerged as one of the strongest proponents of what might be considered the social legacy of the Haskalah: as an advocate of solving the Jewish question by transforming backward Jews into productive laborers, Beilin oversaw the establishment of vast networks to productivize Jews and intensify Jewish labor that far exceeded the fantasies of nineteenth-century maskilim. Even as he repudiated the cultural dimension of the Haskalah, he helped to realize its underlying bourgeois vision of universal productivization for itinerant Jews. For traditional Jews, this invariably looked like all of the chaff, and none of the wheat, from the promise of the Haskalah, and even the haskole.

In the grand scheme of things, Abram Beilin proved to be a remarkably lucky individual. Having been purged and excluded from the party, he appealed the decision of the Control Commission. In his complaint, he stressed his long service to the revolution, his longstanding devotion to the Bolsheviks, repeated arrests as a Bolshevik activist, and dedicated party service after the revolution. Beilin claimed, moreover, that the charges against him had been trumped up by Belorussian chauvinists in the party ranks, including Aleksandr Cherviakov, Dmitri Zhilunovich, and other Belorussian nationals, who themselves faced purge trials for national opportunism in 1930.[97] The Control Commission eventually accepted Beilin's appeal and restored him to the ranks of the party, but the reprieve proved short-lived. Arrested again during the Great Terror of the 1930s, Beilin miraculously survived the mass death of the interwar period and lived out the rest of his days nonpolitically, until his death in 1980.

Beilin's story serves as an important corrective to prevailing conceptions of Jewish politics in the first Soviet decade. In particular, it challenges the notion that Jewish party activists remained reluctant Bolsheviks, secret oppositionists, or hidden "traditional" Jews in Bolshevik garb. Beilin was none of these. Like many of the young Jewish Bolsheviks who followed his path away from the promise of Bolshevik haskole and toward the politics of Bolshevik universalism, Beilin was convinced that only a full amalgamation with the party and its goals could lead to the social and existential salvation of the Jews. Judaism, religion, and explicitly Jewish politics appeared to him as relics of a prerevolutionary age that needed to be overcome. He believed fervently in the Bolshevik promise that labor would wash away the "sin" of Jewishness. Beilin's fall demonstrated how elusive this promise remained.

This chapter opened with a trial and ended with a trial. The first trial, a spectacle of the Jewish Revolution, took place in a Jewish public sphere. Popular Jewish opinion, however, rallied behind Bontshe Shvayg as a representative of all the ills that proletarianized Jewry faced in its struggle to become part of the newly reborn human family. The gallery wailed its support for the defendant, even as Bolshevik prosecutors found the accused guilty for being too much of an old-fashioned Jew. In 1929 the Bolshevik party cast the same verdict on Abram Beilin, even if the proponents of the Jewish Revolution would have disagreed profoundly. Unlike in the trial of Bontshe Shvayg, no voices from the gallery rose to defend the accused.

5
BUNDISM AND THE NATIONALITIES QUESTION

ON OR ABOUT Thursday, January 21, 1926, state and party policy toward the political, social, and cultural life of Belorussian Jewry began to change discernibly. On that day the Bureau of the Central Committee of the Belorussian Communist Party (TsK KPB) gathered for its regular meeting to discuss three pressing items of business. The meeting opened with a report on the state of kustar' production throughout Belorussia in light of the Fourteenth Party Congress in December 1925, during which the party leadership in Moscow dedicated itself to the industrialization of the Soviet Union. Stressing the need to promote rapid industrialization, the report recommended the swift expansion and reorganization of kustar' production "on the basis of cooperatives" to combat unemployment, expand the availability of market goods, and allow for the more efficient coordination of production in the face of "the peculiarities of the current market conditions."[1] Next the Bureau moved to the second order of business, approving republic-wide pay increases for party workers, soviet administrators, skilled workers serving soviet and party apparatuses, and white-collar workers.[2] Finally, the Bureau turned toward its last major order of business, the reading of a "political letter" by Sergei Mikhailovich Gessen on behalf of the TsK KPB, concerning the need to eradicate the vestiges of non-Bolshevik political traditions within the party ranks.[3]

A leading Bolshevik activist who cut his teeth in revolutionary Petrograd as a close collaborator of Grigorii Zinoviev, Sergei Gessen was brought to Minsk in late 1925 to serve as the head of agitation and propaganda.[4] His arrival coincided with a total overhaul of party personnel in the republic, beginning with the appointment of the thirty-two-year-old Aleksandr Ivanovich Krinitskii, a young Russian party activist from Tver' and a budding Stalin loyalist, as secretary of the KPB in late 1924.[5] The change in political leadership coincided with a major overhaul of "Jewish work" in the newly renamed Belorussian Soviet Socialist Republic (BSSR), the first hints of which began to surface in late 1925.[6] Gessen's political letter, approved by the party and distributed to all corners of the republic, signaled a new phase in the party's position toward Jews and Jewishness.[7]

Drafted on behalf of the Central Committee of the KPB with approval from Moscow, Gessen's letter opened with a warning about the lingering, pernicious influence of individuals who "previously left petit-bourgeois parties" to join the Bolshevik party. "The largest and most typical of these parties in Belorussia," Gessen noted, "is the Bund." Given the Bund's strength, as well as its leading position among the prerevolutionary working class, "the question of the struggle against the Bundist tradition carried special significance." Despite the ominous tone, Gessen insisted that the struggle against Bundism was not to be directed at any individuals, per se: "the subjective sincerity and revolutionary conviction of those comrades who entered our party from the ranks of the Bund stand beyond any doubt." Since entering the party four and a half years earlier, many former Bundists, Gessen stressed, had undergone considerable "evolution," overcome traces of Bundism, and completely comprehended the ideology of Bolshevism. "Despite that fact," he warned, "the Bundist tradition must not be considered completely eliminated in the present moment."[8]

Bundism, according to Gessen, entailed a series of ideological deviations that, taken together, constituted a primary threat. First, those afflicted with Bundism excessively idealized the place of the Bund in the revolutionary movement. In doing so, they overlooked the Bund's "Menshevik"—and thus reactionary—"essence." Second, Bundism manifested "national narrowmindedness" (natsional'naia ogranichennost'); the guilty took an interest in "Jewish work" only and proved unable and disinclined to work "among the mass of other nationalities." This narrow-mindedness appeared most clearly in the "mistaken policy" that required all Jewish children to attend Yiddish schools. Third, Bundist deviants "did not understand the role of the proletariat as a class hegemon," and failed to assimilate the party's nationality policy and position toward the peasantry; consequently they were completely indifferent to peasant issues and the countryside in general. Finally, those guilty of "Bundism" exhibited a pronounced tendency toward "tailism," or the tendency to follow the demands of the most backward, petit-bourgeois elements within the Jewish milieu. Gessen called for systematic propaganda work to make clear the Bund's "opportunistic and nationalistic character" and to ensure that former Bundists became "complete Leninists."[9]

Gessen's political letter against Bundism coincided with a series of events that decisively reshaped party policies toward "Jewish work" throughout Belorussia. In late 1925, Abram Grigor'evich Beilin, a former woodworker from Mstislav, replaced Yankel Levin, the old Bundist turned Bolshevik, as head of the Belorussian evsektsii.[10] Shortly thereafter, the Grosser Club, a workers' club and Bundist fixture from the prerevolutionary period, was renamed the Lenin club. In March 1926 the evsektsiia changed the name of the daily Yiddish organ from the Bundist-inspired *Der Veker* to the more acceptable *Oktyabr*.[11] Between late February and the end of April, the party conducted mass meetings across the republic to educate workers about the dangers of Bundism. The struggle against "Bundism" had begun.

Far from being a localized event, the political campaign against "Bundism" reverberated across the Soviet Union and, consequently, has attracted considerable attention in the historiography. The campaign against Bundism has generally been interpreted as a final settling of scores in the ongoing, tenuous political drama between Jewish Bolsheviks and Bundists in the party ranks. Viewed within the contours of Jewish politics, the campaign against Bundism appears as the beginning of the end of the last vestige of Jewish political autonomy in postrevolutionary Soviet society.[12] Yet Gessen's political letter suggests that the factors driving this anti-Bundism campaign were far more complicated than a simple question of retribution and consolidation of power. The campaign engulfed the upper echelons of the party leadership, pitting Moscow evsektsiia members against local Jewish party activists and leaders in the provincial cities of the former Pale of Settlement.

While the language of the campaign focused on the political meaning of Bundism, the actual agitation campaign targeted the shop floor.[13] Unsurprisingly, the mass propaganda campaign focused on those factories and workshops with large numbers of Jewish workers and former Bundists, including the leatherworking, shoemaking, sewing, and woodworking industries. At the same time, discussions about the history of the Bund and the nature of Bundism were overwhelmingly conducted in party cells with few former Bundists, or Jews in general. Far from being simply a "Jewish" matter, the anti-Bundism campaign constituted an intranational, mass phenomenon.[14] Moreover, as Gessen's political letter made clear, the campaigns' critical core focused not on the question of political power but rather upon the attitude of alleged Bundists toward questions of nationality policy. From the concern over Jewish education, to the overvaluing of Jewish work, to the accusations of downplaying or ignoring the social and political concerns of the Belorussian peasantry, discourses about Bundism focused more on issues of integration and equality between peoples and less on questions of party politics.

As the protocol that introduced the anti-Bundism offensive indicated, the campaign, while undeniably political in nature, developed in a context of acute social and economic change. The proposal to expand kustar' production in order to increase the availability of consumer goods on the market—a driving concern of the evsektsiia under Abram Beilin—indicated the degree to which the Central Committee continued to operate under the economic presuppositions of the NEP era. Simultaneously, the proposal to use kustar' cooperatives to promote industrialization foreshadowed the turn to rapid, state-driven industrialization that would constitute the social core of the emerging Stalinist industrial order. The plan to implement wage increases likewise spoke to economic turbulence and the trend of system-wide inflationary pressures evident from late 1925. In short, the period in which the campaign against Bundism unfolded was not simply that of the political consolidation of Bolshevik power; it simultaneously marked the demise of the social, economic, cultural, and political synthesis of the NEP and the emergence of the Stalinist managed economy.

Rather than focusing on the meaning of the anti-Bundism campaign in the specifically Jewish milieu, this chapter frames the campaign as a critical moment in the trajectory of nationalities policies in postrevolutionary Belorussia. It argues that in the midst of the structural transformation separating NEP and Stalinist society, discourses concerning the cultural assimilability and political reliability of Jews changed rapidly and radically, reflecting deeper change in nationality politics. At the high-water mark of NEP society—roughly culminating in Bukharin's ill-fated call for peasants to "enrich yourselves" in 1925 and Abram Beilin's ascendancy in the evsektsiia—Jewish nationality was of interest, but not inherently problematic to Soviet and Party authorities. The party actively promoted Jewish national cultural life provided it was atheistic (or at least highly ambivalent about religion), not too nationalist, and sufficiently proletarian in orientation.[15] The turn against Bundism in intraparty practice signaled a change, as the idea of cultivating a modern soviet Jewish national culture as a desirable endpoint gave way to ambivalence, if not outright hostility, toward the particularity of nationalism. Among its proponents, this change was viewed as a progressive return to the internationalism inherent in the revolutionary project from the outset. From the standpoint of its critics, the turn against nationality appeared as an abrupt reversal and attack on national autonomy for the sake of universalizing socialist construction.[16]

In viewing the campaign against Bundism through the lens of nationality, this chapter argues that the "nationality" and "Jewish" questions in Belorussia were bound together inextricably. Despite efforts to delimit discussion of both issues to language policy, schools, national soviets, and the like, the question of nationality and Jewishness permeated all aspects of party and Soviet decision making. With the outlawing of antisemitism in the aftermath of the revolution, however, excessive focus upon the particularity of Jews within Soviet society came to be viewed as politically suspect. Open discussions of "Jews" and "Jewishness" consequently appeared in muted fashion within party policy and debate, particularly outside of the ranks of the evsektsii. In this context, discussions of ostensibly political categories became a mechanism for discussing proscribed questions of nationality. Discourses about "Bundism" became a linguistic mechanism for discussing Jewishness and Jewish ethnicity without discussing Jews.

Jewish Questions and the Nationalities Question

Among the many atypical nations (*natsii*), nationalities (*narodnosti, natsional'nosti*), tribes (*plemena*), and clans (*rodi*) that populated the Soviet lands, the Jews were particularly atypical. The prerevolutionary tsarist state classified Jews—along with Kalmyks, Samoeds, and other nomadic populations—as *inorodtsy*, literally "aliens," or "foreigners." As a conceptual category, the inorodtsy were necessarily juxtaposed to the empire's cultured and civilized *narodnosti*, a term derived from *narod* ("people" or "folk"), that connoted authentic and essential Russian or Slavic identity in nineteenth-century thought.[17] Unlike other inorodtsy groups, viewed as "primitive," "barbarous," or "uncultured" populations in need of civilizing measures, tsarist-era official policy viewed Jews as too cultured, too civilized, or too clever in comparison to the local populations among whom they resided. The idea that Jews constituted an economic, social, and existential threat to neighboring populations provided the "logical" basis for the voluminous anti-Jewish legislation that restricted Jewish settlement, economic practice, and social life.[18] Moreover, a series of theological presuppositions that attributed to Jews a litany of offenses, ranging from moral turpitude, to spiritual degradation, to deicide, reinforced their peculiar status.[19] While all inorodtsy and foreigners were categorized as aliens, Jewish alienation was embedded in the fundamental theological presuppositions of the Christian Orthodox Russian state.[20]

Bolshevik policy, while theoretically sympathetic to the plight of the Jewish working class, remained highly ambivalent toward the broader question of Jewish nationality. Conflicts about Jewish national claims, including persistent debates with specifically Jewish political parties, namely the Bund, played a formative role in shaping Bolshevik nationality policy in the prerevolutionary period.[21] Following the theories of Otto Bauer and the Austro-Marxists, prerevolutionary Bundists stressed the principles of self-identification and extraterritoriality in defining nationality; in their estimation, Jews should have the right to identify as a national group despite their diasporic existence. Early Bolshevik missives, including Joseph Stalin's 1913 much-cited *Marxism and the Nationalities Question*, explicitly rejected these principles.[22] Early Bolshevik theory stressed that nations were not constructed, imaginary, or fluid communities based on conviction but rather concrete groups sharing certain traits, customs, history, language, and (most importantly, when considering the Jews) territory. Prior to the revolution, moreover, the party took an inflexible line against claims for "national" emancipation, arguing that the emancipation of labor from capital would resolve the domination of hegemonic nationalities over subject nationalities. These positions drew sharp rebukes from Bundists and other socialists with national inclinations, who argued that national emancipation could not be subordinated to the politics of class emancipation.[23]

Once in power, the Bolsheviks' confronted the reality of governing a massive territory populated by groups claiming the right to political self-determination based on the principle of nationality—a right famously championed by Lenin in the context of the First World War. While Cold War–era scholarship stressed the Bolshevik suppression of nationality, recent works have focused instead on the role that the newly established Soviet government played in promoting nationality.[24] Hypercognizant of the threat posed by unleashed nationalism, the Bolsheviks sought to manage nationalist pressures rather than wait for nationalist tensions to blow apart the Soviet territories—as they had done to the Austro-Hungarian, Ottoman, and, indeed, Russian Empires. Thus the Bolsheviks reversed course and began to promote the cause of subject nationalities, implementing mass programs of social mobility and cultural development for previously oppressed national minorities in the hopes of averting autoemancipation from below.

This shift toward national promotion constituted the core of what Terry Martin has described as Soviet "affirmative action."[25] In the broadest terms, Soviet affirmative action meant the promotion of individuals hailing from any exploited minority group of the defunct Russian Empire. This group was constructed loosely enough to include virtually every group of the old Empire, except Russian nationals.[26] In theory, affirmative action policies promoted the construction of schools and cultural institutions for minority nationalities; encouraged language instruction and publication in the languages of minority nationalities; established independent national soviets, courts, and other administrative units for national minorities; championed the creation of new national elites for subject populations; and pursued the active recruitment of national minorities into all aspects of building Soviet society.[27] Moreover, despite earlier misgivings, the Bolsheviks extended national minority rights and privileges far beyond "natural" territorial borders, effectively allowing the formation of local national institutions at any administrative point where a national minority constituted a significant local presence.[28]

The decoupling of nationality and territory opened the path for Jewish national cultural institutions to expand over the course of the 1920s. In addition, the Bolshevik party, soviet state, and official ethnographers included Jews among the officially designated narodnosti of the Soviet lands following the revolution.[29] In doing so, the Soviet regime affirmed the idea that Jews constituted a nationality equal in rights to any other nationality. Throughout the 1920s, state and party institutions promoted the development of Jewish national soviets, national courts, Yiddish cultural institutions, newspapers, literary journals, institutes of Jewish research, schools, university departments, workers' clubs, and theaters to encourage the development of Jewish culture in the Ukrainian and Belorussian republics. Minsk, in particular, developed into a site of vigorous affirmative action policies to promote new Jewish cultural institutions.

Although designated a distinct minority in need of affirmative action policies, Jews remained a peculiar nationality. While party and ethnographic institutions rejected the conflation of religious and national categories for classifying Muslims, Christians, and other religious groups, the terms "Jew," and "Jewish," (evrei, evreiskii) were recognized in all of their ambiguity as acceptable national designations.[30] Consequently, the promotion of nationality frequently conflicted with the logic of antireligious campaigns targeting the practices of Judaism, and vice versa.[31] These tensions became most manifest in language politics, as the state, party, and evsektsiia attacked Hebrew as the language of clericalism, obscurantism, and class domination but promoted Yiddish as the authentic language of healthy, proletarian, Jewish national culture.

In addition, Jews constituted a particularly marked group in the Soviet lands because of ascendant antisemitism across Europe. Ignited by postwar economic collapse, Jews became a conspicuous target and a perceived nefarious source of destabilizing economic crisis and social unrest across the continent. The visible participation of Jewish radicals in revolutionary movements in Russia, Germany, Hungary, Poland, and beyond fueled conspiratorial narratives attributing to Jews the power to make political and social revolution. Across the continent, rightist, antirevolutionary, and anticommunist political parties mobilized populations under the banner of antisemitism.[32] The political meanings attributed to the concept of "the Jews" in postwar Europe unmistakably shaped Soviet policy toward Jews in ways that differed markedly from policy toward other national groups.[33]

Finally, Jews stood out for the fact that they persistently formed "overrepresented" populations in urban locales and institutions, especially when compared to the local titular nationalities among whom they resided. In Belorussia, some 2.96 million Belorussians resided in the 1923 boundaries of the Republic of Belorussia, constituting 70.9 percent of the population of the Republic. The republic's 447,667 Jews constituted just under 11 percent of the population. While Belorussians constituted a decisive majority, Jews formed over 44 percent of the Republic's urban population. The 260,044 urban-dwelling Jews constituted the single largest urban population, far surpassing the regions 240,060 urbanized Belorussians (and 62,730 Great Russians).[34] Jews, likewise, formed pluralities or majorities in a number of key state and party institutions, as well as in economic sectors and professions.[35]

While rarely stated in explicit terms, the soviet government and Bolshevik party undertook measures over the course of the 1920s to "normalize" Jewish representation in party, state, and economic institutions in order to "normalize" national relations. Despite being a nontitular national minority living among titular nationalities, Jews faced policies that mirrored forms of "positive discrimination" usually enacted against the group that Lenin had viewed, suspiciously, as the primary colonizing power—the "Great Russians." Terry Martin's insistence that "in the Soviet case, where all non-Russians were to be favored, Russians alone bore the brunt of positive discrimination" simply did not hold in Belorussia;[36] throughout the mid-1920s, policies of affirmative action overwhelmingly entailed balancing the political weight of the Belorussian population by curtailing the influence, representation, and political weight of the Jewish population. Consequently, although constituting a minority in need of affirmative action policies, Jews were simultaneously viewed as a quasi-colonial power and potential source of domination in relation to titular nationalities. Concerns about the power and influence of over-represented Jews replicated tsarist-era anxiety regarding the ability of Jews to exert power over guileless neighbors.

The promotion of Jewish nationality consequently came into direct conflict with policies promoting *korenizatsiia*, or indigenization, which emphasized the need to expand the cultural, social, and political development of the "root" or "core" nationality in each republic of the USSR. Introduced in 1923 and intensified with the official founding of the Union of Soviet Socialist Republics in April 1924, policies of indigenization in Belorussia became synonymous with policies of Belorussianization. Belorussianization involved policies intended to bring "enlightenment" to the general Belorussian population through the construction of Belorussian schools, theaters, and the like. At the same time, Belorussianization brought the slow demise of multilingualism adopted at the outset of the revolution. A smattering of official documents not directly related to nationality affairs continued to be published in Yiddish and Polish; most government correspondence, however, began to be written almost exclusively in Russian and Belorussian. *Zvezda*, the official Communist Party organ, shifted from monolingual Russian publication, to bilingualism, to the fully Belorussianized *Zviazda* over the course of the mid-1920s; all other

Russian newspapers in Belorussia followed suit. Between 1924 and 1928, the program of linguistic Belorussification was carried out to a remarkable degree, with virtually every important state and party institution—including, ultimately, the evsektsiia—switching to Belorussian in official correspondence (although Russian continued to be the primary language of conversation). The rapid and widespread linguistic shift made the process of Belorussianization among the most successful of the affirmative action programs undertaken in the mid-1920s.[37]

Despite, or, in fact, because of, the success of Belorussianization and other korenizatsiia programs, Soviet officials in Moscow abruptly reversed nationality policy during the last years of the 1920s and began denouncing the excesses of local nationalisms. Seemingly overnight, Soviet policies toward Belorussianization shifted from energetic support to outright suppression through widespread terror. In mid-1929, after a similar turn in Ukraine, investigators from Moscow and local officials began to denounce the supposed seething nationalism and bitter anti-Russian sentiments evident in the Belorussian republic. An investigation from the Moscow Central Control Commission from May 1929 warned, "the degree of animosity toward Moscow that oozes out at every gathering of writers or academics here is greater by several degrees than the most frenzied nationalism of the *Petliurovshchina* in 1918."[38] However hyperbolic the comparisons, the denunciation carried dire consequences. Moscow subsequently conducted a purge of the Belorussian Communist Party leadership, arresting scores of leading Belorussian communists, including Dmitrii Zhilunovich, Aleksandr Adamovich, and Anton Balitskii, for alleged anti-Soviet, nationalist agitation. Arrests of hundreds of other activists, cultural figures, and writers followed, including the leading writers Yanka Kupala, Yakob Kolas, and the Belorussian historian Vsevolod Ignatovskii.[39] Some (like Yanka Kupala and Kolas) recanted their deviations and were awarded respites. Others endured far grimmer fates, including Ignatovskii, who shot himself in 1931 following interrogation at the hands of the GPU.[40]

Policies toward Jewish national culture and institutions exhibited a similar trajectory, if less fateful immediate end. The resurgence of antireligious campaigns across the Soviet Union in 1928 led to the closure of many synagogues (and churches) that had survived earlier antireligious onslaughts in Belorussia following the revolution.[41] The party also suppressed the last remnants of non-Bolshevik Jewish political organizations, banning remaining Poalei Tsion institutions in 1928. Allegations of Jewish national chauvinism among the ranks of the evsektsiia proliferated throughout 1929, culminating in the dismantling of the Jewish sections of the Communist Party in 1930 and the purge of leading "sectionists," including Abram Beilin.[42] Yet, unlike with Belorussian institutions, the turn against nationalist tendencies within the Jewish milieu was not accompanied, initially, by widespread terror. Rather, Jewish cultural institutions generally succumbed to pressures toward "Sovietization" and ideological conformity that accompanied the Stalinist "Great Break" and the Cultural Revolution of the late 1920s.[43] In the words of one historian, "as the party came to dictate the shape of culture building, the Soviet Yiddish intelligentsia lost its ideological power."[44] Jewish national themes and cultural points of reference that flourished in the 1920s increasingly ceded to universal themes of proletarian political struggle, albeit in Yiddish but with suppressed "Jewish" content.[45] The more forceful repression of Jewish culture builders within the party would not come until the Great Terror in the mid-1930s.

The reason for the abrupt turn in nationalities policy at the end of the 1920s has engendered sharp disagreement in recent scholarship. In his field-defining work, Terry Martin attributed the reversal to two key factors. The first was Stalin's decision to launch "his Socialist Offensive, which involved forced industrialization, collectivization, the abolition of the market, increased centralization, and terror against 'bourgeois' population categories."[46] Economic centralization, chosen by Stalin and his hardline followers, drove the campaign against the centrifugal forces of korenizatsiia. The second factor, Martin argued, was the unintended consequences of affirmative action policies in and of themselves. Initially implemented to ameliorate national conflict between the historic "centers" of Russian imperial power and the titular nationalities in the peripheries, the policies of affirmative action actually intensified national conflict in the western borderlands. Alarmed, Stalin and hard-liners in the party leadership chose to reverse course and suppress nationalist manifestations among the titular nationalities of the western borderlands.[47] For Martin, the turn in nationality policies that occurred between 1928 and 1929 reflected a deliberate reversal of policy made necessary by Stalin's equally deliberate choice to introduce rapid industrialization and the "Socialist Offensive."

Francine Hirsch, in her recent study of soviet ethnographic practices and the development of nationalities policies, articulated an important challenge to Martin's compelling analysis. Employing a Foucauldian interpretation stressing the governmental imperatives to rationalize, categorize, and control populations, Hirsch rejected Martin's claim that the 1928 shift in nationality policy constituted a departure for Soviet policymakers. Rebuffing Martin's affirmative action paradigm, Hirsch argued that the party's primary intention was always to build socialism, not promote nationality. When the party promoted national culture and the category of nationality, it did so only to drive forward social and cultural development according to a traditional Marxist developmental logic that viewed the nationalist "phase" as a necessary precursor to the full realization of socialism and, eventually, communism. Thus the Bolsheviks accepted nationality and national culture as a temporary capitulation for the sake of ultimately overcoming nationality. Far from being a reversal or retreat, the change in nationality policy at the end of the 1920s amounted to a return to the first principles of the revolution.[48]

The productive disagreement between Martin and Hirsch has clarified points of tension within the formative period of Soviet nationality policy. While the nuances of their respective differences deserve greater attention than can be afforded here, both authors share certain points of agreement directly relevant to the subject at hand. First, despite their disagreements, both Martin and Hirsch stress the guiding role of ideological motivations and intentionality of political action. While each stresses the importance of "economic" factors in shaping policy, both view economy as subservient and secondary to ideology and politics.[49] For Martin, the primacy of politics is explicit: the change in nationality policy followed as a necessary corollary to Stalin's (individual) decision to implement the "Socialist Offensive." For Hirsch, Bolshevik developmentalist interpretations of Marxist ideology drove nationality policy.

Second, while both studies stress the internal tensions inherent to Soviet nationalities policy, both implicitly accept official party and state definitions concerning the categorization and limitations of that policy. Both authors focus upon areas and topics that the Soviet regime explicitly designated as falling under the rubric of nationality. This acceptance of officially designated categories has served, in turn, to replicate frequently arbitrary distinctions separating "nationality" policy from other areas of policy debate. Tellingly, the Soviet regime explicitly designated questions about Belorussianization as an issue of nationality, but often classified policies toward Jews as separate issues, due in part to the slippery categorization of Jews within discourse and policy. Consequently, campaigns against Belorussian nationalism fit uncomplicatedly under the nationality question while issues involving aspects of Jewish national culture—including issues of Hebrew, religious practice, and so forth—fell under the designation of religious policy. Similarly, in designating "Bundism" as a political deviation, Soviet officials implicitly placed the campaign beyond the limits of nationality.

Third, while Martin and Hirsch point to the prominent place of Jews within Soviet society and discourse on nationality policy, both treat policies toward Jews as either incidental or analogous to policies enacted toward other groups. Given the scope of their studies, it is understandable, perhaps, if questions of Jewish policy are addressed in passing, often in relation to anti-Jewish sentiment among other nationalities.[50] However, in largely bracketing off the question of the Jews, Martin in particular constructs a model of nationality that accepts a binaristic relationship between "Russian" policy makers and peripheral "titular nationalities." In the context of the western borderlands, however, nationality policy was never a binary opposition. Negotiations between titular nationalities and national minorities, particularly the significant Jewish populations, played as critical a role in shaping local policies as did relations between titular nationalities and Moscow.

More fundamentally, Soviet policy concerning Jews never simply stopped at the discursive boundaries of "nationality." Rather, all aspects of revolutionary society in Belorussia—from the politics and relations of labor, to the formation of party cadres and trade unions, to the development of economic policy, to the totality of cultural policy—were inflected with the "nationalities question" and, in turn, an implicit "Jewish question." The bracketing off of the Jewish question from the nationalities question, moreover, has resulted in a skewed periodization of changes in nationality policy. By stressing the relationship between discourses about "Bundism" and the question of nationality, this study argues that the turn in nationality policy began not in the 1928–1929 period, as Martin and Hirsch assert, but in 1926 with the anti-Bundist campaign in Belorussia. The rhetoric and logic of the anti-Bundism campaign simultaneously bring into focus the critical role economic restructuring of the late NEP era played in shaping discourses about nationality. Nationality policy was not simply determined by political ideas, Marxist principles, and ideology; it was simultaneously shaped by the compulsions, pressures, and constraints imposed by the brewing structural crisis that would transform not only Soviet society but also the entire global political culture of the 1930s. Changes in discourses concerning nationality simultaneously articulated changes in the temporal dynamic of the Soviet and global economy. In the Soviet context, as in the totality of Europe, discourses concerning the particularity of the Jews proved the most sensitive seismograph of structural change.

The language of "Bundism" became a language through which the party and party members discussed problems of nationality, nationalization, and ultimately Jewishness. Debates over "Bundism" took place in a context charged with questions of constructing nationalities and becoming national. Discussions of Bundism necessarily converged with questions of Jewish nationality; yet at the same time, the concept of Bundism provided the ideological foil against which Belorussian nationals conducted their own process of nationalization. As party members and policy makers articulated what it meant to be a Bundist, they simultaneously shaped the contours of an emerging Belorussian nation. Belorussianization, in short, became the antithesis of Bundism in the grand drama of Soviet national construction in the western borderlands.

Belorussianization and the "Normalization" of Nationality

From the very first days of the revolution, the nationality question divided the Bolshevik ranks in Belorussia. The first official meeting of the Central Bureau of the Belorussian Communist Party in December 1918 ended with a row between Dmitry Zhilunovich and the party leadership over Belorussian national autonomy. Zhilunovich, a Belorussian poet and leading Belorussian Communist, requested that the party recognize the formation of a separate "Belorussian section" of the party to promote Belorussian national autonomy, along the lines of the evsektsiia created for the Jewish population. His request summarily denied by the Central Bureau, Zhilunovich stormed out of the meeting and resigned his post.[51]

The struggle between Zhilunovich and the Central Bureau reflected a deep fissure in the party leadership at the time of the revolution. Zhilunovich represented one faction of self-identified party members who joined the party while living in Russia before and during the revolutionary events of 1917–1918. They returned to Belorussia following the revolution to encounter an emerging local party administration forged during the period of war, occupation, and revolutionary upheaval. Tensions between these two factions continued unabated throughout the early Revolution. In the most general terms, the local party leadership was pronouncedly multinational and distinctly non-Belorussian. Following the reassignment of Aleksandr Miasnikov, a prominent Armenian-born Bolshevik who briefly served as the first secretary of the Bolshevik party in Belorussia, the leading party position was filled, successively, by Vil'gel'm Knorin, a Latvian, Vatslav Bogutskii, a Pole, Adol'f Getner, a Latvian, and Aleksandr Krinitskii, a Russian. The highest levels of party leadership reflected this commitment to multinationalism, with key posts filled by a combination of Latvian (P. P. Tsel'man, Karl Lander, Getner, Knorin), Jewish (Shepshel Khodosh, El'ia Raichuk, Yankel Levin, Il'ia Osherovich, Sergei Gessen), and Russian (Krinitskii) politicians. Following the pattern repeated in most of the Soviet Republics, Belorussians—as representatives of the titular nationality—were largely absent from the leading party ranks, but far more visible in the Soviet state administration. Thus Zhilunovich gained a prominent position on the Central Executive Committee (TsIK) of the governing Council of People's Commissars (*Sovnarkom*), where he was joined by leading Belorussian Communists, including Aleksandr Cherviakov (Chairman of the Sovnarkom, 1920–1924), Nikolai Goloded (Chairman Sovnarkom, 1927–1937), Vsevolod Ignatovskii (Commissar of Agriculture, Commissar of

Enlightenment, 1920–1926), and Ivan Aleksandrovich Ivanov (Commissar for Internal Affairs).[52]

Belorussian party members also constituted a relatively small portion of the entire party structure. Archival materials concerning the national breakdown of party membership during the first postrevolutionary years are fragmentary. The sheer chaos of local conditions, particularly until the end of the Civil War and the Polish-Soviet War in 1921, explains, in part, the sparse data. At the same time, evidence suggests that such data, if available, presented an uncomfortable reality for the newly established regime, due in large part to the high concentration of Jews in the party leadership and rank and file, particularly in the cities.[53] Such data would have played directly into the hands of antisemites, who insisted that the revolution constituted a Jewish conspiracy from the outset. Tellingly, the party only began to keep detailed records concerning the national composition of party ranks once "imbalances" in representation began to be resolved.

Existing evidence nevertheless points to the unmistakable "normalization" of national representation in the party ranks throughout the early 1920s. While the absolute number of Jews within the party continued to grow, the proportional weight of Jews within the party fell steadily in relation to Belorussians. A March 1923 evsektsiia report concerning national representation in the Minsk city oblast counted 735 Jewish party members and candidates in the oblast, out of a total of 1,660 members (45 percent).[54] The following year, with the founding of the Soviet Union, the regional districts were rejiggered, redefined, and renamed. In the newly formed Minsk city okrug, the number of Jewish party members and candidates rose slightly to 795 by mid-1924, but their percentage within the party as a whole fell to 28.8 percent. By October 1925 the Jewish party members and candidates in the okrug numbered 1,252 of 4,127 (30 percent).[55]

A secret report filed by the evsektsiia in early 1927 reveals the growing marginalization of Jewish actors in the uppermost ranks of the party organization and nonparty apparatuses.[56] Between January 1, 1923, and January 1, 1926, the percentage of Jewish members of the Central Bureau of the KPB fell from 46 percent to 12 percent. Simultaneously, the party also relaxed the informal restriction limiting the representation of titular nationalities in the ranks of the republic's party leadership. By 1926 leading Belorussian communists, including Goloded, Cherviakov, Adamovitch, and Ignatovskii, dominated the Central Committee, as well as the Sovnarkom.[57] Jewish representation within party, state, and productive apparatuses fell sharply. Among okrug secretaries, the percentage of Jews fell from 30 percent to 10 percent; by the end of 1926, there were no remaining Jewish okrug secretaries in the entire republic. Among the full and deputy members of the Sovnarkom, Jewish representation fell from 29 percent to 13 percent. Within the Presidium of the Soviet of Trade Unions, Jewish representation fell from 65 percent to 35 percent.[58] The one notable exception to demographic marginalization remained the trade unions themselves. Concentrations of Jewish workers in the primary "Jewish" industries—leatherworking, needleworking, and woodworking—remained stable through 1925, as did Jewish representation in other unions.[59]

No invisible hand regulated this fluctuating market in demographic and political power. Within soviet apparatuses, the curtailment of Jewish representation resulted, perhaps unintentionally, from policies that disenfranchised significant numbers of Jews as *lishentsy*—those deprived of voting rights as politically, socially, or economically questionable actors.[60] Likewise the shift in the national composition of party ranks resulted directly from policies of Belorussianization and the active recruitment of Belorussians, which began with the so-called Lenin Levy inaugurated in 1924. Between January 1 and the opening of the Eighth Congress of the KP(b)B in May of 1924, the total number of Belorussian party members climbed from 3,998 to 10,438.[61] A secret Central Committee report from April 1926 celebrated the fact that the percentage of Belorussian nationals climbed from 30.3 percent of the party membership in February of 1924 to over 50 percent on January 1, 1926.[62] In the meantime, the percentage of Jewish actors flattened. By 1927, the 6,012 Jewish party members constituted about a quarter of the republic's total Communist party membership of roughly 25,000.[63] As Abram Beilin acknowledged in an atypically frank assessment, "if in the first postrevolutionary years the participation of Jews in our apparatus significantly exceeded the objective specific weight of the Jews in the country, in the present period this discrepancy has been leveled."[64] Stated otherwise, Jews were being demographically swallowed in the party.

The growth of Jewish party members was effectively controlled through the instrument of the Party Review of 1924–1925. Unlike the purge of 1921, which proceeded openly in front of party cells, the party review of 1924–1925 took place behind closed doors before small panels from the party's Central Control Commission (TsKK), the primary institution charged with regulating party membership and weeding out undesirables. According to instructions distributed to local party cells, the stated goal of the party review was to identify four types of "nonproletarian" elements and other suspect members. First, the party singled out individuals with a history of noncomradely relations with other party members, as well as drunkards, fighters, and general lawbreakers. Second, the party ordered the expulsion of party members who, "although ideologically close to the party," were either influenced by the "negative conditions of the NEP" or had ties to "NEP-elements." This group included party members who maintained relations (usually family relations) with unhealthy elements from NEP society, particularly traders. The third included the vague category of "ideologically or socially alien elements," including individuals who infiltrated the proletarian party from other social milieus, particularly the "petite bourgeoisie." It also targeted those who continued to practice religious rites. The final suspect group included individuals who remained loyal to defunct, nonproletarian political parties, including (in theory) the Belorussian Socialist Revolutionaries (BSR), the general Socialist Revolutionaries, and the Mensehviks. In practice, this measure was employed, overwhelmingly, against former Zionists, and, above all, Bundists.[65]

While a detailed breakdown of the final results of the party review is unavailable, the Control Commission reported to Moscow that it had reviewed 4,738 party members over the course of 1924–1925, excluding 1,018, including 508 sluzhashchii, 387 workers, and 123 peasants. While a full breakdown of the nationality of the excluded members does not appear to have been kept, it is almost certain that Jews constituted a significant majority, given the preponderance of Jews among the sluzhashchii and working class.[66] In Minsk, where nationality was recorded, the party excluded 150 Jewish party members, compared to 128 from all other nationalities.[67] Combined with the mass recruitment drive of the Lenin Levy, the Party Review of 1924 effectively served to "balance" national representation in the party by curtailing Jewish representation quantitatively.

The Party Review, moreover, transformed Jewish representation in the party ranks qualitatively. While Jews alone did not face exclusion for questionable political pasts, older Jews in particular were far more likely than their non-Jewish conationals to have a background in non-Bolshevik parties. According to one estimate, former Bundists alone accounted for some 9 percent of the 3,998 declared party members in February 1924.[68] At a minimum, they composed a sizable share of the 1,253 Jewish members of the KPB in early 1924.[69] Former Bundists and Poalei Tsionists came under intense scrutiny, as did Jews with questionable family backgrounds.

To cite but a few examples, on July 14, 1924, the TsKK reviewed appeals from eleven excluded members of the Central Party School Cell; of the seven Jewish members who appealed for reinstatement, three had been Bundists and two members of Poalei Tsion.[70] Two days later, the TsKK reviewed another batch of twenty-one appeals for reinstatement; of the fifteen excluded Jews, five had been Bundists, two Poalei Tsionists, and three maintained connections with "petit-bourgeois" families.[71] On July 17, the TsKK reviewed appeals from fourteen members expelled from the Belorussian State University cell, including eleven Jews, among whom were three former Bundists and five members with ties to "petit-bourgeois families." The former Bundists won reinstatement, but the TsKK upheld the expulsion of those with ties to NEP elements.[72] In August the TsKK approved the expulsion (among many others) of former Bundists Kh. M. Gorsman (thirty-seven years old) and Sh. Ia. Elinevich (thirty-three years old) due to "poor political development;"[73] M. A. Mar'iasin, a forty-one-year-old former member of the United Jewish Socialist Party who maintained ties with his *meshchanstvo* merchant family;[74] V. I. Chaplinskii, a thirty-six-year-old former Bundist and SR member;[75] V. M. Zel'dinaia, a thirty-six-year-old former Bundist and seamstress, due to her "complete political illiteracy;"[76] N. L. Katz, a thirty-four-year-old, longstanding Bund activist and shoemaker, for refusing to carry out party directives;[77] M. Ia. Kagan, a twenty-eight-year-old former Bundist with close ties to his petit-bourgeois trading family;[78] and M. B. Mogilevskii, a thirty-three-year-old former Bundist who worked in the school system but could explain neither the difference between Menshevism and Bolshevism, nor the causes of the Kronstadt Rebellion.[79] Not all former Bundists were excluded from the party. Il'ia Osherovich, Boris Orshanskii, Abram Beilin, and other former Bundists continued to hold prominent party positions. Nevertheless, lower ranking former Bundists who demonstrated passivity, a lack of political knowledge, or ties to questionable family members faced increasingly long odds.

Even as the party expelled significant numbers of older Jewish members, it simultaneously recruited new Jewish party members from the ranks of younger, previously nonpolitical Jews. Despite the expulsion of some 150 Jewish party members in Minsk, the number of Jewish party members in the Minsk Okrug reportedly climbed from 795 to 832 during the 1924–1925 period.[80] A 1925 report regarding an all-Belorussian conference of evsektsiia activists likewise hinted at the demographic transformation within evsektsiia ranks. Of the 118 delegates to the conference, 90 were full members, 20 candidates, and 8 nonparty komsomol members. In this once-Bundist dominated organization, the total number of former Bundists had fallen to 39, or roughly a third of the participants. Of the delegates, 40 percent were twenty-five years old or younger; a full 65 percent were under the age of thirty. Not surprisingly, the thirty-five former komsomol members nearly outnumbered former Bundists among the activists.[81]

The quiet purge of older Jewish party members, especially those with Bundist pasts, sharply reduced the number of party members qualified for "Jewish work."[82] All party institutions carrying out Jewish work, particularly the evsektsiia, faced perpetual shortages of qualified cadres, even before the review decimated their ranks.[83] Yet the most crucial effect of the party review transcended the issue of Jewish work; in the context of the review, the concept of what it meant to be "Bolshevik" came to be fundamentally recast in nationally discreet terms. The principle of multiethnic fluidity that characterized the early period of the revolution increasingly gave way to nationally derived identities of hierarchy and exclusion.

With the 1924 party review, the party increasingly determined what constituted a good Bolshevik by what it was not; and what it was not was Jewish, or at
least problematically so. The conflation of Jewishness and political dubiousness
was stated, implicitly but unmistakably, in the very instructions distributed
by the TsKK. To facilitate comprehension of the instructions and the review
process, Comrade Bende, the TsKK secretary, provided positive and negative
examples of ideal types. As a positive prototype, Comrade Bende apparently
decided upon the most exemplary model of Bolshevik-ness he could imagine:
himself. Comrade Bende, the model party candidate, was a twenty-eight-year-
old worker in a printing press who had joined the Bolsheviks in 1914. He served
in no other party, fought in the Red Army, accepted political work after being
demobilized, and worked his way up to the position of Secretary of the Control
Commission. While the real Comrade Robert Martsevich Bende was a Latvian
by nationality (as one could learn from his real 1929 purge record), the imaginary ideal of Comrade Bende was unmarked by nationality.[84] Needless to say,
Comrade Bende, the head of the Control Commission, recognized in Comrade
Bende an ideal type of Bolshevik propriety, fully worthy of his party card.[85]

As a negative type, Comrade Bende chose the presumably fictitious Comrade X, party number 121303, who joined the Russian Communist Party in
1919. By assigning his comrade the name "X" and a properly meaningless but
sufficiently random identification number, Comrade Bende rhetorically suggested that this Bolshevik was an abstraction, a perfectly interchangeable variable in the long list of party comrades. But Comrade X was anything but a
random, unmarked, abstract variable. Old enough to have lived through the
revolution and to have fought in the Civil War, Comrade X did not join the
Bolsheviks at the time of the Revolution and avoided fighting in the Red Army
"due to illness." By social position, Comrade X was a sluzhashchii and a bookkeeper by profession. In other words, he was "*intelligent*," despite having only
a middling education. The hypothetical Comrade X worked, moreover, in the
financial management department of the People's Commissariat for Economy
for Belorussia (VSNKh). He displayed a purely formal relationship to party
work and was not interested in political life. Finally, prior to joining the Bolsheviks, Comrade X had been a member of the Bund for three years. Far from
being an abstract, interchangeable variable of a Bolshevik, Comrade X was a
very concrete Bundist and thinly veiled Jew.[86]

Anti-Bundism as a Cultural Code

The culling of Bundists and other allegedly unreliable Jewish party members
occurred behind closed doors, with little public fanfare, without missives in
the press or a sustained agitation campaign. Between the launching of the

Lenin Levy in 1924 and the completion of the Party Review in late 1925, the overall composition of the KPB was radically reconfigured, as Belorussian nationals became the most significant demographic group in the party ranks. It must, therefore, be viewed as particularly curious that soon *after* the *practice* of anti-Bundism came to an end, the party launched its mass, widespread campaign to enlighten party members about the danger of "Bundism" in the party. Unlike the party review, which targeted Bundists within the party, the anti-Bundism rhetorical campaign unveiled in the ensuing months targeted the Jewish population at large. The campaign against Bundism did not simply entail an attack against the Bund as an historical entity (although it entailed this as well); it involved, at a more abstract level, an attack on the very meaning of "Jewish" labor and Jewish culture.

Inaugurated with Sergei Gessen's political letter, the anti-Bundist campaign unfolded throughout the spring of 1926 as political workers from the party descended on local party cells to organize mass meetings on Bundism. Not surprisingly, the campaign met with great skepticism in cells with heavy concentrations of Jewish workers and former Bundists. Comrade Gershon, the Bolshevik activist cum sacrificial lamb offered up to the leatherworkers union—a Bundist stronghold before the revolution—received an impromptu history lesson from a decidedly ambivalent crowd. Comrade Kremer sharply reminded Comrade Gershon that the Bund had split in the revolutionary period, and that the "proletariat part of [of the Bund] entered into the Communist Party." Several members challenged that the Bund stood at the forefront of the revolutionary movement in the Jewish milieu. "If there had been no Bund," Comrade Rosenberg insisted, "the Jewish workers would have been more backward." "In Belorussia the Bund was a revolutionary party," Comrade Kantsler likewise insisted. Some took the argument further, stressing that the Bund had been chiefly responsible for the Bolshevization of the Jewish working class: "Had there been no Bund," one worker insisted, "then *our* party would have been able to do nothing among the Jewish workers."[87]

Defenses of the historical importance of the Bund in the revolutionary movement were repeated in party cell meetings across the republic. One worker in Vitebsk reportedly claimed "that the Belorussian Communist party was formed out of the Bund." Another worker argued, "the Bolsheviks came forward on prepared ground, and the Bund prepared that ground."[88] Such pronouncements, however, constituted the exception, not the rule, even within the "Jewish" professions. Despite their defense of the Bund's legacy, even the leatherworkers by and large agreed that the Bund lost its relevance after the revolution. Comrade Kremer conceded that those Bundists who entered the party fully embraced the ideology of the Bolsheviks; those who refused to enter the party became irrelevant, as the Bund ceased to exist. Comrade Gordon, another leatherworker, dismissed as incorrect those who argued that the "Bund was the forerunner to the Communist party," emphasizing that the Bolsheviks had been correct in attacking the Bund's national exclusionary ideology.[89] In the debate that took place in the shoemakers' factory cell run by VSNKh, Comrade Ginzburg similarly argued that "the Bund previously, of course, held influence among the workers," but added that "in the present moment, this is completely not the case."[90]

A far greater number of Jewish workers attacked the legacy of the Bund outright. "Of course [the Bund] held great influence," Comrade Novitskii of the Mogilev city party administration argued. As "an organization formed of kustari, artisans, and petit-bourgeois elements," it could not help but exert tremendous influence in the tsarist period.[91] Comrade Maisel' of Union of the People's Commissariat for Provisioning (*Narpit*) made similar associations. As a result of its petit-bourgeois nature, Maisel' argued, there "was not even one single worker" in the Bund. From its "very first day of origin," he continued, "the Bund preached the idea of the separation of the Jewish working mass from the general workers movement."[92] Members of the shoemakers' factory, the leatherworkers union, the needleworkers union, the food makers union, and the metalworkers union articulated similar criticisms of the Bund's separatist tendency. Within the komsomol cell, composed of the youngest and least conflicted party members, the presumed irrelevance of the Bund was not simply asserted in the present, but projected back onto the past as well. It took a considerable deal of historical amnesia to assert, as the *komsomolets* Comrade Gold'man emphatically did, that "the Bund did not have a strong influence among the broad working class," or that the Jewish working class had always looked upon the Bund "as national chauvinists" due to their goal of specifically national work. Thankfully for Comrade Gold'man and others like him, historical forgetting was quickly becoming the order of the day.[93]

If the historical legacy of the Bund constituted the text of the campaign, the question of nationality lurked immediately below the surface. In virtually every recorded worker meeting, discussion quickly moved from debates about the revolutionary pedigree of the Bundist past to the practices, attitudes, and sentiments of Jewish workers and party members in the present. Invariably, debates about Bundism flowed toward conversations about Jewish attitudes toward language, leisure, education, and politics. While workers, both Jewish and non-Jewish, party member or not, frequently struggled to define Bundism, most instinctively understood that Bundism was tied inextricably to language policy.[94] Faced with the question of what, exactly, constituted the "Menshevik essence of the Bund" denounced in Gessen's letter, Comrade Katsilevich of the Mogilev city party administration explained that Bundism "put forward demands of a purely national character, of cultural freedoms for the Jewish population," particularly in "the area of opening schools and issuing literature" in Yiddish.[95] Comrade Gorman of the Commissariat of Labor criticized the fact that "many comrades consider that since they present themselves as Jews (*iavliaiutsia evreiami*), they should only talk in Yiddish, and train their children to do the same."[96] In a needleworkers union meeting, Comrade Teklin denounced as "Bundism" the idea that Yiddish education should be made mandatory for Jewish children—a claim that was frequently and vociferously denounced, even though it had few supporters among even the most aggressive proponents of Yiddish education.[97]

In addition to promoting mandatory monolingual education, ideological Bundists allegedly demonstrated a number of other linguistically bound practices. Bundist "opportunists" insisted on delivering lectures at conferences in Yiddish, Comrade Sadkovskii of the metalworkers union complained, even when only 60 percent of the audience spoke Yiddish.[98] Others used the discussion on Bundism to express their ambivalence about the use of Yiddish generally. "In my opinion," Comrade Fishman of Mogilev declared, "it is completely unnecessary to teach Yiddish, since it is difficult to use and useless in real life."[99] Among the most common recurring themes was the allegation that Jewish party members worked and associated only with other Jews. Such exclusionary tendencies could be seen in the "everyday life of the local Jewish workers in Minsk," charged Comrade Maisel' at the Narpit meeting. The Jewish workers, he observed "concentrate themselves in the Lenin workers' club, the former Grosser Club." The mass of Jewish workers "sitting in that club" he continued, "will not set foot in another club. . . . They love to concentrate themselves in *their* club."[100] Haughtiness constituted the flip side of the exclusionary essence of Bundism. Those displaying Bundist proclivities, Comrade Erofeev stated during the Narpit meeting, "feel that the entire Jewish population should be in the ranks of the Bolshevik party."[101]

The attacks by comrades Fishman, Maisel', and Erofeev—all Jewish—point to the degree to which the critique of Bundism merged with a process of Jewish public self-criticism (or, more precisely, criticism of other, less "politically conscious" Jews). Yet the morphing of attacks on Bundism into general attacks on Jewish cultural institutions provoked considerable consternation among other Jewish party members. Even those willing to criticize the Bundist tradition expressed exasperation over the changing winds of cultural policy. Many objected that the campaign against Bundism attacked the very institutions that the party claimed to promote. When faced with this complaint in the Minsk Bootmaking Workshop, Comrade Volabrinskii, a cultural activist, insisted that the party had no intention of undermining Jewish schools, news-papers, or clubs, but only to fight against "national chauvinism" in these insti-tutions.[102] Such arguments drew swift rebukes. Comrade Keller, a member of the Narpit union, reversed the charge of Jewish chauvinism, arguing that the party "removed good workers who know their work, because they were former Bundists and replaced them with Belorussians." This, he argued, was the true trajectory of the nationality policy in the republic.[103] Other Jewish party mem-bers repeatedly asked why the party attacked Bundism, but remained silent about national chauvinism on the part of Belorussian party members.[104]

Ultimately, the attack on Bundism as an ideological deviation confronted the limits of nationality policy with respect to the Jews. Wherever party mem-bers began to look, the contradictions of cultural policy became evident. "Since the party is now carrying out work to eliminate national separatism," one party member in Mogilev asked during a party meeting, "why does the evsektsiia exist?" In the needleworkers union, a worker accused the evsektsiia of carry-ing out "Bundist work," since they insisted on working in Yiddish.[105] Within the Commissariat of Enlightenment, Jewish and non-Jewish party members debated the logical consistency of the attack in light of the party's unyield-ing promotion of Belorussian language and culture. Comrade Galkin warned that the attack on purported "Bundist" chauvinism was generating "distrust" of the nationality policy in general, particularly given the aggressive policy of linguistic Belorussianization. Comrade Vaitsok responded in a revealing, if feeble, manner. The party previously supported the development of all national cultures that flowed from "general proletarian culture." "Now," he contin-ued, "when the party poses the question of the development of national cul-ture, particular attention is paid to Belorussian culture, because it is the most backward."[106] The inconsistency of the attack on Bundism and simultaneous promotion of Belorussian was thus justified through the ambiguous logic of affirmative action: the needs of the purportedly more backward Belorussian population trumped those of the more culturally "advanced" Jews.[107]

In addition to targeting party cells with high concentrations of former Bundists and Jewish workers, the campaign against Bundism was also per-formed in party cells with few former Bundists or Jewish members at all. On March 9, 1926, to cite one revealing example, the party cell of the Minsk state glassmaking factory Proletarii organized a meeting to warn of the danger of Bundism, despite the fact that the factory employed only two former Bundists and a handful of Jews.[108] Judging by the questions posed by the cell mem-bers, few party members had any real familiarity with the Bund. The meeting began with a reading of Gessen's political letter, followed by lectures from the cell secretaries, Comrade Klionskii (almost certainly Jewish) and Comrade

Tsarenok (almost certainly not) on the history of the Bund and the problems of Bundism. Far from generating opposition, Comrade Klionskii's description of the "petit-bourgeois" history of the Bund met with indifference, due in all probability to the general absence of former Bundists.[109]

The tenor of the conversation shifted dramatically, however, when the subject turned from the historical Bund to the ongoing relationship between Bundism and "tailism," which, as Comrade Tsarenok explained, meant following the lead of nonparty workers and becoming a tail of the nonparty mass. To clarify the nature of "tailism," one worker, Comrade Baranov, drew an example from the everyday life in the glassmaking factory. Some comrades, he suggested, followed reactionary nonparty workers in the factory by demanding vague "nationalist concessions" from the party. Baranov's ambiguous comment drew a sharp reaction from Comrade Kurnovskaia, one Jewish member of the cell (and possibly one of the former Bundists), who decried the enforcement of nationality policy in the factory. In one pioneer cell of the union, she explained, all of the children were Jewish, but the party and union refused to allow the group to operate in Yiddish. Comrade Tsarenok jumped in, explaining that, "in light of the fact that the majority of the population speaks Belorussian, it was necessary to demand that all be able to express themselves in it." When another comrade observed that the discussion of language policy proved the existence of "tailism" in the cell, Comrade Kurnovskaia demanded that her party members drop their niceties: "Tell us, then," she demanded, "from whom does this 'tailism' come?" Comrade Vorotnitskii responded curtly, "it seems from the posed question about the work of the pioneer unit, together with a whole range of similar facts, that we have tailsim among certain women party members (*partiitsi*) in the factory." Within the glassmakers cell, tailism appeared not only, like Bundism, as a Jewish phenomenon, but also a gendered one.[110]

As in the case of the glassmaking factory Proletarii, debates about Bundism exposed building tensions between non-Jews and Jews over questions of "culture," nationality, Jewish policy, and Jews, Bundist or otherwise. The language of "Bundism" provided a sanctioned way for party members to discuss the behavior of Jewish party members without recourse to nationality. In the Commissariat of Agriculture, for example, interparty debates over the danger of Bundism blurred distinctions between political and national categories. One member, comrade Timofeev, accused "Bundists" in the party of engaging in "protectionism." Comrade Maevskii took this idea a step further, stating that he knew "Jewish families in which petit-bourgeois ideologies reverberated." It was hardly surprising, he added, that one noticed "chauvinism" not only among "communists who were former Bundists" but also among the "rest of the mostly Jewish officials" in the party. Comrade Kabailo quickly corrected comrade Maevskii. What Maevskii had noticed was not *Jewish* "chauvinism," he insisted, but rather the precise expression of "Bundism" on the part of certain party members. Comrade Luk'ianchik added that this petty-bourgeois ideology and the spirit of "protectionism" inherent in Bundism were foreign to the spirit of the Bolshevik party. The cell concluded the meeting by passing a resolution calling for the removal from responsible posts of all former Bundists who had not thoroughly broken with their Bundist proclivities.[111]

Reports of tensions between Belorussians and Jews filtered in from meetings around the republic. Rather than parse the line between acceptable Jewishness and inadmissible Bundism, many party members simply stopped drawing distinctions. According to a report to the Central Committee, anti-Bundism frequently devolved into broad attacks against Jewish communists in general. In meetings across the republic, one heard claims that "Jewish party members are not able to break from their nationalist souls," or that "Jews are not able to value peasants as being worthy of power." One worker in the Minsk Railroad factory (always a hotbed of anti-Jewish sentiment) reportedly argued that "any institutions led by Jewish *rabotniki* (party workers) are *Jewish* institutions," and hence, non-Belorussian. A worker in Vitebsk asserted that Jews always form states within states in professional organizations.[112] "In general, among all Jews," one member of the Minsk machine factory Energiia opined, "even members of the party, one notices nationalist deviations. When a Jewish communist marries, it is without fail to a Jewess [*evreika*]."[113] Similar accusations against Jews filtered in from all corners, arguing that they avoided military service, shirked manual labor, engaged only in trade, and the like.

Jewish party members responded to allegations of "Bundism" not as an attack on the legacy of the Bund but for what they in fact were: debates over nationality policy and Jewish identity. They by and large responded by criticizing not the concept of Bundism, but the policies of Belorussianization. One Central Committee report filed in 1926 noted that Jewish workers across the republic routinely objected to the fact that linguistic Belorussianization was introduced "by force."[114] In the Commissariat of Labor cell, one Jewish member responded to charges that "Bundists" refused to send their children to non-Jewish schools by attacking policies of Belorussianization policies. "There have been cases," he argued, "when Jewish children and their parents wanted to study in Russian schools, and this was not allowed" by the Commissariat of Enlightenment, due to the demands of Belorussianization.[115] An early 1927 report from the Minsk Okrug reported that with the intensification of Belorussianization policies, party activists noticed an "increase in nationalism among Jewish workers, and even more so among Jewish sluzhashchii and intellectuals." Across the republic, Jewish workers decried the fact that Jews were being removed from their posts and jobs as a result of these policies. One worker observed that the policy meant "the best positions in the party go to the Belorussians." Another theorized that "Belorussianization was devised to weaken the role of Jews in social life." Another wondered "why is Yiddish not equal to Belorussian" in the eyes of the state.[116]

The swelling wave of nationalist sentiment overwhelmed ideological subtleties distinguishing permissible attacks against Bundism from impermissible attacks against "general" Jewish behavior. In general, the anti-Bundism campaign coalesced with a broad resurgence of anti-Jewish sentiments. The abovementioned Minsk Okrug report warned of growing "signs of antisemitism among non-Jewish workers, white-collar workers, and party members." In a party cell meeting of the Gostorgdel, the department of state trade, one worker wondered "why the main administration" consisted only of Jews? In the glassmaking factory Proletarii, another complained that "*they* only promote Jewish workers" in the factory.[117] A detailed evsektsiia report from October 1926 likewise discerned increases in anti-Jewish sentiments and actions across the republic. Party members in Mogilev reported that local officials in one raion refused to accept any papers from Jewish workers for a local conference, on the grounds that "the Jews have grabbed the entire social and state establishment." In Borisov, workers in the local printers union complained that they had been ordered to use only Russian, despite the fact that 119 of the 125 of the union's workers were Jews, and the vast majority did not know Russian. In Orsha, hostile relations existed between Jewish agricultural workers and the raion party organization. Non-Jewish workers at the Dnevorposk Manufacture factory in Orsha dismissed the idea that they engaged in protectionism, despite the fact that they only allowed Belorussians to work in the factory.[118] An early 1927 report from the shtetl Svisloch stated that relations between Jews and Belorussians had recently become completely "unhealthy." Arguments over taxation, rights to animal pasture, fees for slaughtering, and other issues had driven a wedge between the two populations. The spirit of national separatism between "us" and "them" had devolved to a point that local officials had no choice but to divide the local soviet into two different national soviets.[119]

Taken collectively, allegations of Bundism, Jewish chauvinism, excessive Belorussianization, and antisemitism all point to the fact that by the second half of 1926, intranational relations had begun to simmer. While soviet and party authorities recorded these events in rather detailed fashion, the response proved uneven. Allegations of Bundism, Jewish separatism, and Jewish nationalism received particular attention as the party engaged in systematic campaigns to excise these deviations from the ideological landscape of Belorussia.

No similar action was taken to combat the problem of anti-Jewish agitation, which continued to build until a wave of antisemitic incidents broke across the Republic in late 1928, catching everyone "unaware." Although denounced as a dangerous ideological deviation, the party did not focus on the problem of antisemitism explicitly until it became a functionally useful political language on the eve of the Stalin Revolution.[120] "Bundism," by contrast, became a functionally useful political language with the initial crisis of the NEP system.

Bundism, Nationality, and the NEP

The introduction of the anti-Bundism campaign and seemingly abrupt change in Jewish policy in 1926 perplexed many rank-and-file party members. "Why has the Central Committee, after five years, only now posed this question," wondered Comrade Avrutin during the meeting on Bundism in the Narpit cell. Comrade Iankelevich of the agricultural workers union noted "to me, it's strange, when they begin to talk about the 'Bund,' when, after six years, practically all [former Bundists] have been boiled up into the Bolshevik stock."[121] Among the Jewish rank-and-file party members, some simply threw up their hands in exasperation when considering the campaign's timing. "There's something wrong in the party," Comrade Rosenberg of the leatherworkers union observed during the cells' meeting on Bundism. The party "needed to find a cause" to explain this problem, "and so they found the Bund."[122]

The question of the timing of the shift in nationalities policy has remained as perplexing for historians as for contemporary observers. Terry Martin argued that the politics of affirmative action themselves paradoxically drove the intensification of intranational hostility in the period of 1920s. Instead of damping nationalist sentiments, policies of affirmative action intensified nationalist animosity between titular nationalities and the "imperial" center of Moscow.[123] The events examined in this chapter offer much qualified support to this thesis. In the Belorussian context, affirmative action policies undeniably served to drive the politics of intranational conflict, as the anti-Bundism campaign developed hand in hand with campaigns to promote Belorussianization throughout the republic. The language of Bundism became the mechanism through which the party increasingly characterized opposition to Belorussianization. The campaign indirectly established parameters, a script, and a language for how party members should think about Jews. In a similar fashion, efforts to ameliorate Jewish poverty, to normalize Jewish social organization, and to eradicate "petit-bourgeois" tendencies among Jews by settling them on the land met with acrimony on the part of land-hungry Belorussian peasantry.

Direct political struggle undoubtedly played a role in the degeneration and breakdown of intranational relations. Such explanations, however, are less capable of accounting for the peculiar *timing* of the political and cultural "turn" in intranational relations. Far from inaugurating a campaign to drive Bundists from the party, the rhetorical campaign against Bundism emerged in the *aftermath* of the campaign to marginalize and exclude former Bundists from the party. Antisemitism, similarly, did not emerge as a potentially destabilizing threat in the period when Jews held "disproportionate" position within the party and soviet apparatuses. It spiked, rather, *after* the actual influence of Jews in the party had been reversed. Jewish "chauvinism" and cultural exclusivity, likewise, did not appear as problematic in the period when Jewish cultural activists enjoyed their greatest autonomy—a degree of autonomy that led many to believe the complete reconstruction of Jewish cultural life was a vibrant and imminent possibility. Jewish "cultural exclusivity" became rhetorically problematic only after the suppression of the most overt tendencies toward cultural autonomy in the Jewish milieu. These campaigns did not, in other words, develop when they "should" have developed, if they were structured exclusively by questions of politics and culture. They *did*, however develop simultaneously with the unfolding economic crisis of the NEP.

Stalin would ultimately assert that the increase in national tensions in the late 1920s sprang directly from the restoration of capitalist relations under the NEP. By this, he meant that the revival of capitalist relations (i.e., the market) had fostered the growth of undesirable class enemies and, consequently, promoted the revival of deviant ideologies. In the midst of the anti-Bundist campaign, certain members of the party groped toward a similar explanation. In this, they followed the lead of Aleksandr Krinitskii, whose pro-Stalinist credentials would, by 1928, elevate him to the head of Agitprop for the entire USSR.[124] In interparty meetings, attempts to trace the alleged resurgence of "Bundist" deviations in 1926 to the purported revival of the reactionary "petite bourgeoisie" as a class during the NEP proliferated. Within the food producers union, for example, Comrade Rives, a Jewish defender of the anti-Bund turn, explained the campaign's timing with an eye toward the social "reality." The Bund, he argued, was historically a petit-bourgeois party made up of artisans and kustari, which thrived in the petit-bourgeois milieu of the late imperial period. If the danger of Bundism was reviving in the social context of the present day, Rives argued, this was not the fault of the former Bundists. Rather, it constituted a warning for the party about the danger inherent in the social system created by the NEP.[125] Comrade Rabinovitch in the builders union advanced a similar argument. "The Bund is reviving because of the fact that the conditions exist" for its revival. "The development of the NEP and the development of the petite bourgeoisie that followed from it," he asserted, made the resurgence of the petit-bourgeois ideology of Bundism possible. The fault lay not with the Bundists, per se, but with the economic policy that made the social group they represented—the petty bourgeoisie—once again relevant.

Evidence suggests that the intensification of intranational strife and tension was driven to no small degree by the social contradictions of the NEP, but in a manner rather different than that imagined by the Stalin faction. The campaign against Bundism, upsurge in criticisms about Jewish chauvinism and protectionism—and counterclaims of Belorussian chauvinism, protectionism, and antisemitism—began to bubble forth in the first quarter of 1926. In other words, the anti-Bundism campaign picked up steam as the fleeting moment of market and economic stability engendered by the NEP, which reached its pinnacle in 1925, showed signs of unraveling. The "balance" between nationalities broke down contemporaneously with the unbalancing of the NEP.

The NEP, as a total system of social organization, rested upon the principle of balance. As a system of market exchange and response to the "scissors crisis" of 1923, the functioning of the NEP depended on the maintenance of a series of critical equilibriums, namely maintaining the balance between agricultural prices and prices for manufactured goods. This balance, in turn, rested upon the concept of a *smychka*, or "union" between peasants and urban workers that would balance production between city and countryside. Socialized or cooperative production, likewise, was envisioned as a mechanism for balancing the pressures of private production and distribution necessitated, however grudgingly, by the NEP. In the context of Belorussia (and beyond), these ostensibly economic and social divides were keenly inflected with the politics of nationality, insofar as nationality and social positionality within systems of production mapped onto one another rather precisely. Divisions between Belorussians and Jews, while rhetorically constructed, were not merely rhetorical; they also reflected real prevailing national divisions in processes of production, distribution, and consumption. The NEP promoted tranquility, harmony, and the mutual cultivation of national cultures precisely because the social structure of the NEP depended upon the social balance between populations.

The eruption of renewed conflicts over nationality beginning in early 1926 coincided with the rapid and steady decline in the NEP economy due to a combination of intensified inflationary pressures, subsequent pressures on wages, and heightened conflict between the agricultural and urban economy. In response to these inflationary pressures, the party launched a vigorous deflationary campaign. The structural tensions between these inflationary pressures and deflationary measures ultimately broke apart the system of the NEP. By early 1926 the government had begun to abandon the sound currency policies that served as the driving economic rationale since the early NEP period.

By late 1927, the system of market driven trade had frozen up across the Republic. By 1928, the market system of distribution had broken to the point that the Civil War–era tool of rationing was reimplemented to deal with chronic shortages. In the meantime, the systemic contradictions of the collapsing NEP and the efforts to rein in inflation led to a marked upswing in unemployment across the republic, a significant tightening of the labor market, and a general environment of creeping scarcity.[126]

In the context of intensifying inflationary pressures coupled with the NEP-directed imperative for profitability and economic accountability, the language of nationality began to incorporate the language and logic of scarcity-driven competition. The charges of protectionism expressed in the recriminations of Bundism and related counterrecriminations must be read in the light of this underlying systemic shift. Mounting levels of unemployment likely pushed forward the campaign against Bundism as a mechanism for breaking through ethnic boundaries that kept Belorussians out of "Jewish" industries, and vice versa. Within the context of Belorussia (but by no means *only* in Belorussia), there can be little doubt that, historically, language and "culture" *did* serve as mechanism for "protecting" certain economic sectors and industries from encroachment on the part of outsiders. In the context of the late NEP, national politics intervened decisively in efforts to break ethnic enclaves of production.

A report on national minorities in the labor unions compiled by the Central Committee in 1927 provides evidence suggesting that such intentions played no small role in the overarching logic of the drive against Bundism. From the period of 1925 to 1927, after years of unmitigated growth and numerical predominance, the absolute number of Jewish members in both the leatherworkers and needleworkers unions declined significantly for the first time in the postrevolutionary era.[127] This period marked the very beginning of a five-year period during which the proportional weight of Jews in both unions fell dramatically.[128] In the context of two unions that had overwhelming majorities of Yiddish-speaking members, the politics of anti-Bundism and general attacks on Jewish nationalism clearly constituted a functional mechanism for undermining resistance to workforce integration.

Yet this process was by no means a one-sided affair. While Jewish representation fell sharply in these key "Jewish" professions, the numbers of Jews incorporated into every other trade union increased during the 1925–1927 period. Leading the way, in this respect, were Jewish members of the union for agricultural workers, whose numbers climbed from a scant 347 in 1924 to 2,722 by 1927. The number of Jewish workers in the builders union climbed from 5,078 in 1925 to 5,831 in 1927. Taken together, the total number of Jewish trade unionists grew from 27,593 in 1924, to 37,403 in 1925, to 45,307 in 1927.[129] In the broadest terms, the concentration of Jewish labor in specific enclaves began to be broken during this period, while the overall trend across the unions was toward greater integration. Integration occurred, as it does virtually everywhere, against a background of resistance, animosity, and intragroup rivalry. Bolshevik policy, intended to defuse these rivalries, in fact exacerbated them.

Conclusion

It would be highly reductionist to attribute the growing national acrimony that manifested with the anti-Bundism campaign of 1926 to economic factors alone. To be certain, the politics of nationalism and national resentment remained an ever-present possibility in postrevolutionary society, driven by impulses that can never simply be reduced to "rational" causes. As the interwar period demonstrated beyond a shadow of a doubt, irrational emotion played no small role in driving national conflict across the European continent. Nor were the economic factors that contributed to intensified national acrimony themselves autonomous from the political realm. From the time of the Fourteenth Party Congress of 1925, the all-Russian Communist Party in Moscow devoted itself as vigorously to planned industrialization as it did to the repression of ideological enemies within the party. The language of politics undoubtedly contributed to the restructuring of economy in the subsequent period. Yet even as the party committed itself to the theoretical project of industrialization, it simultaneously devoted itself to industrialization through the system and structures of the NEP. That industrialization could be achieved through the mechanism of the market remained axiomatic in the initial Stalinist (and Bukharinist) attack on the emerging Trotskyist opposition.

Politics, nationality, and "culture" did not operate autonomously; all were bound, fundamentally, to underlying socioeconomic structures. The campaigns for Jewish cultural reconstruction, alongside the korenizatsiia and Belorussianization campaigns, proceeded without generating intensive conflict as long as the NEP economy functioned with some degree of plausibility. At the height of the NEP in 1925, there was little reason to believe that the projects of Jewish cultural construction would necessarily come into conflict with the demands of Belorussianization. That they did was the result of politics, to be certain. But it was a politics inflected with the language of intensified intranational competition, of protectionism, of access to employment and of scarcity.

Intranational tension and antagonism between social groups erupted as the NEP economy began to slide into crisis. By highlighting the relationship between nationality policy and the emerging structural change of the late 1920s, the anti-Bundism campaigns suggest three important correctives to recent historiographic framings of Soviet nationality policy. First, attempts to characterize the change in nationality policy at the end of the 1920s as either a "reversal" of affirmative action policies or as the return to or continuation of the original revolutionary intention of the Bolsheviks vis-à-vis nationality policy appear, in this context, as one-sided. The party, it might be argued, was as sincere in promoting national self-determination as a desirable end in the early 1920s as it was ambivalent by the end of the decade. What changed was not simply party policy, but the totality of the social order that nationality policy sought to regulate, shape, and guide.

Second, in the context of the Western Borderlands, the problem of nationality manifested itself, first and foremost, in a renewed and reconstituted "Jewish question." Far from being incidental, the question of Jewish policy remained absolutely integral to the resolution of nationality conflict in postrevolutionary society. By largely bracketing off questions of Jewish nationality from the history of Soviet nationality policy, recent historiography has tended to treat the question of nationality as a binary relationship between "Russian" Soviet hegemons in Moscow opposed by "titular nationalities." Yet as the case of the anti-Bundism campaign in Belorussia demonstrated, the politics of nationality was driven as much by the intrinsic social and economic tensions of the late NEP era as the extrinsic relations between the "center" of Moscow and the national republican peripheries.

Third, while formulated within the official language of nationality, interparty discussion persistently pushed against, and frequently beyond, the proscribed linguistic boundaries of nationality. The multivalent meanings embedded in the concept of "Bundism" ranged from an explicitly political meaning targeting a historically discreet political entity, to questions of language policy, to ephemeral, deeper, and fraught questions of the supposed "essence" of Jewish identity. The contestation of Jewish identity that emerged in the context of the anti-Bundism campaign was not simply a process of ascribing identity; rather, Jews themselves frequently played a primary role in determining and teasing out implied and contested meanings of an ostensibly political category. Debates over Bundism, moreover, were always framed in the language of cultural traits and practices. From the outset of the campaign, "Bundism" was understood, theoretically, as an affliction that even former members of the Bund could overcome through proper thought and practice. Bundism became a language through which Jewish and non-Jewish party members discussed and debated a form of affective Jewish identity grounded in purported cultural practices that was opposed to healthy, "national" soviet Jewish identity. In other words, Bundism became a marked category through which the party discussed and debated the reemergent "problem" of Jewish ethnicity.

PART IV

THE POLITICS OF CRISIS

6

THE POLITICS OF CRISIS: ECONOMY, ETHNICITY, AND TROTSKYISM

Anti-Semitism raised its head with . . . anti-Trotskyism.

Leon Trotsky *My Life*

Without time-discipline we could not have the insistent energies of industrial man; and whether this discipline comes in the form of Methodism, or of Stalinism, or of nationalism, it will come to the developing world.

E. P. Thompson "Time, Work Discipline, and Industrial Capitalism"

FOLLOWING THE EXPULSION from the party ranks of Trotsky, Zinoviev, and Kamenev during the Fifteenth Party Congress in December 1927, the Belorussian Communist Party (KPB) undertook a sweeping campaign to wipe out the last vestiges of "Trotskyist" Opposition across the Belorussian Soviet Socialist Republic (BSSR). From November 1927 until January 1928, the party organized mass meetings to draw Oppositionists into open debate and force them to recant their oppositional ideas or face expulsion.[1] Records of these debates reveal an unmistakable pattern. In Minsk 144 party members voted against or abstained from voting on a resolution supporting the expulsion of Trotsky and Zinoviev; of these, 116 were Jews.[2] In Vitebsk Jewish party members accounted for 55 of 72 identified Oppositionists.[3] In Bobruisk, 46 of the 49 party members opposed to the expulsion of the Opposition leaders were Jews.[4] In total, some 326 party members in Minsk, Vitebsk, Bobruisk, and Gomel abstained from voting or voted against the expulsion of the Opposition leaders and/or the theses supporting the First Five-Year Plan and collectivization—resolutions strongly championed by the Stalinist camp. Of these, 264 (81 percent) were Jews. At the conclusion of the anti-Trotskyist campaign, the KPB resolved to expel thirty-six recalcitrant Oppositionists;

of these, twenty-three were Jews, including eight of the nine party members identified as primary ringleaders.[5]

The marked concentration of Jews among the supporters of the United Opposition in Belorussia suggests two commonsensical explanations. First, it is possible that Jewish party members gravitated toward the Opposition out of a sense of ethnic or national solidarity. Perhaps it was natural that in Belorussia, where Jews constituted half of the urbanized population and the most influential nontitular nationality, Jewish party members should have sided with the "Jewish" triumvirate of Leon Trotsky, Grigorii Zinoviev, and Lev Kamenev.[6] Second, antisemitism in the party mainstream may have driven Jewish members into the Opposition camp. Indeed, records of the anti-Trotskyist campaigns in Belorussia lend credence to Trotsky's assertions that antisemitism played a critical role in the campaign against the Opposition.[7] In either case, the prevalence of Jews in the Opposition ranks seems to suggest a struggle defined by nationality.[8]

A radically different picture emerges, however, if one turns from the question of nationality to that of the occupations of the accused Oppositionists. Of the thirty-seven Jewish party members who voted with the Opposition in Vitebsk, virtually all were workers at the bench. Their ranks included ten tailors and seamstresses, a furrier, a builder, a baker, a shoemaker and four apprentices, three locksmiths, three joiners, three house painters, and a handful of unemployed workers.[9] Of the 122 Jewish Oppositionists in Minsk, 22 were university students, while 10 served as white-collar workers (sluzhashchii).[10] The remaining Jewish Oppositionists included twenty leatherworkers (nine leather finishers, a leather cutter, two tanners, a joiner, a folder, and several unskilled laborers), sixteen shoemakers, a handful of shoemaker assistants, seven bristle makers, seven carpenters, three joiners, three milliners, six tailors and seamstresses, three typesetters, and assorted mechanics, unskilled laborers, and unemployed workers.[11] Shoemakers, tailors, and seamstresses likewise dominated the Opposition in Bobruisk.[12] In short, the data suggests a pattern familiar in the history of labor radicalism in Europe: the Opposition drew its strongest support from industries resting on the unstable fault line separating artisanal and petty manufacturing from full-blown industrial production.[13]

Far from being coincidental or incidental, the tension between ethnic and social identities proved critical to the development of the political concept of "Trotskyism" in Belorussia. While most often associated with the realm of high politics, I argue that the concept of Trotskyism in Belorussia emerged as a discourse tied directly to the realm of economy. Specifically, the political language of "Trotskyism" developed as a direct response to the economic crisis that erupted across the republic in 1926–1927. Faced with the collapse of international grain prices, falling trade revenues, saturated industrial capacity, inflationary pressures, and renewed monetary instability, the Belorussian state (following Moscow) sought to overcome the spreading economic crisis by intensifying labor productivity, by further rationalizing production processes, and by suppressing wages. The Belorussian Communist Party combated economistic agitation against such "rationalizing" initiatives by labeling it as a counterrevolutionary political deviation: namely, "Trotskyism." The invented concept of "Trotskyism" served the function of driving through politics of economic productivization in the midst of profound economic crisis.

Ethnicity played a critical role in the process of economic rationalization. At the most apparent level, the anti-Trotskyism campaign fell heavily on Jewish labor because Jewish laborers constituted the vast majority of workers in industries that experienced the brunt of the campaign to intensify industrial production. In this context, ethnicity entered into political language as a mechanism to further intensify industrial rationalization. By associating economic opposition with political and, ultimately, ethnic nonbelonging, the language of "Trotskyism" itself became a mechanism for suppressing resistance to economic rationalization. As ethnicity came to be reinterpreted as the ontological cause of political and economic deviation, conceptions of Jewish identity began to harden. Jewishness increasingly appeared less as an affective identity grounded in culture and increasingly as a form of ascribed identity asserted from without. The example of Trotskyism suggests that in Belorussia, economy structured political language; political language, in turn, became a mechanism for reconstituting not only economy but also concepts of ethnicity and, ultimately, race.

Oppositions Everywhere

Political opposition, real and imagined, formed a purported threat from the first days of Bolshevik power in Belorussia.[14] In the earliest months of Soviet rule, party organs inveighed against the Belorussian Rada, the Belorussian Party of Socialist Revolutionaries, and other nationalist opponents.[15] Throughout the 1920s, the party kept close tabs on Belorussian and Polish underground nationalist groups who supposedly threatened the state. As the Bolsheviks consolidated power, however, attention focused increasingly on specifically Jewish political opposition.

Jewish political opposition constituted a conceivable threat in Belorussia for three seemingly logical reasons. First, Jews composed a significant, politically active portion of the population, forming pluralities or majorities in most major cities and countless shtetlekh. Second, Jews made up a considerable portion of the Bolshevik party ranks. Despite being thinned and "corrected" over the first postrevolutionary decade, Jews continued to constitute one-quarter of the total party membership in 1927.[16] Finally, the Jewish populations of Belorussia had a long and developed history of non-Bolshevik political activism. In addition to the extensive campaign against Bundism that raged throughout the mid-1920s, the party, largely through the evsektsiia, campaigned tirelessly to stamp out the influence of nationalism, Zionism, and explicitly Jewish politics on the so-called Jewish street.[17]

Concern over Jewish political opposition was by no means simply illusory. The cities of Belorussia had been prerevolutionary strongholds of the Bund, and former Bundists continued to form sizable contingents of workers on shop floors. Indeed, the same industries that previously formed the core of support for the Bund reemerged as volatile sites of labor unrest during the early years of the NEP.[18] When labor disturbances broke out in workshops across Belorussia during the second half of 1923, the evsektsiia functionary Samuil Agursky attributed the waves of strike agitation to "Bundist-Menshevik tendencies" within the labor force.[19] Evsektsii activists routinely blamed social unrest on a myriad of alleged enemies, including Mensheviks, representatives of the American Relief Agency, petit-bourgeois nationalists, practitioners of "clericalism," and, above all, Zionists.[20] Glaringly absent from the list of enemies, however, was the group that constituted the primary political threat in the centers of Russian politics during the 1923–1924 period: the Left Opposition.

The evsektsii was hardly alone in minimizing the threat posed by the Left Opposition. Compared to Moscow and Leningrad, where significant groups of intellectuals, functionaries, students, and workers lined up behind Trotsky and the signatories of the "Platform of the 46," support for the Left Opposition remained marginal in Belorussia during the 1923–1924 period.[21] Central Control Commission (TsKK) records from the 1924 party review, launched to eliminate "nonproletarian elements" from the party ranks, excluded some 1,018 individuals across Belorussia.[22] Particular cells—most notably that of the Belorussian State University (BGU) in Minsk—came under scrutiny as hotbeds of support for the Left Opposition.[23] One leading historian claimed that the party excluded sixty-five members across Belorussia for support of the Left Opposition during the period of the review.[24] Yet unlike in 1927–1928, when a coordinated anti-Trotskyist campaign was carried out across the republic, the party did not stage a systemic campaign to wipe out support for the Left Opposition. Quite to the contrary, the TsKK went so far as to send a secret memo condemning local Okrug Control Commissions (OKK) for expelling "party members and candidates who speak in defense of Trotskyism."[25] Compared to the perceived challenge posed by Bundists and Poalei Tsionists, "Trotskyism" appeared as a minor threat in Belorussia.[26]

This changed dramatically two years later, with the outbreak of renewed economic crisis in the summer of 1926. The crisis that swept away the economic institutions of the NEP and generated new tensions between nationalities also engendered a profound transformation of political discourse across the Soviet territories. In Belorussia, the crisis fused multifarious forms of worker opposition into a singular political specter, labeled retroactively as Trotskyism.

The fact that the name of Trotsky came to be associated with politics of opposition to industrial rationalization appears ironically incongruent with the usual characterization of Trotskyism. It was, after all, Trotsky who vociferously championed the "mass conscription of labor," the "fully efficient allocation of living labor power," and the "dictatorship of industry" in the early years of the Revolution.[27] It was Trotsky, likewise, who led the charge against independent, nongovernment trade unions during the Workers' Opposition of the early 1920s. Given Trotsky's purportedly unrelenting support for the "militarization of labor," how did the allegations of Trotskyism come to be associated unmistakably with a full-throated critique of labor rationalization? The answer to this paradoxical question begins to emerge if the concept of Trotskyism is viewed not as a cause of political deviation, but rather as a discursive by-product of the general economic crisis that ended the era of the NEP.

The Economics of "Trotskyism"

The nature of the economic crisis that began to break in mid-1926 can be sketched here in only the broadest strokes.[28] Following a brief period of restabilization brought about by the full introduction of the gold-backed *chervonets* currency in 1924, inflationary tendencies resurfaced abruptly in mid-1926. The collapse of international grain prices, which plummeted in the mid-1920s due to postwar agricultural recovery, played a primary role in fermenting economic instability.[29] Faced with a constricting grain market and falling rates of profitability, Soviet grain exports fell unexpectedly and precipitously in 1925–1926.[30] Foreign currency and gold reserves, upon which the stability of the chervonets depended, ran short. In March of 1926, faced with depleted reserves, falling exports, and falling international confidence in the stability of the currency, the People's Commissariat of Finance (*Narkomfin*) effectively abandoned its defense of the chervonets, ending the brief experiment with the gold standard.[31]

The "snapping" of the interwar "gold thread," to use Karl Polanyi's phrase, radically loosened the fiscal straightjacket imposed by gold and opened the pathway toward rapid, credit-fueled industrial expansion.[32] As in the Civil War era, the Soviet state turned once again toward deliberate inflationary monetary policy as a mechanism for revolutionary restructuring. Beginning in mid-1926, the state steadily increased both credit and monetary supply. Means of payment increased some 6.6 percent from 1925 to 1926, jumped an additional 17 percent in 1927, and rose another 25 percent the following year. In short, the Soviet Union once again began to use the printing press to cover fiscal shortfalls and economic expansion.[33]

Expansionary fiscal policies undermined the chervonets monetary reform and intensified inflationary pressures. The output of industrial goods could not keep pace with increasing demand; rapidly expanding supplies of money chased increasingly scarce goods. On the private market, prices for manufactured goods began to rise sharply; one estimate indicates an increase of more than 117 percent from 1926 to early 1929.[34] Workers, in turn, began to call for wage increases to offset increases.[35] Within state-run institutions, price controls provided added incentive to dump devalued currency for goods with stable values.[36] The buying up of goods created widespread shortages; the resulting "goods famine" constituted the logical outcome of repressed, or cryptoinflationary pressures.[37] The widening crisis broke in full in late 1927 as the domestic circulation of goods dropped off dramatically and basic commodities disappeared from shelves. By mid-1928, the state was forced to reintroduce widespread rationing as a response to the crisis.[38] Complicating matters further, falling revenues from declining export profits strained abilities to service foreign loans, which drove the state toward increasingly severe austerity measures.[39]

The unfolding crisis generated intensive debate in the party organs concerning the roots of the seemingly irrational breakdown of market functions. As during earlier periods of market disequilibrium, explanations based upon structural factors lost out to explanations based upon malignant human agency. Voices in the party and the press increasingly attributed the economic crisis, including shortages and price increases, to the deliberate actions of hoarders, speculators, and economic counterrevolutionaries. Yet despite the rhetorical tendency to blame nefarious human agency for the crisis, the state response at the level of industrial policy implicitly accepted the structural nature of the crisis. In Moscow, the party center moved decisively toward the promotion of rapid industrialization and planning as mechanisms to overcome economic rupture. Industrial expansion would, in theory, expand the availability and drive down the cost of consumer goods, thereby restabilizing price levels and restoring economic equilibrium. Far from constituting a deliberate rejection of market principles on ideological grounds, the turn toward economic planning developed as a direct reaction to the economy of crisis.[40]

Viewed against the backdrop of the global economic crisis that broke in 1929, the turn to the managed economy appears as an early stage of the broader shift toward autarkic "Fordist" economies that took place throughout the industrial world.[41] Indeed, the Soviet response to the global economic crisis prefigured in critical ways the policies that would come to be associated in the post–World War II era with the economic policies of economic Keynesianism.[42] In the face of acute disequilibrium, Soviet policymakers reactively implemented controls on international capital flows by suspending the convertibility of the currency and implemented massive public works programs intended to combat rampant unemployment. Rapid industrial expansion and the development of fixed capital, the economic cornerstones of the unfolding Stalin Revolution, likewise served the social function of integrating surplus labor. From October 1926 to the end of 1929, state budgetary expenditure for the expansion of fixed capital more than doubled (jumping from 485 million rubles to more than 1.165 billion), an expansion that could hardly have been imagined under a system of tight monetary policy.[43]

In pursuing industrial expansion, the Soviet system demonstrated the greatest affinity for the type of industrial mechanization that formed the foundation of production in the capitalist world.[44] Yet the Soviet path to the managed industrial economy differed qualitatively from the capitalist model in critical respects. In the capitalist world, where rule of private property trumped social concerns, the economic crisis of 1929 led to a sharp curtailment of industrial production and the shedding of excess labor force in the hope of restoring equilibrium and profitability. The Soviet response to economic crisis was to expand industrial production and the industrial labor force for the sake of social stabilization and industrial expansion itself.

While constituting the central core of the economic restructuring unleashed by the Stalin Revolution, the policy of combating economic crisis through industrial expansion was a theoretical innovation of the Trotsky camp. The basic blueprint owed its origins to Evgenii Preobrazhenskii, the iconoclastic economist and close associate of Trotsky, who advocated for intensified industrialization as a mechanism of breaking through crises of overaccumulation.[45] Preobrazhenskii insisted that the brunt of this industrialization campaign should be borne by the peasantry, a proposal supported by Trotsky and the Left Opposition. The pro-NEP Bukharin faction warned, with good reason, that the social cost of industrialization expansion would prove devastating to the peasantry. Following the political defeat of the Bukharin camp and the turn to collectivization, the Stalin camp embraced Preobrazhenskii's logic of appropriating wealth from the peasantry as a mechanism of "primitive socialist accumulation," implementing this vision with ruthless brutality.

Despite the undeniable severity of the assault on the countryside, the innovation of the Stalin industrialization policy lay precisely in its willingness to extend the burden of forcible "primitive socialist accumulation" across the entirety of the social spectrum. The coercive extraction of wealth from the countryside coincided with the extreme devaluation of labor through increases in productivity norms and wage reductions. The productivization and devaluation of industrial labor, in short, constituted a primary weapon with which the Soviet Union combated economic crisis. The devaluation of labor came to be understood as the foundation for the establishment of, in Stalin's parlance, a "regime of economy" that would in turn lead to industrial "rationalization."[46]

Wherever possible, industrial rationalization occurred through the replacement of outdated plants and the introduction of new "labor-saving" (or, more correctly, labor-intensifying) technology in existing industries. Where this possibility did not yet exist, factory administrators (backed by state and the party directives) drove labor to greater levels of productivity in the old-fashioned way: they pressed for industry speed ups, higher productivity norms, and the more efficient exploitation of labor time. Taken together, these measures aimed at driving down costs of industrial production, and, in theory, restabilizing price levels throughout the economy. Productivization, in short, materialized as an alternative antidote to price instability and general economic crisis.[47]

In the course of the interparty struggles, the issue of labor productivization emerged as a central pillar of the Trotskyist critique of the Stalinist industrial policy. Notwithstanding his close association with the theories of Preobrazhenskii, his earlier defense of the "militarization of labor," and his repeated calls for economic planning, Trotsky became an increasingly blunt critic of the industrial policies adopted by VSNKh, Gosplan, and the party mainstream. Specifically, he attacked the Stalinist insistence that the fulfillment of increased productivity norms should constitute a precondition for any wage increases.[48] As inflationary pressures became evident in 1926, the Trotsky camp repeatedly called for wage increases for industrial workers, staking its claim to legitimacy on the basis of support from the industrial proletariat. The party center decisively rejected this call for a programmatic shift in priorities, insisting that workers shoulder the burden of short-term sacrifice in livelihood for long-term socialist construction.[49]

The resulting rapid devaluation of labor was a phenomenon that exceeded the most extreme fantasies of owners of industrial capital in the capitalist world. Tellingly, real wages were driven down by roughly 50 percent across the USSR during the first four years of the Stalin Revolution.[50] By contrast, real wages increased in the United States during the first years of the Great Depression, despite, or rather because of, the massive reduction in labor force.[51] In 1927 the Stalin bloc sought to further intensify production through the introduction of a seven-hour workday designed to streamline production, combat unemployment, and slow wage inflation. Taken in sum, rationalization entailed the radical devaluation of labor, which materialized as an integral part of the solution to price instability and general economic crisis.[52]

Throughout the Soviet territories, the party and state responded to the multifarious manifestations of economic crisis by introducing ever more intensive policies of rationalization and productivization. In Belorussia, the implementation of industrial rationalization exhibited tensions visible throughout the USSR. In theory, when officials spoke of the need to rationalize production, they stressed the ideal of intensified production through expanded mechanization. A March 1927 Belorussian Sovnarkom report stressed the need for a two- to threefold increase in industrial investment to rationalize production.[53] Building new factories and refurbishing outdated ones would allow Belorussian enterprises to "keep pace with the industry of the entire [Soviet] Union and offer competitive prices on the all-Union market."[54] Capital investment for new and refurbished plants doubled between 1925–1926 and 1926–1927,[55] and quadrupled again the following fiscal year.[56]

In practice, the emphasis on industrial investment masked the flip side of rationalization, which entailed a particularly selective process of labor devaluation. As consumer prices began to rise noticeably in 1926, workers in Belorussia agitated for wage increases to keep pace with inflation. Soviet and party organs in Minsk, following the Central Committee in Moscow, initially insisted that wage increases be predicated upon proportionate increases in industrial productivity.[57] Under pressure from Trotsky and the United Opposition, the Central Committee in Moscow acquiesced and agreed to increases in August 1926.[58] In October, the Belorussian Sovnarkom followed suit, but introduced telling discrepancies in the rates of increase. In a number of industries—including the linen, chemical, and distilling industries—the Sovnarkom ordered wage increases ranging from 10 to 12 percent; in the sewing, leatherworking, and metalworking industries, however, increases were to be capped at 3 percent.[59] The discrepancy reflected a broader pattern: between 1924–1925 and 1926–1927 wage increases significantly outpaced the growth in industrial productivity in the metalworking, minerals, food production, and paper industries; by contrast, productivity increases outpaced wage growth in the leatherworking, shoemaking, needleworking, and woodworking industries.[60] The underlying logic of this discrepancy stemmed from questions of equality; in general terms, the industries that received the highest rates of increase were those that historically offered the lowest wages. High-wage industries experienced the sharpest wage erosion. Coincidentally or otherwise, the industries targeted for restricted wage growth were also precisely those with the highest concentration of Jewish laborers.

The ratcheting up of productivist pressure was intensified further by sub-stantial investment in industrial plants.[61] Beginning in mid-1926, the Belorus-sian state inaugurated a broad campaign to mechanize and expand industrial production. The construction of the Krasnyi Metallist machine plant in Vitebsk in the summer of 1926 was followed by the refurbishment of the Energiia met-alworks in Minsk,[62] matchstick factories in Borisov (Krasnaia Berezina) and Gomel (Vezuvii), the Dvina linen factory in Vitebsk, and the paper factory Geroi Truda in Gomel.[63] A significant portion of new construction focused on the clothing, textile, and leather industries. New mechanized garment fac-tories were established in Vitebsk (Profintern) and Gomel (Gomshvei). In Minsk, a new shoemaking factory in the Nemiga market district reached full capacity in 1926.[64] In August 1927 Minsk welcomed the opening of the brand new Bolshevik tannery on the appropriately named Lekert Street.[65] Zviada, the main party organ, celebrated the new state-of-the-art facility, hygienic ven-tilation system, worker cafeteria, and five-hundred-horsepower engine capable of powering the production eighty-five-thousand high-quality hides per year.[66]

In addition to horsehides and box calf, however, the Bolshevik factory began to produce a less conventional by-product: Trotskyists. Over the course of 1926–1928, the factories and industries that experienced the most intensive brunt of the rationalization campaign became primary flashpoints of alleged Trotskyist Opposition in Belorussia. Of the above-mentioned factories, all but the Energiia and Dvina factories came to be identified as main centers of support for the United Opposition. Of the seventy-two identified Opposition-ists in Vitebsk in 1928, seventeen were members of the party cell at Profin-tern; sixteen were members of Metprom 3 at the Krasnyi Metallist works.[67] In Minsk, twenty-three of the identified Oppositionists were party members at the Bolshevik tannery; sixteen more worked at the Minsk shoe factory or the affiliated boot-making workshop.[68] In Gomel, the Vezuvyi matchstick factory, Trud' shoe factory, and the recently mechanized bristle-making factory were identified as centers of Opposition support in late 1927.[69] As the economic cri-sis unfolded, the Opposition gained its strongest footholds in industries sub-jected most intensively to the devaluation and mechanization of labor. Once again, the targeted industries tended to be those with high concentrations of Jewish labor.

Making Workers Trotskyists

The first hints of the anti-Trotskyist campaign in Belorussia coincided with the onset of economic crisis in the spring and summer of 1926. The campaign ini-tially began with broad investigations into allegations of oppositional activity in local party cells. By late 1926 the campaign against Trotskyism had reached

the highest circles of political power in Minsk when Sergei Mikhailovich Gessen, a leading Belorussian Bolshevik (and fervent anti-Bundist crusader), was
driven from his position as the head of Agitprop due to his outspoken support
for Trotsky. The anti-Trotskyist offensive gained steam through 1927, as the
Central Committee of the Party (TsK KPB), and particularly the Okrug and
Central Control Commissions, took the lead in ferreting out supporters of the
Opposition across the republic. The campaign climaxed in the months sur-
rounding the expulsion of Trotsky, Zinoviev, and Kamenev from the party in
December of 1927, as the KPB organized mass meetings and votes throughout
Belorussia to demonstrate support for the expulsions.[70]

Notwithstanding the broad political campaign, internal party correspondence suggests that self-understood Oppositionists remained a distinctly limited group until a rather late date. In July 1927 Secretary of the Central Control
Committee Pavel Grigor'evich Vilenstovich sent an atypically frank report
to Emel'ian Mikhailovich Iaroslavskii, the secretary of the all-Union TsKK,
assessing the state of the Opposition across Belorussia. The report delineated
two distinct forms of anti-Party activities.[71] On one hand, Vilnestovich identified a handful of "conscious" Oppositionists, drawn mostly from the intelligentsia, who carried on active political agitation against the party. Included
in this group were Gessen, Fedor Tikhonovich Volvok, a university lecturer
at BGU in Minsk, Ia. M. Drapkin, a museum curator in Gomel, and several
students and low-ranking party officials dispersed across the Republic. On the
other hand, he identified a second, much broader threat: workers with no formal ties to the Opposition who nevertheless expressed increasingly sharp criticisms of party policy. These "hidden oppositionists" (*skrytye oppoztitsionery*),
for the most part "nonconscious" and "politically illiterate" workers, expressed
oppositional sentiments even though they did not consciously support the
United Opposition. Many had previous ties to other parties, particularly
the Bund; many others came from a "petit-bourgeois-trading environment,"
(*meshchansko-torgovaia sreda*) with strong Bundist influence. Dropping euphe-
misms, Vilenstovich cut to the chase: "Characteristically for these groups, particularly among former members of Jewish parties, there still appears to be
hidden sympathy for the figure of Trotsky."[72]

By attributing support for the Opposition to latent ethnic solidarity, Vilenstovich prefigured what would ultimately become the party consensus. Yet the
more nuanced sections of his report suggested a far more complicated reality,
detailing a litany of worker complaints about falling wages, pressures of industrial rationalization, unemployment, and rising prices. Records from party
meetings convened across Minsk during the summer of 1926 to discuss the
danger of the Opposition further accentuate the predominantly economistic

nature of worker demands. While outright support for the United Opposition remained muted, concerns over wages and rising prices were rife.[73] A list of eighty-four questions about the Opposition gathered from rank-and-file party members from the Minsk Tannery focused almost exclusively on economic issues. Among the workers' questions were the following: "Why do productive norms for workers increase, while wages stay at the same level?" "Doesn't the increasingly high cost of everything amount to an actual lowering of wages?" "How much has unemployment increased . . . as a result of the 'Regime of Economy'?"[74] In the cell of the Minsk glassmaking factory Proletarii, workers called for wage increases to keep up with rising prices, while defenders of the party line argued that wage increases would only intensify inflationary pressures.[75]

Concerns over wages likewise constituted a primary theme in the clash that took place during a mass meeting convened in the Minsk Shoemaking Factory cell in August 1926 to discuss the danger posed by the Opposition. Comrade Shafer (who would eventually turn against the Opposition) asked the leaders of the cell specifically about disagreements within the party leadership over wages. "Why," he pointedly asked the cell leadership, "did [the party] not think about increasing wages until the Opposition [raised the issue]?"[76] The debate within the shoemakers' cell, which raged over the ensuing year, revealed a good deal of consideration of the issues at hand, as many workers proved remarkably well versed in both questions of economy and the central points of political dispute between the Stalinist and Opposition camps.[77] One shoemaker, a certain Comrade Edinovich (likely a non-Jew, and certainly a non-Oppositionist), took a critical and perceptive stance toward the call for increased wages. "For us, in the given moment," Edinovich argued, "it doesn't make any sense to talk about increasing wages, because our chervonets *is sinking* and the workers are not able to purchase products, because they are more expensive."[78] Comrade Klionskii disagreed: "We would be able to purchase more, if they increased our wages, but only if this did not fall as a burden on our chervonets." To this, Comrade Shneider chimed in to note that the "they could pay the workers five rubles if they would lower the prices on products, so that we could live on five rubles a month." The problem, he suggested, was that prices were not falling, but increasing. Moreover, he chastised party leaders for denying pay increases to rank-and-file workers while amply rewarding "executives" in the factory. "A few of the executives receive up to 183 rubles salary, and their wives also receive 150 rubles—from where do they get the money," Comrade Shneider wondered. Ultimately, he drew his own conclusion: "the economic regime is always deflected onto the shoulders of the workers."[79]

Faced with widespread worker anger over stagnant wages and rising prices, the Belorussian Sovnarkom finally pushed through wage increases in October

1926. Yet as noted above, wage increases exhibited marked differentials, privileging industries with the lowest paid workers.[80] Overt anger remained most pronounced in industries targeted for restricted wage growth, notably the leatherworking, shoemaking, needleworking, and woodworking industries.[81] Over the course of 1927 worker grievances in these industries expanded to include broader criticisms of the rationalization and streamlining of industrial production. Increasingly, worker agitation converged with criticisms of industrial policy articulated by the United Opposition, blurring the line between "conscious" and "hidden" opposition.

In Moscow, the high-water mark of support for the Trotskyite Opposition in the metalworking industry occurred in 1923–1924. The United Opposition experienced a revival of support in the summer of 1926 but saw their influence decline thereafter.[82] Archival records suggest that in Belorussia this trend did not hold. As noted above, far from reaching its pinnacle in the mid-1920s, alleged opposition of a Trotskyite variety was rather muted, to say the least, in Belorussia in the 1923–1924 period. With the formation of the United Opposition of Trotsky, Zinoviev, and Kamenev in 1926, the Opposition gained steam in Belorussia. The party mainstream, in turn, took increasingly aggressive measures to stamp out grassroots opposition. During the closing months of 1928, as the party organization in Moscow debated and decided the fate of the Oppositionists, the Belorussian party staged mass party cell meetings across the republic. These meetings revealed significant support for the Opposition message, at least in specific pockets. In addition to these meetings, the party Control Commission carried out extensive investigations into alleged Opposition cells across Belorussia, claiming to have discovered widespread underground networks in Minsk, Bobruisk, Gomel, Borisov, and Vitebsk, among other locales. These measures led to the public expulsion of an array of alleged Oppositionists throughout the late 1927–1928 period.

While it might be tempting to suggest that the alleged upsurge in oppositional sentiment was but a figment of a paranoid collective Soviet imagination, evidence suggests otherwise. Oppositional voices increased in number and volume during the 1926–1927 period, due to a variety of factors. As stated, disputes over wages played a primary role in fermenting a rebellious mood. Similarly, the United Opposition alliance between Trotsky and his erstwhile rivals, Zinoviev and Kamenev, gave greater rhetorical weight to the movement and helped build the ranks of the Opposition; while the former Menshevik Trotsky always remained an outsider in the party, Zinoviev and Kamenev had been Old Bolsheviks with longstanding (if sometimes quite volatile) ties to Lenin. A third, related factor resulted from the breakdown of the agricultural market and the drying up of goods in the city. As prices rose, workers voiced increasingly strident criticisms of kulak elements in the countryside, purported to be responsible for the shortages by jacking up prices and selling grain to speculators.[83] Evidence suggests that agitation over price inflation and wages continued to mount throughout 1927, particularly as the market seized up and goods disappeared from shop shelves in the autumn. A report from a mass meeting held within the builders union in late 1927 emphasized the role that such issues played in fueling opposition in the union. One worker, the report noted, summed up the basic condition: "the private trader (*chastnika*) near my apartment raised prices, but my pay hasn't gone up, so everything is more expensive at the bazaar."[84]

Cryptoinflationary pressures, which already generated agitation over the issue of wages, introduced a fourth factor into this volatile mix. As price pressure crept upward, economic policy makers emphasized the need to lower prices through price controls and the rationalization of production. Oppositional agitation raised its head with the intensified campaign to productivize labor and drive down prices. Opposition within the furniture makers workshop run by LesBel, the Belorussian lumber administration, gained strength over the course of 1926–1927. A Control Commission investigation into the situation at LesBel attributed the intensely agitated mood to the political activity of the "infamous Oppositionist" Fedor Tikhonovich Volkov. Among the most active members of the Opposition underground in Belorussia, Volkov purportedly returned to the furniture workshop repeatedly to stir up workers and members of the governing board of the woodworkers union, converting a number of union leaders, as well as rank-and-file members from the "petit-bourgeois milieu" to the cause of the Opposition. While couched in terms of agent-driven political deviation, the Control Commission report hinted at underlying concerns over the effort to productivize labor. "Comrade Volkov came out against the introduction of rationalization [policies]. In his speeches he said that the party line on rationalization would bring about an increase in unemployment, and, following this, the worsening of conditions for laborers." Rather than strengthen the union between workers and peasants, "rationalization," Volkov allegedly continued, was the path to the "splitting of the union between the city and countryside."[85] His criticism of the vaguely defined program for rationalization won over an unspecified number of workers and several dozen komsomol members associated with the union. Nevertheless, the union ultimately voted to exclude Volkov, along with one other Oppositionist and four komsomol members (identified as coming "from the kustari"), from the party ranks in late 1927.[86]

What, exactly, "rationalization" meant in the eyes of the oppositional workers can be gleaned from the Control Commission report from the investigation of the Minsk leather mill Bolshevik. The report emphasized that worker hostility within the cell spiked in July and August 1927. Again, the Control Commission blamed oppositional agitation on politics alone. The infamous Comrade Volkov and Comrade Gol'man, another "well-known Trotskyite," allegedly infiltrated the cell, rousing the rabble. The primary rallying issue, the Control Commission insisted, was the question of whether the party should exclude Trotsky and Zinoviev from its ranks.[87] Yet the report on the Bolshevik leather mill also noted a myriad of other concerns tied to the question of rationalization. The mill, and the leather industry in general, the report noted, recently experienced massive reorganization. Leather production had previously been dispersed over four small, separate workshops around Minsk. In early 1927 the Belorussian Leather Administration built a new, large leather mill in Minsk, closed the four small shops, and consolidated production. As a result, the leatherworkers experienced widespread layoffs. Wages for lower-skilled workers were, on top of this (or, in part, as a result of this) extremely low, the report frankly acknowledged; yet such grievances were dismissed as a failure of workers to understand the correct party line.[88] To the familiar complaints relating to the rationalization of production, the report on the leatherworkers mill added another. Opposition speeches, the report emphasized, repeatedly focused on the problem of the "compression" (*uploteniia*) of the workday. Oppositional leatherworkers, in other words, denounced the attempt to speed up and compress the labor process, focusing much of their wrath on efforts to further rationalize production through the introduction of a seven-hour workday.[89]

Among the many proposals to intensify labor productivity, the plan to introduce a seven-hour workday generated particular animosity among alleged Oppositionists. Initially proposed by Bukharin in the hopes of outflanking the Opposition in the scramble for worker support, the seven-hour day was imagined as a testament to the progressive labor policies of the Soviet Union.[90] By implementing the seven-hour day, the Soviet Union would free workers to focus on projects of self-improvement, education, or other pursuits. In theory, the cutting of the workday below that of the normative eight-hour day in the advanced capitalist world would have occurred without a corresponding cut in total compensation.[91] The policy was also intended to alleviate unemployment by drawing more workers into factory production to make up the reduced hours.

As envisioned, the seven-hour day was imagined as a move toward that time in the unspecified socialist future when workers could return to a life of hunting in the morning, fishing in the afternoon, and criticizing in the evening. Yet the responses from supporters of the Opposition suggest that workers understood the proposed policy as anything other than the long-awaited emancipation from unnecessary labor time envisioned by Marx. One metalworker in Metprom factory No. 3 in Vitebsk challenged the productivist math of the Central Committee, noting that the proposed factory norms called for an 11 percent increase in productivity, but only a 9 percent increase in wages. The same worker scoffed at the notion that the proposal would lead to the shortening of the workday: "It is no secret that among us, 30 percent work overtime." Rather than lighten the labor load, the seven-hour workday would intensify the labor burden. Comrade Zabezhinskii, a self-proclaimed and outspoken Oppositionist, added "the seven-hour day gives us nothing; it is only agitation. We need to correctly enforce the eight-hour day."[92] In the eyes of these Vitebsk metalworkers, the promise of the seven-hour day appeared as little more than an illusory ploy to intensify the already fictitious eight-hour working day.[93]

The metalworkers of Vitebsk had no monopoly on skepticism concerning the ulterior motives underlying the rhetoric of the seven-hour day. They were joined by leatherworkers and shoemakers in Gomel,[94] boot makers in Minsk,[95] and shoemakers in Bobruisk.[96] Workers in the "Tomskii" woodworking factory in Gomel rose up in unison to denounce the proposed measure. "The workers are against the seven-hour work day," Comrade Moisei Naumov Freidlin declared. Comrade Polovinkov dismissed the proposal as a "manifest display of showing off for foreign governments." Comrade Perstin brushed aside claims that the seven-hour day would help to solve the problem of unemployment. "We move toward the worsening of conditions for the workers," he warned. Comrade Bykhovskii concurred: "In the present time we produce in eight hours what we used to produce in twelve; and if we further introduced the seven-hour day, then all of these hours would still remain on the neck of the workers." Even if production intensified in this fashion, Comrade Bykhovskii lamented, "we will still not be as efficient as mechanized production."[97]

Comrade Bykhovski's despondent observation pointed to the underlying, crucial social reality. Trotskyism, or allegations of Trotskyism, spread most broadly in those industries that faced the fundamental turbulence that the shift to mechanized production necessarily unleashed on artisans and petty handworkers everywhere. This was hardly a novel phenomenon. At the dawn of the machine age in England, such social groups stood at the forefront of agitational activism in the form of machine breaking, strikes, demonstrations, and the like.[98] In revolutionary Belorussia, on the cusp between the collapsing world of handwork and the rise of the Soviet Industrial Revolution, the expression of such anxieties and concerns frequently came to be understood by authorities as political opposition.[99] This was no mere exercise in discourse construction. Discourse fused with the politics of productivization.

One clear example of the melding of opposition to productivization with the language and politics of the Opposition occurred in the Bobruisk needle-workers factory (Bobrshvei) during the second half of 1927. Reports from the Control Commission investigation stated that opposition in the cell of twenty-nine workers broke out in late 1926. Workers in the cell, the report continued, pointed to their material hardship to explain their support for the Opposition. The anonymous reporter dismissed these claims out of hand, noting that "lack of material means among the party members and candidates must not be considered a source of opposition." These workers, the report asserted "receive the very highest pay for workers."[100] Rather, the report attributed the oppositional mood as an emphatically political deviation. The real source of the Opposition, the report continued, was "the presence [in the cell] of workers who emigrated from other parties." In particular, the report stressed the presence of two unidentified Bundists in the cell, along with the worker El'ia L'vovich, who was reported to have had direct ties with the opposition.

The situation in Bobrshvei, already tense in 1926, became more divisive over the summer of 1927. The report blamed the spike in Opposition activity on a worker Oppositionist studying in Moscow, Gdali Kitaichik, who purportedly stirred up trouble following his return to Bobruisk for his summer break. Following the arrival of Kitaichik, "workers became more animated," and he reportedly recruited half of the Bobrshvei union—including the cell secretary, Moisei Girshi Feigin—to the Opposition. The Control Commission once again emphasized the role that political agitation played in fermenting opposition in the workshop. A separate Control Commission report likewise blamed Kitaichik, along with fellow MBTU students Vikhman and Faivusovich, for fermenting Trotskyism and oppositional attitudes among the members of the Bobruisk shoemakers' cell.[101]

It is most likely that political agitators did indeed play a key role in building opposition within Bobrshvei. Reports on the situation within the tumultuous union repeatedly stressed politics in order to explain oppositional tendencies. Echoes of underlying economic grievances, however, repeatedly bubbled up to complicate simple explanations derived from politics alone. Bobrshvei reports noted that opposition to the seven-hour workday constituted the primary issue around which workers in the sewing industry united during 1927. Workers decried the policy as a measure to pave the way for the introduction of a third work shift into the workshop.[102] One unidentified worker denounced these proposed policies, decrying the fact that the "rationalization and the compression of work is placed on the shoulders of the workers and further intensifies the exploitation of the workers." Such sentiments found open ears among the rank and file of the cell, and even greater support among the nonparty workers in the workshop, many of whom trumpeted the expulsion of Oppositionists as a victory against Soviet rule. "You exclude them from your [Bolshevik] family," one nonparty needleworker reportedly declared, "and they return to us in our family."[103]

Whatever the cause, members of Bobrshvei responded to official indifference to their concerns by becoming explicit and unrepentant Trotskyists. The circumstances in the Bobruisk needleworkers workshop came to a head in late 1927, beginning with the local celebration of the tenth anniversary of the October Revolution. To commemorate the victory, the Bobruisk needleworkers made a pointed collective decision. They pooled donations from party and nonparty workers and honored the historic event by purchasing an iconoclastic collective gift to the workshop—a bust of Trotsky. After proudly placing the bust in the front window of the workshop, the needleworkers unsuccessfully attempted to purchase a matching present—a picture of Trotsky from his Red Army period—to hang on the workshop wall. Needless to say, things had gotten out of hand. Local party leaders from the Bobruisk city party committee accused the workshop members of partaking in the "idolization of Trotsky" and demanded that the bust be removed. The needleworkers grudgingly complied. One Oppositionist, S. G. Kazimirovskii, took the bust of Trotsky and put it on display inside his apartment.[104]

Rather than abating, tensions continued to rise in Bobruisk through the Fifteenth Party Congress in December. A Central Committee resolution from Moscow calling for the exclusion of the Oppositionists gained minimal support in the Bobrshvei cell, with six workers voting against the resolution and twelve abstaining, meaning that eighteen of twenty-nine workers expressed sympathy, if not support, for the Opposition.[105] The party responded with direct measures by rounding up Trotskyist agitators. When dragged before the Bobruisk Control Commission, Comrade Kazimirovskii defiantly refused to capitulate. While he "voluntarily defended Soviet power in the past," Kazimirovskii declared before the commission that he "would no longer do so, since Soviet power and the party have degenerated."[106] The Control Commission expelled Kazimirovskii, along with L'vovich, the other organizer of the Trotsky idolization festival, who left town without turning in his party card.[107]

As reports concerning the Bobrshvei collective suggest, a critical tension existed in official interpretations of the growing worker unrest that spread throughout the second half of 1927. Read against the background of the rapidly deteriorating economic situation, worker agitation appeared as a comprehensible response to deepening economic and structural crisis. As the Central Committee line swung decisively toward austerity and intensified rationalization as mechanisms for combating the crisis, such explanations proved politically unacceptable. Control Commissions across the republic exhibited remarkable uniformity in reducing manifestation of worker anger to politics alone and attributing opposition to the pernicious influence of malignant political agents. Despite detailing the critical role that economic restructuring played in triggering worker agitation at the Bolshevik tannery, for example, the Minsk Okrug Control Commission ultimately blamed opposition in the tannery on the malignant influence of outside troublemakers—the "infamous" Comrades Volkov and Gol'man—who allegedly incited the disgruntled workers into full rebellion.[108] The OKK placed the remainder of the culpability squarely on the shoulders of the leatherworkers themselves. Rather than addressing the legitimacy of worker economic grievances, the OKK attributed Oppositional stirrings to the "weak political development of a large portion of party members, and the presence of a significant number of workers who come from the petit-bourgeois milieu/former kustari."[109] In other words, the fundamental problem stemmed from the manipulations of political wreckers and the debased social origin of the workers in question, not the deterioration of labor conditions.

It was not, however, the "social" origins of recalcitrant workers alone that came under question. Rather, the unspoken, and in certain respects unspeakable, reality was that a significant portion of the Oppositionists were marked ethnically. Returning to a familiar script, party officials gravitated toward the category of "Bundism" to account for the overrepresentation of Jews in the ranks of the Opposition.

Making Trotskyists Jews

Events like those that transpired in Bobruisk—including anti-Trotskyite campaigns, meetings, hearings, expulsions, and the like—took place across Belorussia throughout 1927–1928. In Gomel, Vitebsk, Minsk, Bobruisk, Mogilev, and other cities, as well as many shtetlekh, the party undertook extensive campaigns to drive from its ranks the supporters of the Opposition.[110] In local cells throughout the republic, the party carried out an extensive campaign to warn of the danger of Trotskyism. In the months surrounding the Fifteenth Party Congress of December 1927, party cells throughout the republic held mass meetings to put to a vote two key resolutions from the congress. The first resolution, "On Work in the Countryside" outlined plans for collectivization in the villages and intensified productivization in industry. The second resolution concerned the expulsion of Trotsky and Zinoviev. Voting against or abstaining from the vote for either measure was taken as a sign of support for the Opposition. Consequently, the party kept close tabs on the results of these votes, compiled lists of Oppositionists from them, and used them to track and at times expel members of the Opposition.[111]

In the end, only a handful of members of the party faced formal accusations of supporting the Opposition. A concluding report placed the total number of party members who demonstrated their support of the Opposition by voting against either one of the resolutions at eighty-six people, of a party of about thirty-two thousand total members in 1928.[112] An estimated 254 additional members abstained from one or both of the votes in question.[113] In total, thirty-six members of the Belorussian Communist Party were excluded following the Fifteenth Party Congress.[114] A composite report from the Minsk Okrug likewise maintained that less than 1 percent of the more than eight thousand local party workers supported the Opposition in 1927.[115]

Based on the archival records, however, these numbers should be taken with a grain of salt. The numbers for Minsk, at the very least, appear to be severely underreported.[116] Moreover, the official numbers at most reflected only the hard core of Oppositionists who refused to recant under pressure from the party organization. Many workers who initially joined the United Opposition or voted for the Opposition platforms ultimately reversed their position under pressure. Following the Fifteenth Party Congress, the seven Oppositionists left in the Minsk Bootmaking Workshop all repudiated their previous support for the Opposition, following the expulsion of four ringleaders.[117] The five Opposition members of the Minsk builders union—all identified as young, unemployed members of the union—recanted after a stern talking to from the Control Commission.[118] In the party organization in the city of Rechitsa, fourteen of the fifteen initial Oppositionists—all of whom supported the Opposition due to the issue of the seven-hour day—were convinced to change their position and vote with the majority in a second round of voting.[119] Clearly, the motives behind these professed rejections of the Opposition were mixed, insofar as loss of party membership entailed loss of privileges. In the Bobruisk shoemakers cell, for example, cell leaders complained that they received a number of "insincere" letters from members condemning their own previous oppositional activity.[120] In addition, evidence suggests that for each outspoken Oppositionist, there were certainly several who remained quiet. One worker for Gomel stated the problem succinctly: "it is difficult to enter into the debates, because the regional committee (*raikom*) will sack us."[121] The United Opposition consequently claimed, plausibly, that their support would have been greater if allowed to operate openly.[122]

The final official numbers of Oppositionists ultimately reflected the state of affairs after all measures had been taken to isolate hard-core Oppositionists from the more malleable rank and file. Moreover, the demographic weight of the professed Opposition mattered far less than the weight of their arguments in worker meetings, and it is clear that they had the ears of many fellow workers. Finally, and most importantly, the number of Oppositionists may have been small in relation to the party as a whole, but they were substantially more pronounced among the ranks of party workers within productive apparatuses in the light industry sector. It should be noted that there existed virtually no opposition among certain rather crucial industries, such as railroad workers, sanitation workers, glassmakers, and workers in the chemical industries. The patterns of opposition arguably reveal as much about the absolute stratification of the labor force in Belorussia as it does about any other contributing factor.

Support for the Opposition in Belorussia cut across national boundary lines. However, given the peculiarities of the labor force, support for the Opposition came overwhelmingly from Jewish workers. In Vitebsk, for example, all but three of the forty party members who voted against the expulsion of Trotsky and Zinoviev were Jews; of these, all but two were workers at the bench.[123] Twenty-eight of them had joined the party between 1925 and 1927, suggesting that they were, on the whole, quite young. All but six were men. In Minsk, of the 144 or so party members who voted against or abstained from voting on the expulsion of Trotsky and Zinoviev in the third district, 116 were Jews (80 percent).[124] Jewish shoemakers, tailors, and seamstresses dominated the list of Oppositionists in Bobruisk. As in Minsk and Vitebsk, Jews constituted some fifty of the sixty-odd identified Oppositionists and sympathizers in Bobruisk.[125] Included among the Jewish Oppositionists in Bobruisk were Comrades Kitaichik, Kazimirovskii, Feigin and virtually all of the members of the Opposition.[126]

Jews likewise figured prominently among those individuals who were ultimately kicked out of the Belorussian Communist party for oppositional work. Of the thirty-six party members excluded from the party, twenty-three were Jews (63 percent). Of those identified as being prominent ringleaders of the Opposition—Fedor Volkov and two shoemakers, Levin and Fuks (Minsk), Feigin and L'vovich (Bobruisk), Kalman Zalmanovich Kaplan (Vitebsk), and Drapkin, Kuskin, and the shoemaker Gorelik (Gomel)—all but Volkov (Russian) were Jews. Seven of the excluded Jewish members had previously been members of the Bund (including Fuks, Levin, Kaplan, and Gorelik) and one, Kuksin, had been a Poalei Tsionist. Tellingly, seventeen of the twenty-three excluded Jewish Oppositionists joined the party *before* 1922, meaning that they were most likely among the older members of their party cells. In addition, almost half of the expelled Jewish Oppositionists were white-collar workers, suggesting that the party proved more lenient with workers at the bench who objected to the party line.[127]

The overwhelming presence of Jewish activists among the ranks of the Oppositionists immediately suggests a number of commonsensical observations. It was probably the case that a number of Oppositionists and sympathizers voted with the United Opposition because Trotsky, Zinoviev, and Kamenev were understood to be Jewish Communists locked in a struggle with *goyish* Communists. Yet such conjectures find little evidence in the archival record, at least on the part of the Oppositionists themselves. Among the reported speeches of Oppositionists, one is hard-pressed to find evidence suggesting that ethnic solidarity shaped voting patterns. Of course, it should be understood that a separation likely existed between sentiments stated in public forums and those uttered unrecorded behind closed doors. Nevertheless, the recorded speech suggests, at the most, the belief that Trotsky, Zinoviev, and Kamenev had been singled out unfairly for alleged mistakes, while the mistakes of non-Jewish Communists like Stalin, Bukharin, and Tomskii went unexamined.

From the other side of the fence, there exists substantial evidence suggesting that antisemitic attitudes at times fueled antioppositional sentiment. One report recorded a variety of typical comments made during a meeting on the Opposition at metalwork shop Metprom No. 1 in Vitebsk: "To the devil with Trotsky!; It serves him right; Trotsky—king of the yids (*zhidovskyi tsar'*); it should have happened a long time ago," and so forth.[128] Several reports on the popular mood in the party ranks in Minsk emphasized the prevalence of antisemitic sentiments among some party members. One Professor Turnel'taub, in a lecture on the subject of antisemitism delivered before party members in Minsk in January of 1928, claimed to have heard the repeated comment that "all of the Oppositionists are petty shopkeepers who hang on the words of Lev Davidovich [Trotsky]." When asked about their sentiments, the mutterers of such sentiments invariably responded, the lecturer noted, in the following fashion: "Why is there antisemitism? . . . The Opposition brought it about."[129] Another worker in Minsk reportedly noted that "the majority of the Oppositionists are Jews—they want to grab the whole party in their hands."[130]

Such expressions of outright anti-Jewish sentiment fell beyond the limits of acceptable party discourse, but they were hardly isolated utterances.[131] By all accounts, the period of the anti-Trotskyite campaigns coincided with a significant resurgence in antisemitic agitation across Belorussia.[132] Cognizant of the growing threat, the party launched widespread rhetorical campaigns against antisemitism. Yet even as it sought to combat antisemitism in its most explicit forms, party discourse about the nature of Trotskyism explicitly linked the political deviation with the stigma of Jewishness. Internal party reports occasionally stated the matter openly. A 1928 report from the Control Commission in the Orshansk Okrug, for example, explained away the large number of Jews in the local Opposition as evidence of ethnic allegiance. The Jews of the region, the report claimed, supported the Opposition out of a sense of ethnic solidarity, since "the Central Committee is composed only of 'goyim.'"[133]

Most frequently, the inference that Trotskyism constituted a particularly Jewish deviation was articulated in subtler tones. Internal party reports attributed oppositional positions not to economic concerns or even political principle, but to ontological social categories, which were themselves laden with ethnic associations. A secret report from the secretary of the TsKK to the okrug offices explained that "one always notices petit-bourgeois leanings on the part of the comrades" in the shoemakers and needleworkers cells, "among whom the largest part come from the kustari."[134] Others, like the aforementioned Pavel Vilenstovich, blamed the weak political development of Oppositionists on "the petit-bourgeois, trading milieu" from which Oppositionists invariably seemed to originate. The categories utilized to delegitimize the Opposition were, of course, abstract class designations. Yet in the context of Belorussia, where the overwhelming bulk of kustari and merchants were in actuality Jewish, social categories necessarily suggested ethnic marking and ethnicized meaning.

The utilization of purportedly objective social categories to explain away the persistence of opposition left room for ethnic ambiguity. Such ambiguity was absent from the most common rhetorical tactic utilized to undercut the legitimacy of the Opposition. Defenders of the emerging party orthodoxy increasingly sought to delegitimize the Opposition by associating it with discredited, non-Bolshevik political parties—in particular, the Jewish Bund. Far from being simply a designation of previous political affiliation, the charge of Bundism carried with it a series of unmistakable and undesirable connotations. Bundists allegedly promoted narrow trade unionism, emphasized nationality over internationality, rejected state campaigns toward linguistic Belorussianization, sought to "protect" the labor market in "their" industries by speaking Yiddish on the shop floor, and generally opposed efforts to integrate the Jewish labor force into the general labor force.[135]

As anti-Trotskyist campaigns spread, party observers repeatedly attributed oppositional leanings to the persistence of Bundist influence in the party. A 1928 report from the TsKK to the Executive Committee of the Party minced few words, explaining that cities like Minsk, Gomel, and Bobruisk had become hotbeds of Opposition precisely because they had previously been Bundist strongholds. "Former members of Jewish parties," the report asserted, "display secret sympathy for Trotsky."[136] The Bobruisk Okrug Control Commission blamed the strength of the local Opposition on the prevalence of "former Bundists" among the local, largely kustar' working class. These Bundists, the Bobruisk OKK complained, disrupted a local party conference with shouts of "Long Live Trotsky" and managed to bring a number of komsomol members under their influence.[137] A report on the Bobruisk shoemakers cell likewise attributed the groundswell of support for the Opposition on the "persistent Bundist–petit-bourgeois (*meshchanskii*) smell (*dushok*)" in the cell.[138] The party kept close tabs on former Bundists in the Opposition ranks and publicized these affiliations, noting repeatedly that seven of the thirty-six members ultimately expelled from the party for their dogged oppositionism had been former Bundists.[139]

Insofar as the Bund, historically speaking, stressed the primacy of nationality, it is entirely probable that some former Bundists felt drawn to the United Opposition out of a sense of national solidarity, despite Trotsky's own notoriously hostile views toward the Bund. Whether these groups of former Bundists drove the politics of opposition on the floor in "Jewish" industries remains, however, a different matter. From archival records, there is little doubt that while former Bundists did indeed join the ranks of the Opposition, the overwhelming bulk of those Jews who sided with the Opposition had no previous party affiliation. Of the 264 Jewish party members who either voted with or abstained from voting against the United Opposition position across Belorussia during the Fifteenth Party Congress, about two dozen had previously been members of the Bund. Nearly 70 percent of all Jewish active and passive supporters of the Opposition across Belorussia joined the party following the Lenin Levy of 1924, meaning that they were likely younger workers without previous political experience.[140] Of the thirty-seven or so Jewish workers who voted with the Opposition in Vitebsk, only one had been a Bundist. Of the 122 Jewish Oppositionists in Minsk, 15 had Bundist backgrounds.[141] Even in Bobruisk, the purported hotbed of Bundism, only three of the identified Oppositionists had previously been Bundists.[142]

In sum, a rather significant disjuncture existed between allegations of Bundist influence and the actual presence of former Bundists in the Opposition ranks. Regardless of the reality, the association of the Opposition with Bundism served a discernible functional role. The appellation of Bundism marked the Opposition as being recalcitrant, nonintegrated, and definitively Jewish. As the anti-Trotskyist campaign unfolded, party activists at all levels increasingly stressed the "ethnic" dimension of Trotskyism through outright assertion, association, or innuendo. Ignoring the economic tensions that drove Jewish workers into the ranks of the Opposition, the political language of Trotskyism asserted, subtly or otherwise, that the problem lay not with the economics of intensified rationalized production, but with the ontological difference of those who opposed such overwhelming rationality.

As the campaign against Trotskyism intensified, assertions concerning the primacy of "ethnicity" within the oppositional ranks took on an increasingly ascribed character. Unlike the initial campaigns against Bundism, wherein many Jewish members of the party acknowledged, embraced, or repudiated the historical relationship between the Bund and Jewish working class identity, few, if any, Jewish Oppositionists justified their political choice by pointing to purported cultural affinities or practices. Rather, the fact of "ethnic" belonging and solidarity was increasingly asserted from without, suggesting the murky line at which a language of ethnicity began to bleed into a language of race. In the era of fundamental structural instability and rising antisemitism, such language played the functional role of disciplining labor. By marking political resistance—as well as the array of economic concerns that framed the Opposition—as not simply ethnically dubious, but ontologically different, the rhetoric of anti-Trotskyism silenced and undercut economic grievances on "Jewish" shop floors.

Unsurprisingly, as opposition became ethnically marked, many Jewish laborers turned into vociferous defenders of the party line. Comrade Slonimskii, a rather typical worker from Minsk, joined the majority in denouncing the Opposition during a mass meeting in 1927. "It is necessary to say to Zinoviev and Trotsky," he declared, "for the betrayal of the party, you get your just desserts."[143] Another party member, Rubinskii, declared during a 1927 meeting in Bragin, "Factionalism destroys our party, and in the goal of expanding the unity of the party, the most decisive measures should be taken to against the Opposition."[144] Comrade Shafer, the shoemaker introduced above as an early supporter of the United Opposition in the Minsk Shoemaking Factory under VSNKh, broke with the Opposition early and eventually became a fierce critic. During an open meeting of the Minsk shoemakers union in 1927, Shafer went on the offensive, calling on the party to stamp out deviation: "it is necessary for us to carry out an urgent struggle against the Opposition. At the present time, we don't need discussion; we need a unified, unbroken idea of what should be—not a schism (*raskol*). Down with the Opposition!"[145] Comrade Gol'blat forcefully seconded this opinion: "the Opposition thinks that they represent the point of view among the whole working mass . . . because they use pay increases as bait." The workers, however, do not follow them, Gol'blat continued, "because they know that the Opposition is mistaken in their beliefs."[146]

In denouncing the economic policies of the Opposition, Comrade Gol'blat asserted the superiority of a regime of rationalized, intensified production. By making this claim on behalf of "the workers," a fully universal abstraction, Comrade Gol'blat implicitly sided against the purportedly particular claims of Trotskyist labor—which is to say implicitly petty-bourgeois, Bundist, and Jewish labor. As opposition became marked with the stigma of ascribed ethnicity, the only way forward for a shoemaker in Minsk was to transform himself into a proponent of a regime of abstract, undifferentiated labor. Or, stated otherwise, into a Stalinist.

Conclusion

Between 1926 and the end of 1928 the Bolshevik party in Belorussia waged a determined and aggressive campaign to wipe out alleged support for the United Opposition in the ranks of the party. Despite the full-scale offensive, the party steadfastly insisted that only a handful of members supported the Opposition. Yet regardless of the final calculations, Trotskyism was discursively understood to be a far-reaching and intractable problem. It was not, however, a socially general phenomenon.

The Opposition gained its strongest degree of proletarian support from specific sectors of the Belorussian economy. Opposition flourished among leatherworkers, shoemakers, boot makers, woodworkers, tailors, dressmakers, carpenters, and metalworkers. In other words, opposition flourished precisely in semiartisanal, labor-intensive industries most directly threatened by the onrush of mechanized production. The forms of compulsion faced by workers in these industries were not simply political; they were simultaneously structural. The precarious state of labor-intensive handworkers confronted with the social reality of industrial revolution was hardly a novel phenomenon. At the dawn of the machine age across Europe, such social groups played critical roles in the development of radical activism, ranging from machine breaking, to strikes, to political organization.[147] What was novel, however, was that these workers faced suppression not from a nascent class of industrialists and owners of private capital, but from the guarantors of an ostensible workers' state that proved willing to marshal all available coercive methods to drive through economic restructuring.

In addition to being drawn primarily from the ranks of handworkers and petty producers, the overwhelming bulk of Oppositionists throughout the republic were Jews. In the context of the western borderlands of the Soviet Empire, where nationality and social position frequently converged, the large contingent of Jews among the ranks of the Opposition could be traced to multifarious causes, ranging from a sense of ethnic solidarity with the leadership of the Opposition to the pronounced grouping of Jewish laborers in those industries targeted for rapid and massive restructuring with the Stalin Revolution. Whatever the cause, the politicized language of ethnicity proved critical to the process of economic restructuring. The initial brunt of the campaign to rationalize production fell upon Jewish labor because Jewish labor coalesced in industries that faced the most intensive pressures to rationalize and intensify production. In the face of such pressures, Jewish laborers responded in the way that they had responded to similar pressures throughout the pre- and postrevolutionary periods. They grumbled, held meetings, criticized their bosses, organized themselves, and pushed for reforms intended to redress economic demands. The party and state ultimately responded by rejecting these economistic claims outright. In denying the legitimacy of worker economic grievances, they increasingly attributed worker recalcitrance to the nature of the recalcitrant workers themselves. Workers spoke to the state in the language of class and structure. The state responded by attributing economic and political grievances to ethnic and increasingly essentialized difference.

Interethnic animosity undoubtedly played a role in shaping responses to opposition. Viewed exclusively from the standpoint of culture and "discourse," the conflation of opposition and Jewish ethnicity appears to be a purely political manifestation of the unintended consequences of Soviet nationality policies. To view tensions between Jews and non-Jews through the lens of "nationality" alone is, however, to overlook a crucial, underlying reality. Nationality and ethnicity became patently problematic in the midst of a broader constellation of social pressures. Throughout Belorussia, the fundamental tensions that gave rise to the Opposition were primarily social tensions: they arose from conflicts over wages, the pace of industrialization, and the desirability of implementing new regimes of labor and productivity. The fact that Jews constituted the overwhelming majority of workers in these industries remained largely incidental until the terms of political discussion shifted and ethnicity came to be taken as the cause of political intransigence. Ethnicity was neither a constant nor an ever-primary structuring reality. Economic crisis catalyzed nationality, intensified ethnic division, and ultimately engendered new categorizations of difference in which Jews were asserted to be a group united not simply by affinity and culture, but also by essence. In doing so, the anti-Trotskyist campaigns reinscribed recalcitrant Jews as not simply economically and politically alien elements, or ethnically dubious, but as ontologically different. Unintended or otherwise, the language of essential difference in turn opened space for the reconstitution of race.

The peculiar case of Trotskyism in Belorussia suggests broader claims concerning political language and economic crisis in postrevolutionary Soviet society. That political discourse became more absolute, more totalizing, more "Manichean" on the eve of the Stalin Revolution is hardly to be disputed.[148] The arrival of Stalinism as a fully blown political project announced itself with the linguistic offensive against the kulak, the speculator, the wrecker, and the

Trotskyist. The construction of enemies constituted an elemental core of the culture and ideology of Stalinism. Yet the process of constructing enemies—intimate, distant, or imagined—was structured everywhere by the dynamics of economic and structural crisis that made Stalinism itself a social and political possibility.

1
ANTISEMITISM AND THE STALIN REVOLUTION

READERS OF THE workers' newspaper *Rabochii* likely felt a sense of shock when they opened the November 13, 1928, edition and read of the breaking scandal at the Oktiabr' glassmaking factory in Svisloch, Bobruisk Okrug.[1] On that day, *Rabochii* published an exposé outlining a series of attacks by workers against Dreiza Leibova Barshai, a twenty-year-old Jewish woman working in the Oktiabr' factory. An unskilled laborer with no previous employment record, Barshai had recently moved from a nearby shtetl into the factory village and labor force. Since the summer of 1928, *Rabochii* reported, Barshai had been subject to repeated physical and sexual assaults committed by a group of non-Jewish, mostly male workers in the factory. Downplaying the gendered nature of the violence, *Rabochii* denounced the attacks as evidence of a virulent resurgence of antisemitism within Belorussian factories, party cells, and institutions. As the newspapers of Belorussia churned out follow-up stories, investigations, and editorials, the lurid details of events at the factory came to light. Virtually overnight, the Oktiabr' Affair exploded into a cause célèbre, triggering an examination and condemnation of resurgent antisemitism across Belorussia and the entire Soviet Union.[2]

Soviet officials responded to the antisemitic moment of 1928–1929 by letting loose the rhetorical, political, educational, and coercive power of the party-state. The Oktiabr' show trial in January 1929, which resulted in the incarceration of eight assailants, heralded the arrival of an aggressive offensive to eradicate antisemitism by educating, policing, and punishing antisemites. In komsomol and pioneer cells, schools and universities, activists exposed antisemitic agitation and removed antisemites from organizational ranks. Mass meetings, investigations, and educational sessions in factory party cells and trade unions continued across Belorussia and the USSR throughout 1929. In these spectacles of revolutionary didacticism, rhetorically constructed antisemites took their place alongside kulaks, priests, hooligans, bandits, wreckers, speculators, and swindlers in a growing rogues gallery of enemies of the Soviet state. Like all constructed enemies, the rhetorical antisemite appeared as a one-sided, morally unambiguous creature to be eradicated.

Paradoxically, the Stalin Revolution—which announced itself in Belorussia with anti-Trotskyist campaigns that questioned Jewish political assimilability—transformed the rhetorical defense of Jewish integration in Soviet society into a driving principle of political practice. Far from being incidental, the campaign against antisemitism constituted a fundamental thrust of the Stalin Revolution and the populist Cultural Revolution that erupted in all corners of Soviet life in 1928.[3] Like the war against the kulak, the defense of proletarian women, or renewed avowals of proletarian political power, the struggle against antisemitism exposed fundamental tensions inherent in Stalinism.[4] On one level, the anti-antisemitism campaign constituted a rhetorically powerful device for mobilizing forces for Cultural Revolution and a "return" to the revolutionary principles of 1917.[5] On another level, the campaign was symptomatic of the coalescing rhetorical practices of Stalinism, which sought to manipulate and control political processes and the very language of politics itself.[6] The attack on antisemitism became one mechanism through which the Stalinist state sought to consolidate its hold on domestic power and build social cohesion in a period of acute economic instability.

Internally, policing, punishing, and disciplining racial hatred became fundamental to the project of forging "New" Soviet men and women. Attacking antisemitism, violent nationalism, and the politics of racial animosity likewise became a central part of pressuring populations to learn to "speak Bolshevik," as one historian has put it.[7] However well intentioned, these attempts to excise racial animosities from the souls of populations also masked forms of political control and the exercise of disciplining state power. In combating the scourges of antisemitism and racism, the Stalinist state pursued logics of rule, discipline, and ideological control over subject populations, who in turn resorted increasingly to the rhetoric of race and antisemitism to articulate opposition to new hierarchies of Stalinist power and privilege.[8]

Alongside political control, Soviet policy was motivated by a second critical factor: antisemitism constituted a real and growing global danger. From the virulent antisemitism of the White movement during the Civil War, to the multitude of militant racist parties that vied for power in Admiral Horthy's Hungary, to the acerbic xenophobic nationalism of Roman Dmowski's *Endek* movement in Poland, to the vitriolic Jew-hatred basic to National Socialism in Germany, the 1920s witnessed the violent resurgence of antisemitism across Europe.[9] Reverberations of total war, retrenched postwar nationalism, repeated economic paroxysms, hyperinflation, persistent unemployment, extreme and expanding wealth disparities, and universal political fragmentation found contorted expression in forms of modern, "redemptive" antisemitism.[10] More threateningly from the standpoint of the Stalinist regime, these political movements uniformly fused antisemitism and radical anti-Bolshevism. Insofar as right-wing political reaction and counterrevolution announced itself across Europe through the language of antisemitism, the sudden eruption of antisemitism in the Soviet context presented a clear, if inchoate, threat.

While foregrounding local histories, this chapter reframes the Soviet antisemitic moment of the late 1920s—and the resurgence of grassroots antisemitism throughout the Stalin era—against the transnational, interwar antisemitic turn. Soviet nationality policy, intergroup competition for resources and positions, interparty struggles, and gender and class dynamics all contributed to the outbreak of antisemitism across Belorussia and the USSR. Such factors alone, however, cannot explain why the upsurge in the Soviet space coincided with, and frequently preceded, the pan-European antisemitic turn. In light of this, it will be argued that the eruption of antisemitism on the eve of the Stalin Revolution formed one part of a socially general phenomenon that crossed geopolitical boundaries. The proximate cause originated in the global economic crisis of the late 1920s. The antisemitic storm that engulfed Europe during the 1930s broke first in the Soviet lands in the late 1920s because it was precisely there and then that the global crisis first surfaced, tearing apart the market-mediated economy of the New Economic Policy and ushering in the Stalinist planned economy. Drawing on critical analyses of race and interwar antisemitism, this chapter argues that antisemitism became the modality through which the structural transformation from liberal capitalism to the managed, productivist economy was realized in the Soviet Union within the framework of Stalinism.[11]

Economic shock alone, however, cannot account for the sudden resurgence of antisemitism, whether in the Soviet, Polish, or German context. As this chapter argues, antisemitic discourses across Soviet Belorussia returned repeatedly to a dichotomy of political power and powerlessness. However unformed and politically reactionary, the antisemitic eruption across Belorussia fixated upon the loss of political and economic power by the "working class" at a moment of profound political change and astounding social restructuring.[12] Paradoxically, the Stalinist political revolution ultimately sought to resolve this crisis of legitimacy by absorbing and channeling the violent politics of resentment unleashed by the Stalinist social and economic revolution.

Faced with the eruption of grassroots race hatred, the Stalinist state confronted a stark political choice. As events of the 1930s would make explicit, the open embrace of antisemitism as a mobilizing principle of political rule presented an unmistakable opportunity. From the standpoint of Jewish history, the fact that the Stalinist regime (regardless of Stalin's own ambivalences) ultimately rejected the global antisemitic turn ranked among the most significant political choices of the era. Yet like all aspects of the Stalin Revolution, the campaign against antisemitism was thoroughly double-sided. Even as the state defended the principle of integration, it simultaneously attacked "Jewish" deviations of Bundism and Trotskyism in the party and ordered the final closure of all independent Jewish political parties and groups, including Poalei Tsion and the remaining left-Zionst youth organizations.[13] Finally, in 1929, as part of a growing offensive against national deviations, the Communist party disbanded the evsektsii, bringing an end to the last quasi-independent Jewish voice within the party.[14] Taken together, the defense of social integration and constriction of political options offered an implicit, new social contract for Soviet Jewry: the state effectively guaranteed social inclusion and security of Jewish individuals at the expense of autonomous Jewish politics and collective life.

The Oktiabr' Affair and the Criminalization of Hatred

Prior to the fall of 1928, few signs indicated that the Bobruisk Okrug would suddenly become *the* epicenter of antisemitic rupture in Belorussia. To be sure, Bobruisk was hardly a model Soviet town. A poor, agriculturally dependent region with staggering levels of unemployment, little industry, and a highly diverse population of Jews, Belorussians, Poles, Russians, Ukrainians, and Tatars, the region had a deep history of intranational strife.[15] During the Civil War the okrug had been the site of some of the worst pogroms in Belorussia, and party investigators reported ongoing animosity between Poles and Jews over questions of schools and Jewish agricultural settlements throughout the 1920s.[16] For most of this period, however, local evsektsiia activists downplayed intranational tensions and focused instead on what they considered the far more pressing issue of internal Jewish politics, including the threat posed by Bundists, Trotskyists, Zionists, and religious Jewish organizations in the region.[17]

As late as mid-1928, the local Bobruisk *evburo* (Jewish Bureau) continued to prioritize the threat posed by Jewish parties over that of intranational conflict. Reports to the Minsk evsektsiia from the local evburo secretary, Comrade Leizer Isaakovich Pam, sounded alarms about internal Jewish political dangers. An upwardly mobile evsektsii activist, vigilant class warrior, and enthusiastic promoter of "godless" campaigns and antireligious festivals, Comrade Pam filled his reports with calls for relentless class war in the Jewish milieu.[18]

Throughout most of 1928 he devoted the bulk of his attention to organizing anti-Passover campaigns,[19] aggressively combating vestiges of Bundism,[20] and suppressing Zionist and clerical elements who purportedly preyed on Jewish kustari and young, unemployed workers.[21] Stressing the presence of counter-revolutionary threats in the Jewish milieu, Pam paid rare and passing attention to the issue of antisemitism.[22]

The tenor of Comrade Pam's reports changed dramatically in September 1928, when he began to write of sudden, widespread outbreaks of social unrest throughout the okrug.[23] While lauding the expansion of local arteli and kustar cooperatives, Pam outlined a litany of growing problems in these undertakings. Of late, cooperatives across the region had begun to complain simultaneously of growing wage inequalities between workers; shortages in raw materials, credit, and orders; and idle workforces. Living and work conditions throughout the okrug remained woefully cramped, degraded, and unsanitary. Despite earlier efforts to relocate Jews to agricultural settlements, the establishment of new Jewish colonies in the region ground to a halt. Everywhere arteli, workshops, and settlements teemed with "nonlaboring" populations, a vague category that grouped together declassed and disenfranchised elements, as well as the unemployed. Wherever one looked, Pam claimed, one saw proliferating signs of division between wealthy and poor, between wealthier kustari and itinerant hired laborers, and between skilled and unskilled producers. In short, after several years of stasis, social conflict seemed to erupt everywhere overnight.[24]

More alarmingly, intensified social conflict appeared to unleash pent up intranational animosity. "The exacerbation of class struggle has called forth unhealthy phenomena, like antisemitism and chauvinism," Comrade Pam warned. Such sentiments had become "particularly sharp" across Bobruisk, despite the fact that the okrug party committee paid "great attention to this question."[25] In Glusk, evsektsii activists reported a marked spike in national antagonism in mixed-nationality arteli after the party ordered the establishment of a single, uniform day of rest for all artel' members. The town's numerous Jewish kustari, many from local shoemaker arteli, won the vote to designate Saturday as the day of rest; in response, Belorussian kustari staged open antisemitic demonstrations, denouncing "the evil Jews, because of whom 'we have to work on Sunday.'"[26] In Parichi, tensions between Jews and Belorussians over the Sabbath became so acute that both groups refused to establish integrated agricultural settlements.[27] Jewish agriculturalists in Svisloch complained that Belorussian peasants refused them access to pastures, while the Belorussian-dominated village soviet denied funds to build new workshops for Jewish arteli. In general, the Svisloch evsektsii lambasted the "strong national narrow-mindedness" of both populations, each of which tended to view all events in the shtetl as a struggle between "'us' and 'them'—that is, Jews and Belorussians."[28] The lone bright spot in Svisloch, Comrade Pam reported, was the glassmaking factory Oktiabr', which boasted an international labor pool of Belorussians, Ukrainians, and Jews, and helped to combat the perpetual problem of youth unemployment by "swallowing some two hundred youths" into its expanding labor force.[29] Six weeks after the Minsk evsektsii considered Pam's report, this ostensible site of integration became, overnight, the focal point of antisemitic intolerance in Belorussia.

As later investigations would make clear, tensions had in fact been building at the Oktiabr' factory for many months.[30] In the immediate aftermath of the scandal, the local procurators office completed an investigation that uncovered escalating incidents throughout 1928. Conflicts first broke out in the spring, when a group of women workers resolved to form a canteen in the women's factory dormitory. Shortly after opening, the canteen fell apart when organizers denied access to Jewish women and refused to eat alongside Jewish workers. The dispute over the dormitory canteen, investigators argued, reflected rampant antisemitic tendencies in the factory. Workers routinely used the derogatory terms *zhids* and *zhidovkas* to refer to Jews, at times chiding Jewish workers with even cruder slurs. During the dispute over the canteen, one organizer reportedly declaimed, "We will never build socialism until we slaughter (*vyrezhit'*) the yids." Workers in the factory regularly sang antisemitic songs, including one about "slaughter[ing] all the Jews on the streets," and engaged in rather bald abuse of Jewish coworkers.[31]

Into this environment stepped Dreiza Barshai, the daughter of paupers from Svisloch, who was hired at the Oktiabr' works in the spring of 1928. Born and raised in the shtetl, Barshai spoke only Yiddish and a smattering of Russian, leading investigators to repeatedly label her an illiterate. She had no formal education and entered the factory as a nonparty, unskilled day laborer, drawing the minimum monthly salary of twenty-five rubles.[32] Shortly after her hire, a group of young workers—Aleksei Tochilin, Aleksandr Gladkov, Gavril Gruzdev, Ivan Tuliakov, and Tatiana Nitsievskaia—began to verbally abuse Barshai with antisemitic slurs. All of the participants, excluding Tuliakov, were members of the komsomol. One morning in early July, verbal abuse turned into physical abuse and sexual assault as Tochilin, the master of the factory's iron shop, grabbed Barshai, threw her down onto a bench, pulled up her skirt, and threw water on her. Several weeks later, on July 25, Tochilin and another worker, Gruzdev, attacked Barshai again; the pair threw her to the ground and tore off her clothes and underclothes, while a woman worker, Nitsievskaia, threw water on Barshai's genitals. They called Krasnianskii, a security worker, to gawk at Barshai, who at this point began to scream out for help. Upon hearing the screams, three Jewish workers, Iaakov Elentukh, Aron Margolin, and Mota Rubinchik, ran over, and a shouting match broke out; Tochilin began swearing, called Elentukh a "Jew-face" (*zhidovskaia morda*), and screamed that "yids stand up for yids." Eletukh, Margolin, and Rubinchik filed a written complaint with Karonin, one of the factory's administrators, who gave Barshai, Gruzdev, and Tochlin a stern warning for "horsing around."[33]

The attacks on Barshai continued. In the ensuing months, the same group of assailants repeatedly assaulted, mocked, and tormented her. Finally, in October 1928, Tochlin cornered Barshai and beat her with a wooden shoe until she suffered a broken arm requiring medical attention. At that point, word of the repeated assaults on the remote shop floor reached the editors of *Rabochii*. Following initial reports, the Bobruisk Okrug Committee (Okruzhkom) of the party condemned the events at the Oktiabr' factory and ordered an immediate investigation of the conditions and activities in the factory.[34]

Breaking news of events at the Oktiabr' factory generated immediate and emphatic reaction across the republic. "The crimes at the Oktiabr' factory are the bestial salvos of the class enemies of the Soviet state," proclaimed *Rabochii*.[35] On November 16, the newspaper printed resolutions from the Lenin Communist University (*Komvuz*) and the second shoemakers collective in Minsk, the Borisov city works combine, members of the Belorussian glassmakers trust, various komsomol cells, and other institutions across the republic demanding severe punishment for the "antisemitic animals."[36] On November 19, the workers of the Belorussian Metal Trust denounced the antisemitic and "counterrevolutionary" crimes in Svisloch, which in their opinion "clearly show the class face of the enemies of the working class."[37] In Bobruisk, the okrug committee similarly denounced antisemitism as the "mask" behind which the class enemies sought to destabilize and undermine the revolution.[38] The Okruzhkom likewise issued a public proclamation stressing the expressly political nature of the attacks in Svisloch and warned of the dangers of antisemitism and intranational hatred.[39] In these missives, antisemitism appeared to be caused simply by the presence of antisemites, counterrevolutionaries, and secret political enemies who infiltrated the proletarian ranks.[40]

While the Borbruisk Okrug Committee stressed the "great political meaning" of the attacks, local investigations detailed a number of social stresses that contributed to the factory's hostile environment.[41] In particular, they pointed to the marked intensification of productive pressures as an underlying source of worker resentment. During 1927 and 1928, the factory's total output levels reached 150 percent of the 1926–1927 levels, while worker productivity increased 23 percent. The number of workers likewise increased more than 30 percent, reaching a level of 582 employees by mid-1928. Many of the 135 or so new workers came from surrounding shtetlekh, including a significant number of Jews.[42] By October 1928, according to a second report by the Bobruisk Okruzhkom, the number of Jewish workers had climbed from an insignificant handful to eighty-nine people, or some 15 percent of the factory labor force.[43]

In addition, the Okruzhkom emphasized ongoing wage conflicts as a key flashpoint. During the preceding year, rank-and-file workers experienced acute wage erosion as a result of a revised pay structure intended to increase productivity. Under the new terms, masters in the workshop received a piece rate for the work of their employees, while workers received a simple day wage. The masters consequently sought to speed up production, leading to vast pay discrepancies. Higher-paid masters made 100–140 rubles a month, while the bulk of workers received only 22 to 25 rubles—poverty rates even before one factors in mounting inflation. These dynamics created high turnover and a sharply stratified labor force split between skilled and unskilled laborers. Such divisive conditions, the report concluded, fostered an environment in which the "crude abuse" flourished.[44] In sum, rather than simply attribute the outbreak of antisemitism to malignant political actors, Bobruisk investigators explained the upsurge as a response to eroding wages, overcrowded work conditions, and a general ratcheting up of productive pressures. As such, investigators tacked directly into the storm of the Stalin Revolution, which transformed ever-intensified production into an end in itself.

Unsurprisingly, the Central Committee of the Communist Party in Minsk took a less reflective position far more in line with prevailing winds blowing from Moscow. After condemning the Bobruisk Okruzhkom and Svisloch Raikom for insufficient oversight of the Oktiabr' factory, the Central Committee called for an additional investigation and the full prosecution of all perpetrators.[45] A resolution from the end of November glossed over social tensions in the factory, emphasizing instead the absolutely political nature of the crime. Antisemitism, it asserted, constituted the "form" of "political banditism" through which ever-present "reactionary, class enemy elements" carried out their struggle against the party and soviet policies.[46] Two weeks later, the Central Committee issued an even more robust denunciation of antisemitism as a crime undertaken by class enemies to undermine the "dictatorship of the proletariat." Antisemitism found fertile ground in the Oktiabr' factory not because of adverse social conditions, the proclamation continued, but because of the failure of trade union, party, and komsomol activists to carry out effective agitation campaigns against antisemitism as a class ideology. The Central Committee castigated local political institutions and factory administrators for failing to confront this ideological crime and likewise chastised the editors of *Oktyabr, Savetskaia Belarus'*, and *Chyrvonaia Zmena* for failing to recognize the manifestly political nature of antisemitism.[47]

The wheels of reasserted revolutionary justice turned quickly. On January 15–19, 1929, eight accused perpetrators in the Oktiabr' Affair stood trial for hooliganism (article 84) and counterrevolutionary agitation under the infamous article 107-b of the criminal code. Tochilin, Gladkov, Gruzdev, Tuliakov, Nitsievskaia, and Krasniankii received sentences ranging from six months in prison to three years, for Tochilin.[48] By forcefully punishing the perpetrators, the party utilized administrative measures to suppress future Tochilins and Gladkovs and dissuade them from giving quarter to counterrevolutionary race hatreds. Over the ensuing months, activists organized mass meetings in dozens of factory cells to enlighten workers of the dangers of antisemitism and inoculate them against Jew-hatred. In other words, the party sought to combat antisemitism through a republic-wide talking cure.

Antisemitism and the Great Break

Based on reports by okrug investigators, local and national procurators, and the Central Committee in Minsk, there is little doubt that Tochilin and his coassailants formed an unsavory and rather despicable lot. Local procurators in Bobruisk questioned twenty witnesses during their investigation, virtually all of whom reported seeing at least one assault against Barshai. Witnesses uniformly supported the claim that Tochilin and other assailants verbally attacked Barshai and other Jewish workers.[49] In stressing the perpetrators' debased political motivations and counterrevolutionary intentions, the Central Committee simultaneously established acceptable parameters for understanding the phenomenon of antisemitism itself. By rejecting any connection between events in the Oktiabr' factory and the unfolding social tumult of the Great Break, the party leadership effectively drove itself into a paradox. Even as they decried the antisemites as class enemies, they took the profoundly anti-Marxist turn of denying a relationship between ideology and society. Unmoored from the social context, political language was attributed simply to the base motives and politics of debased individuals.

As such, the party leadership interpreted the events in Svisloch as an isolated event made possible by poor local leadership. While plausible in isolation, such explanations could not explain why antisemitism might erupt across a spectrum of social actors in a given period. In other words, such explanations could not account for the socially general nature of antisemitism as a movement.[50] Ample evidence indicates that—far from being an isolated event—the occurrences at the Oktiabr' factory did indeed reflect a socially general outbreak of antisemitism building across Belorussia. In December 1927, *Komsomol'skaia*

Pravda, the party's youth organ in Moscow, reported on efforts of Belorussian schoolchildren in Mozyr to organize a boycott of Jewish candidates for a local pioneer troop.[51] In early 1928 officials in Vitebsk denounced komsomol members from the local Veterinarian Institute, who allegedly openly read antisemitic poems at a university event.[52] In July 1928 a band of komsomol "hooligans" engaged in an antisemitic riot in Mogilev, drunkenly harassing and beating Jewish shopkeepers, pedestrians, and train passengers.[53] Jewish students at the Kalinkovichi Railroad School near Mozyr reportedly encountered systemic harassment and physical violence.[54] Throughout the summer of 1928 *Der Yunger Arbeter*, the Minsk Yiddish komsomol newspaper, published letters from Jewish komsomol'tsy who experienced antisemitic violence in local cells. One anonymous author claimed that fellow komsomol'tsy attacked him, stripped him to determine whether he was circumcised, and strangled him to near asphyxiation before pronouncing him "saved."[55] Trade union investigations conducted after the Oktiabr' Affair also revealed widespread antisemitic agitation and violence in factories and workshops across the republic.[56]

Far from being specific to Belorussia, the surge in antisemitic incidents mirrored conditions across the entire Soviet Union. Internal party reports throughout 1927 warned of surging antisemitism in party and komsomol cells across Russia, Ukraine, and Belorussia.[57] In early 1928 the gathering wave broke. In March, *Proletarii* reported that a Jewish student at Kharkov University had been subjected to almost daily antisemitic assaults.[58] A month later the Moscow artistic scene was shaken by the suicide of a Jewish violinist from the Bolshoi Theater who reportedly took his life because of antisemitic actions by the theater's artistic director, Nikoali Golovanov.[59] In November, shortly after news of the Oktiabr' Affair surfaced, a Jewish student at Voronezh University committed suicide after experiencing antisemitic harassment; two alleged perpetrators were arrested and eleven students expelled from this "nest of antisemitism."[60] That same month an anti-Jewish pogrom broke out in Rudna, near Smolensk, leading to the arrest of twelve perpetrators.[61] In December, *Rabochaia Gazeta* reported that virtually all of the 2,789 Jewish coal miners previously employed in the Don coal mines between 1920 and November 1928 had been driven out by antisemitism—a case leading to a show trial in February 1929.[62] Later that month the Soviet and international press carried the scandalous story of a Russian factory worker and komsomolets in Pskov who murdered a Jewish coworker and fellow komsomol member with an axe in front of five other komsomol'tsy, a crime leading to another sensational trial in April 1929.[63] By the summer and fall of 1929 the press was awash with stories of antisemitic violence, including accusations of Jewish ritual murder in the town of Poltava,[64] reports of antisemitic riots in Zhitomir,[65] murderous pogroms against Jewish colonists in Ukraine,[66] attempted komsomol-led boycotts of Jewish students at the University of Kiev,[67] the grisly murder of two Jewish women by a group of peasant women in Repka, near Mogilev,[68] and the torture of two Jewish girls who worked at the *Geroi Truda* paper factory near Gomel.[69]

While officials in Minsk stressed the alleged role that old-regime, counterrevolutionary elements played in stoking the antisemitic revival, the wave of violence prompted others to seek more nuanced explanations. In November 1927 the journalist, Bolshevik nationalities theorist, and "godless" militant Emel'ian Iaroslavskii published an editorial in *Pravda* blaming Stalin and the party leadership for mobilizing antisemitism as part of their war against the Trotskyist Opposition.[70] Iurii Larin, a former Menshevik turned Bolshevik economic theorist, responded by blaming renascent antisemitism on intensified social competition between national groups brought about by urbanization and breakneck industrialization, as well as the machinations of hidden class enemies.[71] Mikahil Gorev, a frequent contributor to *Komsomol'skaia Pravda*, argued that resurgent antisemitism was tied directly to the consumer crisis and basic goods shortages of the late 1920s. As consumer prices rose and goods disappeared during the crisis of the NEP, popular anger turned not against the state, but against merchants and middlemen who, in the popular imaginary, came to be conflated with Jews.[72] Writing from exile long after the fact, Trotsky attributed the antisemitic surge to the crude intrigues of Stalin and the instinctive hatred of the proletariat for the growing Stalinist bureaucracy; insofar as Jews played a visible role in the bureaucratic ranks, manifestations of antisemitism, he argued, reflected growing animosity toward the very institutions of Stalinist rule.[73]

Despite their differences, Iaroslavskii, Larin, Gorev, and Trotsky each offered "rational" explanations for antisemitism based upon local Soviet conditions. Archival evidence from the late 1920s offers ample support for each of these explanations, pointing to the degree with which antisemitism defied monocausal explanation. Economic, social, and political pressures, as well as vestiges of underlying, if supposedly cast-off, religious drives contributed to the sudden eruption of antisemitism in the Soviet context.[74] Nevertheless, insofar as these explanations stressed local tensions and interest-group conflict, as well as internal Soviet political factors, each necessarily implied that Soviet antisemitism was somehow separate and genetically different from the contemporaneous plague of antisemitism spreading across interwar Europe. Given that European antisemitism was understood to be a classed phenomenon produced by capitalism in crisis, the roots of antisemitism in ostensibly postcapitalist Soviet society necessarily had to be found elsewhere.[75]

This insistence on the distinctiveness of Soviet antisemitism, however, ran diametrically counter to the dominant Bolshevik interpretation articulated by Lenin during the years of revolution and civil war. Lenin's most famous statement on the subject, a 1919 gramophone recording made to combat antisemitism in the ranks of the Red Army, laid out the basic contours of the Bolshevik critique of antisemitism. First and foremost, he insisted that antisemitism constituted a manipulative ideological tool used by entrenched elites for the sake of deflecting popular anger away from their failing regimes: "When the accursed tsarist monarchy was living its last days," Lenin explained, "it tried to incite the ignorant workers and peasants against the Jews . . . The landowners and capitalists tried to divert the hatred of the workers and peasants who were tortured by want against the Jews." Yet while stressing the particularity of tsarist conditions, Lenin insisted that conditions in Russia mirrored those found elsewhere. "In other countries, too, we often see the capitalists fomenting hatred against the Jews in order to blind the workers, to divert their attention from the real enemy of the working people, capital."[76]

Superficially, Lenin's characterization of antisemitism as an ideology fomented by manipulative elites seemed to provide a firm basis for subsequent attempts to attribute antisemitism to malignant, hidden class enemies. Yet in identifying the "real enemy" of the working class not as the "capitalist"—that is, an agentive actor—but rather as "capital," which is to say a set of social relations, Lenin, in actuality, suggested a far more complex understanding.[77] Unlike his posthumous interpreters, who would emphasize the need to fight against agents of antisemitism, Lenin underscored that the "enemy" to be overcome was, in fact, a structural problem, that is, the social relations of capital. While seemingly semantic, the subtle difference in meaning was, in fact, extraordinary, as were the implications for later Soviet society. As the Stalin Revolution unfolded, the Soviet regime sought to annihilate the phenomenon of antisemitism by attacking supposed counterrevolutionary agents; yet the social program of the Stalin Revolution simultaneously unleashed the full productive potential of capital by organizing production under the direction of an increasingly totalizing state. In other words, even as the Stalin Revolution attacked antisemitism politically and rhetorically, it produced antisemitism socially. This constituted one central contradiction at the heart of the Stalinist project that drove it toward a dynamic of perpetual violence.

This contradiction of Soviet antisemitism pointed, in turn, to the fundamental question at the absolute center of the entire Soviet project: the nature of capital itself. In theory, the Bolshevik Revolution had been made in the name of overcoming and abolishing capital. In practice, the Bolshevik regime could never definitively determine whether this meant abolishing reified things (such as money and banks), or institutions (such as the market), or people (capitalists, bankers, traders, or "speculators"), or "capitalist social relations," by which the traditional Marxists of the Bolshevik party invariably meant private property. Throughout the first revolutionary decade, every critical social and industrial policy debate revolved around these multivalent meanings of what it meant to abolish capital in practice. In certain moments, such as the era of War Communism, policy turned decisively against concrete and reified manifestations of capital: money, the market, and alleged "agents" of capitalism. Under the NEP, the party sheepishly sought to evolve its way to a post-capitalist existence by establishing new sites of production, including arteli, worker collectives, and collective farms, ostensibly "free" from capitalist social relations insofar as they were collectively owned, or owned by the state, but definitively free from the stigma of private property.

Yet faced with the onset of economic crisis between mid-1926 and 1928, the state swung decisively back toward attacks on reified sites of capital and "concrete" manifestations of capitalism. In light of collapsing international grain prices, constricting international grain markets and Soviet exports, and increasing pressure on Soviet monetary reserves followed by the unraveling of "sound" monetary policy and the return of inflation, the Stalinist state made a virtue of necessity and turned decisively against the NEP. Taxation policies turned confiscatory as the state increased taxes on private traders and private workshops, driving all but the most insignificant producers and traders out of business. As in the era of the Civil War and early NEP, the state once again threw its full administrative and coercive apparatus against purported economic criminals, including "speculators," "contrabandists," "hoarders," and the like. As a partial result, the market itself, viewed as the central defining institution of NEP policy, shriveled over the course of 1927–1928. Goods disappeared from shelves, industries throughout the Soviet Union reported shortages, and the state, beginning in 1928, was forced to reintroduce rationing. Finally, in place of the unpredictable, crisis-prone, and increasingly malfunctioning market, the state turned definitively to the planned economy. Insofar as the state effectively abolished the market and the last vestiges of private property in production, it appeared to have broken through the morass of the NEP to renew its assault on the most reified conception of capital imaginable. With the Stalin Revolution, capital and capitalism again came to be envisioned as tangible things to be "smashed" and the concretized agents who controlled them annihilated.[78]

Rather than eradicating antisemitism, the Stalin Revolutionary assault upon reified capital appeared to unleash it everywhere. Such, for example, was the case at the massive Dvina linen factory located outside Vitebsk, where a series of antisemitic episodes exploded in November 1928. Prior to and following the Bolshevik Revolution, the factory had been a rock solid stronghold of Belorussian labor. Like the many glassmaking factories of Belorussia, it employed an almost exclusively non-Jewish labor force until the onset of the Stalin Revolution. As with the Oktiabr' factory, rapid industrialization drew hundreds of new workers into the labor force, driving forward ethnic integration in the factory. By November 1928 the factory employed some 1,755 workers, including 1,487 Belorussians, 151 Poles, and 22 Latvians. The demand for labor created by forced industrialization additionally drew some 95 Jewish workers, almost all women, into the ranks of some 1,300 women textile makers employed in the factory.[79] From the outset, Belorussian workers viewed these new Jewish workers with decided hostility. They appeared as interlopers who took jobs from Belorussians, drove down wages, and allegedly shirked work responsibility. Jewish women workers, investigators argued, likewise shunned the Dvina factory, preferring instead to seek out better-paying work in city garment factories. Yet by 1928, with unemployment rife and the garment industry, like all consumer goods industries, in disarray, young Jewish women found themselves pulled into the Dvina factory orbit.[80]

Events surrounding one such worker, Comrade Khrapunova, came to light in the days after the Oktiabr' Affair broke. One day Khrapunova heard a crash coming from the machine sector, investigated, and found Comrade Likhavidov, a male Belorussian worker, standing over a broken machine belt. An argument broke out over the accident. Likhavidov reportedly cursed at Khrapunova, who, without a hint of timidity, lifted up her skirt, telling Likhovidov to "kiss my ass" (*"potselu mne tuda"*). Incensed, Likhavidov began to shout antisemitic slurs, calling Khrapunova a "kike" and "Jew face" and accusing her of being a "slacker, who doesn't want to work." In another incident, a non-Jewish worker, Stepanova, and a Jewish worker, Tsirkin, got into a fight after Stepanova hit Tsirkin in the leg with a cart. Tsirkin burst into tears, Stepanova berated her, and as the two women cursed each other, Stepanova hurled antisemitic epithets.[81]

Unsurprisingly, given preexisting tensions, the allegations of antisemitism in the factory set off a firestorm. Alarmed, the factory committee, trade union, and party cell convened a mass meeting on November 26 to deal with antisemitism in the Dvina factory. Trade union reports noted extremely high turnout, as the factory hall filled with women workers, komsomol'tsy, and party members. Rather than participate in the scripted proceedings, however, the workers in the Dvina factory revolted en masse. As soon as the meeting opened to remarks from the shop floor, worker after worker came forward to speak out against the antisemitism campaign. One worker reportedly argued that the entire "question of antisemitism is inflated and puffed up (*razdut i razman*)." Multiple workers defended Likhavidov and Stepanova, objecting to their possible exclusion from the union, firing, or any other proposed punishment. In general, the workers insisted that nothing serious had happened in the factory. The workers then voted down, by large majorities, two successive resolutions condemning the actions of Comrades Likhavidov and Stepanova. Having been rebuffed on the factory floor, the factory committee resolved to move Likhavidov to another department, but allowed both of the accused to continue working. They then sent the entire matter to the local procurator to investigate.[82]

Workers clearly viewed the skirmishes as business as usual, and in all likelihood they were exactly that. Internal investigations revealed a long list of antisemitic incidents predating the November episodes.[83] As a result, the factory committee organized additional mass meetings for workers and komsomol members to further inform them of the antisemitic danger. These, too, however, produced unsettling results. In the komsomol meeting held on December 2, young party members reportedly gave a series of speeches condemning antisemitism and the actions of Comrade Stepanova and Likhavidov. In the discussion that followed, however, several young factory members reportedly tried to turn the conversation, stressing the need to "carry out a decisive struggle with Jewish chauvinist-nationalism, which is obscured by the struggle with antisemitism presently, since antisemitism exists among workers in a rather sharp form." In the general factory meeting that followed workers, likewise, demanded punishment for Tsirkin and Khrapunova equal to that given to Likhavidov, on the grounds that they had supposedly demonstrated Jewish chauvinism during the skirmishes. Rather than condemning antisemitism, the problem turned back to the question of the Jews.[84]

Judging solely by these discussions, the affair at the Dvina factory appears as an eruption of old hatreds and racial animosities on the factory floor. Yet internal investigations conducted by the factory committee uncovered widespread troubles and countless immediate grievances that seemed to trigger events. At the start of 1928 wages in the factory, which relied almost exclusively on piece rates, were notoriously low. Most workers earned between three to five rubles a week, while the most skilled struggled to earn ten. The vast majority of the factory's workers had only recently left the countryside. Alcoholism was rife among both men and women workers. Investigators found that alcoholism and destitution had forced several women workers into prostitution within the factory. Women workers, moreover, complained bitterly of maternity policies, decrying the fact that administrators invariably laid off pregnant workers and refused to rehire them after their pregnancy until a sewing machine "opened up."[85]

Already tense, factory conditions turned grievous in mid-January 1928, after the factory administration cut wages again but continued to increase the labor force. Wage cuts, the factory administration insisted, had been necessary to meet budgetary demands for ongoing capital improvements to the industrial complex, continued investment in new machinery, and repair of dilapidated worker dormitories, cafeterias, schools, and so forth. Even as it cut wages, the factory committee attempted to implement bonus structures, night work, and other measures to intensify worker productivity, all of which reportedly found widespread resistance among the women workers. Moreover, even as the factory sought to intensify productivity, it was beset by acute shortages of materials, orders, and markets for goods produced, leading to long furloughs and irregular work for employees.[86] In short, the Dvina factory experienced the same pressures toward industrial rationalization, intensified production, and austerity that sparked the turn to Trotskyism across the Belorussian Republic. Yet if Trotskyism emerged as a movement of "conscious" workers who came to conceptualize the changing structural conditions in political terms, antisemitism seemed a spasmodic reaction to structural pressures.

Officially, internal investigations stopped short of drawing a direct correlation between intensified productive pressures and antisemitism. In fact, the reports made only passing reference to antisemitism at all, stressing instead the general atmosphere of worker anger. The factory committee predictably rejected such interpretations. Having failed to cajole workers to collectively condemn her outburst, the factory committee fired Comrade Stepanova on charges of hooliganism after she circulated a petition demanding the overturning of Likhavidov's punishment. Following this, the factory committee redoubled its political campaign against antisemitism, hoping to combat the phenomenon through more forceful repression.[87] The Dvina factory committee ultimately had little choice but to dismiss the argument linking antisemitism to intensified structural pressures in the factory. Asserting such a linkage challenged the logic of productivism, which is to say the very logic of the Stalin Revolution.

Soviet Antisemitism and the Language of Power

Discourses about Jews and antisemitism became a primary political language through which Soviet society conceptualized radical structural change and the dynamics of power itself in the midst of a social rupture that appeared both total and inexplicable. Insofar as the social roots of the crisis became politically unspeakable, the party attributed the resurgence of antisemitism to the same groups that purportedly drove the economic crisis: the kulak, the Nepmen, the international capitalist, and the crypto-tsarist. Official proclamations and press coverage of antisemitism relied rhetorically upon tropes of Jewish victimhood. Narratives of Jewish victimization were, moreover, manifestly intensified by the gendered nature of the attacks in the Oktiabr' factory, the Dvina factory, and other similar episodes. Newspaper reports, internal investigations, and public proclamations repeatedly stressed the frailty, physical weakness, diminutive stature, and "illiteracy" of Comrade Barshai and other targets of violence and harassment. In stressing the victims' passivity and vulnerability, the party, and through it, the state, positioned itself as the defender of the weak and guarantor of equality and revolutionary justice. Insofar as many of these incidents also involved defending the rights of the Soviet woman, the representation of women in the anti-antisemitism campaign dovetailed precisely with the gendered logics rife in propaganda of the Stalin Revolution.[88]

Clearly not all episodes of antisemitism targeted Jewish women. Episodes of victimized male workers, however, rarely aroused the same degree of coverage or sympathy in the press. Indeed, when Jewish men did appear as primary actors in public narratives about ethnic violence, it was overwhelmingly as malignant agents of purported Jewish chauvinism and intolerance. In keeping with the gendered structure of passivity and agency, such stories frequently focused upon the victimization of non-Jewish women at the hands of Jewish men. Such, for example, was the case at the local tannery in the shtetl Orsha, in eastern Belorussia, where a young, recently hired Russian worker in the tannery, Comrade Sharai, experienced repeated harassment at the hands of three Jewish workers, Faerman, Naiman, and Gurvich. In December 1928 representatives from the leatherworkers union reported patterns of systematic verbal abuse of Sharai and other non-Jewish workers. According to investigators, the accused made repeated sexual jokes at Sharai's expense, referred to her and other workers as "goys" and "goyishe kep" (literally, non-Jewish heads, a term of abuse meaning "stupid people,"), and denigrated other non-Jews in the factory. Following the investigation, the tannery immediately fired all of the accused.[89]

Rhetorically, party members routinely emphasized the danger of Jewish chauvinism as comparable to that posed by antisemitism. In actuality, the two forms of national chauvinism differed sharply. In quantitative terms, reported episodes of antisemitic attacks vastly outnumbered similar episodes of Jewish chauvinism.[90] Qualitatively, as in the Dvina factory, charges of Jewish chauvinism frequently emerged as a reaction to charges of antisemitism. Consequently, claims of Jewish chauvinism came to be deployed to support the logic of antisemitic discourses, insofar as both insisted upon the malignant agency of Jews. Finally, while charges of Jewish chauvinism could be used either to press for integration or subtly oppose it, acts of antisemitism invariably opposed integration. As such, they brought their espousers into immediate and direct conflict with administrative and coercive organs of the state.

Official narratives of antisemitism stressed the role played by enemies of the working class in fermenting intranational hatred. In practice, the campaign against antisemitism overwhelmingly targeted the factory floor. As with earlier campaigns against Bundism, Trotskyism, and the like, the mass meeting became the weapon of choice in this ideological struggle. Between the end of 1928 and mid-1929, party activists held meetings and brought to light episodes of antisemitism at glassmaking and paper factories, textile mills, chemical and machine works, and numerous other locales across the republic.[91] By targeting productive sites with recently integrated labor forces, the party effectively acknowledged in practice what it denied in public: that antisemitism was a social phenomenon driven largely by workers, komsomol members, and party members. In theory, the mass meetings were intended to engage workers in criticism, as well as self-criticism, for the sake of bringing to consciousness unrecognized animosity and excising the pathology of race hatred from the ranks of the proletariat. In practice, the airing of grievances let loose the passions, animosities, bitterness, and rage of the repressed.

Across the republic, mass meetings revealed different stories, ranging from name-calling, verbal abuse, and acts of physical violence. In many locations, workers performed the public ritual as planned, condemning antisemitic utterances and practices as an existential threat to the revolution. In the builders union of Bobruisk, workers denounced Alesia Bazileva Bazhichko for repeatedly berating Comrade Shpeer, a Jewish white-collar worker in the insurance office. In particular, they chastised Bazhichko for allegedly informing Shpeer that his "place is in the synagogue" and for repeatedly telling Shpeer that, "nowadays, it's your regime," meaning that the Jews had taken over.[92] At the state glassmaking factory *Dombal'* in the Borisov raion, union members decried Comrade Gaisenkov, a member of the executive committee, for verbally abusing a Jewish woman worker, calling her a "Jew face" (*zhidovskaia morda*), and generally complaining about the "kike antics" of the factory's small group of Jewish workers.[93] At the Stalin machine factory in Bobruisk, the mass meeting rebuked one group of "hooligans" for attacking Jewish workers on Yom Kippur, and condemned one komsomol member for refusing to study with Jewish students.[94] Union members at the Il'ich glassmaking factory in Novy Bykhov condemned Comrades Zheltkov and Sirmanom, who reportedly went to the apartment of one Jewish worker late at night, woke him up with violent shouts, hit him in the face with a cow liver, and threatened to hang him from a noose they had brought along. The accused claimed the whole event was a prank; the union members responded by expelling both for hooliganism.[95]

In many locations, however, mass meetings took on unexpected dynamics and proved difficult to control. Such transpired during a meeting at the second brickmaking factory in Bobruisk, convened in early December to address events from November 14, the day after news of the Oktiabr' Affair broke. On that day, a group of Belorussian workers requested an advance of six rubles from the factory, spent the money getting smashed on alcohol, and beat up a group of Jewish kustari in the factory. The group of twenty-something workers, almost all seasonal workers, then poured onto the streets screaming, "beat the Jews, save Russia," and "slaughter all the Jews and Tatars, get four years," and launched a mini-pogrom in the town before being arrested on charges of hooliganism. Defying the script that called for them to condemn these acts of "antisemitic banditry" in their ranks, union members instead sided with the accused. "The Jews sit in power," one worker reportedly said. Another chimed in, "the Jew won't get his hands dirty, but sits at the table." A third, "for hooliganism, punishment is necessary, but why drag antisemitism into this? They're just following Oktiabr';" and still another corrected him, "they're pulled along by the Yids."[96] Rather than condemn the antisemites, members of the brickmaking factory affirmed their logic, without consequence.

The turn of events at the second brickmaking factory in Bobruisk served as an early indicator of widespread resistance to changing political winds. While the campaign against antisemitism took the same form as earlier initiatives against Bundism and Trotskyism, the underlying dynamics of political power had reversed completely. Previous campaigns overwhelmingly targeted Jews in the party ranks, finding widespread support among non-Jews and resistance among pockets of mostly Jewish workers. The didactic campaign against antisemitism, unsurprisingly, reversed the tides. In numerous locales, non-Jewish workers subverted the intended narrative by transforming meetings into discussions about the purported problems of the Jews. Across the republic, workers turned time and again to a central trope: that of Jewish political and social power.

A striking example occurred in the trade union meeting held at the Torg-Stroi brickmaking factory, also in the Bobruisk Okrug.[97] On December 1 party and trade union leaders gathered the forty-five members of the labor force to discuss events in the Oktiabr' factory. Following the reading of a report about the events, the party and union organizers opened the floor. Rather than performing the expected script by condemning the antisemitic events in Svisloch, the almost exclusively non-Jewish workforce immediately began to justify the events. The opening question by Comrade Khoban'ko set the tone: "Why do Jews now have to work in the fields and factories, when before they were able to live without working, had a shop, and lived magnificently?" Comrade

Shevelevich followed by stating that the TorgStroi workers should refuse to issue a strong resolution condemning the events, since the accused perpetrators were "ignorant workers who acted out of a lack of consciousness." Then Comrade Dem'ianovich jumped in: "If they shoot those people," referring to the accused in the Oktiabr' factory, "then I will go and slaughter Jews, too."

Rather than sparking outrage, Dem'ianovich's shockingly blunt comment seemed to embolden other workers. Comrade Khokhlov followed: "They pampered that girl in the Oktiabr' factory because she's a Jewess, and then inflated this to antisemitism and counterrevolution. But if she had been a Russian, than nothing would have happened, and we would not be speaking out against these workers." Comrade Kutsenko then chimed in, demonstrating a clear familiarity with old peasant yarns, if a complete lack of historical knowledge: "Soon, things are going to be here just as they were in Austria, back when the queen was a Jewess, and everyone had to kiss the Jew's ass, because he was a Jew, and no one was allowed to say anything about this."[98] Comrade Savchuk, while decrying the failures of the Oktiabr' factory committee and the local party cell, argued against taking any action against the accused perpetrators. If the party punished them, then "the bourgeoisie will say to their workers, that they [the Bolsheviks] put Russian workers on trial for the sake of one Jewess, but we would never put them on trial." Tellingly, Savchuk then blamed the whole affair on the press: "every day, the newspapers write about antisemitism, and this doesn't improve the situation, but rather makes matters worse." Comrade Bogin, by contrast, placed the blame on a different culprit: the Jews themselves. "The Jews kick up a row and blame the Russians," he argued, before launching into a long story about his brother-in-law (who, he assured the meeting, was "no kind of counterrevolutionary") who had been arrested after an altercation in a market with a Jewish woman. The woman had bought eggs, Bogin explained, broke ten of them, and then demanded to be reimbursed. When the brother-in-law refused, the Jewish woman supposedly told the police he had said, "beat the Jews, save Russia," and was promptly thrown in jail. "And there are many such pieces of evidence that the Jews themselves incite the Russian workers against them." Comrade Zhivitsa agreed, "The Jews bring these attacks on themselves, and when someone touches them, it's antisemitism, etc., and then they try the workers as counterrevolutionaries."

All in all, the trade union recorded only two instances of factory workers speaking against antisemitism or the events at the Oktiabr' factory. Comrade Shelkov criticized his fellow workers, particularly Kutsenko and Shevelevich, for treating the events as a joke or a fabrication made up by the press. "We must reeducate all workers and peasants," he concluded, "since not one worker, nor one peasant, says anything good about the Jews." Comrade Meleshevich likewise condemned the prevailing spirit in the factory, pointing to underlying political questions. "Thanks to the October Revolution," he argued, "we achieved the unity of nationalities; therefore, when Comrade Dem'ianovich says, 'go and beat the Jews,' he says this from a lack of consciousness, because Jews, Russians, and Poles have one interest, and in the case of war we will all defend the October victory." In making this argument, Meleshevich sought to reassert official narratives of nationality and national cooperation in an environment festering with the logics of race. As the prevailing tenor of the comments in the factory made clear, however, the gains of October appeared in the process of being swallowed up by the ideological by-products spewing from the Oktiabr' factory.

Viewed as a collective political text, the TorgStroi meeting offers a rich glimpse into the construction of an emerging collective psychology in one locale. Collectively, the members of the factory told a story of Jewish power and worker powerlessness. According to their interpretation, the attacks on Comrade Barshai became an issue only because of her Jewishness (a claim that simultaneously revealed the utter normalcy with which this particular shop viewed violence against woman workers). The Jewess, moreover, likely incited the events herself, or made the whole event up to discredit "Russian" workers. If not the Jews themselves, then at least the press, and through it, the party stood behind the events and effectively caused antisemitism by talking about it. As for the culprits themselves, the workers in the TorgStroi factory collectively denied their agency completely: as "nonconscious" workers, they could hardly be blamed for systematic assault. Agency and responsibility lay with the victim; the perpetrators, in turn, became the victim of insidious forces. This, of course, was the fundamental logic of antisemitism on full display in the factory cell.

The close proximity between the Bobruisk brick factories and the Oktiabr' factory suggests that local conditions fueled animosities. As noted above, local factors clearly made Bobruisk a particularly fertile region for antisemitic agitation. Yet the same logics and tensions that flourished there with particular vibrancy simultaneously surfaced in towns and locales across the republic. Whether affirmed or condemned, mass meetings across the republic collectively revealed distinct patterns of thought and arguments about the power Jews supposedly held in Soviet society. In meetings at the First State Printing Press in Minsk in December 1928, workers branded Comrade Breinzen as a class enemy for repeatedly referring to "our Palestinian masters, the Yids." They chastised another printer, Kostiuk, who reportedly told Comrade Rodshtein, another (non-Jewish) worker, "when the Poles come, I myself will personally massacre twenty-five Jews," adding "don't worry, we have a fascist organization in the printing press."[99] At the matchstick factory Vezuvii in Gomel, one woman worker by the name of Sergeenko reportedly interrupted a mass meeting on antisemitism in early 1929, declaring that she "spit on the factory committee and the soviets, since only Jews sit there." Having already ensured her own exclusion from the mostly Jewish factory, she proceeded to implicate her husband, who, she insisted, was a communist, despite the fact that he hated Jews and believed it was necessary to drive them out of Russia.[100] In the glassmaking factory in the northern town of Trudy, party members organized mass meetings throughout the summer of 1929 in response to a series of antisemitic attacks, including several physical assaults. During one meeting one worker, Rygor Krytski, launched a long tirade blaming the ongoing agricultural crisis and the policies of collectivization on the Jews. One of Krytski's accusers laid bare the conspiratorial logic of his claims: "in the present we are living through many crises, and the interpretation of Krytski reduces all of these to the power of Jews in the Communist party, adding that the liquidation of the Jews would resolve all of these crises."[101] Concluding that a "secret antisemitic agitation circle had infiltrated the union," the party cell ordered the expulsion of numerous members.[102]

As it did across interwar Europe, the language of antisemitism in the Soviet context revealed fundamental anxieties about power and the perceived loss of power on the part of the working class. In ascribing overarching agency to Jews, discourses of antisemitism on the shop floor simultaneously asserted, in subverted form, the workers' loss of power. Confronted by the growing political onslaught of the Stalin Revolution, workers faced dwindling options to reverse this sense of political helplessness. Having thoroughly routed "conscious" political opposition through the assault on Trotskyism, the party had declared war on "unconscious" and reactionary opposition through the politics of race. To openly embrace antisemitism, or any form of "national chauvinism," was to invite the power and punitive weight of the administrative state. Moreover, despite the eruption of antisemitism across the republic, many workers either rejected those politics outright on principled grounds or at least remained ambivalent about embracing them openly. As the centralized state asserted its power on an unprecedented scale, the only viable path back from the wilderness of helplessness and political powerlessness was to swim with the tide and embrace the Stalin Revolution.

Nowhere was this process enacted as clearly as on the very shop floor that launched the antisemitic moment in Belorussia: the Oktiabr' factory. Rather than suppressing worker rage on the shop floor, the crackdown on antisemitism and the punishment of antisemitic culprits continued to reverberate in the glassmaking factory. Less than three weeks after the Oktiabr' Affair broke, another episode of worker conflict broke out on the factory floor. Early in the morning of December 1 a foreman in the workshop, Aron Badanin, a Jew, and Abram Tabenko, a non-Jew, got into an altercation with a young Belorussian apprentice named Sobol.[103] According to investigators, Badanin and Tabenko approached Sobol's station shortly before the end of the shift and began to stir the molten ash mixture in his cauldron. When Sobol tried to drive them away from his workbench, a fight broke out. Badanin threw a lamp at Sobol, hitting his arm, while Tabenko took a piece of hot glass and struck Sobol in the face, leaving him with a light burn on his cheek, according to doctors.[104] Badanin and Tabenko stated after the fact that they had provoked the fight with Sobol because he had disobeyed orders by using techniques learned from other masters in the workshop.

"As soon as the facts became known, the mood of the workers in the factory took a sharply negative turn," reports noted. Workers immediately asserted that Badanin and Tabenko had been motivated by the Barshai affair. They furthermore claimed that Tabenko and Badanin, a witness in the Barshai affair, would not be punished. "Now we'll see how the party organization treats this," one worker reportedly seethed, "especially since they're komsomol members and Jews." Another worker, Comrade Tishkevich, added, "*nu*, now let them go ahead and write in their newspapers." In fact, the response in the factory was instantaneous. The factory committee ordered an immediate investigation and called an emergency mass meeting to address the counterrevolutionary actions in the factory. The committee charged with organizing the meeting set the tone in their report from the morning of December 2. "Having reviewed the facts, it is absolutely clear that the actions of Badanin and Tabenko against Sobol were conscious actions to ignite national hatred among workers." Moreover, the actions were connected, it insisted, "to the offensive of the class enemy, who in the present case has utilized Badanin and Tabenko, who have fallen under the influence of shtetl Nepmen and kulaks."[105]

Workers turned up in droves for the mass meeting on December 2. Comrade Kren', the chairman of the organizing committee, opened the meeting by describing the attack before elaborating on the political meaning. Badanin, Kren' explained, was the son of a meat dealer from Svisloch, while Tabenko was the son of a blacksmith. The attack on Sobol, was, therefore, a salvo launched by the class enemy, "the second attack of the class enemy in our factory," referring to the Barshai affair. In framing the events in relation to the Barshai affair, Kren' made explicit what everyone in the room knew: from the outset, the second Oktiabr' Affair had the strong stench of retribution about it. Yet workers clearly learned a lesson about how to deploy the language of the Stalin Revolution to press their claims, as became clear when the floor opened for discussion.

Initially, several members of the factory briefly attempted to defend Badanin and Tabenko on the grounds of worker discipline. One, Petrushkevich, insisted that it was the duty of workers to listen to masters, and that masters had the right to intervene to correct a worker. "It was as a result of these events," he argued, "that Tabenko and Badanin became angry." Comrade Orlov agreed: "a subordinate needs to listen to what the master says, and if he doesn't listen, he gets burned." A number of workers immediately objected, revealing deep divides in the factory over the question of workplace conditions, worker authority, and management. Along with Comrade Petrovskii, they denounced the idea that a master had the right to burn a worker, even a bad worker. "But the whole matter has a deeper character," Comrade Petrovskii continued, turning the discussion. "Badanin is the son of a speculator. During his breaks he helps his father trade." Rather than denouncing him as a domineering master, or as a Jew, Petrovskii attacked Badanin in the language of Stalinism, as a class enemy.[106] At the same time, by harkening back to the language of speculation, Petrovskii simultaneously made it clear to all that this class enemy was simultaneously a Jew.

One by one, workers came forward to condemn Badanin in similar terms. Comrade Iandul'skii denounced him as the "son of a trader," adding that it was imperative to "cut off those workers who bring us harm." Comrade Zin'kevich detected in Badanin's actions the "hand of the enemy, who tries to stir up nation against nation." Comrade Ianchikovskii dug deeper still, explaining that Badanin affirmed the truth that "Lenin bequeathed to us, that differences between nations do not exist, and that every separate incident like this forces us to search with great attention for the tricks of the class enemy."[107] By the following day, internal investigations produced additional evidence of Badanin's essential nature as a class enemy by revealing that his brother and sister were underground Zionists, that his speculator father regularly supplied him with money, and that Badanin himself routinely skipped work details on Saturdays, presumably to engage in clerical activities. In short, the factory collectively exposed Badanin as a class enemy and a Jew, even as the fact of his Jewishness was never stated explicitly.

As for Tabenko, workers found him guilty of complicity in the affair, while simultaneously stressing his lack of agency, despite the fact that it was Tabenko who actually assaulted Sobol. Tabenko, one worker asserted, was the "son of a worker, and we should consequently regard this as hooliganism resulting from a lack of consciousness."[108] Comrade Gromov, in a separate meeting of professional activists, further emphasized Tabenko's lack of agency. "Badanin, the son of a speculator, used the worker Tabenko for his goal" of spreading national conflict. "This was a matter of the shtetl Nepman; through the hand of the worker Tabenko, the class enemy repeated his attack."[109] The investigative committee effectively agreed, arguing that Tabenko, the son of a blacksmith, had "acted the entire time under the control of Badanin."[110]

The denunciations of Badanin and Tabenko, in short, reproduced precisely the logic of antisemitic discourse, yet without mention of the Jews. Workers in the factory collectively branded Badanin a class enemy tied to speculators, clericalism, Zionism, and the shtetl. Similarly, they asserted his function as an agent of distant, powerful forces and ascribed to him the power to control the actions of workers, incite violence, and provoke national hatred. Yet unlike instances of antisemitic agitation, which asserted similar claims unsuccessfully, the worker revolt against the class enemies Badanin and Tabenko found nearly unanimous approval from the factory committee, the workers, the party, and the komsomol. In asserting the power of the Stalinist collective, workers once again recovered political agency, provided they wielded it in the direction of state power.

Among the scores of workers who stepped forward to denounce Badanin and Tabenko during the worker mass meeting, two, in particular, stood out. Aaron Isaakov Margolin and Mota Tsalev Rubinchik had been two of the Jewish workers who first came to Dreiza Barshai's defense during the initial affair. Now, confronted with the rapidly changing circumstances in the factory, they faced a political choice. Given the terms of the debate, the repeated evocations of the Barshai affair, and the demand that the two attacks be viewed as equal despite the rather unequal severity of the episodes, both Rubinchik and Margolin undoubtedly recognized the retributive nature of the second Oktiabr' Affair. To protest against this retributive dimension assuredly would have reverberated back in the charge of Jewish chauvinism or hypocrisy. The Stalin Revolution had demanded punishment of Barshai's attackers on the grounds of revolutionary justice and integration. Margolin and Badanin repaid the debt.

"Badanin executed the business of the speculator," Margolin informed the crowded room, "trying to call forth hatred between nations." "But," he added, "the most recent event should in no way be understood as a matter of revenge; rather, the recent event carries the character of the class enemy. We demand that Badanin and Tabenko be brought to justice. We once and for all disassociate from such workers." The room erupted in applause. Rubinchik followed, addressing the second accused. "Tabenko did what he did under the direction of Badanin," Rubinchik asserted, adding that Badanin was, in turn, "sufficiently developed to understand that he made a horrible decision." Rubinchik stressed, "this does not exclude the possibility of ascribing blame to both of them. They both did a horrible act. We must exclude them from our workers' family." The room erupted in applause again, as the workers moved to expel

Tabenko and Badanin from the factory, the union, and the party. Having overcome the particularity of national myopia, the collectivist power of the Stalin Revolution was unleashed.

The Jewish Revolution was over in Svisloch.

Conclusion

Anti-Jewish attitudes, conspiratorial thought about Jewish power, violence against Jews, and the language of hatred did not disappear following the revolution of 1917. While antisemitism remained a constant presence in post-Revolutionary society, as even the most optimistic Bolshevik would certainly have admitted, the force of the ideology ebbed and flowed. Suppressed in certain moments, such attitudes and actions bubbled up repeatedly in periods of economic and social crisis throughout the 1920s. For the most part, these incidents flew under the radar or were explained away as vestiges of prerevolutionary reactionary thought. Antisemitism, as a particular form of racial thought, regained coherence in the specific social context of the upheaval wrought by the crisis of NEP society and the Stalin Revolution; it returned as a social fact when the state actively construed such sentiments and acts as a discernible ideology to be uprooted ruthlessly. Cynically, it might be argued that antisemitism returned as a fundamental problem of Soviet society during the Stalin Revolution only because the regime said it was so. Moreover, in delineating official antisemitism, the Soviet state simultaneously placed its own policies toward Jews, including the myriad forms of overt and subtle exclusion practiced under the language of class and political struggle, beyond the realm of suspicion. By designating certain practices as antisemitism, the state exonerated its own web of policies toward speculators, *lishentsy*, Zionists, Trotskyists, Bundists, and other suspect groups that tended to be largely, if not exclusively, Jewish.

The campaign against antisemitism cannot be divorced from the rhetoric and practices of Stalinist political rule. Despite this fact, antisemitism also constituted a real threat, both internationally and domestically. From the standpoint of the Soviet workers' state, the most alarming aspect of the antisemitic outbreak of the late 1920s was the degree to which this ideology seemed to resonate with the industrial working class. While the state attributed the movement to class enemies, the evidence base clearly indicates that in Belorussia and beyond, shop floors, factories, and workshops became the primary site of antisemitic revival, agitation, and violence. Far from proving to be the vanguard of an antiracist, postnational international proletariat of Marxist mythology, the Soviet working class seemed to become, on the eve of the Stalin Revolution, the primary social base for the antisemitic resurgence.

Writing on the eve of World War II as an exile from Nazi Germany, the iconoclastic Marxist critic Max Horkheimer emphasized the similarly troubling role the working class played in supporting the fascist authoritarian turn across Europe. Challenging myths concerning the instinctive class consciousness, international solidarity, and antiracism of the working class, Horkheimer stressed that the social and political breakdown of the 1920s made demoralized workers susceptible to the appeals of authoritarianism, even as the new statist order subjected them to unprecedented forms of domination.[111] Antisemitism resonated within the demoralized working class, he argued, precisely because it gave vent to the hostilities and psychic anger produced by the ruthless suppression of the promise of revolutionary change and human emancipation.[112] The repression of pan-European worker revolutions, the murder of leading revolutionaries, the perpetual crises of the interwar period, and the devastating unemployment catastrophe unleashed by the global crisis reverberated back onto the collective psyche of the proletariat. "Unconsciously," Horkheimer asserted, "the workers realize the horror of their existence, which they are nevertheless unable to change."[113] This intuitive realization of fundamental political powerlessness, fueled by the repression of emancipatory aspirations, became a driving dynamic of modern antisemitism. "The rage produced by misery, . . . the deep, fervent, secret rage of those dependent in body and soul, becomes active where opportunity presents itself . . . that is, against the weak and dependent itself."[114] Violence against Jews became a mechanism through which repressed populations vented rage at their own powerlessness, and in doing so affirming an "ideological practice in which people tend to demean the objects of social injustice all over again in their own minds, so as to give the injustice a veneer of rationality."[115]

The antisemitic moment that erupted hand in hand with the Stalin Revolution exhibited similar dynamics and logics.[116] The utterances of workers accused of antisemitic agitation, as well as general conversations about the topics of antisemitism and the Jews in Soviet society reveal a preoccupation with the question of power and powerlessness. Antisemitism became a language through which workers expressed an instinctive realization of their own loss of political power, however crudely formulated. While the rhetoric of antisemitism stressed the supposed power wielded by Jews within the Soviet system, antisemitic action targeted individuals like Dreiza Barshai, who were themselves utterly marginal figures on the fringes of social networks and far removed from the halls of power. In attributing fundamental power to the Jews, antisemitic articulations acknowledged, however distortedly, the very real loss of power and position experienced by workers run over by the combined force of the Stalin Revolution and the Great Break. Politically, the Stalin

Revolution demanded the total organization of power from above, effectively abolishing spaces for oppositional worker politics from below. Socially, the Great Break ushered in radical social upheaval and construction intended to build socialist society, yet the price of socialist construction was borne in no small part by the working class itself, which experienced ever more intensive pressures to rationalize and increase productivity. Stalinist society produced antisemitism socially everywhere, insofar as the policies of austerity, credit-driven industrialization, and labor regimentation coalesced in the new system of scarcity-driven production. Both abstract coercive pressure to intensify production and the direct coercion of the state's growing repressive apparatus came to be interpreted and explained in the language of antisemitism. As an ideology, it appeared to account for the paradoxical fact that the revolution made in the name of the emancipation of the working class brought instead unprecedented forms of social and political domination.

In Belorussia, antisemitism became one, but by no means the only, mechanism through which workers attempted to reverse the loss of power by opposing the Soviet project of transcending "national" and "cultural" difference through the integrative practice of ceaseless labor. Opposition to the march of social integration entailed an implicit rejection of the Soviet conception of progress. The campaign *against* antisemitism, consequently, emerged as a political weapon to further the project of social integration in the factory and forge new types of abstract, undifferentiated, universal labor. Ultimately, the campaign against antisemitism was, then, like that against shop-floor Trotskyists, also a campaign to productivize labor. The obliteration of "cultural" impediments to the intensified integration and application of abstract labor was fundamental to Stalinism, as it was to driving ideologies of all nonfascist, advanced industrial societies. Antisemitism and anti-Trotskyism emerged as twinned discourses, raising their heads together with campaigns to productivize, rationalize, and intensify labor.

The struggle over antisemitism simultaneously played a role in directly shaping new forms of Soviet subjectivity. The process of talking through the problem of antisemitism produced a predictable response. Reacting to their own discrimination against minorities, the majority bound together and succeeded in dragging, coercing, and educating recalcitrant party members until they relented into the consensus. The language of antisemitism was reversed in many locations into a language about Jewish willingness to integrate, about their haughtiness or dubious loyalty. Jews, in turn, faced a choice: to renounce politics, fight until excluded, or dive into the consensus. Insofar as they accepted this consensus, Jews made an implicit Faustian bargain with the Stalin Revolution, exchanging "power" for security and support. Despite recurrent surges in antisemitic sentiments throughout the 1930s, the Stalinist state effectively upheld its end of the bargain. Unlike in much of Europe, where entrenched elites took cover behind discourses about the "problem" of the Jews, the Stalin Revolution, for all of it numerous failures, rejected the pan-European antisemitic turn. Antisemitism continued to exist, but it would not overtly rule the law of the state. That difference proved absolute.

Examined against the broad sweep of Jewish history, the social contract offered by the Stalinist state appeared as a return to what Yosef Yerushalmi understood to be the dominant paradigm of Jewish politics in the premodern world: as vulnerable minorities, Jews necessarily sought alliances with the state for protection, at the cost of autonomous politics.[117] Superficial resemblances notwithstanding, the Stalinist social contract reflected, in actuality, the emergence of a decidedly new arrangement under a radically new form of total political state. Within the Stalinist state, Jews ceased to function as politically autonomous agents because political autonomy outside of the Stalinist collective ceased to exist. Stalinization became the only avenue for Jewish political participation because it became the only avenue for legitimate politicization for all Soviet citizens. Forcefully reasserting an imperial logic of power, the Stalin Revolution obliterated the politics of regionalism and local autonomy. In their place, it asserted the hegemony of the center. The collectivity stood on the verge of trampling out of existence the subjective vestiges of the small-minded and constrained bourgeois individual. Judaism, excessive Jewishness, and certainly nonconfessional secular Yiddish culture would have to go.[118] The Soviet Union became "good" for the Jews in body, provided they accept the collective efflorescence of the Stalinist crowd in spirit.

CONCLUSION

THE INAUGURATION OF the sweeping campaign against antisemitism in 1928 marked the opening of a primary front of Cultural Revolution in Belorussia. Unleashed at the moment of the Great Break, the proponents of Cultural Revolution harkened back to the intellectual fervor, bellicose language, and "style" of the Civil War (1918–1921) in the hopes of purifying the *proletarian* revolutionary project. Cultural Revolution spasmodically attacked "bourgeois specialists," "petit-bourgeois" writers, cultural producers, professors, and intellectuals of all types who allegedly infiltrated party ranks and institutions to sabotage the revolution internally. Cultural Revolutionaries everywhere demanded war on overt class enemies who purportedly sought to undermine and overturn the revolution.[1] Across Belorussia campaigns to "purify" the revolution called for renewed attack on hidden social enemies in the form of petit-bourgeois elements, speculators, and middlemen; ideologically, campaigns demanded the eradication of deviations of Bundism, Trotskyism, and antisemitism.

As examined throughout this work, each of these problematic categories was bound, implicitly or explicitly, with questions of "Jewishness." That the twinned ruptures of the Great Break and Cultural Revolution should have triggered renewed, rancorous debate about the place of Jews in revolutionary society was anything but surprising; throughout the 1920s, every episode of social and economic crisis triggered reconsiderations of the place of Jews in Belorussia. At the heart of these recurrent debates stood the underlying issue of the integration and assimilability of Jews within postrevolutionary society. With the Stalinist mass campaign against antisemitism—one-sided though it was in the given moment—the party leadership sought to resolve the issue

238

once and for all by visibly defending the full integration of Jews within all spheres of Soviet life. In this context, the party adamantly defended the principle of integration at a moment fraught with resurgent national, ethnic, and racial animosity. For Belorussian Jewry, continued integration necessitated the implicit acceptance of a new social contract: the initial Bolshevik promise of relatively autonomous national collective identity was displaced by a curiously liberal defense of cultured individuality predicated on the assimilation of Jews into an increasingly universalizing "Soviet" identity.[2]

Pressures to embrace emerging, universalizing forms of "Soviet" identity did not, of course, effect Belorussian Jewry alone. Rather, the campaign against antisemitism coincided with a dramatic, razor-sharp reversal of nationalities policy across the republic and the western borderlands of the Soviet Union. The language of conciliation and compromise in nationality policy gave way to the language of unyielding struggle against nationalist deviants as class enemies. Revitalized by radicalized, young militants, the revolution threw its full might against the constructed boundaries of nationality. Beginning in late 1929, as the Cultural Revolution built toward the politics of the purge and the practices of terror, the Bolshevik regime unleashed "administrative" measures to bring a forceful end to the politics of nationality introduced during the NEP. Among the first victims of this repression were alleged Belorussian nationalist deviants and purported members of nationalist conspiratorial parties, whom the state accused of plotting to overthrow Soviet power to reestablish a "bourgeois" nation-state in White Russia. The purge of Belorussian nationalists swallowed mass numbers of alleged conspirators. Scores of leading Belorussian communists, including Vsevolod Ignatovskii, Dmitrii Zhilunovich, Aleksandr Adamovich, and Anton Balitskii were driven from their positions in the party and the state apparatuses. Arrests of hundreds of other activists, cultural figures, and writers, including the leading writers Yanka Kupala and Yakob Kolas, followed. Some recanted their deviations and were awarded brief respites. Others met dire ends. On February 4, 1931, the Belorussian historian and Bolshevik cultural activist Vsevolod Ignatovskii shot himself following interrogation at the hands of the GPU.[3] Dmitrii Zhilunovich, arrested in 1936, committed suicide in a psychiatric hospital shortly thereafter.[4] As it unfolded, the Great Terror wiped out virtually every prominent party activist of the 1920s in Belorussia, whether Belorussian by nationality or otherwise. Nikolai Goloded, who became chairman of the Sovnarkom in the late 1920s, was shot in 1936. Vil'gel'm Knorin, who briefly returned to Minsk as a party secretary in the late 1920s before becoming a full-time historian, was arrested in 1937 and shot the following year. Aleksandr Krinitskii, recruited to Moscow to become the head of agitation and propaganda for the entire USSR, was shot in 1937.

Aleksandr Cherviakov was shot in 1938. They constituted the tip of the tip of the iceberg.[5]

The abrupt turn in nationality policy unleashed with the Great Break held similarly devastating consequences for alleged national deviationists in the Jewish camp. Throughout 1929 the leading figures of the evsektsiia in Belorussia came under attack for allegedly promoting national chauvinism and opportunistic petit-bourgeois political movements. The evsektsiia itself was closed in 1930. In February of that year Abram Beilin was purged from the party, but ultimately survived the terror of the 1930s; he was an exception, but not a solitary one. Samuil Agursky was arrested in 1938 and sent to the Gulag before dying of natural causes in Grodno in 1947. Shepshel Shepshelevich Khodosh died of natural causes in 1951. Few others were so lucky. Semen Dimanshtein was shot in 1937, as were Il'ia Osherovich, Moisei Kalmanovich, and Boris Orshanskii, the editor of the Yiddish newspaper *Oktyabr*. Yankel Levin was arrested in 1937 and shot the following year. Ester Frumkin, arrested in 1938, died in the Gulag. Rakhmiel Vainshtein was arrested and shot in 1938.[6] The fates of many rank-and-file party members encountered here remain unknown. Yet it is likely that many perished in the purges of the 1930s, particularly those with Bundist or Trotskyite pasts. Many lesser figures who did survive the 1930s were doubtlessly murdered in the Holocaust.[7]

The Jewish Revolution in White Russia ended long before the German army and killing apparatuses brought forth the destruction of Eastern European Jewry. The Great Break brought a dramatic end to the project of Jewish cultural and social reconstruction in revolutionary White Russia. Unlike the regimes of Central Europe, which increasingly fell with lockstep precision behind the explicit politics of antisemitism, the Stalin regime remained steadfast in its opposition to antisemitism, at least on paper, throughout the 1930s. Yet the absolute social upheaval unleashed by the Great Break completely eviscerated the possibility for the type of cultural transformation envisioned by proponents of Jewish Revolution in the heady days of revolution. In place of this vision of individuals emancipated within national communities and local political structures, the Stalin Revolution violently imposed modernizing, homogenizing universalism.

* * *

In his pioneering study of Jewish politics in the Soviet Union, Zvi Gitelman long ago stressed the crucial relationship between Stalinist industrialization and Jewish integration. For Gitelman, the story of the Soviet Jewish experience was a narrative of top-down modernization. Driven by a commitment to Marxian conceptions of class revolution, the Bolsheviks, from the outset of the revolution, consciously sought to break down local Jewish institutions, traditional life, and autonomous politics for the sake of forcibly integrating Jews into Soviet society. To this end, promoters of Jewish "national" politics and cultural autonomy within the Bolshevik movement and the evsektsii—however sincere in their intentions for cultural transformation—unwittingly served as the agents of Bolshevization and Soviet domination on the Jewish street by breaking apart traditional communities, structures, and politics. Despite these attempted measures, Gitelman stressed that full integration only came with the top-down, state-driven industrialization campaign, which finally succeeded in breaking down communities and integrating Jews socially.[8]

This work largely confirms Gitelman's emphasis on the absolute centrality of the industrialization drive that began in the late 1920s for understanding the process of Jewish integration.[9] At the same time, it challenges the claim that dynamics of either the Jewish or the Bolshevik Revolution can be understood simply as a process of top-down, state-driven modernization. From the outset, the Bolshevik Revolution spoke the language of integration and equality between national groups. These commitments emerged directly from local contexts brutalized by global war and ravaged by ethnically and politically driven civil war. Throughout the region of central and eastern Europe, the Great War and its aftermath left millions dead or maimed, entire regions decimated, and populations devastated physically and psychologically. Across Europe the war created new and galvanized existing forms of antidemocratic, militarized, populist political movements predicated upon integral nationalism and the violent exclusion of minorities, especially, but not exclusively, Jews. The Bolsheviks understood their revolution to be a repudiation of the Great War and the world that produced this descent into modernist savagery. In light of this context, this work began from the premise that the Bolshevik commitment to intranational reconciliation, the eradication of national hatred, and the overcoming of the debased politics of racial exclusion were real and unprecedented. Rather than being imposed from above through processes of statist modernization, this revolutionary transformation found widespread support from across war-torn regions. Belorussia, moreover, constituted an ideal-typical site to carry out this grand experiment in overcoming nationalist barbarism through the democratic promotion of nationality.

Despite these commitments, the Bolshevik experiment ended up producing intranational conflict and ethnic division across the western borderlands of the Soviet Union over the course of its first decade. In Belorussia the revolution that began with the premise of overcoming divides between peoples descended into seething intranational hostility by the late 1920s. Between 1926 and the full onset of Stalinism, the republic experienced successive mass campaigns, ostensibly targeting political deviations of Bundism, Trotskyism, and antisemitism, that opened space for the outpouring of increasingly feverish expressions of animosity. While the reasons for this reconsolidation of national, ethnic, and, ultimately, racial hostility were of course multifarious, this work has argued that the root causes of the reethnicization and racialization of politics in Belorussia were fundamentally structured by economy. The recurrent, systemic economic crises of the 1920s, I have argued, produced intensified social pressures that reanimated discourses of difference, generated intensified conflict, and ultimately drove the reconsolidation of racialized forms of thought and hatred.

Rather than resulting from the "Marxist" or "socialist" nature of Bolshevik economic policy, this work has stressed that the root of revivified intragroup animosities lay, paradoxically, in the persistence and intensification of underlying, core structures and relations of production that constituted the very heart of the supposedly abolished system of capitalism: specifically, the social production of value based upon waged labor, for the sake of producing more value still. Rather than being driven by an intended process of state-directed modernization, the Soviet planned economy emerged in reaction to the perpetual crises generated by contradictions emanating from this basic social relation at the heart of soviet production. The Bolshevik experiment sought to overcome capitalism by attacking markets, by eradicating private property, by annihilating the capitalist class, and by nationalizing production under state control. Yet despite these measures, the Bolsheviks left in place, and progressively expanded, the fundamental social relation at the absolute core of the system of capitalist production—the process of workers alienating, or selling, their labor power in exchange for wages. The Soviet state responded to each moment of economic crisis in Belorussia by reconfiguring the relations of labor; in moments of crisis, overproduction, and disequilibrium, state apparatuses turned to familiar mechanisms to rationalize and discipline labor: they cut labor force, closed workshops, pushed workers onto "flexible" secondary labor markets or labor reserves, and drove down wages, all in the name of rationalizing productivity to restore equilibrium. In the context of socialized ownership of the means of production, extracted surplus labor was, in theory, poured back into society to build the workers state. Yet the experienced, everyday reality for most workers, particularly in the depths of the crises, remained unchanged. Rather than social emancipation, the revolution brought intensified labor, marginal existence below the line of penury, want, shortage, and a perpetual cycle of ever more intensified labor. For Marx, the core vision at the heart of socialism was the abolition of alienated labor; the Bolshevik regime, by contrast, transformed alienated labor into the end and goal of "socialist" production.

The persistence of waged labor as the basis of Soviet production held implications that extended far beyond the strict realm of economy. State responses to economic crisis fueled local animosities across the Belorussian republic. In "liberal" moments of response, such as those that predominated during the NEP, the state turned to tried and true mechanisms of shedding labor force—thereby intensifying intragroup competition for positions and resources, expanding scarcity, and exacerbating inequality between skilled and unskilled, protected union and unregulated labor. Such measures exacerbated animosities not only between national groups but also within groups. In periods of "statist" response, embodied in the emerging Stalinist system, the primary response to crisis involved deploying all administrative means to effect the massive intensification of labor productivity through industrial speedups, the sharp devaluation of labor through wage reductions, the destruction of worker organizations for collective security, and the application of increasingly widespread technology to drive up productivity and reduce productive costs. Each of these forms of response to crisis generated not only intensified anger between laboring populations caught in the vortex of violent restructuring, but also a general seething resentment toward the state, as well as against the abstract pressures to produce ever more quantities of goods through ceaseless labor.

In the context of crisis, economy increasingly "articulated"—to use the terms of Stuart Hall—with renewed forms of antagonistic, constructed difference on the shop floor and beyond.[10] In Belorussia, as elsewhere across Europe and the Soviet Union, each moment of structural crisis generated new conceptions of identities and social dangers that congealed increasingly around the multivalent figure of the Jew. Each episode of crisis hypostatized a certain manifestation of "Jewishness" and took this manifestation to be a malignancy on the body politic. Economic crisis in the form of price spirals and shortages generated tropes of speculation and economic chicanery that once again normalized the idea of the Jew as a predatory, parasitic agent of trade. Crises in the labor market brought Jews into direct conflict with non-Jewish labor, leading to charges of protectionism, exclusion, and aloofness—all of which came together under the rubric of "Bundism." Inflationary crises likewise drove the ever-escalating demand for the productivization of labor; resistance to productivization brought new allegations of non-Jewish-Jewishness in the form of Trotskyism. Each moment of crisis broke apart supposed qualities of "Jewishness" and magnified, demonized, or criminalized deviant parts. The Jew-in-and-of-himself/herself rarely came under direct attack in this process, at least not officially. But their phenomenal manifestations did. Despite the promise of inclusion, Bolshevik practices continually reinscribed Jews as anomalies.

With the Revolution, Bolshevik power avowed the full and final emancipation of the Jew, predicated upon the total reconstruction of Jewish social life. The program for the reconstruction of Jewish social and economic life, however, repeatedly ran up against the economic, social, and political limits of the NEP. In the repeated episodes of economic and political crisis that plagued the 1920s, the reconstitution of Jews as distinct and recognizable anomalies came to be interpreted as evidence of inherent nonassimilability. Initially, the purported unwillingness of Jews to integrate socially was read as evidence of persistent, if unspoken or hidden "cultural" affinities, labeled as "Bundism," that prevented Jews from fully entering into the newly constituted collective. As the crisis of the NEP deepened, assertions of Jewish difference hardened; as manifest within party debates about "Trotskyism," such discourses increasingly posited internal, ontological, and essential Jewish difference.

Thus, as I have shown, debates concerning Jewish identity and the possibility of integration existed on a continuum. As economic and social crises intensified and deepened over the 1920s, conceptions of Jewish identity morphed from valorized ideas of officially affirmed collective national identity, to dubious but affective conceptions of ethnic identity grounded in culture, and finally to ascribed assertions of difference grounded in essence or ontological difference. In other words, over the course of the 1920s, conceptions of Jewish identity exhibited a clear and pronounced example of what Eric Weitz described as the "slide from nation to race."[11] Race, in this context, was not constructed through the language of biological or genetic difference, as it was, most ominously, in Nazi Germany. Rather, in the context of the Soviet Union, the reconstruction of race and racialized conceptions of ontological difference emerged from the inherent and intensifying contradictions of economy. Even as the Bolshevik party sought to suppress the language of race politically, the contradictions of society and economy reproduced the logics of race socially.

While the party played no small role in driving this slide from nation to race through the anti-Trotskyist campaigns, the speed and vehemence with which the resurgent logics of race caught fire—particularly among members of the working class—provoked genuine alarm. In the context of interwar Europe, where insurgent right-wing, antirevolutionary parties sought power through the logics and politics of race, the surge of grassroots antisemitism fueled by working-class anger constituted an existential threat to the workers' state. The state responded by changing course, unleashing its full arsenal against the espousers of race, and redoubling its commitment to the principle of integration. This process of integration entailed a full assault against the peculiarities and particularisms of Jewishness, because it was predicated on the full eradication of all particularism. Unlike the Belorussianization and anti-Bundism campaigns of the mid-1920s, which attacked the concrete particularities of Jewishness from the standpoint of the concrete particularities of Belorussian-ness, the Stalin Revolution attacked Jewishness (and Belorussian-ness) from the standpoint of abstract, universalizing labor. Rather than being driven by the always present, if hidden, end goal of modernization and the erasure of difference, the attack on all forms of national difference emerged, in other words, from the very sudden and very real threat of race and racial politics. In this moment, the Jewish Revolution was subsumed and eviscerated not simply as a function of the Stalinist industrial Revolution, but also in the conscious assault on the politics of race.

* * *

The sharp reversal of Jewish policy at the end of the 1920s, as well as the ultimate, horrific fate that awaited many participants, has led numerous observers to view the attempted Jewish Revolution within the Soviet experiment as a failure a priori. Rather than examine the Jewish Revolution in the language of success and failure, this work has focused upon the presuppositions of the Jewish revolutionaries, taken on their own terms, and the intentions and practices of the state. Ultimately, these programs for Jewish reform broke down under pressure of the repeated economic and social crises of the NEP. The fate of the Jewish Revolution was tied to the fate of the NEP and structured by the policies of that era. They imploded simultaneously.

The shortcomings, reversals, and limitations of the Jewish Revolution have been well documented, here and elsewhere. It is, of course, exceedingly easy to find shortcomings in a program that promised nothing short of total redemption. Yet the list of achievements accomplished by these Jewish cultural revolutionaries was remarkable: the Bolshevik state opened unprecedented numbers of secular schools for Jewish children; removed the restrictions on university entry for Jewish students; established schools and informal programs for Jewish workers; formed and supported state- and party-run literacy centers, libraries, theaters, worker clubs, and other cultural meeting centers; produced unprecedented volumes of printed materials in Yiddish; encouraged the opening of local artistic venues of all varieties; staged lectures, classes, and performances; and carried on a ceaseless press barrage of polemical debates with real and imagined opponents of Bolshevik reform. The unprecedented accomplishments of the regime defy simple quantification (although the numbers support the claim). What distinguished the Bolshevik reform of Jewish life from those undertaken at earlier historical moments across Europe was not mathematical, but philosophical. In place of older notions of reform—which imagined and sought to implement programs of modern, worldly, rigorous, and secular education for a select part of the Jewish community—the Bolshevik program understood itself from the outset in universalizing, democratizing terms. Many aspects of this outward transformation of Jewish cultural institutions lasted well into the 1930s, long after the spirit that brought them into existence had been extinguished.

This project of Jewish cultural transformation was not incidental, but rather intrinsic to a new, postbourgeois conception of Jewish emancipation born in the Soviet experiment. The success of the project was predicated upon the success of social revolution. The fact that the revolution promised a different form of emancipation for Jews, particularly nonelites, was recognized from the outset by the most marginalized of Jewish actors. These actors were, however, never simply, exclusively, or even primarily Jews. The revolution opened a broad variety of possible identities—identities of class, of occupation, of gender, of nationality, and of religion. To treat these actors exclusively as Jews is to privilege a rather essentialized conception of identity that many of the individuals in question would likely have rejected. This work has consequently sought to understand these actors in their multiplicities and complexities, arguing that social categories frequently mattered as much as, if not necessarily more than, "ethnic" ones. Yet the logics of ethnicity, and increasingly race, reemerged steadily over the course of the first postrevolutionary decade, to obstruct and delimit *social* revolution.

Alongside the ubiquitous intellectuals, at the forefront of the Jewish Revolutionary project stood the Jewish artisans—the shoemakers, tailors, cabinetmakers, watchmakers, and others. Following the pattern of revolutionary and evolutionary social movements across Europe, revolutionary change at the grassroots level within the Jewish milieu was driven by artisans confronted by the onrush of industrial revolution. The Jewish Revolution, moreover, arguably constituted the clearest example in the long, tumultuous history of Eastern European Jewry in which the popular classes—the unlettered, frequently illiterate, poor, marginal, and nonaristocratic—attempted to rise up and overturn the dominant social order within the Jewish communities. This revolt from below was undoubtedly only made possible by the broader revolutionary process that engulfed the region. Yet ample evidence points to the fact that many in the revolutionary rank and file enthusiastically undertook the project of social revolution and the remaking of the Jewish social order. In light of its plebeian nature, we should not be much surprised that this revolutionary project received the condemnation of traditional elites within the Jewish community.

The Jewish Revolution in White Russia was ultimately engulfed and overwhelmed by the broader trajectory of the Bolshevik Revolution. Over the course of the 1920s the Jewish Revolution lost ground because the initial social revolution that made it possible was reversed. This social revolution was neither a "socialist" nor a "communist" revolution, if these terms are taken to be synonymous designations for the type of state-centered, productivist, centralizing state that emerged in the aftermath of the Great Break. It was a petit-bourgeois revolution, if one takes the existence of market relations to be the quintessence of the petit-bourgeois experience. It was a democratic revolution, if one takes direct action of citizens at the most local level to be the definition of democracy. It was a collectivist revolution, if one takes the establishment of organizations for mutual support and welfare to be the basis for collectivism. And, truth be told, it was no stranger to the principle of anarchism, insofar as the state, when it lurched its head, tended to bring repression under one name or another.

The Jewish Revolution was necessarily Janus-faced. It was made by social groups that were on the losing side of the historical march of progress, at least from the standpoint of the emerging industrial, Fordist state of ever more intensified, ever more rationalizing productivism. It looked forward to the promise of a new cultural and social order, but ultimately clung to the idea that the new social order should look a lot like an improved version of the old. In the final analysis, there can be no doubt that the Jewish Revolution proved incapable of fulfilling the initial visions of its most committed practitioners. Yet to pronounce the project a failure in retrospect is to fail to recognize that in a world where "success" is guaranteed at the end of the bayonet and the machine gun, or through the marshaling of ever-greater productive powers for the sake of ever-greater destruction, or through the perpetual domination and repression of one social group or imagined community over another, failure is not always the worst option.

APPENDIX: TABLES

Table 1. Composition of Unions in Belorussia, by Nationality, 1921

Union	Membership		Of these									
	Absolute	%	Belorussian		Russian		Jewish		Polish		Other	
			abs.	%	abs.	%	abs.	%	abs.	%	abs.	%
Agricultural	9,491	100	8,828	93.0	168	1.8	292	3.1	131	1.4	77	0.8
Metalworkers	463	100	83	18.0	87	18.7	251	**54.2**	37	8.0	5	1.1
Woodworkers	2,892	100	1,132	33.1	300	10.4	1,405	48.0	42	1.4	13	0.5
Needleworkers	1,626	100	17	1.0	14	0.8	1,592	**97.9**	2	0.2	1	0.1
Food Producers	1,410	100	200	14.2	228	16.2	927	**65.8**	44	3.1	11	0.7
Leatherworkers	1,636	100	164	10.0	126	7.7	1,215	**74.2**	85	5.2	46	2.5
Chemical	1,821	100	559	30.5	51	2.8	331	18.1	876	47.9	14	0.7
Printers	774	100	66	8.9	36	4.8	619	**83.2**	18	2.4	5	0.7
Builders	2,741	100	1,253	45.7	372	13.5	1027	37.5	42	1.6	47	1.7
Transport	1,303	100	145	11.0	235	18.0	875	**67.3**	32	2.4	16	1.2
Communications	1,934	100	1,713	88.5	95	5.0	22	1.2	50	2.6	54	2.7
Provisioning	1,485	100	201	13.5	172	11.6	984	**66.3**	112	7.5	16	1.1
Komkhoz	2,225	100	1.072	48.2	198	8.8	747	33.6	95	4.3	113	5.1
Medical	4,747	100	1,816	38.3	650	13.7	1,912	40.2	264	5.6	105	2.2
Enlightenment	8,798	100	5,288	60.1	815	9.3	2,187	24.9	367	4.1	141	1.6
Artists	1,088	100	392	36.0	183	16.8	460	42.3	42	3.9	11	1.0
Sovrabotniks	8,052	100	2,736	34.0	888	11.0	4,133	**51.3**	140	1.8	155	1.9
Total	52,466	100	25,665	48.9	4,618	8.9	18,979	36.0	2,379	4.6	825	1.8

Source: Report on National Composition from the Central Soviet of Trade Unions, *Natsional'nyi Akrkhiv Respubliki Belarus'* f. 265, op. 1, d. 666, l. 13. Bold print indicates unions with Jewish majorities; italics indicate Jewish pluralities.

Table 2. Composition of Unions in Minsk *Uezd*, by Nationality, 1921

Union	Membership		Of these										
			Belorussian		Russian		Jewish		Polish		Other	
	Absolute	%	absolute	%	abs.	%	abs.	%	abs.	%	abs.	%
Agricultural	3,468	100	3,138	90.4	54	1.6	174	5.0	62	1.8	40	1.15
Metalworkers	250	100	41	16.4	32	12.8	**147**	**58.8**	24	9.6	5	2.0
Woodworkers	569	100	19	3.3	208	36.6	**329**	**57.8**	13	2.2	--	
Needleworkers	856	100	2	0.2	12	1.4	**839**	**98.0**	2	0.2	1	0.1
Food Producers	897	100	90	10.0	139	15.5	**622**	**69.3**	37	4.1	9	1.0
Leatherworkers	1,073	100	114	10.6	102	9.5	**742**	**69.2**	69	6.4	46	4.3
Chemical Workers	267	100	82	30.7	13	4.9	**141**	**52.8**	25	9.4	6	2.2
Printers	473	100	64	13.53	29	6.13	**361**	**76.3**	14	2.3	5	1.14
Builders	987	100	208	21.0	284	28.8	*457*	*46.3*	26	2.6	12	1.2
Transport Workers	815	100	98	12.0	205	25.2	**466**	**57.2**	30	3.7	16	2.0
Communications	984	100	894	90.9	20	2.0	4	0.4	18	1.8	48	4.9
Provisioning	761	100	105	13.8	106	13.9	**433**	**56.9**	102	13.4	15	2.0
Komkhoz	1,576	100	841	53.4	180	11.4	360	22.8	83	5.3	112	7.1
Medical Workers	2,794	100	982	35.1	316	11.3	*1,191*	*42.6*	211	7.6	94	3.4
Enlightenment	3,684	100	1,820	49.4	387	10.5	1,130	30.6	222	6.0	125	3.4
Artists	457	100	147	32.2	78	17	*208*	*45.5*	13	2.8	11	2.4
Sovrabotniks	3,960	100	1,038	26.2	326	8.2	**2,979**	**75.2**	80	2.0	137	3.5
Total	23,871	100	9,683	40.6	2,491	10.4	*9,983*	*41.8*	1,032	4.3	682	2.9

Source: *Natsional'nyi Arkrkhiv Respubliki Belarus'* f. 265, op. 1, d. 666, l. 1A–1V Compiled by the Central Soviet of the Trade Unions of the BSSR. Bold print indicates unions with Jewish majorities; italics indicate Jewish pluralities.

Table 3. Jewish Population in Belorussian Territories

Year	Jewish Population	Percentage of Total Population
1815	200,000 (estimated)	5 %
1850	500,000 (estimated)	12 %
1897	910,900 (1897 Census)	14.2%
1926	407,000 (1926 Census, within Soviet BSSR borders)	8.2 %

Source: Gershon Hundert, ed., *The Yivo Encyclopedia of Jews in Eastern Europe*, vol. 1 (New Haven: Yale University Press, 2008), 140.

Table 4. Jewish Populations of Major Urban Centers, 1897, 1926

City	Jewish Population (1897)	Total Population (1897)	Jewish Population as Percentage of Whole (1897)	Jewish Population (1926)	Jewish Population as Percentage of Whole (1926)
Minsk	47,561	90,912	52.3 %	53,686	40.8 %
Bobruisk	20,759	34,336	60.4 %	21,558	42 %
Borisov	7,722	15,063	51.2 %	8,358	32.4 %
Gomel	20,385	37,800	53.9 %	37,475	44 %
Mogilev	21,539	41,100	52.4 %	17,105	34.1 %
Mozyr	5,631	8,076	69.7 %	6,901	71.7 %
Slutsk	10,264	14,349	71.5 %	8,538	53 %
Vitebsk	34,420	65,719	52.4 %	37,013	37.5 %

Sources: Compiled from L. A Katsenel'son and D. G. Gintsburg, eds., *Evreiskaia entsiklopediia*, 16 vols. (Moscow: Terra, 1991), 5: 638 (Vitebsk), 11: 81 (Minsk), and 11: 152 (Mogilev); Gershon Hundert, ed., *The Yivo Encyclopedia of Jews in Eastern Europe*, vols. 1–2 (New Haven: Yale University Press, 2008); and G. G. Branover, ed, *Rossiiskaia evreiskaia entsiklopediia*, tt. 4–6 (Moscow: Epos, 2000–2007).

NOTES

Introduction

1. Needless to say, the process of emancipation in "the West" was variegated, complex, and conflicted. On the twisted roads to Jewish integration, see Jonathan Frankel and Steven Zipperstein, eds., *Assimilation and Community: The Jews in Nineteenth-Century Europe* (New York: Cambridge University Press, 1992), and Pierre Birnbaum and Ira Katznelson, *Paths of Emancipation: Jews, States, and Citizenship* (Princeton: Princeton University Press, 1995). On the contradictions of anti-Jewish legal discrimination in the Russian Empire, see Benjamin Nathans, *Beyond the Pale: The Jewish Encounter with Late Imperial Russia* (Berkeley: The University of California Press, 2004).

2. On the consternation engendered by the promise of liberal emancipation itself, particularly among liberal Jewish nationalist intellectuals, see Simon Rabinovitch, *Jewish Rights and National Rights: Nationalism and Autonomy in Late Imperial and Revolutionary Russia* (Stanford, CA: Stanford University Press, 2014).

3. On the centrality of labor to Soviet conceptions of citizenship, see Golfo Alexopoulos, *Stalin's Outcasts: Aliens, Citizens, and the Soviet State, 1926–1936* (Ithaca, NY: Cornell University Press, 2003).

4. According to the 1918 Constitution of the Russian Soviet Federative Socialist Republic (RSFSR), the rights of citizenship through labor applied not only to "native" populations, but also to foreign laborers residing in Soviet lands. On the expansive citizenship policies of the early regime, see Eric Lohr, *Russian Citizenship from Empire to Soviet Union* (Cambridge, MA: Harvard University Press, 2012), 132–134.

5. The concept of the "Jewish Revolution" employed here is informed by formulations articulated in Benjamin Harshav, *Language in Time of Revolution* (Stanford, CA: Stanford University Press, 1993), and Yuri Slezkine, *The Jewish Century* (Princeton: Princeton University Press, 2004). For Slezkine, the "Jewish Revolution" constituted, primarily, a revolt against Judaism and Jewishness. This work, in turn, stresses that proponents of the "Jewish Revolution" in Belorussia understood themselves as continuing longstanding trajectories of explicitly Jewish political and cultural revolt in the Pale of Settlement.

6. Harshav, *Language in Time of Revolution*, 5–6.

7. Prior to the end of the eighteenth century, the region of Belorussia existed entirely within the confines of the Polish-Lithuanian Commonwealth, the remarkably tolerant early-modern state

forcibly dismembered during the Partitions of Poland in 1772, 1793, and 1795. For recent accounts of the cultural implications of partition for Jews, see Israel Bartal, *The Jews of Eastern Europe, 1772–1881*, trans. Chaya Naor (Philadelphia: University of Pennsylvania Press, 2005), and Gershon Hundert, *Jews in Poland-Lithuania in the Eighteenth Century: A Genealogy of Modernity* (Berkeley: University of California Press, 2004).

8. Gershon Hundert, ed., *The YIVO Encyclopedia of Jews in Eastern Europe*, vol. 1 (New Haven: Yale University Press, 2008), 140.

9. According to the 1926 census, the Jewish population for the major cities of Belorussia was as follows: Minsk—53,686 (40.8 percent of total population); Gomel—37, 475 (44 percent); Vitebsk—37,013 (37.5 percent); Bobruisk—21,558 (42 percent); and Mogilev—17,105 (31 percent). Data compiled from Hundert, *The YIVO Encyclopedia of Jews in Eastern Europe*, vols. 1–2.

10. At the time of the 1897 Census, Jews formed roughly 75 percent of all artisans in the Vitebsk, Minsk, and Mogilev *gubernii* of the Russian Empire. See L. A. Katsenel'son and D. G. Gintsburg, eds., *Evreiskaia entsiklopediia*, 16 vols. (Moscow: Terra, 1991), 5: 638 (Vitebsk), 11: 81 (Minsk), and 11: 152 (Mogilev).

11. According to the 1897 Census, Jews constituted approximately three quarters of traders in the region. Yuri Slezkine suggests that by the 1920s, Jews constituted 90 percent of all private traders in Belorussia. See Slezkine, *The Jewish Century*, 218.

12. The resurgence of intranational animosities at the end of the 1920s is interrogated in Terry Martin, *The Affirmative Action Empire: Nations and Nationalism in the Soviet Union, 1923–1939* (Ithaca: Cornell University Press, 2001), 254–269.

13. On the Russian case, see John Klier, *Russia Gathers Her Jews: The Origins of the "Jewish Question" in Russia, 1772–1825* (DeKalb: Northern Illinois University, 2011); John Klier, *Imperial Russia's Jewish Question, 1855–1881* (Cambridge: Cambridge University Press, 2005); and Hans Rogger, *Jewish Policies and Right-Wing Politics in Imperial Russia* (Berkeley: University of California Press, 1986). On Ukraine, see Elias Tcherikower, *Di ukrainer pogromen in yor 1919* (New York: YIVO Institute for Jewish Research, 1965); Amelia Glasser, *Jews and Ukrainians in Russia's Literary Borderlands: From the Shtetl Fair to the Petersburg Bookshop* (Evanston, IL: Northwestern University Press, 2012); and Yohanan Petrovsky-Shtern, ed., *Jews and Ukrainians (Polin*, Volume 26) (Oxford: Littman Library, 2014).

14. Despite significant discrepancies in breadth and intensity, pogroms were by no means absent in Belorussia during the Civil War. In terms of numbers of victims, they were significantly over-shadowed by the Ukrainian pogroms, which killed between 70,000 to 200,000 Jews. On the Civil War pogroms, see Oleg Budnitskii, *Rossiiskie evrei mezhdu krasnymi i belymi (1917–1920)* (Moscow: Rosspen, 2005). For official investigations of the Civil War conducted by the Belorussian government, see *Natsional'nyi Akrkhiv Respubliki Belarus'* (NARB) fond 684, opis 1. On the pogroms, see also L. B. Miliakova, ed., *Kniga pogromov: pogromy na Ukraine, v Belorussii i evropeiskoi chasti Rossii v period grazhdanskoi voiny, 1918–1922: Sbornik dokumentov* (Moscow: Rosspen, 2007).

15. The radical modernity of the nation and nationalism is stressed, most emphatically, in Eric Hobsbawm, *Nations and Nationalism: Programme, Myth, Reality* (Cambridge: Cambridge University Press, 1990).

16. In this, my work challenges interpretations put forward by Terry Martin, as well as the classic argument in Yuri Slezkine, "The USSR as Communal Apartment, or How a Socialist State Promoted Ethnic Particularism," *Slavic Review*, 53: 2 (Summer, 1994), 414–452.

17. In this respect, the work departs from Zvi Gitelman's classic study of Jewish politics in the first postrevolutionary decade. Zvi Gitelman, *Jewish Nationality and Soviet Politics: The Jewish Sections of the CPSU, 1917–1930* (Princeton: Princeton University Press, 1972). The present study, while critical of some of Gitelman's conclusions, remains thoroughly indebted to this pioneering research.

18. In theoretical and methodological terms, this work draws on the tradition of social history introduced with E. P. Thompson, *The Making of the English Working Class* (New York: Vintage, 1966). It is also indebted to the generation of Soviet "revisionist" historians who rewrote Soviet history in light of the archives. It is impossible to cite them all individually, but collectively they produced works that laid the foundation for this study, including Sheila Fitzpatrick, Alexander Rabinowitch, and Richard Stites, *Russia in the Era of NEP: Explorations in Society and Culture* (Bloomington: Indiana University Press, 1991); Diane Koenker, William G. Rosenberg, and Ronald Suny, *Party, State, and Society in the Russian Civil War: Explorations in Social History* (Bloomington: Indiana University Press, 1989); and Lewis Siegelbaum and Ronald Grigor Suny, *Making Workers Soviet: Power, Class, and Identity* (Ithaca, NY: Cornell University Press, 1994).

19. My understanding of the relationship between antisemitism and capitalism in crisis is informed, first and foremost, by analyses of the Frankfurt School of critical theory and its successors. Of the many works that inform my analysis, the most influential remain Max Horkheimer, "The Jews and Europe," reprinted in Stephen Eric Bronner and Douglas MacKay Kellner, *Critical Theory and Society: A Reader* (New York: Routledge, 1989); Max Horkheimer and Theodor Adorno, *Dialectic of Enlightenment* (New York: Continuum, 1989); Moishe Postone, "Anti-Semitism and National Socialism: Notes on the German Reaction to 'Holocaust,'" *New German Critique*, No. 19, Special Issue 1: Germans and Jews (Winter, 1980), 97–115; Shulamit Volkov, Antisemitism as a Cultural Code: Reflections on the History and Historiography of Antisemitism in Imperial Germany," *Leo Baeck Yearbook XXIII* (1978), 25–46; and the endlessly provocative reading of antisemitism in Hannah Arendt, *The Origins of Totalitarianism* (San Diego: Harcourt Books, 1973).

20. This was, of course, by no means simply a Soviet phenomenon. For a recent, brilliant comparative analysis of the relationship between economic crisis and populist animosities, see Mark Loeffler, "Producers and Parasites: The Critique of Finance in Germany and Britain, 1873–1944" (PhD diss., University of Chicago, 2011).

21. Unlike recent works, which view Soviet opposition to antisemitism as a mere myth masking the history of antisemitism on the left, this work takes the position that the campaigns against antisemitism were real, important, and utterly contradictory. For a countervailing argument, see Robert Wistrich, *A Lethal Obsession: Anti-Semitism from Antiquity to the Global Jihad* (New York: Random House, 2010).

22. On the transformation of the region of Belorussia into the heart of the Nazi killing fields, see Timothy Snyder, *Bloodlands: Europe Between Hitler and Stalin* (New York: Basic, 2010).

23. The designation "White" emerged during the period of the Mongol suzerainty to refer to regions that did not pay tribute to the Khanate. The term increasingly came to designate lands that were generally "free" or exempt from the payment of tribute. Far from referring to an "essential" or "natural" quality, "White"-ness referred to a relational, social, and malleable quality. See Nicholas P. Vakar, "The Name 'White Russia,'" *American Slavic and East European Review* 8, No. 3, (Oct., 1949): 201–213. On the amorphousness of Belorussia as a political and national space, see Timothy Snyder, *The Reconstruction of Nations: Poland, Ukraine, Lithuania, and Belarus, 1569–1999* (New Haven: Yale University Press, 2003).

24. Bound together by dynastic union from the fourteenth century, the lands of Poland and Lithuania entered into official union with the Treaty of Lublin in 1569.

25. For recent accounts of the cultural implications of partition for Jewish cultural life, see Israel Bartal, *The Jews of Eastern Europe, 1772–1881*, trans. Chaya Naor (Philadelphia: University of Pennsylvania Press, 2005), and Gershon Hundert, *Jews in Poland-Lithuania in the Eighteenth Century: A Genealogy of Modernity* (Berkeley: University of California Press, 2004). On the "absence" of pogroms in Belorussia, see Claire Le Foll, "The Missing Pogroms of Belorussia, 1881–1882: Conditions and Motives of an Absence of Violence," in Jonathan Dekel-Chen, David Gaunt, and Nathan M. Meir, *Anti-Jewish Violence: Rethinking the Pogrom in East European History* (Bloomington: Indiana University Press, 2010).

26. The spread of the Haskalah constituted a significant portion of Simon Dubnow's canonic work on Jewish history in Russia and Poland. See, for example, Simon Dubnow, *History of the Jews in Russia and Poland from the Earliest Times Until the Present Day*, trans. Israel Friedlander (Philadelphia: Jewish Publication Society of America, 1916). An apologetic defense of the movement can be found in Jacob Raisin, *The Haskalah Movement in Russia* (Philadelphia: Jewish Publication Society of America, 1913). Recent scholarship has stressed the crucial importance of place and social change in thinking about the diffusion of the Haskalah. See, for example, Steven J. Zipperstein, *The Jews of Odessa: A Cultural History, 1794–1881* (Stanford: Stanford University Press, 1986); David Fishman, *Russia's First Modern Jews: The Jews of Shklov* (New York: New York University Press, 1995); and Benjamin Nathans, *Beyond the Pale: The Jewish Encounter with Late Imperial Russia* (Berkeley: University of California Press, 2002). On the centrality of place in the Haskalah in Galicia, particularly in cities like Brody and L'vov (known as Lemberg in Yiddish, Lviv in Ukrainian, and Lwow in Polish), see Nancy Sinkoff, *Out of the Shtetl: Making Jews Modern in the Polish Borderlands* (Providence, RI: Brown Judaic Studies, 2004).

27. On the fundamentally peripheral nature of Belorussia and its capital city, Minsk, see Elissa Bemporad, *Becoming Soviet Jews: The Bolshevik Experiment in Minsk* (Bloomington: Indiana University Press, 2013).

28. Located on the east-west line linking Moscow to Warsaw and the north-south line linking the Baltic and Black Seas, Minsk particularly benefited from the coming of the railroad.

29. On the social and economic function of the *shtetl*, see Yohanan Petrovsky-Stern, *The Golden Age Shtetl: A New History of Jewish Life in Eastern Europe* (Princeton: Princeton University Press, 2014). On the economic and social effects of the Great Reforms (especially the 1861 emancipation of the serfs) on Jewish social life, see Arcadius Kahan, *Essays in Jewish Social and Economic History*, ed. Roger Weiss (Chicago: University of Chicago Press, 1986).

30. The relationship between industrialization and the pogroms has been stressed in Charters Wynn, *Workers, Strikes, and Pogroms: The Donbass-Dnepr Bend in Late Imperial Russia, 1870–1905* (Princeton: Princeton University Press, 1992). While social rupture undoubtedly played a key role, the pogroms were fueled, politically, by the emergence of modern, right-wing populism, as stressed by various contributors to John Klier and Shlomo Lambroza, eds., *Pogroms: Anti-Jewish Violence in Modern Russian History* (Cambridge: Cambridge University Press, 1992).

31. Jonathan Frankel, *Prophecy and Politics: Socialism, Nationalism, and the Russian Jews, 1862–1917* (Cambridge: Cambridge University Press, 1981), 200–209.

32. Henry Tobias, *The Jewish Bund in Russia: From Its Origins to 1905* (Stanford: Stanford University Press, 1972), 75–80.

33. Frankel, *Prophecy and Politics*, 311.

34. For the formation of this movement, headed by S. V. Zubatov, the head of the Moscow secret police, see Tobias, *The Jewish Bund*, 141. For the actions of the Independent labor movement in Belorussia, see N. A. Bukhbinder, *Di geshikhte fun der Yidisher arbeter bavegung in Rusland: loyt nit gedrukte arkhiv materyaln* (Vilne: Farlag Tomor, 1931), 211–232.

35. In addition to the above-cited works, Eric Haberer stressed the importance of Minsk and other Belorussian cities as sites of mediation between Jewish and broader revolutionary politics. See Eric Haberer, *Jews and Revolution in Nineteenth-Century Russia* (Cambridge: Cambridge University Press, 1995), esp. 93, 169, and 202–203.

36. On the Bund's role as practical organizers, see Leonard Schapiro, "The Role of the Jews in the Russian Revolutionary Movement," *Slavonic and Eastern European Review*, 40: 94 (Dec. 1961), 148–167.

37. G. Aronson, S. Dubnov-Erlich, I. S. Herts, E. Novogrudski, H. S. Kazdan, and W. Sherer, *Di Geshikhte fun Bund*, Vol. 2 (New York: Farlag Unzer Tsayt, 1962), 9.

38. The schism is examined extensively in Frankel, *Prophecy and Politics*, 210–246. On the position of the RSDWP leadership during the 1903 congress, including the actions of Iulii Martov,

who had earlier played a formative role in the formation of the Bund, see Leopold Haimson, *The Russian Marxists and the Origins of Bolshevism* (Boston: Beacon, 1955), and Israel Getzler, *Martov: A Political Biography of a Russian Social Democrat* (Cambridge: Cambridge University Press, 1967), 63–95.

39. Within the Polaei Tsion movement, however, the Minsk branch eventually gained a reputation for stressing national liberation over class struggle, a fact eventually derided by Borochov himself. Frankel, *Prophecy and Politics*, 347.

40. On the massacre at Station Square, see Frankel, *Prophecy and Politics*, 149.

41. On 1905 in the region, see Bukhbinder, *Di geshikhte fun der yiddisher arbeter-bavegung*, 329–344.

42. The increasingly pro-Bolshevik atmosphere over the summer of 1917 was recorded in the memoirs of the Polish socialist, Vatslav Solskii. See Vatslav Solskii, *1917 god v zapadnom oblasti i na zapadnom fronte* (Minsk: Tesei, 2004).

43. Oliver H. Radkey, *Russia Goes to the Polls: The Election to the All-Russian Constituent Assembly* (Ithaca: Cornell University Press, 1977), 148.

44. While anti-Jewish violence proved limited compared to the absolute devastation in parts of Ukraine, pogroms also spread to Belorussia, where more than 800 Jews were killed in several weeks of anti-Jewish violence. For a history of pogroms in Belorussia, see Leonid Smilovitsky, *Evrei Belarusi: iz nashei obshchei istorii, 1905–1953* (Minsk: Arti-Feks, 1999), 21–37.

45. This project of national reconstruction is stressed in Martin, *The Affirmative Action Empire*.

46. The official postrevolutionary Bolshevik position largely followed Lenin's famous 1919 gramophone speech against antisemitism, which was distributed to Red Army units. For a transcript, see Hyman Lauer, ed., *Lenin on the Jewish Question* (New York: International Publishers, 1974), 135. In practice, individual Bolsheviks and Red Army units proved far from inoculated against the scourge of antisemitism.

47. Among the outstanding works of émigré activists turned historians, see Yakov Lestschinsky, *Dos Sovetishe Yudentum* (New York: Poalei Tsion, 1941); Solomon M. Schwarz, *The Jews in the Soviet Union* (Syracuse: Syracuse University Press, 1951); and Jacob Frumkin, Gregor Aronson, Alexis Goldenweiser, and Joseph Lewitan, *Russian Jewry (1917–1967)* (New York: Thomas Yasseloff, 1969). Lestschinsky was a member of Poalei Tsion, Schwarz had been an active Menshevik, and the group of authors in the third volume had strong ties to the Bund. Other later works stressing decline and repression include Salo Wittmayer Baron, *The Russian Jews Under Tsars and Soviets* (New York: Macmillan, 1976); Lionel Kochan, ed., *The Jews in Russia Since 1917* (London: Oxford University Press, 1970); and Nora Levin, *The Jews in the Soviet Union since 1917: Paradox of Survival*, 2 vols. (New York: I. B. Tauris, 1988).

48. Gitelman, *Jewish Nationality and Soviet Politics*; Mordechai Altshuler, *Ha-yevsektsiya bi-vrit ha-mo'atsot: beyn komunizm ve leumiyut* (Tel Aviv: Sifriyat po'alim, 1981); and Benjamin Pinkus, *The Jews of the Soviet Union: The History of A National Minority* (Cambridge: Cambridge University Press, 1988).

49. David Shneer, *Yiddish and the Creation of Soviet Jewish Culture, 1918–1930* (Cambridge: Cambridge University Press, 2004); Jeffrey Veidlinger, *The Moscow State Yiddish Theater: Jewish Culture on the Soviet Stage* (Bloomington: Indiana University Press, 2000); and Anna Shternshis, *Soviet and Kosher: Jewish Popular Culture in the Soviet Union, 1923–1939* (Bloomington: Indiana University Press, 2006). For a more sanguine view, which examines the cacophony of purportedly authentic Jewish culture within the revolutionary cauldron and the impossibility of meaningful Jewish culture under Bolshevism, see Ken Moss, *Jewish Renaissance in the Russian Revolution* (Cambridge, MA: Harvard University Press, 2009).

50. Bemporad, *Becoming Soviet Jews*. Continuities between pre- and postrevolutionary culture are likewise stressed in Jarrod Tanny, *City of Rogues and Schnorrers: Russia's Jews and the Myth of Old Odessa* (Bloomington: Indiana University Press, 2011).

51. Slezkine, *The Jewish Century*, esp. 152–167.

52. The concept of culture employed in this study is highly influenced by Clifford Geertz, *The Interpretation of Cultures: Selected Essays* (New York: Basic, 1973).

53. In this sense, this work agrees with many of Gitelman's argument concerning the role of "modernization" in integrating Jews into the Soviet system. Yet whereas Gitelman interprets modernization as a deliberate ideologically driven policy intentionally pursued by the Bolshevik party and Soviet state, this work views the policies of rapid industrialization and social integration as an unanticipated Soviet response to the global crisis of the late 1920s. For a recent excellent reworking of Gitelman's theory in light of archival materials, see the outstanding study of the Vitebsk province under soviet power presented in Arkadii Zel'tser, *Evrei sovetskoi provintsii: Vitebsk i mestechki, 1917–1941* (Moscow: Rosspen, 2006).

54. In addition to Martin, *The Affirmative Action Empire*, see Ronald Suny, *The Revenge of the Past: Nationalism, Revolution, and the Collapse of the Soviet Union* (Stanford: Stanford University Press, 1993); Ronald Suny and Terry Martin, eds., *A State of Nations: Empire and Nation-Making in the Age of Lenin and Stalin* (Oxford: Oxford University Press, 2001); and Francine Hirsch, *Empire of Nations: Ethnographic Knowledge and the Making of the Soviet Union* (Ithaca, NY: Cornell University Press, 2005).

55. Hirsch, *Empire of Nations*, 10.

56. As Hirsch notes, official Soviet nationality policy originally divided Jews into five *narodnosti* by region, before amalgamating them into a single *narodnost'* in 1938. Ibid., 132–133, 289–290.

57. See, in particular, Veidlinger, *The Moscow State Yiddish Theater*, 2; Bemporad, *Becoming Soviet Jews*, 81–84; and Zel'tser, *Evrei sovetskoi provintsii*, 121–147.

58. See, for example, the important but acrimonious 2002 debate in *Slavic Review*, which greatly informs my understanding of the complexities of the Soviet case. See Eric Weitz, "Racial Politics Without the Concept of Race: Reevaluating Soviet Ethnic and National Purges," in *Slavic Review* 61:1 (Spring, 2002), 1–29; Francine Hirsch, "Race Without the Practice of Racial Politics," *Slavic Review*, 61:1 (Spring, 2002), 30–43; Amir Weiner, "Nothing but Certainty," *Slavic Review*, 61:1 (Spring, 2002), 44–53; and Alaina Lemon, "Without a 'Concept?' Race as Discursive Practice," *Slavic Review*, 61:1 (Spring, 2002), 54–61. In addition to these seminal works, addressed below, see Alastair Bonnett, "Communists Like Us: Ethnicized Modernity and the Idea of 'the West' in the Soviet Union," *Ethnicities*, 2:4 (2002), 435–467; and Nikolai Zakharov, *Race and Racism in Russia* (London: Palgrave Macmillan, 2015).

59. The terms *natsional'nost'* and *narodnost'* were used interchangeably in the early 1920s; over the course of the ensuing decade, *natsional'nost'* came to refer to a fully formed nation, while *narodnost'* took on the connotation of a cultural nationality, or something approximating an ethnic group. In the text, I differentiate between these concepts when the specificity of the concept is in question; yet generally, I refer to the Jews and Jews as a nationality when speaking of their official status.

60. Max Weber, *Economy and Society* (Berkeley: University of California Press, 1978), 389; and Anthony Smith, *The Ethnic Origins of Nations* (Malden, MA: Blackwell, 1988), 3.

61. This constructivist definition parallels that offered in Eric Weitz's provocative essay and rearticulated more forcefully in his reply to Hirsch, Weiner, and Lemon. See Eric Weitz, "On Certainties and Ambivalense: Reply to My Critics," *Slavic Review*, 61:1 (Spring 2002), 62–65.

62. My understanding of linguistic practices in the reconstitution of race in the Soviet sphere is greatly indebted to Alaina Lemon's theoretically sophisticated contribution to the *Slavic Review* debate. My definition of race is further informed by various critical studies, including Thomas C. Holt, *The Problem of Race in the 21st Century* (Cambridge, MA: Harvard University Press, 2000); Stuart Hall, "Race, Articulation, and Societies Structured in Dominance," in *Sociological Theories: Race and Colonialism* (Paris: UNESCO, 1980), 305–345; Etienne Balibar and

Immanuel Wallerstein, *Race, Nation, Class: Ambiguous Identities* (London: Verso, 1991); and David R. Roediger, *The Wages of Whiteness: Race and the Making of the American Working Class* (London: Verso, 1991).

63. Weitz, "Racial Politics without the Concept of Race," 3.

64. For a remarkable recent treatment of the particular question of the underlying issues of race within Soviet antiracist policies, see Brendan Francis McGeever, "The Bolshevik Confrontation with Antisemitism in the Russian Revolution, 1917–1919" (PhD Dissertation, University of Glasgow, 2015).

65. In Weitz's words, certain groups became "racialized" insofar as "their suspect characteristics were seen to inhere in each and every member of the group bar none and were transmitted across generations." Weitz, "Racial Politics without the Concept of Race," 5. This process was not simply one of top-down ascription; as Brigid O'Keefe has demonstrated in her outstanding case study of Soviet gypsies, national groups frequently articulated their own sense of "essential" qualities for the sake of gaining support and resources. Brigid O'Keefe, *New Soviet Gypsies: Nationality, Performance, and Selfhood in the Early Soviet Union* (Toronto: University of Toronto Press, 2013).

66. Weitz, "Racial Politics without the Concept of Race," 3.

67. Hirsch, "Race Without the Practice of Racial Politics," 30–32. While Hirsch was absolutely correct in stressing the centrality of biologized theories of race to Nazi thought and practice, contemporary historians of race (as well as Weitz himself), have quite universally rejected and critiqued such biological definitions.

68. Some exemplary works from an enormous literature include Paul Gilroy, *There Ain't No Black in the Union Jack: The Cultural Politics of Race and Nation* (Chicago: University of Chicago Press, 1991); Anne McClintock, *Imperial Leather: Race, Gender, and Sexuality in the Colonial Contest* (New York: Routledge, 1995); Petrine Archer-Straw, *Negrophilia: Avant-Garde Paris and Black Culture in the 1920s* (London: Thames and Hudson, 2000); Matthew Frye-Jacobson, *Whiteness of a Different Color: European Immigrants and the Alchemy of Race* (Cambridge, MA: Harvard University Press, 1998); Thomas C. Holt, *The Problem of Freedom: Race, Labor, and Politics in Jamaica and Britain, 1832–1938* (Baltimore: Johns Hopkins University Press, 1992); Mae Ngai, *Impossible Subjects: Illegal Aliens and the Making of Modern America* (Princeton: Princeton University Press, 2014); and virtually every article included in Frederick Cooper and Ann Laura Stoler, eds., *Tensions of Empire: Colonial Cultures in a Bourgeois World* (Berkeley: University of California Press, 1997).

69. Lemon, in particular, directly employed Michel Foucault's concept of biopower, meaning the deployment of racial logics of power inherent to modern, rationalizing states, to explain the persistence of race in the Soviet sphere. See Lemon, "Without a Concept? Race as Discursive Practice," 54. My emphasis on the relationship between economy and racial reconstitution is informed, in particular, by the interpretive work of Stuart Hall and Thomas Holt.

70. In particular, I am indebted to Alaina Lemon's distinction between official discourses about nationality and underlying linguistic practices of racial "indexing."

71. The centrality of the myth of the so-called *Żydokomuna*, or Jewish Communist, to interwar antisemitism and anti-Jewish violence has been stressed most forcefully in the Polish context in Jan Gross, *Neighbors: The Destruction of the Jewish Community of Jedwabne* (New York: Penguin, 2002). On the conflation of Jewry and Bolshevism in Poland, also see Joanna Michlic, "The Soviet Occupation of Poland, 1939–1941, and the Stereotype of the Anti-Polish and Pro-Soviet Jew," in *Jewish Social Studies*, 13:3 (Spring–Summer, 2007), 135–176. For a recent reconsideration of the persistence of the conflation of Jews and Bolshevism in interwar Germany, see Jan C. Behrens, "Back from the USSR: The Anti-Comintern's Publications on Soviet Russia and Nazi Germany (1935–1941), in *Kritika: Explorations in Russian and Eurasian History*, 10:3 (Summer 2009), 527–556; for the pan-European context, see Howard Sachar, *Dreamland: Europeans and Jews in the Aftermath of the Great War* (New York: Vintage, 2003).

1. Making Jews Bolsheviks

1. *Natsional'nyi Akrkhiv Respubliki Belarus'* (NARB) fond 5, opis' 1, delo 2, list 5.

2. Throughout this work, the terms "Belorussia" and "White Russia" are used interchangeably to designate the territory of the Belorussian Soviet Republic. To avoid confusion, I refrain from employing the modern day terms of "Belarusian" or "Belarus."

3. Vladimir Lenin, *The State and Revolution,* trans. and ed. Robert Service (London: Penguin, 1992), 43.

4. According to the election instructions issued by the Minsk Soviet of Workers' and Red Army Soldiers' Deputies, "the right to vote and to be elected to the Minsk Soviet . . . was held by citizens of either sex who were older than eighteen years, occupied in productive and useful labor, including: workers and employees occupied in trade and industrial enterprises, organized in professional unions or factory committees, and Red Army divisions stationed in the limits of the city." (NARB f. 5, op. 1, d. 3, l. 17).

5. On Menshevik critiques of Bolshevik policies, see Leopold Haimson, *The Russian Marxists and the Origins of Bolshevism* (Boston: Beacon, 1955); Israel Getzler, *Martov: A Political Biography of a Russian Social Democrat* (Cambridge: Cambridge University Press, 1967), 63–95; and Jane Burbank, *Intelligentsia and Revolution: Russian Views of Bolshevism, 1917–1922* (Oxford: Oxford University Press, 1986), 14–34.

6. See Rosa Luxemburg, *The Russian Revolution and Leninism or Marxism?* (Ann Arbor: Ann Arbor Paperbacks, 1961), 41–56.

7. Due, in part, to this pronounced Red Army presence, Belorussia proved to be one of the most ardently Bolshevik regions. The Bolsheviks received 579,087 votes in the Constituent Assembly elections of 1917, far outdistancing the Socialist Revolutionaries, who finished second with 181,673 votes. Oliver H. Radkey, *Russia Goes to the Polls: The Election to the All-Russian Constituent Assembly* (Ithaca: Cornell University Press, 1977), 148.

8. Over the spring and summer of 1917, peasants throughout Belorussia staged uprisings and seized most remaining landowner estates. On the eve of the revolution, peasants held nearly 90 percent of the land in most regions of Belorussia. See Marc Ferro, *The Bolshevik Revolution: A Social History of the Russian Revolution* (London: Routledge & Kegan Paul, 1985), 125–130, and I. M. Ignatenko et al., *Istoriia Belorusskaia SSR* (Minsk: Nauka i tekhnika, 1977), 231.

9. Karl Marx, *The Eighteenth Brumaire of Louis Bonaparte* (Peking: Foreign Language Press, 1978), 126.

10. P. T. Petrikov et al., eds., *Istoriia rabochego klassa Belorusskoi SSR, tom 2* (Minsk: Nauka i tekhnika, 1985), 20. Nicholas P. Vakar placed the total number of workers (union and nonunion) at seventy thousand, a figure that did not include artisanal laborers. Nicholas P. Vakar, *Belorussia: The Making of a Nation, A Case Study* (Cambridge, MA: Harvard University Press, 1956), 35.

11. S. A. Smith, *Red Petrograd: Revolution in the Factories: 1917–1918* (Cambridge: Cambridge University press, 1983), 8.

12. F. S. Martinkevich, ed., *Ekonomika sovetskoi Belorussii, 1917–1967* (Minsk: Nauka i tekhnika, 1967), 22.

13. The reconstituted independent Polish Republic captured the regions of Pinsk and Grodno during the Polish-Soviet War. Vitebsk guberniia was added to the territory of Belorussian Republic in 1924. For figures concerning large industrial enterprises in prerevolutionary Belorussia, see V. I. Ivanov, *Ocherk byta promyshlennykh rabochikh dorevoliutsionnoi Belorussii* (Minsk: Nauka i tekhnika, 1971), 31.

14. Martinkevich, *Ekonomika sovetskoi Belorussii,* 15, 62.

15. The technical difference between artisans and kustari lay in the fact that the former were contracted to produce a specific good while the latter engaged in hand production—either individually, in collectives, or with minimal hired labor—for the market.

16. For classic studies of artisanal radicalism in nineteenth-century Europe, see E. P. Thompson, *The Making of the English Working Class* (New York, Vintage, 1966); Joan Scott, *The Glassworkers of Carmaux: French Craftsmen and Political Action in a Nineteenth-Century City* (Cambridge, MA: Harvard University Press, 1974); and William H. Sewell, *Work and Revolution in France: The Language of Labor from the Old Regime to 1848* (Cambridge: Cambridge University Press, 1980). Victoria Bonnell has stressed the leading role of artisans in the Russian context. See Victoria Bonnell, *Roots of Rebellion: Workers' Politics and Organizations in St. Petersburg and Moscow, 1900–1914* (Berkeley: University of California Press, 1983), 454.

17. L. A Katsenel'son and D. G. Gintsburg, eds., *Evreiskaia entsiklopediia*, 16 vols. (Moscow: Terra, 1991), 5: 638 (Vitebsk), 11: 81 (Minsk), and 11: 152 (Mogilev).

18. Ibid., 11: 80. Nokhum Bukhbinder, working in the Leningrad archives in the 1920s, argued that the percentage of Jewish artisans and small producers in Minsk was significantly higher, constituting roughly 65 percent of the total population. N. Bukhbinder, "Evreiskoe rabochee dvizhenie v Minske, 1895–1903 gg." *Krasnaia Letopis'* 5 (1922), 122.

19. Unfortunately, records of the 1921 party purge in the Minsk Oblast archive are incomplete. Party cells examined include those of the administration of the Central Bureau of the Communist Party (TsB KP(b)B); the Commissariat of Enlightenment (*Narkompros*); the Commissariat of Social Security (*Narkomsobez*); the Commissariat of Internal Affairs (*NKVD*); the Commissariat for Military Affairs (*Narvoenkomat*); the Commissariat for Agriculture (*Narkomzem*); the Commissariat for Provisioning (*Komprod*); the Minsk city militia; the Minsk City Executive Committee (*Mingorispolkom*); the Minsk House of Labor; the Minsk party cells of the trade union for People's Food Provisioning (*Narpit*) and the Food Workers Union (*Profsoyuz pishchevnikov*); the Central Union of Belorussian Consumer Societies (*Tsentrobelsoyuz*); the United Consumers Society (*Edinoe potrebitel'skoe obshchestvo* [EPO]); the Jewish Party School (*Evpartshkola*); the Jewish Pedagogical Institute (*Evpedkurs*); the trade unions for woodworkers (*Derevoobdelochniki*); railroad workers; a state-run shoemaking workshop; a tailoring and shoemaking workshop run by the Cheka; and the heating-materials union. All records are from *Gosudarstvennyi Arkhiv Minskoi Oblasti* (GAMO) f. 4704, op. 1, d. 1–5. Where possible, biographical materials have been augmented with records from the 1924 party review of the KPB in NARB f. 15-P (Control Commission), op. 2, d. 104 (Bobruisk), 113 (Minsk), and 125–126 (Slutsk).

20. Isaac Deutscher, *The Non-Jewish Jew and Other Essays* (London: Oxford University Press, 1968).

21. On the Plekhanov cell and the development of the Social Democratic Workers' Party, see Leopold Haimson, *The Russian Marxists and the Origins of Bolshevism* (Boston: Beacon, 1955).

22. GAMO f. 4704-P, op. 1, d. 2, ll. 427 ob., 438, 438 ob.

23. Vatslav Solskii, *1917 god v zapadnom oblasti i na zapadnom fronte* (Minsk: Tesei, 2004). Solskii, a Polish socialist, opposed the Bolsheviks but sympathized with their platform.

24. Vakar, *Belorussia*, 97.

25. Aside from Lipets, only one other individual among the 297 Jews analyzed in this chapter claimed to have joined the Bolsheviks before 1917, compared to six Mensheviks, three SRs and three Anarchists. According to Zvi Gitelman, there were, according to a 1922 census, a total of 958 Jews in the entire Bolshevik party at the start of 1917. Zvi Gitelman, *Jewish Nationality and Soviet Politics: The Jewish Sections of the CPSU, 1917–1930* (Princeton: Princeton University Press, 1972), 105. Jewish actors were far more numerous among the Mensheviks. See Leonard Schapiro, "The Role of Jews in the Russian Revolutionary Movement," *The Slavonic and Eastern European Review* 40, no. 94 (December 1961): 148–167.

26. Events in Belorussia followed closely the broader pattern of Jewish political action in 1917. See Simon Rabinovitch, "Russian Jewry Goes to the Polls: An Analysis of Jewish Voting in the All-Russian Constituent Assembly Elections of 1917," *East European Jewish Affairs* 39, no. 2 (August 2009): 205–225.

27. G. Aronson et al., *Di geshikhte fun bund*, 4 vols. (New York: Unzer tsayt, 1966), 3: 110.

28. The Constituent Assembly, charged with drafting a constitution for postrevolutionary Russia, convened on January 18, 1918; the Bolsheviks shut down the assembly after one day of operation.

29. Radkey, *Russia Goes to the Polls*, 148–153, and Gitelman, *Jewish Nationality and Soviet Politics*, 80–81. Bemporad omitted the vote for the Bund-Menshevik alliance from the tally of Jews voting for socialist parties, due in all likelihood to the impossibility of votes cast for the Bund from votes for the Mensheviks generally. Elissa Bemporad, *Becoming Soviet Jews: The Bolshevik Experiment in Minsk* (Bloomington: Indiana University Press, 2013), 24.

30. Concerning likely Kadet support from the Jews of Minsk, see Rabinovitch, "Russian Jewry Goes to the Polls," 211–212.

31. This interpretation was argued most forcefully and convincingly in Gitelman, *Jewish Nationality and Soviet Politics*.

32. NARB f. 4-P, op. 1 (Central Bureau), d. 228, ll. 19–19 ob.

33. NARB f. 265, op. 1, d. 666, l. 13.

34. Despite party disapproval, such practices continued to endure within sections of the Jewish work force well into the 1930s. See Elissa Bemporad, "Behavior Unbecoming a Communist: Jewish Religious Practice in Soviet Minsk," *Jewish Social Studies* 14, no. 2 (Winter 2008): 1–31.

35. Opposition, particularly in the economic and cultural realms, is examined in chapters 2 and 3.

36. E. Tsherniovski, *Der yidisher arbeter in Vaysrusland: Bam baginen fun der yidisher arbeter bavegung* (Minsk: Melukhe-farlag fun Vaysrusland, 1932), 159. The period between 1894 and 1897 witnessed the outbreak of 54 strikes.

37. Henry Tobias, *The Jewish Bund in Russia: From its Origins to 1905* (Stanford: Stanford University Press, 1972), 38.

38. Ezra Mendelsohn, *Class Struggle in the Pale: The Formative Years of the Jewish Workers' Movement in Tsarist Russia* (Cambridge: Cambridge University Press, 1970), and Bukhbinder, "Evreiskoe rabochee dvizhenie v Minske, 1895–1903 gg.," 122.

39. Israel Kolatt, "Zionist Marxism," in Shlomo Averini, ed., *Varieties of Marxism* (The Hague: Springer, 1977), 230–232.

40. On the early anarchist cells in Bialystok, Minsk, and the Jewish milieu of the Pale of Settlement, see Paul Avrich, *The Russian Anarchists* (New York: W.W. Norton, 1978), 17–20, 40–49.

41. Zubatov began his career as a secret police (*okhrana*) informer within the socialist movement before organizing the "independents," with tsarist approval. On Zubatov, see Jeremiah Schneiderman, *Sergei Zubatov and Revolutionary Marxism: The Struggle for the Working Class in Tsarist Russia* (Ithaca: Cornell University Press, 1976).

42. On the early formation of the Bund and its relationship to Plekhanov's émigré group, see Tobias, *The Origins of the Bund*, and Jonathan Frankel, *Prophecy and Politics: Socialism, Nationalism, and the Russian Jews, 1862–1917* (Cambridge: Cambridge University Press, 1981), 211–213.

43. The relationship between the early Jewish followers of Plekhanov's movement, particularly Pavel Aksel'rod, and the Narodnik movement has been brilliantly analyzed in Erich Haberer, *Jews and Revolution in Nineteenth-Century Russia* (Cambridge: Cambridge University Press, 1995).

44. Frankel, *Prophecy and Politics*, 255.

45. Much to the chagrin of future Soviet historians, who generally took the Second Congress of 1903, which witnessed the split between Bolsheviks and Mensheviks, as the true founding congress.

46. Aronson et al., *Di geshikhte fun Bund*, 2: 144.

47. For the geographic ties between the early region of Bundist activity and leather-producing regions of the Russian Empire, see the article on the "Bund" by the historian Elias Tsherikover in Katsenel'son and Gintsburg, eds., *Evreiskaia entsiklopediia*, 5: 93–94, and Sofiia Dubnova-Erlikh, *Garber-Bund un Bershter Bund: Bletlekh geshikhte fun der yidisher arbeter-bavegung* (Warsaw: Kultur-Lige, 1937).

48. On the failed assassination attempt on Governor General Viktor von Wahl, see Tobias, *The Jewish Bund in Russia from Its Origins to 1905*, 150–151.

49. The one exception to the trend of Bund support within "Jewish" industries were those related to food production, which came to be widely regarded in Belorussia as a stronghold of *Poalei Tsion*.

50. The exact membership at the height of its popularity in mid-1917 is difficult to determine, but it is doubtful the party had more than 1,500 active members in Minsk. Membership had declined rapidly by the end of the year. Minsk representatives attending the Bund party conference in Petrograd in December 1917 claimed to represent 1,050 party members (compared to 1,060 members in Bobruisk, 900 members in Gomel, and 790 members in Vitebsk). Aronson et al., *Di geshikhte fun Bund*, 2: 144, 3: 176.

51. Aronson et al., *Di geshikhte fun Bund*, 3: 129.

52. Paviel Urban, "The Belorussian Soviet Republic: A Brief Historical Outline," *Belorussian Review* 7 (May 1959): 4.

53. NARB f. 4-P, op. 1, d. 19, l. 10.

54. NARB f. 4-P, op. 1, d. 19, ll. 8–10.

55. NARB f. 4-P, op. 1, d. 3, ll. 19–22.

56. On the debates surrounding the formation of the EKP, see Samuil Agursky, *Der yidisher arbeter in der komunistisher bavegung, 1917–1921* (Minsk: Melukhe-Farlag fun Vaysrusland, 1925), 63–67; and Gitelman, *Jewish Nationality and Soviet Politics*, 177–183.

57. NARB f. 4-P, op. 1, d. 3, l. 21a.

58. Gitelman described the organization as "nothing but a paper organization." Gitelman, *Jewish Nationality and Soviet Politics*, 179.

59. A party report from Bobruisk stated that since the creation of the EKP "the influence of the party spread very quickly among the Jewish working class, which until now had been strongly under the influence of the Bund." The report argued that EKP activists helped the Bolsheviks to win 80 percent of the seats in local soviet elections in Bobruisk. NARB f. 4-P, op. 1, d. 19, l. 6.

60. For a list of elected representatives, see NARB f. 4-P, op. 1, d. 70, ll. 8–12 ob. The elections seem to have been fairly open. The SRs, however, were allowed to participate only if they agreed to a "repudiation of the term 'Constituent Assembly'" and recognized Soviet (i.e., Bolshevik) power.

61. *Der Shtern*, January 6, 1919.

62. *Der Shtern*, January 16, 1919, 3.

63. *Der Shtern*, January 30, 1919, 4.

64. *Der Shtern*, February 19, 1919, 4

65. *Der Shtern*, March 2, 1919, 4.

66. Benedict Anderson, *Imagined Communities: Reflections on the Origins and Spread of Nationalism* (London: Verso, 1983).

67. Thirty-five members claimed to have come from the *meshchanstvo*. Unsurprisingly, a large number of applicants simply left this question blank.

68. Culled from the files listed in footnote 19.

69. NARB f. 4-P, op. 1, d. 19, l. 5 ob.

70. L. I. Volokhovich, *Partiinoe stroitel'stvo v Belorussii v pervye gody nepa (1921–1924 gg)*. Minsk: Izdat. Minister. Prof. Obraz., 1962), p. 5.

71. Norman Davies, always willing to downplay anti-Jewish violence in "Poland," emphatically insisted the event was "not a pogrom," which is quite true, insofar as victims of pogroms occasionally live. Norman Davies, *White Eagle, Red Star: The Polish-Soviet War, 1919–1920* (New York: St. Martin's, 1972), p. 47.

72. Among the victims of summary counterrevolutionary violence in Vilna was Stanislaw Berson, the Polish-Jewish socialist who chaired the Minsk Revolutionary Committee in 1918.

73. For details of the attacks in Minsk and other locations, see the article outlining the findings of the official American investigation into Polish pogroms headed by Henry Morgenthau in *The New York Times*, January 19, 1920.

74. Detailed reports concerning the pogroms in these regions can be found in NARB f. 684. For the pogroms in southern Belorussia, see NARB f. 684, op. 1, d. 5, ll. 1–12, and NARB f. 684, op. 1, d. 7.

75. While the archival records attribute almost all of the pogroms to "outside" perpetrators, the local Belorussian population was not immune to the perpetration of anti-Jewish violence. As Polish forces encroached on the town of Znamenka in southern Belorussia in May 1919, the local population carried out a massive pogrom on May 19–20, killing forty-two Jews. NARB f. 684, op.1, d. 5, l. 47.

76. Among the forty Jewish members of the Narkompros party cell, nine had been arrested for revolutionary activity during the Polish occupation, and only one during the German occupation. Among the sixty-four Jewish members of the Central Bureau of the Communist Party cell, fifteen emphasized the Polish occupation as a formative period in their political development, against one member who emphasized the German occupation. A similar trend seems to hold across the board.

77. GAMO f. 4704-P, op. 1, d. 2, l. 241.

78. GAMO f. 4704-P, op. 1, d. 5, l. 243.

79. Despite its nationalist goals, Petliura's Directorate forces in Ukraine remained nominally aligned with Poland during the war. Although Petliura's army operated almost exclusively in Ukraine, it entered southern Belorussia during the spring of 1919. The army arrived in Mozyr on March 27 and remained until April 2, killing three people but wreaking devastation on the Jewish community. NARB f. 684, op. 1, d. 7, l. 1–4. Given its proximity to the Ukrainian and Polish borders, Mozyr was pogromized repeatedly during the Polish-Soviet War and Russian Civil War, including particularly horrific pogroms at the hands of the army of Bulak-Balakhovich in June and October of 1921. NARB f. 684, op. 1, d. 7, ll. 16, 64–64 ob.

80. GAMO f. 4704-P, op. 1, d. 5, ll. 13–13 ob.

81. NARB f. 4-P, op. 1, d. 3, l. 118.

82. Oleg Budnitsky, "Jewish National Units in the Red Army: Discussion, Formation, Disbandment," in Zvi Y. Gitelman and Ya'acov Roi, eds., *Revolution, Repression, and Revival: The Soviet Jewish Experience*, (Lanham, MD: Rowman and Littlefield, 2007).

83. GAMO f. 4704-P, op. 1, d. 5, ll. 51–51 ob.

84. GAMO f. 4704-P, op. 1, d. 2, l. 9.

85. GAMO f. 4704-P, op. 1, d. 1, ll. 236–236 ob.

86. GAMO f. 4704-P, op. 1, d. 1, ll. 33–33 ob.

87. NARB f. 4-P, op. 1, d. 225, l. 23.

88. Of the twenty-two male Jewish members of the Minsk city militia party cell in 1921, fifteen (nearly 70 percent) had served in the Red Army. The numbers of Red Army soldiers fell off in nonsecurity cells, but remained considerable. Thus, one-third of the members of the Jewish party school cell in 1921 had previously served in the Red Army, the majority of these being Bundists mobilized after 1920.

89. NARB f. 4-P, op. 1, d. 226, l. 70.

90. NARB f. 4-P, op. 1, d. 226, l. 72.

91. GAMO f. 4704-P, op. 1, d. 5, ll. 29–29 ob.

92. Five of the eight members of the party cell of the woodworkers union in 1921 claimed to have entered the Bolshevik party between 1919. GAMO f. 4704-P, op. 1, d. 1, ll. 790–792.

93. During his 1924 party review, Beilin denied having been a member of the Bund; he later claimed to have broken with the Bund as a fourteen-year-old in June of 1905. For his 1924 party review, see NARB f. 15-p., op. 2, d. 94, ll. 13–14 ob.

94. For Agursky's 1924 party review record, see NARB f. 15-P, op. 4, d. 113, l. 354. For Osherovich, who joined the party in 1919, see his 1924 part review record (NARB f. 15-P, op. 4, d. 113, l. 360 ob.)

and his 1929 purge record (NARB f. 15-P, op. 4, d. 311, l. 4 ob.). For Orshanskii, who entered the party in October of 1918, I was able to locate only the very brief autobiography in his 1929 Purge Record (NARB f. 15-P, op. 4, d. 311, l. 11 ob.).

95. On the circumstances surrounding the party split and reactions within the Bund, see Gitelman, *Jewish Nationality and Soviet Policy*, 193–197.

96. NARB f. 4-P, op. 1, d. 238, l. 11.

97. V. I. Brovikov, ed. *Kommunisticheskaia partiia Belorussii v rezoliutsiiakh i resheniiakh s'ezdov i plenumov TsK, tom 1, 1918–1927* (Minsk: Belarus', 1983), 65, 78.

98. For records of the Central Bureau debates from August 8–12, see NARB f. 4-P, op. 1, d. 109, l. 7–11.

99. Agursky based his claim concerning the percentage of intellectuals among the Bundists on numbers from Moscow. Samuil Agursky, ed., *Di yidishe komisaryatn un di yidishe komunistishe sektsyes: protokoln, rezolutsyes, un dokumentn (1918–1929)*, (Minsk: Vaysruslendisher melukhe farlag, 1928), 415.

100. NARB f. 4-P, op. 1, d. 228, l. 19. Similar numbers were reported in L. I. Volokhovich, *Partiinoe stroitel'stvo v Belorussii v pervye gody nepa*, p. 59.

101. NARB f. 4-P, op. 1, d. 362.

102. Moreover, the party cells examined here excluded a number of critical unions, including the Minsk needleworkers union and leatherworkers union, which were historic strongholds of the Bund. In addition to the Bundists, there were also fifteen former members of Poalei Tsion among the 297 members examined in the purge records.

103. By 1923, there were, according to one report, 735 Jews in the entire Minsk party organization, plus another 261 in the rest of the Minsk *uezd*. NARB f. 4-P, op. 1, d. 804, l. 15. According to a different report, the number of Jewish communists in the city apparatus grew to 847 members and candidates by April of 1924. GAMO f. 12-P (Minsk Okrug KPB), op. 1, d. 138, l. 20.

104. In general, Jewish party members made up majorities of all party members in each of these cells. The EPO cell (GAMO f. 4704-P, op. 1, d. 3, ll. 12–33 ob.) was composed entirely of Jews; Jews constituted three-fourths of the Dom Truda (GAMO f. 4704-P, op. 1, d. 2, ll. 427–458) and TsB KP(b)B (GAMO 4704-P, op. 1, d. 5, ll. 1–98 ob.) cells, 85 percent of the Narkomsobez cell (GAMO f. 4704-P, op. 1, d. 3, ll. 83–101 ob.), half of the Narkompros cell (GAMO f. 4704-P, op. 1, d. 5, ll. 336–446), 65 percent of the woodworkers cell (GAMO f. 4704-P, op. 1, d. 1, ll. 790–793), and the entire membership of both the shoemakers (GAMO f. 4704-P, op. 1, d. 1, ll. 743–43 ob.) and Cheka workshop (GAMO f. 4704-P, op. 1, d. 1, ll. 573–576) cells.

105. Concern over "petit-bourgeois" elements reflected underlying anxieties about the unfolding policies of economic liberalization introduced with the New Economic Policy (NEP) of 1921. On the NEP, see chapters 2 and 3.

106. My italics. GAMO f. 4704-P, op. 1, d. 2, l. 6.

107. In most of the purge records, it is difficult to discern the exact date of entry into the party if they entered during the merger, as their dates of entry were frequently recorded as "1920" retroactively.

108. Given the fact that the purges frequently took place within party cells similarly populated by Bundists, there is little ground to support the idea that, in Minsk at least, Bundists were disproportionately targeted for expulsion during the 1921 purge. Moreover, according to Volokhovich, only 148 people who previously belonged to other parties were excluded throughout the entirety of the BSSR in 1921. See Volokhovich, *Partiinoe stroitel'stvo v Belorussii*, 62.

109. GAMO f. 4704-P, op. 1, d. 2, l. 7.

110. Unfortunately, only the seven-page report from the purge preceding itself remains intact. The prepurge applications for this cell do not seem to have been preserved, which makes it impossible to determine the exact occupation of all cell members.

111. On Jewish radicalism as a revolt of sons against Jewish fathers, see Yuri Slezkine, *The Jewish Century* (Princeton: Princeton University Press, 2004).

112. The story of one parent (usually a father) who emigrated to the United States in search of work and was never heard from again is a repeated trope in the purge records.

113. GAMO f. 4704-P, op. 1, d. 2, l. 7 ob.

114. GAMO f. 4704-P, op. 1, d. 2, l. 7.

115. GAMO f. 4704-P, op. 1, d. 2, l. 9

116. GAMO f. 4704-P, op. 1, d. 2, l. 7.

117. Volokhovich states that 465 of 1,512 party members were removed from the Minsk city organization in 1921, meaning that over 30 percent of the local party was purged. Based on the purge records under consideration in this chapter, this percentage seems extremely high. Volokhovich, *Partiinoe Stroitel'stvo v Belorussii*, 60–63.

118. See GAMO 4704-P, op. 1, d. 2, l. 7 ob.

119. In the end, eighteen voted for his renewal, seventeen voted against, and fourteen abstained altogether.

120. GAMO 4704-P, op. 1, d. 2, l. 8.

121. GAMO f. 4704-P, op. 1, d. 2, l. 8 ob.

122. GAMO f. 4704-P, op. 1, d. 2, l. 6.

123. GAMO f. 4704-P, op. 1, d. 2, l. 9.

124. GAMO f. 4704-P, op. 1, d. 2, ll. 8–9.

125. Moreover, two members—Comrades Movshovich and Tsygel'nitskii—quickly jumped to Fainbukh's defense to vouch for his discipline. GAMO f. 4704-P, op. 1, d. 2, l. 8 ob.

126. GAMO f 4704-P, op. 1, d. 2, l. 9 ob.

2. Speculators, Swindlers, and Other Jews: Regulating Trade in Revolutionary White Russia

1. D. N. Ushakov, ed., *Tolkovyi slovar' russkogo iazyka, tom. 4* (Moscow, Sovetskaia entsiklopediia, 1940), 429.

2. *Slovar' sovremennogo russkogo literaturnogo iazyka, tom 14* (Moscow: Akademii nauk SSSR, 1963), 490.

3. *Gosudarstvennyi Arkhiv Minskoi Oblasti* (GAMO) fond 413 (People's Court), opis' 1, delo 321, listy 14–14 ob., 19.

4. GAMO f. 413, op. 1, d. 321, l.12. Gantman acknowledged that he gave Fitershtein money for the transaction but insisted that the real culprit was Gantman's sister, not himself. GAMO f. 413, op. 1, d. 321, ll.29–30.

5. On February 18, 1922, the third district court released Fitershtein from custody early, in accordance with the general amnesty announced in November of the previous year.

6. GAMO f. 413, op. 1, d. 689, ll. 6–6 ob., 12. The bilingual Russian-Hebrew *Ketubah* is preserved as supplemental material in the fond.

7. GAMO f. 413, op. 1, d. 689, ll. 17–17 ob.

8. This thesis, which mythicizes and ultimately naturalizes Jews as perpetually modern "Mercurian" boundary crossers living among rooted, land-bound "Apollonians," lies at the heart of Yuri Slezkine's *The Jewish Century* (Princeton: Princeton University Press, 2004).

9. Statistical reports on criminal activity by nationality do not seem to have been kept, an unsurprising fact given the official nationality-blind treatment of criminality in the SSRB. This conclusion is based, therefore, on a broad analysis of the fonds and opisi of the second, third, and fourth district People's courts in Minsk. The proportion of Jews among those tried on suspicion of engaging in speculation ranged from roughly two-thirds of all suspects in the third district to over 80 percent of all suspected speculators in the second district.

10. See, for example, the records for the first district court in Borisov, which suggest a pattern similar to (if even more pronounced) to the one observable in Minsk. GAMO f. 431, op. 1.

11. The one major exception to this trend seems to be the crime of contraband smuggling, which, while undeniably an "economic crime" (at least in part), seems to have been a rather equal-opportunity pastime for inhabitants of all nationalities on the borderlands.

12. The central importance of the struggle against speculation was evident in the full title of the Cheka, the Extraordinary Commission to Fight Against Counterrevolution, Speculation, and Official Malfeseance (*chrezvychainaia komissiia po bor'be s kontr-revoliutsiei, spekuliatsiei i prestupleniiami po dolzhnosti*).

13. The sense of randomness is captured vividly in reminiscences, recorded by Anna Shternshis, of one Jewish woman from a Ukrainian shtetl: "There was a song which people in Kasatin sang about Moyshe Stoliar (a Jewish soldier from her town). The GPU took him because he did not pay his taxes or something. At that time people were arrested for nothing, they called it 'speculation.' . . . So he probably sold something wrong." Recorded in Anna Shternshis, *Soviet and Kosher: Jewish Popular Culture in the Soviet Union, 1923–1939* (Bloomington: Indiana University Press, 2006), 127.

14. For the percentage of Jewish private traders, see Slezkine, *The Jewish Century*, 218.

15. Zvi Gitelman's account remains the definitive work on the extremely influential role the *evsektsii* played in Soviet attempts to reconstruct Jewish social and economic life. See Gitelman, *Jewish Nationality and Soviet Politics: The Jewish Sections of the CPSU, 1917–1930*.

16. The Oxford English Dictionary credits H. Walpole with the earliest known usage in English of speculation in this economic sense, in 1774. As the quote from Pushkin, borrowed from Voltaire, suggests, the French "*agioteur*" was clearly in use at a far earlier date.

17. Adam Smith, *An Inquiry into the Nature and Causes of the Wealth of Nations* (Chicago: University of Chicago Press, 1976), 127.

18. The speculator is thus "a corn merchant this year, and a wine merchant the next, and a sugar, tobacco or tea merchant the year after. He enters into every trade when he foresees that it is likely to be more than commonly profitable, and he quits it when he foresees that its profits are likely to return to the level of other trades." Ibid.

19. John Markoff, *The Abolition of Feudalism: Peasants, Lords, and Legislators in the French Revolution* (University Park: Pennsylvania State University Press, 1996), 243–246.

20. George Rudé, *The Crowd in the French Revolution* (London: Oxford University Press, 1972), 119.

21. "Petition to the National Convention Concerning a Special Jury Against Hoarders" (September 29, 1793) in Keith Michael Baker, ed., *The Old Regime and the French Revolution* (Chicago: University of Chicago Press, 1987), 337. On antimerchant and antispeculation in the initial years of the revolution, see Georges Lefebvre, *The Coming of the French Revolution* (Princeton: Princeton University Press, 1986), 105; for the intensification and centrality of antispeculation rhetoric among the sans-culottes, see Albert Soboul, *The Sans-Culottes* (Princeton: Princeton University Press, 1980), 14–20.

22. Dmitri Shlapentokh, *The French Revolution and the Russian Anti-Democratic Tradition* (New Brunswick, NJ: Transaction Publishers, 1997).

23. In particular, through Marx's extremely ambiguous essay on the "Jewish Question," republished in Robert Tucker, ed., *The Marx-Engels Reader* (New York: W.W. Norton, 1978). Such a line emphasizing the relationship between socialist and Marxian anticapitalist critiques and the emergence of modern antisemitism has been stressed in Robert Wistrich, *A Lethal Obsession: Anti-Semitism from Antiquity to the Global Jihad* (New York: Random House, 2010).

24. Lenin was still struggling with the issue when he announced the turn to the New Economic Policy in 1921. "Correct trade, which doesn't evade state control, we must support, as it is beneficial to us. But *it is impossible* to separate speculation from 'correct' trade, if speculation is understood in the sense of political economy. Free trade is capitalism, capitalism is speculation. To close one's eyes towards this is laughable." V. I. Lenin, "O prodovol'stvennom naloge (znachenie novoi politiki i ee usloviia)," in V. I. Lenin, *Sochineniia, tom 32* (Moscow: Gos. izdat., 1952), 336.

25. The 1918 Soviet Constitution rather infamously deprived the bourgeois class of political rights. This group of disenfranchised individuals, known as *lishentsy* (the deprived) included, among others, former traders, clerics, and former tsarist officials. See Golfo Alexopoulos, *Stalin's Outcasts: Aliens, Citizens, and the Soviet State, 1926–1936* (Ithaca: Cornell University Press, 2003).

26. On the retrospective application of the term "War Communism" to the policies of 1918–1921, see Lewis Siegelbaum, *Soviet State and Society Between Revolutions, 1918–1929* (Cambridge: Cambridge University Press, 1992), chapter 1.

27. Alec Nove, *An Economic History of the USSR, 1917–1991* (New York: Penguin Books, 1992), 23.

28. *Natsional'nyi Akrkhiv Respubliki Belarus'* (NARB) f. 5, op. 1, d. 2, l. 2.

29. The decision to fix prices for goods of "prime necessity" at levels "not higher than those market prices, which existed at the time of the evacuation by the Germans" was decided upon in the Minsk *guberniia* revolutionary committee meeting on December 10. NARB f. 5, op. 1, d. 3, l. 2.

30. NARB f. 5, op. 1, d. 3, ll. 19, 26. A similar order allowing for the free trade of foodstuffs into Mogilev was passed by the Mogilev *Guberniia* Committee on January 4, 1919.

31. From the dedication of his book *Paper Money in the Epoch of the Proletarian Dictatorship*, quoted in A. Arnold, *Banks, Credit and Money in Soviet Russia* (New York: Columbia University Press, 1937) 95.

32. Report to the Minsk *Guberniia* Commissariat for Internal Affairs, NARB f. 4-P, P: 1, d. 19, l. 38 ob.

33. NARB f. 4-P, op. 1, d. 19, ll. 37 ob.–38 ob.

34. NARB f. 4-P, op. 1, d. 19, l. 39 ob.

35. *Der Shtern,* January 31, 1919, 4.

36. TsB KP(b) Protocol No. 16, February 10, 1919, in NARB f. 4-P, op. 1, d. 3, ll. 49 ob.–50.

37. Reports of speculation were, by contrast, rather rare and subdued in the pages of the Russian language party organ, *Zvezda*.

38. "Di pogrom agitasie un di spekulatsie," *Der Shtern* February 14, 1919, 2. An article by Miasnikov, warning that the Cheka would begin to shoot speculators and other counterrevolutionaries to "defend the revolution," appeared in *Zvezda* several days beforehand. See *Zvezda*, February 11, 1919, 1.

39. During a TsB KP(b)B meeting on February 16, Miasnikov urged the party to adopt new emergency measures to combat speculation, noting that "in the past few days, some bandits and speculators were shot." As a result, he reported, "the situation in Minsk has eased." TsB KP(b)B protocol No. 19, February 16, 1919, in NARB f. 4-P, op. 1, d. 3, l. 76 ob.

40. "Der kamf mit spekulatsye," in *Der Shtern*, February 19, 1919, 2.

41. *Zvezda*, March 6, 1919, 4.

42. *Zvezda*, March 9, 1919, 3.

43. *Zvezda*, March 12, 1919, 4.

44. "Ver iz shuldik?," *Der Shtern*, March 16, 1919, 3.

45. In general, archival materials pertaining to the Cheka prior to 1921 are extremely rare. Most were likely destroyed during the evacuation of Minsk in 1919 or are currently housed in the closed archives of the Belarus KGB.

46. TsB KP(b)B Protocol No. 11, September 20, 1920, in NARB f. 4-P, op. 1, d. 109, l. 20.

47. Of the 812 inmates whose records remain in place, 61 were incarcerated for speculation; of these, 53 were Jews. See GAMO f. 146, op. 1.

48. *Der Shtern*, May 20, 1919, 1.

49. The Yiddish original, "*handlen mizrekhn*," conveys a more complicated meaning. Here, the author criticizes the practice of buying and selling the "best" seats in the synagogue—those by the eastern (*mizrekh*) wall—for profit. The term became an idiomatic expression for swindling, as rendered here. My thanks to Ben Sadock for helping me to clarify this line.

50. *Der Veker*, February 20, 1923, 3.

51. A. Ball, *Russia's Last Capitalists: The Nepmen, 1921–1929* (Berkeley: University of California Press, 1988).

52. J. Hessler, *A Social History of Soviet Trade: Trade Policy, Retail Practices, and Consumption, 1917–1953* (Princeton: Princeton University Press, 2004).

53. TsB KP(b)B Protocol No. 23, May 15, 1921, NARB f. 4-P, op. 1, d. 243, l. 65.

54. TsB KP(b)B Protocol No. 23, May 15, 1921, NARB f. 4-P, op. 1, d. 243, l. 65.

55. *Der Veker*, the former organ of the Bund, became the primary Yiddish party daily following the merger of the Bolshevik party and the left Bund in 1920. On the merger between the Bolsheviks and the Bund.

56. *Der Veker*, May 14, 1921, 1–2.

57. *Der Veker*, July 19, 1920, 1.

58. This trend was not absolute, as indicated by an article blaming speculators for an ongoing famine in southern Belorussia published in the late summer. See *Der Veker*, September 15, 1921.

59. Shapiro's rather self-satisfied description of the good life in Minsk clearly caught the eye of the censors; the letter was detained en route and sent to the TsK KP(b) for review and possible disciplinary action. NARB f. 4-P, op. 1, d. 252, l. 409–410 ob.

60. NARB f. 4-P, op. 1, d. 252, l. 191–191 ob.

61. GAMO f. 413, op. 1, d. 322, l. 15.

62. GAMO f. 413, op. 1, d. 322, l. 1 ob.

63. GAMO f. 413, op. 1, d. 322, l. 27-27 ob.

64. While violations for the sale of sugar, saccharin, and other items are common, salt speculation remained the most common nonmonetary form of speculation throughout 1920–1922.

65. NARB f. 192, op. 1, d. 77. On leather speculation, also see GAMO f. 412, op. 1, dd. 613, 1865.

66. GAMO f. 413, op. 1, d. 764, ll. 11–11 ob., 27–28 ob., 31–31 ob.

67. No law prohibiting speculation appeared on the books until a 1927 addendum added the infamous article 107, which would come to be used as a tool in the offensive against traders and kulaks in the late 1920s.

68. In doing so they introduced a whole series of excise taxes that had been abolished by the Russian Empire in 1881. See E. H. Carr, *Socialism in One Country, 1924–26*, vol. 1 (London: Macmillan, 1958–1964), 465.

69. Code 139a, referred to euphemistically as the controlling of "private business activities" (*Chastnopredprinimatel'skaia deiatel'nost'*), policed various forms of tax evasion. See O. T. Rayner, *The Criminal Code of the Russian Socialist Federative Soviet Republic* (London: NP, 1925).

70. Based on the *opis'* records, Jews made up roughly 70 percent of the hundred or so people accused under article 139a from 1922 to 1923 in the third city district which, compared to the second district (which included the Nemiga) contained a far higher number of non-Jewish shops.

71. Rayner, *The Criminal Code*, 33. See, for example, the case against thirty-six-year-old Aron Borshch, who was arrested and fined for selling unstamped playing cards in the lower market. GAMO f. 413, op. 1, d. 1926.

72. Quoted in Carr, *The Bolshevik Revolution, 1917–1923*, vol. 2 (New York: Macmillan, 1952), 345.

73. V. I. Lenin, "O znachenii zolota," in Lenin, *Sochineniia*, Vol. 33, 89.

74. The Soviets were, of course, not alone in turning back to the gold standard in hopes of miraculously reconstructing the pre-World War I economy. As Karl Polanyi long ago noted, the attempted return to the gold standard became the socially general trend that guided macroeconomic policy throughout interwar Europe. Karl Polanyi, *The Great Transformation: The Political and Economic Origins of Our Time* (Boston: Beacon, 2001).

75. GAMO f. 414, op. 1, d. 2252.

76. GAMO f. 414, op. 1, d. 2127.

77. GAMO f. 414, op. 1, d. 2238.

78. GAMO f. 414, op. 1, d. 2242.

79. NARB f. 192, op. 1, d. 64, ll. 5–19, 36, 36 ob.

80. See GAMO f. 414, op. 1, dd. 2513–2530, 2608, 2617–2618.

81. GAMO f. 414, op. 1, d. 2526, l. 11.

82. GAMO f. 414, op. 1, d. 2518.

83. GAMO f. 414, op. 1, d. 2524.

84. Interestingly, two of the largest "fish" caught by the Cheka during this sweep were Elena Mitskevich and Nikolai Suchkin, both Russians, who were nabbed for holding 90 and 145 gold rubles, respectively. See GAMO f. 414,op. 1, dd. 2519, 2617.

85. GAMO f. 414, op. 1, d. 2513.

86. NARB f. 192, op. 1, d. 71, ll. 1, 1 ob., 78.

87. NARB f. 192, op. 1, d. 71, ll. 8–8 ob.

88. The monopoly on the holding and trading of gold, silver, and precious stones, lifted in April, was partially restored from October of 1922 through 1923, as the government outlawed the use of these items as a medium of payment for domestic transactions. See Yuri Goland, "Currency Regulation in the NEP Period," *Europe-Asia Studies* 46, no. 8 (1994): 1251–1296.

89. NARB 192, op. 1, d. 76, l. 39.

90. Ginzburg stated that she had built the false wall to hold personal items during the Polish occupation. The gold coins, she insisted, she held with the intention of having false teeth made out of them—a repeated, if ineffective alibi. NARB f. 192, op. 1, d. 66.

91. Originally diagnosed by Trotsky, this explanation of the crisis been widely accepted in the historiography. See, for example, Carr's extremely influential short history of the revolution, *The Russian Revolution from Lenin to Stalin 1917–1929*.

92. From 1921 until 1922, the amount of paper sovznak rubles in circulation increased from sixteen trillion rubles to two quadrillion rubles, indicating the rate of hyperinflation. Arnold, *Banks, Credit, and Money in Soviet Russia*, 126.

93. The rate of exchange of the sovznak against the chervonets fell from 16,700,000 to 1 on January 1, 1923, to 32,800,000,000 to 1 on March 1, 1924, right before the sovznak was taken out of circulation. Ibid., 180.

94. The explanation, always simplistic, failed to account for the complexity of the situation. Numerous sources suggest that the availability of goods in Belorussia, as well as the price of those goods on the market, had increased dramatically, and that commodity prices were actually falling. Shoes, for example, were in overabundant supply, further gumming up market. See V. A. Arkhipov, L. F. Morozov, *Bor'ba protiv kapitalisticheskikh elementov v promyshlennosti i torgovle 20-e nachalo 30-x godov* (Moscow: Mysl', 1978). Rather than a unique form of crisis specific to socialist economies, the "scissors crisis" appears, in retrospect, to have been very much like the rather familiar crises of over-accumulation fueled by overabundant currency issue and collapsing markets that spread across the capitalist countries of Europe during the period of 1922–1924 (especially in France, Germany, and Poland).

95. All of those sentenced to death, save Kozerski, were Jews. *Der Veker*, April 13–May 8, 1923.

96. See GAMO f. 412, op. 1, dd. 3582, 3670, 3732, 3771, 3793, 3797, 3799, 3801, 3817, 3828, 3901, 3952, 3977, 4019, 4020, 4038, 4070, 4109, 4135, 4197, 4290, 4318, 4359, 4447.

97. *Der Veker*, February 7, 1923, 3.

98. *Der Veker*, January 10, 1924, 3.

99. Emile Durkheim, *The Division of Labor in Society* (New York: Free Press, 1984), 62–63.

3. Jewish Proletarians and Proletarian Jews: The Emancipation of Labor in NEP Society

1. For protocols and speeches from the conference, see Samuil Agursky, ed., *Di yidishe komisaryatn un di yidishe komunistishe sektsyes: protokoln, rezolutsyes un dokumentn, 1918–1921* (Minsk: Vaysruslendisher melukhe farlag, 1928), 19–68.

2. Ibid., 48–49.

3. Ibid., 51.

4. The circumstances surrounding the death of Shimeliovich and the other members of the Vilna Soviet were recorded in M. Daniel's novella *Iulius* and dramatic play *4 Teg*, which debuted to critical acclaim at the Moscow Yiddish Theater in 1931. Solomon Mikhoels played the role of Shimeliovich. See Jeffrey Veidlinger, *The Moscow Yiddish Theater: Jewish Culture on the Soviet Stage* (Bloomington: Indiana University Press, 2000). During the 1952 secret trial of the Jewish Anti-Fascist Committee members, Boris Shimeliovich, Iulius's brother, contested the account of the collective suicide, testifying that his brother had been shot by Polish legionnaires. Joshua Rubinstein and Vladimir P. Naumov, eds., *Stalin's Secret Pogrom: The Postwar Inquisition of the Jewish Anti-Fascist Committee* (New Haven: Yale University Press, 2001), 236). The Yiddish writer Sh. An-skii, who had fled from Petrograd to Vilna in September 1918, delivered the eulogy for Shimeliovich. David Roskies, introduction to *The Dybbuk and Other Writings*, by S. Ansky (New Haven: Yale University Press, 1992), xxi.

5. Agursky, *Di yidishe komisaryatn*, 148.

6. Ibid., 153.

7. For two very different treatments of Jewish agricultural projects, see Robert Weinberg, *Stalin's Forgotten Zion: Birobidzhan and the Making of a Soviet Jewish Homeland: An Illustrated History, 1928–1996* (Berkeley: University of California Press, 1998), and Jonathan Dekel-Chen, *Farming the Red Land: Jewish Agricultural Colonization and Local Soviet Power, 1924–1941* (New Haven: Yale University Press, 2005).

8. Canonical works stressing processes of top-down transformation include Yakov Lestschinsky, *Dos sovetishe Yidntum: zayn fargangenhayt un kegnvart* (New York: Yidisher Kemfer, 1941), and Zvi Gitelman, *Jewish Nationality and Soviet Policy: The Jewish Sections of the CPSU, 1917–1930* (Princeton: Princeton University Press, 1972).

9. For a recent work stressing the "choice" Jews had to make between national and class allegiances, see Arkadii Zel'tser, *Evrei Sovetskoi provintsii: Vitebsk i mestechki, 1917–1941* (Moscow: Rosspen, 2006).

10. There was, of course, nothing particularly "Belorussian" about the prevalence of factional struggle and competing interests in production. Path-breaking works by Diane Koenker, Lewis Siegelbaum, S. A. Smith, Victoria Bonnell, and William Chase, among others, demonstrated the contingent nature of class and social identity throughout the revolutionary period. See, for example, Diane Koenker, *Moscow Workers and the 1917 Revolution* (Princeton: Princeton University Press, 1981) and *Republic of Labor: Russian Printers and Soviet Socialism, 1918–1930* (Ithaca: Cornell University Press, 2005); Victoria Bonnell, *Roots of Rebellion: Workers' Politics and Organizations in St. Petersburg and Moscow, 1900–1914* (Berkeley: University of California Press, 1983); Lewis Siegelbaum, *Soviet State and Society Between the Revolutions, 1918–1929* (Cambridge: Cambridge University Press, 1992); S. A. Smith, *Red Petrograd: Revolution in the Factories, 1917–1918* (Cambridge: Cambridge University Press, 1983); William Chase, *Workers, Society, and the Soviet State: Labor and Life in Moscow, 1918–1929* (Urbana: University of Illinois Press, 1990); and the path-breaking collection of essays in Lewis Siegelbaum and Ron Suny, eds., *Making Workers Soviet: Power, Class, and Identity* (Ithaca, NY: Cornell University Press, 1994). Ronald Suny's study of the relations between ethnicity, politics, and production in Baku constitutes a still-unsurpassed thinking together of

the categories of nationality and class. See Ronald Suny, *The Baku Commune, 1917–1918: Class and Nationality in the Russian Revolution* (Princeton: Princeton University Press, 1972).

11. Marx, "Wage Labor and Capital," in Robert C. Tucker, ed., *The Marx-Engels Reader* (New York: W. W. Norton and Co., 1978), 209.

12. For the young Lenin, the kustarnichestvo constituted a "hopelessly indefinite" social designation resting between precapitalist and industrial production. See V. I. Lenin, *Razvitie kapitalizma v Rossii: protsess obrazovaniia vnutrenniago rynka dlia krupnoi promyshlennosti*, in *Sochineniia, tom 3* (Moscow: Gos. izdat., 1951), 286 n.

13. The liminal status of kustari is productively examined in Hirokai Kuromiya, "Workers' Artels and Soviet Production Relations," in Sheila Fitzpatrick, Alexander Rabinowitch, and Richard Stites, eds., *Russia in the Era of NEP: Explorations in Soviet Society and Culture* (Bloomington: Indiana University Press, 1991).

14. Ibid., 288.

15. Protocol No. 39, July 16, 1926, "Theses on Jewish Population in Shtetlekh (*mestechki*)," in the *Natsional'nyi Akrkhiv Respubliki Belarus'* (NARB) fond 4-P, opis' 3 (Executive Committee), delo 14, list 711.

16. The estimate of the percentage of Jews among the kustari is taken from an undated report on "Party Work Among Kustari and Women Kustari," likely written in early 1926, NARB f. 4-P, op. 5, d. 204, l. 44.

17. Ibid.

18. See chapter 1.

19. This observation, first postulated by the iconoclastic socialist Zionist thinker Ber Borochov, has been corroborated in Ezra Mendelsohn, *Class Struggle in the Pale: The Formative Years of the Jewish Workers' Movement in Tsarist Russia* (Cambridge: Cambridge University Press, 1970), and Yoav Peled, *Class and Ethnicity in the Pale: The Political Economy of Jewish Workers' Nationalism in Late Imperial Russia* (New York: St. Martin's Press, 1989).

20. The details of the 1903 factory inspector report are examined in Z. E. Abezgauz, *Rabochii klass Belorussii v nachale XX v.* (Minsk: Nauka i Tekhnika, 1977), 82–86.

21. Ibid., 73–76.

22. NARB f. 265 (Trade Unions), op. 1, d. 666, l. 13. See chapter 1 for a complete breakdown of Jewish representation in Belorussian unions.

23. 1925 Report from the *Glavburo* of the Belorussian *Evsektsiia* to the Central Committee of the Communist Party, NARB f. 4-P, op. 10 (Evsektsii), d. 7, l. 39.

24. F. S. Martinkevich and V. I. Dritsa, *Razvitie ekonomiki Belorussii v 1921–1927 gg.* (Minsk: Nauka i Tekhnika, 1973), 4.

25. S. M. Malinin and K. I. Shabuninia, eds., *Ekonomicheskaia istoriia BSSR* (Minsk: Vysheishaia shkola, 1969), 136.

26. On general policies toward cottage production, see E. H. Carr, *The Bolshevik Revolution*, vol. 2 (New York: The Macmillan Company, 1952), esp. 174–175, 229–232.

27. NARB f. 4-P, op.1, d. 226, l. 65. Circular TsB *Evsektsiia* RKP, 1920.

28. V. I. Lenin, *Sochinenie, tom 32*, 326–327.

29. On the discussion over trade and speculation, see chapter 2.

30. TsB KP(b)B Protocol No. 23, May 15, 1921, in NARB f. 4-P, op. 1, d. 243, ll. 87–88.

31. By the end of 1921, the state had managed to turn only 42 of 277 previously nationalized industrial undertakings back to arendators. M. E. Shkliar, *Bor'ba Kompartii Belorssii za ukreplenie soyuza rabochego klassa i trudiashchegosia krest'ianstva v vosstanovitel'nyi period (1921–1925 gg.)* (Minsk: Gos. izdat. BSST, 1960), 122–123.

32. On the general introduction of the policy of *khozraschet* and its effect, see Siegelbaum, *Soviet State and Society Between the Revolutions, 1918–1929*, 100–113.

33. Minsk oblast party report from 1924 on "The Work of the KPB among the Jewish Laboring Masses," *Gosudarstvennyi Arkhiv Minskoi Oblasti* (GAMO) fond 12-P (Minsk Okrug KPB), opis' 1, delo 1, l. 96. Similar instances of mass unemployment were reported throughout the republic. See, for example, the 1924 evsektsiia report on conditions in Minsk, Gomel, and other cities, in "Report TsB RKP Evsektsiia to All-Russian Conference of Evsektsii, activities from Feb. 1923–Feb. 1924," in NARB f. 4-P, op. 10, d. 2, ll. 7–8.

34. By 1897, 70 percent of Shislevish's 400 Jewish families were employed in the tanneries. Abraham Ain, "Swislocz: Portrait of a Jewish Community in Eastern Europe," in *Yivo Annual of Jewish Social Science*, Vol. 4 (New York: YIVO, 1949), 101–102. Khayim Frenkel's tannery in Shavel, established in 1879, would become the largest leather factory in the entire Russian Empire. Sofiia Dubnova-Erlikh, *Garber-Bund un Bershter Bund: Bletlekh geshikhte fun der yidisher arbeter-bavegung* (Warsaw: Kultur-Lige, 1937), 11.

35. Dubnova-Erlikh, *Garber-Bund un Barshter Bund*, 14.

36. 1921 report from the All-Belorussian Soviet of Trade Unions, NARB f. 265, op. 1, d. 666. L. 13.

37. Arthur B. Butman, "Shoe and Leather Trade in Russia," *Department of Commerce and Labor: Bureau or Foreign and Domestic Commerce, Special Agents Series no. 68* (Washington: Government Printing Office, 1913), esp. 22. According to one estimate, handmade shoes accounted for 94 percent of all shoes produced in Belorussia before the war. D. Shapiro, *Kustarnaia promyshlennost' i narodnoe khoziaistvo SSSR* (Moscow: Gos. izdat., 1928), 44.

38. Dubnova-Erlikh, *Garber-Bund*, iii.

39. See chapter 1.

40. E. J. Hobsbawm and Joan Wallach Scott, "Political Shoemakers," *Past and Present* 89 (November 1980), 86–114.

41. One typical Yiddish proverb advised, "*Az men iz a sheygets, git men op far a shuster*"—if one is like a gentile boy (i.e., unlearned), make him a shoemaker's apprentice. Robert A. Rothstein, "The Folkloristic Shoe: Shoes an Shoemakers in Yiddish Language and Folklore," in Edna Nahshon, *Jews and Shoes* (Oxford: Berg, 2008), 109–110.

42. While Raichuk claimed to have joined the Bund in 1892, the organization was not founded until 1897. For Raichuk's 1924 party review, see NARB f. 15-P, o. 4, d. 113, l. 4.

43. Kats, who served in the Bund from 1905 to 1918 and had been conscripted into the tsarist Army during the First World War, eventually became the Chairman of the Administration of the Central Workers Committee (TSRK) and was a member of the Central Bureau of the Minsk Okruzhkom by 1929. See GAMO f. 4704-P, op. 1, d. 3 and NARB f. 15-p. op. 4, d. 311, l. 6 ob.

44. See, for example, the fierce inner-party debate recorded in NARB f. 4-P, op. 1, d. 243, ll. 12–13.

45. Report to the leatherworkers union on "The Conference on Factory Manager Committees and Manager Administration, Together with Administration Trade Unions BelKozha," May 5, 1921, in NARB f. 265 (Trade Unions), op. 1, d. 213, l. 2.

46. NARB f. 265, op. 1, d. 213, l. 20.

47. NARB f. 265, op. 1, d. 213, ll. 20–20 ob.

48. In Vitebsk, for example, leather-preparing factories constituted seven of the thirty factories turned over to arendators in 1922. Shkliar, *Bor'ba kompartii Belorussii*, 123.

49. NARB f. 265, op. 1, d. 213, l. 62.

50. Arrests for trading in leather contraband exploded during the early NEP period. See, for example, the cases of Iosif Meerov Gorovoi, a shoemaker in a military leather plant in Minsk, arrested by the Cheka in September of 1921 for speculating in leather (Cheka Report, NARB f. 192, op. 1, d. 67, ll. 3–3 ob., 7–177, 26–26 ob.); Iakov Zendeleva Rakovshik, a volunteer in the Minsk fire department arrested by the Cheka on leather contraband charges in October of 1921 (NARB f. 192, op. 1, d. 77, l. 18); and Khaia Margolis, an illiterate widow, arrested in March (but ultimately exonerated) for holding two sacks of contraband leather in her apartment (People's Court, Third District, GAMO f. 413, op. 1, d. 764, l. 1, 11, 31–31 ob.).

51. See, for example, reports about shortages of wood bark (NARB f. 265, op. 1, d. 213, l. 2); productions stoppage in the Minsk boot-making shop due to lack of materials (NARB f. 265, op. 1, d. 211, l. 8); and the closing of shoe workshops in Mozyr due to absence of raw materials (NARB f. 265, op. 1, d. 211, l. 27).

52. Leatherworkers Union Report, July 1921, NARB f. 265, op. 1, d. 280, l. 1 ob.

53. Martinkevich and Dritsa, *Razvitie ekonomiki Belorussii v 1921–1927 gg.*, 28. The shuttering of state industrial enterprises was more acute in the sewing industry, where thirty-seven out of forty-two factories closed and the workforce plummeted from 4,392 to 656 workers (85 percent).

54. NARB f. 265, op. 1, d. 280, ll. 1 ob., 4–4 ob.

55. Ibid.

56. NARB 265, op. 1, d. 213, l. 83.

57. NARB f. 265, op. 1, d. 211, l. 14.

58. NARB f. 265, op. 1, d. 211, l. 27.

59. Secret Central Bureau Report on conditions in the Mozyr' *uezd*, summer of 1921, NARB f. 4-P, op. 1, d. 283, ll. 30–32.

60. NARB f. 4-P, op. 1, d. 283, ll. 30–32.

61. NARB f. 265, op. 1, d. 806, l. 34.

62. Similar spikes in productivity were reported in similarly "rationalized" undertakings across Belorussia. See Shkliar, *Bor'ba kompartii Belorussii . . .*, 127.

63. NARB f. 265, op. 1, d. 452, l. 14.

64. NARB f. 265, op. 1, d. 806, l. 13.

65. NARB f. 4-P, op. 1, d. 585, l. 46.

66. GAMO, f. 12-P, op. 1, d. 1, l. 97.

67. GAMO, f. 12-P, op. 1, d. 1, l. 96.

68. NARB f. 4-P, op. 10, d. 42, l. 48.

69. Report on "Party Work Among Kustari and Women Kustari," undated, but likely written in the summer of 1926, NARB f. 4-P, op. 5, d. 204, l. 44.

70. MinGub Leatherworkers Union Protocol No. 36, December 25, 1922, NARB f. 265, op. 1, d. 806, l. 43.

71. GAMO 1-P, op. 1, d. 1, l. 11.

72. Glavburo Evsektsiia TsK KP(b)B Report, April 30, 1924, GAMO f. 12-P, op. 1, d. 1, ll. 58–60.

73. Report by Agursky, then an instructor for the evsektsii, delivered to the Central Bureau of the Evsektsiia, April 28, 1924, NARB f. 4-P, op. 10, d. 5, l. 72.

74. Anonymous report "About the Kustar' Societies in the BSSR," undated, but likely mid-1926, GAMO f. 12-P, op. 1, d. 255, l. 110.

75. GAMO f. 12-P, op. 1, d. 1, l. 98.

76. Report by Merezhin on kustari in Gomel, Protocol No. 11, Central Bureau of the evsektsiia of the TsK RKP, September 8, 1923, NARB f. 4-P, op. 1, d. 802, l. 101.

77. GAMO f. 12-P, op. 1, d. 255, l. 110.

78. Merezhin report, NARB f. 4-P, op. 1, d. 802, l. 101.

79. RKP Resolution concerning goals of organizing kustari into kustar' societies, April 14, 1924, NARB f. 4-P, op. 10, d. 3, l. 38.

80. On the central role of kustar' production for filling the "goods hunger" in Vitebsk, see NARB f. 4-p, op. 10, d. 42, ll. 7–15 ob.

81. This, despite the fact that very few kustari actually seem to have produced for "the market." Evsektsiia reports emphasized that the vast majority of ostensible kustar' producers remained, in fact, artisans producing on consignment. See the report "On the Conditions of the Kustari and Measures for the Development of Work Among Them," in NARB f. 4-P, op. 10, d. 42, l. 48.

82. NARB f. 265, op. 1, d. 1178, l. 11.

83. Similar workshops spread to other parts of Minsk and the surrounding areas in the ensuing months. See NARB f. 265, op. 1, d. 1178, l. 28.

84. NARB f. 265, op 1, d. 1178, l. 11 ob.

85. A brief, rather programmatic overview of the scissors crisis can be found in E. H. Carr, *The Russian Revolution from Lenin to Stalin, 1917–1929* (London: MacMillan, 1991), chapter 6.

86. *Der Veker,* No. 58, March 11, 1923, 2.

87. "Far spekulatsye mit gold," *Der Veker,* March 26, 1923, 4.

88. *Der Veker,* April 19, 1923.

89. *Der Veker,* May 16, 1923, 2.

90. "Der shvartser birzhe," *Der Veker,* June 1, 1923, 4.

91. *Der Veker,* June 21, 1923. This was followed by the introduction of regular updates on the price of corn on the market. See *Der Veker,* July 4, 1923.

92. *Der Veker,* August 12, 1923, 1.

93. The next day, on November 22, *Der Veker* began to list its price in relation to the still scarce but expanding chervonets currency.

94. NARB f. 265, op. 1, d. 1175, l. 31.

95. NARB f. 265, op. 1, d. 1175, l. 45a.

96. Needleworkers Union Protocol, December 17, 1923, NARB f. 265, op. 1, d. 1175, ll. 48–48 ob.

97. For later failed efforts to sell manufactured cloth goods on the Moscow market, see the Minshvei protocol from March 22, 1924, NARB f. 265, op. 1, d. 1554, l. 5.

98. Leatherworkers Union Protocol No. 44, January 1, 1923, NARB f. 265, op. 1, d. 1178, ll. 5–5 ob.

99. Leatherworkers Union Protocol No. 40, January 1, 1924, NARB f. 265, op. 1, d. 1556, ll. 5–5a.

100. See, for example, the hearing concerning Comrade Epshtein, brought before the central presidium of Minshvei for engaging in "apartment" work in March 1924, NARB f. 265, op. 1, d. 1554, l. 6.

101. On tensions in Bobruisk, see NARB f. 4-P, op. 1, d. 230, ll. 30–32.

102. Needleworkers Union Protocol No. 16, October 1, 1924, NARB f. 265, op. 1, d. 1554, l 30–30 ob.

103. Nor were workers in privately owned sewing factories spared. A Minshvei report from November argued that the glut of goods on the market had brought about a sharp "liquidationist tendency" in private industry, as industries shed labor force due to an absence of work orders and "material exhaustion." Needleworkers Protocol No. 22, November 19, 1924, NARB f. 265, op. 1, d. 1554, ll. 40–40 ob.

104. For similar trends in the central Russian provinces, see Chris Ward, *Russia's Cotton Workers and the New Economic Policy* (Cambridge: Cambridge University Press, 1990).

105. The economic crisis of the Soviet periphery provided the "push" that accompanied the integrative pull toward internal migration emphasized in Yuri Slezkine, *The Jewish Century* (Princeton: Princeton University Press, 2004).

106. Alan Ball, "Nep's Second Wind: The New Trade Practice," *Soviet Studies* 37, no. 3. (July 1985): 371–385, esp. 376–377.

107. On this campaign, see Deborah Yalen, "Documenting the New Red Kasrilevke: Shtetl Ethnography as Revolutionary Narrative," *East European Jewish Affairs* 37, no. 3 (December 2007): 353–375.

108. GAMO f. 12-P, op. 1, d. 255, l. 110.

109. Tax reform was trumpeted as a major concession to the kustari during okrug-level kustar' conferences held throughout Belorussia in the early summer of 1925. See, for example, the discussion of taxation in the Bobruisk Okrug kustar' conference from late May 1925, NARB f. 4-P, op. 1, d. 17, ll. 66–70.

110. Agursky, for example, labeled the outbreak of widespread strikes among bristle workers in Vitebsk in 1924 evidence of such a Bundist-Menshevik. NARB f. 4-P, op. 10, d. 5, l. 73.

111. Records suggest that concern about the spread of Zionist activity at the time was not entirely mythical. Of the rather voluminous stockpiles of collected (likely confiscated) underground press materials concerning Zionism held in the evsektsiia archives, the vast bulk is from the period of 1924

to 1925. See, in particular, NARB f. 4-P, op. 1, d. 580; NARB f. 4-P op. 10, d. 29; and NARB f. 4-P, op. 10, d. 44.

112. Protocol from the Conference of Evsektsiia Secretaries, December 7, 1924, NARB f. 4-P, op. 10, d. 5, l. 140.

113. NARB f. 4-P, op. 10, d. 5, l. 143.

114. NARB f. 4-P, op. 10, d. 5, l. 140.

115. GAMO 12-P, op. 1, d. 255, l. 111. The estimates of pay scales in this report appear to be on the high end, compared to similar reports.

116. Report from the bureau of the Bobruisk Okrug evsektsiia to the central Bureau of the Belorussian evsektsiia, September 15, 1925, in NARB f. 4-P, op. 10, d. 7, l. 90.

117. See, for example, the discussion of Zionism among kustari in the report of the Central Bureau of the Russian Communist Party to the "All-Russian Conference of Evsektsii" held in Moscow in February 1924, NARB f. 4-P, op. 10, d. 2, ll. 7–8.

118. On the spread of Zionism among the youth in the Vitebsk Okrug, see NARB f. 4-P, op. 10, d. 7, l. 146; concerning similar problems in the Minks Okrug, see GAMO 12-P. op 1, d. 1, l. 103.

119. See, for example, GAMO f. 12-P, op. 1, d. 1, l. 30.

120. See the pamphlet "Three Years" (*tri goda*) an underground newspaper from 1925 presumably confiscated by the OGPU during one of its raids. NARB f. 4-P, op. 10, d. 29, l. 75.

121. NARB f. 4-P, op. 10, d. 42, l. 50.

122. From an underground Zionist newspaper published by the left-wing Hashomer Hatzair, *Pravda Palestine, na smenu: organ severo-zapadnogo okruga gashomer gatsior SSSR*, no. 4 (1925), NARB f. 4-P, op. 10, d. 11, l. 22.

123. Arthur Hertzberg, ed., *The Zionist Idea: A Historical Analysis and Reader* (Garden City, NY: Doubleday, 1959).

4. From Bolshevik *Haskole* to Cultural Revolution: Abram Beilin and the Jewish Revolution

1. "*Gemshpet Bontsie Shvayg*," *Der Veker*, February 10, 1923.

2. For the sad story of Bontshe's life, and one of the finest of Peretz's stories, see "Bontshe Shvayg," in I. L. Peretz, *The I. L. Peretz Reader*, ed. Ruth Wisse (New Haven: Yale University Press, 2002).

3. *Der Veker*, February 20, 1923.

4. As Anna Shternshis has demonstrated, this process was central to the reformation of Jewish culture across the Soviet Union. Anna Shternshis, *Soviet and Kosher: Jewish Popular Culture in the Soviet Union, 1923–1939* (Bloomington: Indiana University Press, 2006).

5. This concept of culture follows Clifford Geertz, who defined culture as "an historically transmitted pattern of meanings embodied in symbols, a system of inherited conceptions expressed in symbolic forms by means of which men communicate, perpetuate, and develop their knowledge about and attitudes toward life." See Clifford Geertz, *The Interpretation of Cultures: Selected Essays* (New York: Basic Books, 1973), 89.

6. David Shneer stressed the novelty of the Soviet Yiddish cultural experiment. David Shneer, *Yiddish and the Creation of Soviet Jewish Culture, 1918–1930* (Cambridge: Cambridge University Press, 2004).

7. The Soviet cultural struggle has constituted one of the richest areas of historical exploration for the past four decades, beginning with the 1978 volume of collected essays, Sheila Fitzpatrick, ed., *Cultural Revolution in Russia, 1928–1931* (Bloomington: Indiana University Press, 1978). Other indispensable works include Richard Stites, *Revolutionary Dreams: Utopian Visions and Experimental Life in the Russian Revolution* (Oxford: Oxford University Press, 1989); Abbott Gleason, Peter Kenez, and

Richard Stites, eds., *Bolshevik Culture: Experiment and Order in the Russian Revolution* (Bloomington: Indiana University Press, 1989); and Katerina Clark, *Petersburg: Crucible of Cultural Revolution* (Cambridge, MA: Harvard University Press, 1998).

8. On struggles between cultural hard-liners and soft-liners, see Sheila Fitzpatrick, *The Cultural Front: Power and Culture in Revolutionary Russia* (Ithaca, NY: Cornell University Press, 1992). In addition, see the useful critical exchange between Fitzpatrick and Michael David Fox in *The Russian Review* 58, no. 2 (April 1999): 181–211. On the Proletkult movement and generational conflicts, see Lynn Mally, *Culture of the Future: The Proletkult Movement in Revolutionary Russia* (Berkeley: University of California Press, 1990), and Anne E. Gorsuch, *Youth in Revolutionary Russia: Enthusiasts, Bohemians, Delinquents* (Bloomington: Indiana University Press, 2000).

9. Sheila Fitzpatrick, *The Commissariat of Enlightenment: Soviet Organization of Education and the Arts under Lunacharsky, October 1917–1921* (Cambridge: Cambridge University Press, 1970).

10. On the overlap between nationality policy and cultural policy, see Terry Martin, *The Affirmative Action Empire: Nations and Nationalism in the Soviet Union, 1923–1939* (Ithaca: Cornell University Press, 2001), and Francine Hirsch, *Empire of Nations: Ethnographic Knowledge and the Making of the Soviet Union* (Ithaca, NY: Cornell University Press, 2005).

11. See, in particular, Robert Weinberg, *Stalin's Forgotten Zion: Birobidzhan and the Making of a Soviet Jewish Homeland: An Illustrated History, 1928–1996* (Berkeley: University of California Press, 1998), and Jeffrey Veidlinger, *The Moscow State Yiddish Theater: Jewish Culture on the Soviet Stage* (Bloomington: Indiana University Press, 2000). For everyday struggles over cultural reformation, in addition to the above-cited works by Shternshis and Shneer, see Elissa Bemporad, *Becoming Soviet Jews: The Bolshevik Experiment in Minsk* (Bloomington: Indiana University Press, 2013).

12. This argument constitutes the provocative central thesis of Yuri Slezkine, *The Jewish Century* (Princeton: Princeton University Press, 2004), 152, 203, 225.

13. For biographical details of Osherovich's life, see his 1924 Party Review report.(*Natsional'nyi Akrkhiv Respubliki Belarus'* [NARB] fond 15-P [Party Control Commission], opis' 4, delo 113, list 75), and his 1929 record from the party purge (NARB f. 15-P, op. 4, d. 311, l. 4 ob.).

14. Il'ia Osherovich, lead article, *Unzer Kultur*, May 7, 1921.

15. Maks Erik, *Etyudn tsu der geshikhte fun der haskole* (Minsk: Melukhe Farlag, 1934).

16. The most sophisticated and nuanced rendering of this argument was made by the iconoclastic Marxist philosopher Georg Lukács in his seminal essay "Reification and the Consciousness of the Proletariat," originally published in 1923 and reprinted in Georg Lukács, *History and Class Consciousness: Studies in Marxist Dialectics*, trans. Robert Livingstone (Cambridge, MA: MIT Press, 1971). Tellingly, the work was condemned by the Communist International following Lenin's death.

17. On early debates over Yiddish, see Gennady Estraikh, *Soviet Yiddish: Language Planning and Linguistic Development* (Oxford: Clarendon Press, 1999).

18. The recurrence of this trope in the broader Soviet context, as well as its own underlying tensions concerning the Jewish question, has been illuminatingly examined in Robert Weinberg, "Demonizing Judaism in the Soviet Union During the 1920s," *Slavic Review* 67, no. 1 (Spring 2008): 120–153.

19. David Sorkin, *The Transformation of German Jewry, 1780–1840* (Detroit: Wayne State University Press, 1999), 31–31, 108.

20. Derek Penslar, *Shylock's Children: Economics and Jewish Identity in Modern Europe* (Berkeley: University of California Press, 2001), 79.

21. David Fishman, *Russia's First Modern Jews: The Jews of Shklov* (New York: New York University Press, 1995).

22. Jacob S. Raisin, *The Haskalah Movement in Russia* (Philadelphia: Jewish Publication Society, 1913), 144–145.

23. The actual legal persecution of Zionists and religious leaders fell to institutions like the GPU, the police, the procurators, and the courts. This is not to say that evsektsii activists played no role

in the process; reports compiled by the evsektsii undoubtedly led to arrests, suppression, and state violence.

24. Sheila Fitzpatrick, "The Soft Line on Culture and It's Enemies," in Fitzpatrick, *The Cultural Front*.

25. The definitive work on this subject remains Fitzpatrick, *The Commissariat of Enlightenment*.

26. Zvi Gitelman, *Jewish Nationality and Soviet Politics: The Jewish Sections of the CPSU, 1917–1930*, (Princeton: Princeton University Press, 1972).

27. In this sense, resistance to Bolshevik cultural policies continued a long tradition of Jewish skepticism toward the intervention of the state that dated back to the earliest decades of the Russian Jewish encounter. See, for example, Michael Stanislawski, *Tsar Nicholas I and the Jews: The Transformation of Jewish Society, 1825–1855* (Philadelphia: Jewish Publication Society, 1983).

28. Given its centrality, the question of educational reform has received considerable historiographic attention. See, for example, Inna Gerassimova, "Evreiskoe obrazovanie v Belarusi v 20–30-x godakh XX v.," *Evrei Belarusi: istoriia i kul'tura* II (1998): 58–73; Leonid Smilovitsky, *Evrei Belarusi: Iz nashei ob'shchei istorii, 1905–1953* (Minsk: Arti-feks, 1999), especially chapter 2; and Galina Zasinets, "Evreiskoe sovetskoe obrazovanie na Gomel'shchine v 20-x godakh XX veka," *Evrei Belarusi: istoriia i kul'tura* VI (2001): 165–171.

29. A fierce critic of "traditional" Jewish education, Mendele himself became headmaster of a reform minded *Talmud Torah* in the 1880s.

30. The Bolsheviks, of course, had no monopoly on animus against the heder. On the imagining of the heder in Zionist thought and practice, see Steven J. Zipperstein, *Imagining Russian Jewry: Memory, History, Identity* (Seattle: University of Washington Press, 1999), 41–62.

31. Protocol from the January 13, 1992, "folks-miting" organized through the Bobruisk Jewish Bureau, NARB f. 4-P, op. 1 (Central Bureau), d. 582, ll. 15–16.

32. *Der Veker*, September 23, 1923, 2.

33. According to a 1924 evsektsiia report, there were an estimated 86,000 school-aged Jewish children. Of these, only 18,727, or about one-fifth, studied in the soviet Yiddish schools in 1924. GAMO 12-P (Minsk Okrug KPB), op. 1, d. 1, l. 100; see also Protocol No. 7, Evburo Minsk Okrug Committee, August 19, 1925, in GAMO 12-P, op. 1, d. 164, l. 22.

34. For a report on the myriad of reactions from Jewish communities across the republic in 1926, see NARB f. 4-P, op. 10 (Evsektsiia), d. 61, ll. 110–128, especially 113–114.

35. The number of Jewish schools operating in the Minsk Okrug, for example, increased from 93 to 105 during the 1924–1925 year, according to one report (GAMO 12-P, op. 1, d. 164, l. 109). A second Minsk Okrug report from the end of 1925 placed the number at 110 (GAMO 12-P, op. 1, d. 164, l. 149).

36. The latter number of students accounted for nearly 64 percent of school-aged Jewish children in 1932. Smilovitsky, *Evrei Belarusi*, 56.

37. To train newly qualified students, the state operated two Yiddish pedagogical institutions, which trained teachers to teach in the local school system. GAMO 12-P, op. 1, d. 1, ll. 100–101.

38. *Der Veker*, April 3, 1924.

39. NARB f. 4-P, op. 1, d. 578, l. 34.

40. NARB f. 4-P, op. 1, d. 810, l. 10.

41. Minsk city evsektsiia report for activities from October to November 1923, in GAMO 12-P, op. 1, d. 1, ll. 8–9.

42. The 1923 antireligious campaign resulted not from "spontaneous" action but from a direct party initiative. In April the party issued a directive calling for the intensification of the antireligious campaign, an action that led to the formation and proliferation of antireligious groups and journals. As Glennys Young and others have argued, these campaigns proved to be of rather dubious efficacy, particularly among the nonconverted. See Glennys Young, *Power and the Sacred in Revolutionary Russia: Religious Activists in the Village* (University Park, Pennsylvania: The Pennsylvania State University Press, 1997), chapters 3–4.

43. *Der Veker,* March 4, 1923.

44. *Der Veker,* March 9, 1923. For the tendency to blame Jewish women for continued religious practices, see Bemporad, *Becoming Soviet Jews,* 142–43.

45. *Der Veker,* March 17–18, 1923.

46. Ibid.

47. In general, the frontal assault against religious practices through antireligious festivals, "humoristic" parodies, show trials, and the like was sharply curtailed after 1923. On the shift in Bolshevik policies, see Young, *Power and the Sacred in Revolutionary Russia.*

48. Gitelman, *Jewish Nationality and Soviet Politics,* 291–318.

49. For an exploration of the dynamics of this counterrevolt in the Jewish milieu, see Elissa Bemporad, "Behavior Unbecoming a Communist: Jewish Religious Practice in Soviet Minsk," *Jewish Social Studies* 14, no. 2 (Winter 2008): 1–31.

50. On the planning for the festival, see the Evsektsiia Central Bureau Protocol No. 12, March 20, 1922, in NARB f. 4-P, op. 1, d. 578, l. 6.

51. NARB f. 4-P, op. 1, d. 580, l. 46.

52. In September of 1923, religious Jews from Minsk sent a letter to the Central Executive Committee of the USSR in Moscow denouncing the action, preserved in NARB f 4-P, op. 1, d. 802, ll. 276–279.

53. Aside from mass demonstrations, opponents of Bolshevik cultural policy wrote petitions and letters of complaint. See, for example, the letters written to the Sovnarkom or the Council of the People's Commissariat complaining about the destruction of two Jewish cemeteries in Minsk to make way for new construction projects in 1925 (NARB f. 7 (Sovnarkom), op. 1, d. 251, ll. 244–247).

54. A point stressed in Bemporad, *Becoming Soviet Jews,* 112–144.

55. NARB f. 4-P, op. 1, d. 802, l. 192.

56. See, for example, the article "Tsu vos darf men hobn di kor-shul in Minsk," in which the author, a komsomol member named Shteynman, unleashed a litany of attacks against the speculators who used the synagogue and demanded that it be turned into a worker club. *Der Veker,* January 28, 1923.

57. See, for example, the regional report from the Borisov region discussing the coordination of the antisynagogue campaign in the surrounding shtetlekh, in NARB f. 4-P, op. 1, d. 809, l. 51.

58. NARB f. 4-P, op. 10, d. 46, l1. 211–228 ob.

59. NARB f. 4-P, op. 10, d. 46, ll. 161–163.

60. NARB f. 4-P, op. 10, d. 46, l. 163.

61. On Levin's political past, see Bemporad, *Becoming Soviet Jews,* 57, 77–79.

62. Her status in the party was attested to by the fact that she was quickly promoted to the central evsektsii administration in Moscow. On Frumkin's rise through the Bund and Bolshevik party ranks, see Shneer, *Yiddish and the Creation of Soviet Jewish Culture,* 26–27.

63. T. S. Prot'ko, *Stanovlenie sovietskoi totalitarnoi sistemy v Belarusi, 1917–1941 g.g.* (Minsk, Tesei, 2002), p. 648.

64. For Orshanksii's biography, included in his 1929 purge record, see NARB 15-P, op. 1, d. 311, l. 11 ob.

65. For Nodel's 1921 purge record, see GAMO 4704-P, op. 1, d. 2, l. 427 ob.

66. GAMO 4704-P, op. 1, d. 5, ll. 62–62 ob.

67. Bemporad, *Becoming Soviet Jews,* 51–80. Zvi Gitelman and David Shneer likewise pointed to the prominence of former Bundists in cultural institutions across the Soviet lands.

68. This process had the effect of keeping the number of "overrepresented" Jews in the party constant, while buttressing the ranks of Belorussian members. Between January 1 and the Eighth Congress of the KP(b)B in May of 1924, the total number of party members climbed from 3,998 to 10,438. See V. I. Brovikov, ed., *Kommunisticheskaia partiia Belorussii v rezoliutsiiakh i resheniiakh s'ezdov i plenumov TsK* (Minsk: Belarus', 1983), 162. For the dynamics of these changes in party composition, see chapter 5.

69. It was from these ranks, primarily, that many of Yuri Slezkine's Jewish *vydiyzhentsy* to Moscow and Leningrad doubtlessly arose. See Slezkine, *The Jewish Century*, 222–23.

70. As Yuri Slezkine has provocatively shown, the revolution found enthusiastic proponents throughout the Pale, or at least among those who chose to leave the Pale. The argument here stresses the social dynamics that transformed Jews, rather reluctantly, into proponents of universalizing "Soviet" identity.

71. From Central Bureau report, "Rabota KPB evreiskikh trudiashikhsia mass," undated, but mid-1924, GAMO f 12-P, op. 1, d. 1, l. 101. For additional complaints about the indifference of the younger generation of Jewish communists to the tasks of "Jewish work," see the report from the conference of Evsektsii Secretaries from December of 1924, in NARB f. 4-P, op. 10, d. 5, l. 149.

72. GAMO f. 12-P, op. 1, d. 1, l. 73. Also see the similar ensuing reports from other students presented to the evsektsiia Central Committee.

73. Erich Haberer deserves credit for returning the Haskalah to the center of his exceptional study of late-nineteenth-century Jewish socialist thought and action. See Erich E. Haberer, *Jews and Revolution in Nineteenth-Century Russia* (Cambridge: Cambridge University Press, 1995).

74. GAMO f. 12-P, op. 1, d. 1, ll. 73–74.

75. GAMO 12-P, op. 1, d. 164, ll. 88–90.

76. The details of Beilin's life are taken from his party review autobiography. See NARB f. 15-P, op. 4, d. 94, ll. 13–15.

77. It is here that Beilin's account, written for the 1924 party review, breaks off. The story is continued through Beilin's archival footprints and fingerprints.

78. Abram Beilin, "Ocherednye zadachi po rabote sredi kustarei," from June 1927, NARB f. 4-P, op. 10, d. 88, ll. 303–308.

79. For a canonical overview of the politics and economy of the NEP era, see Stephen F. Cohen, *Bukharin and the Bolshevik Revolution: A Political Biography* (New York: A. A. Knopf, 1973). Many of Cohen's evaluations of Bukharin, particularly his interpretation of the demise of the NEP economy have, in turn, been critiqued in Robert C. Allen, *Farm to Factory: A Reinterpretation of the Soviet Industrial Revolution* (Princeton: Princeton University Press, 2003).

80. NARB f. 4-P, op. 10, d. 88, l. 303–305.

81. NARB f. 4-P, op. 10, d. 88, l. 304a.

82. From an undated report, likely late 1926, on the political mood in the shtetlekh, NARB f. 4-P, op. 10, d. 55, ll. 41–42.

83. See the response by Knorin and Bailin to the report "Material i vyvody o evreiskoi klerikalizme," heard in the March 31, 1927, meeting of the Jewish Bureau of the Central Committee of the KP(b)B in NARB f. 4-P, op. 10, d. 46, ll. 139–141.

84. Report "Vegn kamf mitn idishn klerikalizm un anti-religyezer propagande," NARB f. 4-P, op. 1, d. 46, ll. 174–186.

85. NARB f. 4-P, op. 10, d. 46, ll. 175–176.

86. NARB f. 4-P, op. 10, d. 46, ll. 182–183.

87. "Borba s klerikalizmom," NARB f. 4-P, op. 10, d. 46, ll. 142–147.

88. NARB f. 4-P, op. 10, d. 46, l. 142.

89. NARB f. 4-P. op. 10, d. 46, l. 180.

90. The specific dynamics of the NEP crisis, as well as the political, social, and economic relationships that produced the Stalin Revolution, are examined in the final three chapters.

91. Yakov Lestschinsky, *Dos sovetishe Yidntum: zayn fargangenheyt un kegnvart*. New York: Yidisher Kemfer, 1941, 128–49.

92. On "godless" shock workers, see Daniel Peris, *Storming the Heavens: The Soviet League of the Militant Godless* (Ithaca, NY: Cornell University Press, 1998), chapter 4.

93. The May 1927 closing of the central synagogue in Zhitomir marked one of the first episodes in the renewed campaign. JTA, "Several Synagogues in Russia Confiscated," May 11, 1927. The

acceleration of the campaigns in the following years could be seen in the closing of synagogues; see JTA, "'Atheist' Gives Figures on Synagogues Closed in Soviet Russia," April 17, 1929. (From *Bezbozhnik* report, April 16.) The crackdown on religious institutions paralleled attacks against Russian Orthodox and Catholic churches. See Young, *Power and the Sacred*, and William B. Husband, *Godless Communists: Atheism in Soviet Society, 1917–1932* (Chicago: University of Northern Illinois Press, 2002).

94. Resolution N. 49, Presidium of the TsKK KP(b)B, February 2, 1930, NARB F. 15-P, op. 5, D. 14, l. 19.

95. A copy of the original version of Beilin's edited text can be found in the purge file from 1930; see NARB f. 15-P, op. 5, d. 14, ll. 12–14.

96. NARB f. 15-P, op. 5, d. 14, l. 30.

97. For Abram Beilin's appeal letter from August 1930, see NARB f. 15-P, op. 5, d. 14, ll. 24 ob.-25.

5. Bundism and the Nationalities Question

1. Bureau of the TsK KPB Protocol No. 8, January 21, 1926, *Natsional'nyi Akrkhiv Respubliki Belarus'* (NARB) f. 4-P (Central Committee of the Communist Party of Belorussia), op. 3 (Executive Committee), d. 11, ll. 11–12.

2. Ibid., ll. 13–14.

3. Ibid., ll. 14–16.

4. In addition to being a leading Bolshevik figure, Gessen was also the nephew of the pioneering historian of Russian Jewry Iulii Isidorovich Gessen.

5. Krinitskii replaced Adol'f Khristoforovich Getner as party secretary, who had in turn replaced Vil'gel'm Knorin in 1922.

6. Krinitskii offered the initial signal for the attack on Bundism during the all-Belorussian evsektsiia conference held in early November 1925, prefiguring many of the same points. For the report on Krinitskii's speech, see evsektsiia Protocol No. 139, November 5, 1925, in NARB f. 4-P, op. 3, d. 8, t. III, l. 227.

7. Gessen's letter, included in the Bureau of the TsK KPB protocol, was widely reproduced; extant copies exist in national and regional evsektsii files, as well as local party files in Minsk. For the original, see NARB f. 4-P, op. 3, d. ll, ll. 14–16.

8. Ibid., 14.

9. Ibid.

10. On the career of Beilin, see chapter 4.

11. Central Committee, TsK KP(b)B, Protocol No. 17, March 19, 1926, in NARB f. 4-P, op. 3, d. 4, ll. 142–143.

12. For treatments stressing the significance of the campaigns as a beginning of the end to autonomous Jewish politics, see Zvi Gitelman, *Jewish Nationality and Soviet Politics: The Jewish Sections of the CPSU, 1917–1930* (Princeton: Princeton University Press, 1972), chapter 8; and Elissa Bemporad, *Becoming Soviet Jews: The Bolshevik Experiment in Minsk* (Bloomington: Indiana University Press, 2013), chapter 3. Arkadii Zel'tser, in his brief treatment of the campaigns, interpreted the attacks as part of a broad attack against manifestations of Jewish nationality. See Arkadii Zel'tser, *Evrei sovetski provintsii: Vitensk i mestechki, 1917–1941* (Moscow: Rosspen, 2006), 141–143.

13. Zel'tser dates the opening of the anti-Bundism campaign to the arrival of Krinitskii as party secretary at the end of 1924. While this claim is correct in terms of internal party rhetoric, it overlooks the fact that the mass campaign against Bundism did not begin in local party cells until 1926.

14. Records of these mass meetings, compiled in NARB f. 4-P, op. 5, d. 409 (On Bundism), form the basis of this chapter.

15. David Shneer, *Yiddish and the Creation of Soviet Jewish Culture, 1918–1930* (New York: Cambridge University Press, 2004).

16. Bemporad, *Becoming Soviet Jews*, 80; Zel'tser, *Evrei Sovetski provintsii*, 143.

17. On the concepts of *narodnosti* and *inorodtsy* and the categorization of the Jews among the latter, see Ronald Grigor Suny, "The Empire Strikes Out: Imperial Russia, 'National' Identity, and Theories of Empire," in Ronald Grigor Suny and Terry Martin, *A State of Nations: Empire and Nation-Making in the Age of Lenin and Stalin* (Oxford: Oxford University Press, 2001), 48–52.

18. As Eric Lohr noted, "nearly every law on naturalization, denaturalization, immigration, or emigration under the old regime included a general clause written in universalistic terms, but followed by a 'commentary' . . . that laid out very different rules for Jews." Eric Lohr, *Russian Citizenship: From Empire to Soviet Union* (Cambridge, MA: Harvard University Press, 2012), 7. A 1914 volume outlining special restrictions concerning Jews in the Russian Empire ran to two volumes and nearly one thousand pages. See Ia. I. Gimpelson and L. M. Bramson, eds., *Zakony o evreiakh* (St. Petersburg: T-va iurisprudentsiia, 1914–1915).

19. For recent reinterpretations of the mechanisms to categorize, control, and exclude Jews from Russian society, see Eugene Avrutin, *Jews and the Imperial State: Identification Politics in Tsarist Russia* (Ithaca, NY: Cornell University Press, 2010).

20. The same claim was true, to a degree, for the Muslim populations of the East; yet Jews, unlike Muslims, occupied a critical antithetical place in the foundational scriptures of Christian Europe, including Russia.

21. See, for example, Francine Hirsch, *Empire of Nations: Ethnographic Knowledge and the Making of the Soviet Union* (Ithaca, NY: Cornell University Press, 2005), 24–30. This recent work reiterates claims concerning the central role Bundist-Bolshevik disagreements played in the shaping of early Bolshevik nationality policy. See, in particular, Henry Tobias, *The Jewish Bund: From Its Origins to 1905* (Stanford: Stanford University Press, 1972); and Jonathan Frankel, *Prophecy and Politics: Socialism, Nationalism, and the Russian Jews, 1862–1917* (Cambridge: Cambridge University Press, 1981), chapter 4.

22. On Stalin and the nationalities question, see Hirsch, *Empire of Nations*, 43.

23. The best treatment of the issues driving the Bund from the ranks of the Russian Social Democratic Workers' Party in 1903 remains Tobias, *The Jewish Bund in Russia*.

24. For a canonical interpretation of the Soviet Union as a "prison house" of nations, see Richard Pipes, *The Formation of the Soviet Union: Communism and Nationalism* (Cambridge, MA: Harvard University Press, 1997). For a diametrically opposed reading, see Ronald G. Suny, *The Revenge of the Past: Nationalism, Revolution, and the Collapse of the Soviet Union* (Stanford: Stanford University Press, 1993).

25. Terry Martin, *The Affirmative Action Empire: Nations and Nationalism in the Soviet Union, 1923–1939* (Ithaca, NY: Cornell University Press, 2001).

26. An argument initially made in "The USSR as Communal Apartment, or How a Socialist State Promoted Ethnic Particularism," *Slavic Review* 53, no. 2 (Summer 1994): 414–452.

27. Martin, *The Affirmative Action Empire*, 9–21.

28. Even as Soviet policymakers continued to reject the Austro-Marxist principle of extraterritorial nationality (Martin, *The Affirmative Action Empire*, 32), this localization and decentralization of nationality policy suggests that the Austro-Marxist principle was embraced, de facto, if not de jure.

29. Even this categorization was contested, as Soviet ethnographers could never quite agree whether the Jews constituted one national group or five separate national groups, due to the language differences between Georgian Jews, Central Asian Jews, Crimean Jews, European Jews, and Mountain Jews. See Hirsch, *Empire of Nations*, 132–133, 289–290.

30. Francine Hirsch noted that during the 1926 census, the party sent instructions warning census takers under "no circumstances to write Muslim, Christian, Bekhaist, or Orthodox" in the census form for nationality (*narodnost'*), as these constituted religious categories, not national ones. Hirsch does not note the peculiar designation of Jews. See Hirsch, *Empire of Nations*, 125.

31. This ambiguous and slippery tension at times fanned latent antisemitic tendencies within Bolshevik discourse. For an illuminating example, see Robert Weinberg, "Demonizing Judaism in the Soviet Union During the 1920s," *Slavic Review* 67, no. 1 (Spring 2008): 120–153.

32. This is not to say that all rightist, antirevolutionary European parties embraced antisemitism in the interwar period—only the most successful ones.

33. The best single-volume work on this period remains Howard Sachar, *Dreamland: Europeans and Jews in the Aftermath of the Great War* (New York: Vintage, 2003).

34. NARB f. 4-P, op. 10 (Evsektsii), d. 7, l. 36. The numbers reflected the demographic situation before the expansion of the Belorussian borders in 1924.

35. On the phenomenon of overrepresentation, see chapters 1 and 3.

36. Martin, *The Affirmative Action Empire*, 17.

37. A point recognized in Martin, *The Affirmative Action Empire*, 261.

38. Central Control Commission report, as quoted in Martin, *The Affirmative Action Empire*, 262.

39. Between 1929 and 1930, some three hundred Belorussian intellectuals were arrested in Minsk alone. Alexander Simirenko, *Professionalization of Soviet Society* (New Brunswick, NJ: Transaction Books, 1982), 76. For the fates of the individuals mentioned, as well as a much broader list of the fates of leading figures in Belorussia, including Belorussian and non-Belorussian activists (but few Jewish actors), see the appendix to T. S. Prot'ko, *Stanovlenie sovetskoi totalitarnoi sistemy v Belarusi* (Minsk, Tesei, 2002).

40. For the record of the party purge of Ignatovskii, see NARB 15-P (Control Commission), O. 5, D. 103.

41. Bemporad, *Becoming Soviet Jews*, 114–119.

42. For the record of Beilin's hearing, see NARB f. 15-P, op. 5, d. 14.

43. A clear example was the increasing party intervention into the affairs of the Moscow State Yiddish Theater, which led to the defection of the theater's director, Aleksandr Granovskii, in 1928, and his replacement by Solomon Mikhoels. On the politics of the theater, see Jeffrey Veidlinger, "Let's Perform a Miracle: The Soviet Yiddish State Theater in the 1920s," *Slavic Review* 57, no. 2 (Summer 1998): 372–397.

44. Shneer, *Yiddish and the Creation of Soviet Jewish Culture*, 216.

45. Recent studies by Veidlinger, Shternshis, and Bemporad have contested the degree of this turn to Stalinist uniformity by demonstrating the ways in which individual Jewish actors sought to preserve aspects of Jewish culture in the midst of this ideological onslaught. That being said, all note a discernible change in the content of Yiddish culture in the 1930s toward greater ideological conformity.

46. Martin, *The Affirmative Action Empire*, 25–26.

47. By contrast, in the eastern borderlands of Central Asia, Martin notes, affirmative action policies for national minorities continued unabated. Ibid., 26.

48. Hirsch, *Empire of Nations*, 8–9, 103–104.

49. Hirsch, in particular, emphasized the role that "economic expediency" played in nationality policy. Her conception of the "economic" dimension, however, focuses exclusively on debates about how to best divide the populations and territories of the Soviet lands geographically in order to maximize industrial output. The concept of economy employed is purely spatial in nature, concerned with the division of economic space to achieve the most rational and efficient output. This study, by contrast, argues that it was the temporal dynamic of economic change over time, driven by structural compulsions, which played the primary role in shaping discourses of nationality. For her distinction between the "ethnographic principle" and the "principle of economic expediency," see Hirsch, *Empire of Nations*, 62–79.

50. See, for example, the treatment of Jewish nationality and antisemitism in Ukraine in Martin, *The Affirmative Action Empire*, 43–44, 388–390. Similarly, sustained consideration of the place of Jews within Soviet society outside of the context of antisemitism is largely absent in Ronald Grigor

Suny and Terry Martin, *A State of Nations: Empire and Nation-Making in the Age of Lenin and Stalin* (Oxford: Oxford University Press, 2001).

51. TsB KP(b)B, Protocol No. 1, December 31, 1918, in NARB f. 4-P, op. 1, d. 3, ll. 3–5.

52. For biographies of these figures, as well as other leading figures in Belorussia during the 1920s and 1930s, see the appendix to Prot'ko, *Stanovlenie sovetskoi totalitarnoi sistemy v Belarusi.*

53. Concerning the high concentration of Jewish actors in party, state, and productive apparatuses, see chapter 1.

54. NARB f. 4-P, op. 1, d. 804, l. 15.

55. GAMO f. 12-P (Minsk Okrug KPB), op. 1, d. 164, l. 141.

56. Secret *evsektsiia* report to the Central Committee on the Conditions of the Jews, 1926–1927, NARB f. 4-P, op. 10, d. 55, l. 58.

57. The only remaining Jewish full member of the Central Committee was Gessen, who was on the verge of being purged as a Trotskyist (see chapter 5). For the complete list of TsK, see NARB f. 4-P, op. 3, d. 13, l. 372.

58. NARB f. 4-P, op. 10, d. 55, l. 58.

59. NARB f. 4-P, op. 5, d. 265, ll. 12–13.

60. On the phenomenon of *lishentsy*, see Golfo Alexopoulos, *Stalin's Outcasts: Aliens, Citizens, and the Soviet State, 1926–1936* (Ithaca, NY: Cornell University Press, 2003).

61. V. I. Brovikov, ed., *Kommunisticheskaia partiia Belorussii v rezoliutsiiakh i resheniiakh s'ezdov i plenumov TsK* (Minsk: Belarus', 1983), 162.

62. NARB f. 4-P, op. 3, d. 13, l. 341.

63. Benjamin Pinkus, *The Jews of the Soviet Union: The History of a National Minority* (Cambridge: Cambridge University Press, 1988), 79. Total party membership in 1927 remains unclear; the Tenth Party Congress of the KP(b)B placed party membership at 30,955, but included members from the Red Army stationed in the region who were not, technically, members of the KPB. See Brovikova et al., *Kommunisticheskaia partiia Belorussii*, 360.

64. Abram Beilin "Report on the Social Structure of the Jewish Population of the BSSR, 1926–7," NARB f. 4-P, op. 10, d. 55, l. 58.

65. For instructions issued by the Control Commission for the Party Review, see NARB f. 15-P, op. 4, d. 87, ll. 17–21, 35–49.

66. NARB f. 15-P, op. 4, d. 131, ll. 21–22.

67. The eighty-three excluded Belorussians constituted the second largest group. For the breakdown by nationality, see NARB f. 15-P, op. 4, d. 114, l. 24.

68. B. Markiianov, *Ukreplenie edinstva riadov kommunisticheskoi partii Belorussii (1921–1937 gg.)* (Minsk: Belarus', 1970), 77–78.

69. NARB 4-P, op. 10 (*Evsektsii*), d. 5, l. 11 (Evsektsiia Galvbiuro report, March 1923–March 1924).

70. NARB f. 4-P, op. 3, d. 3, ll. 446–447.

71. NARB f. 4-P, op. 3, d. 3, ll. 448–450.

72. Interestingly, the report for BGU also included the salaries for all of the members who were excluded from the party, an indication that budgetary concerns may have factored into the decision. NARB f. 4-P, op. 3, d. 3, ll. 451–452 ob.

73. NARB f. 15-P, op. 4, d. 113, ll. 87-87 ob.

74. NARB f. 15-P, op. 4, d. 113, l. 87 ob.

75. NARB f. 4-P, op. 3, d. 3, l. 422.

76. Zel'dinaia was reinstated after appealing on the grounds that her political passivity resulted from the demands of having to take care of a sick child. NARB f. 4-P, op. 3, d. 3, l. 423.

77. NARB f. 4-P, o. 3, d. 3, l. 428.

78. NARB f. 4-P, op. 3, d. 3, l. 500.

79. NARB f. 4-P, op. 3, d. 3, l. 512.

80. GAMO f. 12-P, op. 1, d. 164, l. 141.

81. NARB f. 4-P, op. 3, d. 8, t. III, l. 208.

82. While the exact number of Bundists excluded in 1924 went unrecorded, by 1928 only a reported 107 Bundists remained in the Minsk city party organization, according to Bemporad, *Becoming Soviet Jews*, 77. This number undoubtedly reflected further attrition following the anti-Trotskyist campaigns (see chapter 6), further intensifying the trend toward the exclusion of Bundists from the party ranks.

83. See, for example, Yankel Levin's complaint about shortages of qualified Jewish workers in the evsektsiia, GAMO f. 12-P, op. 1, d. 1, l. 104.

84. For the record of Bende's 1929 purge hearing, see NARB 15-P, op. 4, d. 311, l. 88.

85. NARB f. 15-P, op. 4, d. 87, l. 49.

86. Ibid.

87. NARB f. 4-P, op. 5, d. 409, ll. 63–64.

88. NARB f. 4-P, op. 5, d. 409, l. 1.

89. NARB f. 4-P, op. 9, d. 409, ll. 63–64.

90. NARB f. 4-P, op. 5, d. 88.

91. NARB f. 4-P, op. 5, d. 409, l. 136.

92. NARB f. 4-P, op. 5, d. 409, l. 45.

93. NARB f. 4-P, op. 5, d. 409, l. 102.

94. While Jews and non-Jews joined in on the attack, defenders of Bundism, even ambivalent ones, seem to have been exclusively Jewish.

95. NARB f. 4-P, op. 5, d. 409, l. 136 ob.

96. NARB f. 4-P, op. 5, d. 409, l. 75 ob.

97. NARB f. 4-P, op. 5, d. 409, l. 83.

98. NARB f. 4-P, op. 5, d. 409, l. 90. This charge was likewise articulated by Abram Beilin, the head of the evsektsiia, in a meeting with the builders' union. See NARB f. 4-P, op. 5, d. 409, l. 67.

99. NARB f. 4-P, op. 5, d. 409, l. 137.

100. NARB f. 4-P, op. 5, d. 409, l. 45.

101. NARB f. 4-P, op. 10, d. 409, l. 77.

102. NARB f. 4-P, op. 5, d. 409, l. 125.

103. NARB f. 4-P, op. 5, d. 409, l. 46.

104. See, for example, the comments to this effect in the *Minshvei* meeting, in NARB f. 4-P, op. 5, d. 409, l. 83.

105. NARB f. 4-P, op. 5, d. 409, l. 5.

106. NARB f. 4-P, op. 5, d. 409, ll. 93–94.

107. As Terry Martin stressed, Jews were generally grouped with Russians, Ukrainians, Georgians, Armenians, and Germans as "advanced," in comparison to those populations deemed "culturally backward" (Martin, *The Affirmative Action Empire*, 23). Curiously, in this context, Martin refers to the Jews (as well Germans) as a "titular nationality," which they decidedly were not. The revealing slip points again to the particularly liminal position of Jews within nationality policy.

108. NARB f. 4-P, op. 5, d. 409, ll. 40–41.

109. NARB f. 4-P, op. 5, d. 409, l. 40 ob.

110. NARB f. 4-P, op. 5, d. 409, l. 41.

111. NARB f. 4-P, op. 5, d. 409, ll. 49–50 ob. The resolution was softened during a second meeting on Bundism held in a general meeting of the party cell on the following day. See NARB f. 4-P, op. 5, d. 409, ll. 51–53 ob.

112. NARB f. 4-P, op. 5, d. 409, ll. 5–6.

113. NARB f. 4-P, op. 5, d. 409, l. 176.

114. TsB TsK KP(b)B Protocol No. 45, August 20, 1926, ll. 59–60.

115. NARB f. 4-P, op. 5, d. 409, l. 76 ob.

116. NARB f. 4-P, op. 10, d. 62, l. 30.

117. NARB f. 4-P, op. 10, d. 62, l. 30.

118. NARB f. 4-P, op. 10, d. 61, ll. 112–117.

119. NARB f. 4-P, op. 10, d. 110, ll. 77–79. A separate national Jewish soviet was eventually created.

120. For the political uses of the campaign *against* antisemitism, see chapter 5.

121. NARB f. 4-P, op. 5, d. 409, l. 163.

122. NARB f. 4-P, op. 5, d. 409, l. 63.

123. Martin, *The Affirmative Action Empire*, 26.

124. On Krinitskii's later career, see Fitzpatrick, *The Cultural Front*, 121–124.

125. NARB f. 4-P, op. 5, d. 409, l. 67.

126. For the economic crisis of 1926–1927, see chapter 6.

127. The number of Jewish leatherworkers throughout the Republic, which had risen from 3,001 to 4,177 in 1924–1925, fell back to 3,822 by 1927. The number of Jewish needleworkers rose from 2,837 in 1924 to 3,221 in 1925, but then fell back to 2,823. NARB f. 4-P, op. 5, d. 265, ll. 14–15.

128. By 1932, Jewish representation in both unions had fallen to 56 percent of total membership, down from 1927 levels of 92 percent in the needleworkers' union and 72 percent among leatherworkers. For 1932 figures, see NARB f. 265, op. 1, d. 2385, l. 18; for 1927 figures, see NARB f. 265, op. 1, d. 2386, ll. 3–3a.

129. NARB f. 4-P, op. 5, d. 265, ll. 14–15. By 1932, the total number of Jewish Trade Unionists climbed to just under seventy thousand (NARB f. 265, op. 1, d. 2385, l. 18) before stabilizing at around seventy-five thousand during the mid-1930s.

6. The Politics of Crisis: Economy, Ethnicity, and Trotskyism

1. Throughout this chapter, the capitalized term "Opposition" refers to the various incarnations of the Trotsky Opposition, including the Left Opposition formed in 1923 and the United Opposition forged in 1926; the capitalized version is also used to designate supporters and alleged supporters of these political factions. As a noncapitalized term, opposition is used to refer to sentiments and actions of social and political recalcitrance that did not necessarily lead to participation in and support for the Opposition, as a movement.

2. *Natsional'nyi Akrkhiv Respubliki Belarus'* (NARB) fond 4-P (Central Committee of the Communist Party of Belorussia), opis' 5, delo 656, listy 21–23, and NARB f. 4-P, op. 5, d. 656, ll. 21–23, 40–42 (lists of party members voting for the Opposition, compiled by okrug party committees for the Central Committee of the KPB).

3. NARB f. 4-P, op. 5, d. 656, l. 4–6, 13–14.

4. NARB f. 4-P, op. 5, d. 656, ll. 60–62.

5. For a list of the excluded, see NARB f. 4-P, op. 5, d. 656, ll. 30, 167. In total, among the excluded were twenty-three Jews, six Belorussians, four Russians, one Pole, and three workers "without state nationality."

6. The role that the "Jewishness" of Oppositionists played in the interparty struggles has been debated extensively in the political histories of the 1920s. Isaac Deutscher, following Trotsky himself, argued that antisemitism in the Stalin camp played a strong role in driving the animus toward the United Opposition. Isaac Deutscher, *The Prophet Unarmed, 1921–1929* (London: Verso, 2003). Robert Tucker likewise stressed the primacy of antisemitism in party struggles. See Robert Tucker, *Stalin in Power: The Revolution From Above, 1928–1941* (New York: W.W. Norton, 1990), 41. Other historians, while pulling short of party struggles through ethnicity, nevertheless underscored the importance of ethnicity as a contributing factor. E. H. Carr, for example, treated antisemitism as a secondary factor rather than a primary one. Nevertheless, he observed that "it was not altogether accidental that the principal Opposition leaders . . . were Jews, and that the most prominent

defenders of the official line . . . were not." E. H. Carr, *Foundations of a Planned Economy, 1926–1929*, II (New York: MacMillan, 1972), 396.

7. Leon Trotsky, *Stalin: Volume Two: The Revolutionary in Power* (London: Panther, 1969), 224–225.

8. The primacy of nationality as an analytic for interpreting the politics of the Soviet periphery is stressed in Terry Martin, *The Affirmative Action Empire: Nations and Nationalism in the Soviet Union, 1923–1939* (Ithaca, NY: Cornell University Press, 2001).

9. NARB f. 4-P, op. 5, d. 656, l. 4.

10. Despite the frequently asserted idea that the Opposition was made up primarily of Jewish intellectuals, intellectuals were actually far more pronounced among non-Jewish Oppositionists in Minsk. Of the thirty-two non-Jewish Oppositionists, seven were students and fifteen were white-collar workers.

11. Culled from okrug reports in NARB f. 4-P, op. 5, d. 656, ll. 21–23, and NARB f. f-P, op. 5, d. 656, ll. 40–42.

12. NARB f. 4-P, op. 5, d. 656, ll. 60–60 ob, 62–64.

13. For one particularly pertinent example, see Eric Hobsbawm and Joan Wallach Scott, "Political Shoemakers," *Past and Present* 89, no. 1 (1980): 86–114.

14. The Red Army recaptured Minsk from Polish forces and reestablished Bolshevik rule in July 1920.

15. For the repression of Belorussian nationalist political movements, see T. S. Prot'ko, *Stanovlenie sovetskoi totalitarnoi sistemy v Belarusi (1917–1941 gg.)* (Minsk: Tesei, 2002), 38–51.

16. Of approximately 25,000 total party members in 1927, 6,012 were Jews. Benjamin Pinkus, *The Jews of the Soviet Union: The History of a National Minority* (Cambridge: Cambridge University Press, 1988), 79.

17. For a broad overview, see Ziva Galili, "Zionism in the Early Soviet State: Between Legality and Persecution," in Zvi Gitelman and Ya'akov Roi, eds., *Revolution, Repression, and Revival: The Soviet Jewish Experiment* (Lanham, MD: Rowman and Littlefield, 2007).

18. Unrest mirrored the general upheaval of the NEP, captured in Sheila Fitzpatrick, Alexander Rabinowith, and Richard Stites, *Russia in the Era of NEP* (Bloomington: Indiana University Press, 1991); William Chase, *Workers, Society, and the Soviet State: Labor and Life in Moscow, 1918–1929* (Urbana: University of Illinois Press, 1990); Lewis Siegelbaum and Ronald Suny, eds., *Making Workers Soviet: Power, Class, and Identity* (Ithaca, NY Cornell University Press, 1994); and Diane Koenker, "Factory Tales: Narratives of Industrial Relations in the Transition to Nep," *Russian Review* 55, no. 3 (July 1996): 384–411.

19. "Doklad instruktora glavbiuro evsektsii pri TsK KPB T. Agurskogo o poezdke v Vitebskii raion," May 1924, NARB f. 4-P, op. 10 (Evsektsiia), d. 5, l. 74.

20. See, for example, the report from the July 1924 evsekstii conference on political tendencies among kustari, which stressed the danger posed by each of the above-stated groups. "Protokol soveshchaniia sekretarei Evsektsii pri Okruzhkomakh KPB," July 7, 1924, NARB 4-P, op. 10, d. 5, l. 140.

21. Initiated by supporters of Trotsky, the Platform of the forty-six condemned the party leadership's handling of the unfolding economic crisis of 1923. On Moscow, see Kevin Murphy, *Revolution and Counter-Revolution: Class Struggle in a Moscow Metal Factory* (New York: Berham, 2005), and Darron Hincks, "Support for the Opposition in Moscow in the Party Discussion of 1923–1924," *Soviet Studies* 44, no. 1 (1992), 137–151. On Leningrad, where the Left Opposition was considerably weaker, see Halfin, *Intimate Enemies: Demonizing the Bolshevik Opposition, 1918–1928* (Princeton: Princeton University Press, 2007).

22. "Materialy k dokladu o rabote TsKK," August 5, 1924, NARB f. 15-P (Control Commission), op. 4, d. 131, l. 22.

23. Of the sixteen party members excluded from the party cell of the Belorussian State University, five were excluded in part for their ambivalent positions during discussions about the Left Opposition. Review of the BGU party cell, July 4, 1924, NARB f. 15-P, op. 4, d. 113, ll. 113–120.

24. B. Markiianov, *Ukreplenie edinstva riadov kommunisticheskoi partii Belorussii (1921–1937 gg.).* (Minsk: Belarus', 1970), 77. Based on archival evidence, the claim seems highly dubious. It is probable that Markiianov combined excluded Bundists and Poalei Tsionists into his calculation. Markiianov is alone among Soviet-era Belorussian historians in claiming significant support for the Trotskyist Opposition prior to 1926.

25. Circular from the TsKK to all Okrug Control Commissions and party organizations, January 6, 1925, NARB f. 15-P, op. 4, d. 53, l. 23.

26. Former Bundists and Poalei Tsionists were far more numerous, and faced far greater scrutiny during the party review, than Left Oppositionists. Former Bundists and Poalei Tsionists made up roughly a third of the 150 Jewish party members expelled from the party in Minsk alone.

27. See http://www.marxists.org/archive/trotsky/1920/military/index.htm. On Trotsky's call for the "Dictatorship of Industry" at the Thirteenth Party Congress of 1924, see Maurice Dobb, *Soviet Economic Development Since 1917* (London: Routledge & Kegan Paul Ltd., 1953), 183. On his place within general debates over industrialization, see Alexander Erlich, *The Soviet Industrialization Debate, 1924–1928* (Cambridge, MA: Harvard University Press, 1960).

28. The most indispensable work on the crisis of the late NEP remains E. H. Carr and R. W. Davies, *Foundations of a Planned Economy, 1926–1929*, 3 vols. (London: Macmillan, 1969–1978).

29. Charles B. Kindleberger, *The World in Depression, 1929–1939* (Berkeley: University of California Press, 1986), 61–65.

30. R. W. Davies, *The Soviet Economy in Turmoil, 1929–1930* (Cambridge, MA: Harvard University Press, 1989), 33.

31. Despite official pronouncements to the contrary, the Soviet Union ceased defending the chervonets gold currency on international markets in March 1926, thus allowing for rapid devaluation and the suspension of foreign currency exchange in March of 1928. Carr and Davies, *Foundations of a Planned Economy, 1926–1929*, I: 2, 778. For a detailed examination of the multifarious pressures that combined to push the USSR off gold in early 1926, see Yuri Goland, "Currency Regulation in the NEP Period," *Europe-Asia Studies* 46, no. 8 (1994): 1267–1282.

32. Polanyi's classic critical interpretation of the ill-fated, European-wide return to gold in the 1920s remains the indispensable work on the interwar economy. See Karl Polanyi, *The Great Transformation: The Political and Economic Origins of Our Times* (Boston: Beacon, 2001).

33. Arthur Z. Arnold, *Banks, Credit and Money in Soviet Russia* (New York: Columbia University Press, 1937), 256–257.

34. Carr and Davies estimated that prices on the private market exceeded state prices by more than 10 percent in 1926. Carr and Davies, *Foundations of a Planned Economy*, II: 2, 691. Davies, who provided the figure of 117 percent, later estimated that private prices for industrial goods increased by 28 percent from October 1927 to October 1929, while agricultural prices increased by more than 232 percent on the private market during this period. Davies, *The Soviet Economy in Turmoil*, 71–72.

35. Franklin D. Holzman, "Soviet Inflationary Pressures, 1928–1957: Causes and Cures," *The Quarterly Journal of Economics* 74, no. 2 (May 1960): 167–188.

36. Simon Johnson and Peter Temin, "The Macroeconomics of NEP," *The Economic History Review* 46, no. 4 (November 1993), 750–767; and V. N. Bandera, "The New Economic Policy (NEP) as Economic System," *Journal of Political Economy* 71, no. 3 (June 1963): 265–279, esp. 274.

37. Arthur Arnold utilized the term cryptoinflation to refer to the phenomenon of shortage due to inflationary pressures combined with price controls. Alexander Erlich described the same process as repressed inflation. See Erlich, *The Soviet Industrialization Debate*, 25–26.

38. Sheila Fitzpatrick, "After NEP: The Fate of NEP Entrepreneurs, Small Traders, and Artisans in the 'Socialist Russia' of the 1930s," *Russian History* 13, no. 2–3 (Summer–Fall 1986): 187–234.

39. In particular, the state faced acute difficulties in repaying the three hundred million Deutschmark loan borrowed from Germany only two years beforehand. On balance of payments, deficits, and the turn to austerity, see Oscar Sanchez-Sibony, "Depression Stalinism: The Great

Break Reconsidered," in *Kritika: Explorations in Russian and Eurasian History* 15, no. 1 (Winter 2014): 23–49.

40. In this, I agree in large part with Michal Reiman's argument that—far from being the cause of the crisis—the Stalin Revolution was the *"result* of a deep and all-embracing crisis" that "evolved as a special kind of instrument or means of finding a way out of this crisis." See Michal Reiman, *The Birth of Stalinism: The USSR on the Eve of the "Second Revolution"* (Bloomington: Indiana University Press, 1987), 115.

41. The iconoclastic Marxists associated with the Frankfurt School best understood this global movement toward the convergence of economic and state forms in the midst of economic crisis. See, in particular, the extremely influential essay by Friedrich Pollock, "State Capitalism: Its Possibilities and Limitations," in Andrew Arato and Eike Gebhardt, eds., *The Essential Frankfurt School Reader* (New York: Continuum, 1982).

42. I am deeply indebted to Mark Loeffler for his insights concerning the parallel assumptions underlying interwar and postwar Keynesianism and Soviet economic policies of the 1930s.

43. Davies, *The Soviet Economy in Turmoil*, 70.

44. Without downplaying the significance of the transformation from private to state ownership introduced by the revolution, the underlying logic of production remained in many respects unaffected by the revolution of 1917. E. P. Thompson stressed the persistence of dynamics of capitalist production in the Soviet context, particularly those tied to the regimentation and standardization of concepts of time-discipline. E. P. Thompson, "Time, Work-Discipline, and Industrial Capitalism," *Past and Present*, no. 38 (December 1967): 56–97. Charles Meier also stressed the underlying similarities linking the ideologies of productivization across the political spectrum in interwar Europe; see Charles Meier, "Between Taylorism and Technocracy: European Ideologies and the Vision of Industrial Productivity in the 1920s," *Journal of Contemporary History* 5, no. 2 (1970): 27–61. The degree to which the underlying logic of capitalist production—which is to say, the logic of extracting value from processes of production based upon nominally free wage labor—remained in full force in Soviet society remains to be adequately explored. Any adequate investigation of this phenomenon must begin by rejecting the idea that the abolition of private property and the (partial) elimination of market relations in the distribution of goods constituted the "overcoming" of the capitalist mode of production. For a convincing elaboration of this idea, anticipated in Marx's 1844 manuscripts, see Moishe Postone, *Time, Labor, and Social Domination: A Reinterpretation of Marx's Critical Theory* (Cambridge: Cambridge University Press, 1993).

45. On Preobrazhenskii as a theorist of crisis, see Richard B. Day, "Preobrazhensky and the Theory of the Transition Period," *Soviet Studies* 2, no. 2 (April 1975): 196–219.

46. For the transition from the regime of economy to the project of industrial rationalization, see Carr and Davies, *Foundation of a Planned Economy*, I: 1, 333–344.

47. On the relationship between intensified productivization of labor and the Stalin Revolution from the standpoint of a traditional Marxist (and largely Trotskyite position), see Donald Filtzer, *Soviet Workers and Stalinist Industrialization: The Formation of Modern Soviet Productive Relations, 1928–1941* (New York: M. E. Sharpe, 1986). For an overview of the broad trajectory on questions of labor and productivity within historiography of the Stalin era, see Lewis Siegelbaum, "The Late Romance of the Soviet Worker in Western Historiography," *International Review of Social History* 51, part 3, (December 2006): 463–481.

48. Carr and Davies, *Foundations of a Planned Economy*, I: 2, 488–489.

49. Rykov and Tomskii defended this policy in front of a hostile audience at the Seventh Trade Union Congress, held in December 1926. Tomskii's speech defended the seemingly contradictory policy of a workers' state balancing industrialization on the shoulders of the working class. Ibid., 491.

50. The estimates of falling real wages in the Soviet context—stressed in Alexander Gerschenkron, *Economic Backwardness in Historical Perspective* (Cambridge, MA: Harvard University Press, 1962); Abram Bergson, *The Real National Income of Soviet Russia Since 1928* (Cambridge, MA:

Harvard University Press, 1961); Janet Chapman, *Real Wages in Soviet Russia Since 1928* (Cambridge, MA: Harvard University Press, 1963); and Hiroaki Kuromiya, *Stalin's Industrial Revolution: Politics and Workers, 1928–1932* (Cambridge: Cambridge University Press, 1990)—have been accepted by Carr, Davies, and Filtzer. The claim that real wages fell over the course of the 1930s has been challenged in Robert C. Allen, *Farm to Factory: A Reinterpretation of the Soviet Industrial Revolution* (Princeton: Princeton University Press, 2003). Allen argued that real wages ultimately increased by about one-third over the 1930s if one factors in the movement of peasants into the industrial labor force. This interpretation has drawn sharp criticisms from Kuromiya (see *Enterprise and Society* 9, no. 4 [December 2008]: 514–516) and R. W. Davies (http://eh.net/bookreviews/library/0792).

51. Ben Bernanke and Harold James, "The Gold Standard, Deflation, and the Financial Crisis in the Great Depression," in R. Glenn Hubbard, ed., *Financial Markets and Financial Crises* (Chicago: University of Chicago Press, 1991). Needless to say, this increase in real wages effected those who retained employment, not the quarter of the population thrown out of work at the height of the depression.

52. By devaluation of labor, I am following David Harvey, who argued that economic crises are resolved in part when one sector proves capable of forcing the pain of devaluation onto a differing sector of the economy. See David Harvey, *The Limits to Capital* (London: Verso, 2006), 200–203.

53. "S ratsionalizatsii i sokrashchenii sovetskogo apparata v sviazi s provedeniem rezhima ekonomii," from TsK Bureau, March 5, 1927, NARB f. 4-P, op. 3, D. 25, ll. 136–150, esp. 138–140.

54. Ibid., l. 139.

55. From 8,130 million rubles in 1925–1926 to 15,105 million in 1926–1927. F. S. Martinkevich and V. I. Dritsa, eds., *Razvitie ekonomiki Belorussii v 1921–1927 gg.* (Minsk: Nauka i tekhnika, 1973), 72.

56. F. S. Martinkevich, *Ekonomika sovetskoi Belorussii, 1917–1967* (Minsk: Nauka i tekhnika, 1967), 151.

57. Carr and Davies, *Foundations of a Planned Economy*, I: 2, 488–491.

58. Ibid., 488.

59. See the October 27, 1926, instructions from Sovnarkom BSSR on the increase in pay among industrial workers in V. N. Zhigalova et al., *Industrializatsiia Belorusskoi SSR (1926–1941 gg.) sbornik dokumentov i materialov* (Minsk: Belarus', 1975), 34–35.

60. Between 1924–1925 and 1926–1927, productivity in the metalworking industry increased 119.2 percent, while wages increased 146 percent. Similar increases occurred in the mineral, food, and paper production industries. Among leatherworkers, however, productivity increased 150.9 percent, while wages increased 129.8 percent. Similar patterns existed for shoemakers (productivity, 141.6 percent; wages 123.8 percent), needleworkers (productivity 233.4 percent; wages, 221.4 percent), and woodworkers (productivity 143.0 percent; wages 139.5 percent). F. S. Matrinkevich, *Razvitie ekonomiki Belorussii*, 84.

61. Far from constituting the antithesis of capitalism, the process mirrored and in many respects realized more fully the temporal logic of capitalist production. See Moishe Postone, *Time, Labor, and Social Domination*.

62. G. B. Budai and N. S. Orekhvo, eds., *Khronika vazhneishikh sobytii istorii kommunisticheskoi partii Belorussii*, vol. 1 (Minsk: Belarus', 1970), 184, 190.

63. Martinkevich, *Razvitie Ekonomii Belorussii*, 73.

64. Ibid., 73

65. The street was named after Hirsch Lekert, a shoemaker and Bundist "martyr" executed for attempting to assassinate the governor of Vilna in 1902.

66. "Korrespondentsiia o puske kozhevennogo zavoda v g. Minske," *Zviazda*, August 27, 1927, reprinted in Zhigalova et al., *Industrializatsiia Belorusskoi SSR*, 59.

67. NARB f. 4-P, op. 5, d. 656, l. 4–6, 13–14; TsKK Report on the Opposition in Vitebsk, undated, 1928, NARB f. 15-P, op. 4, d. 254, l. 105–109.

68. NARB f. 4-P, op. 5, d. 656, ll. 21–23, 40–42; TsKK report "Vyvodi po voprosu likvidatsii Trotskistskoi oppozitsii Minskoi organizatsii," undated, 1928, NARB f. 15-P, op. 4, d. 254, l. 29.

69. Report from the TsKK Belorussia to the All-Russian TsKK, filed July 1927, NARB 15-P, op. 4, d. 253, l. 63–67; Okrug KK Report on the *Trud* Shoe factory, March 1928, NARB f. 15-P, op. 4, d. 254, l. 76–77.

70. Records from the Central Control Commission detailing the anti-Opposition campaign from mid-1927 to mid-1928 are compiled in NARB f. 15-P, op. 4, dd. 253, 254, 255, 256, 257.

71. NARB f. 15-P, op. 4, d. 253, ll. 63–73.

72. Ibid., 65.

73. Extant reports of proceedings from the Minsk Okrug Committee of the KPB and Minsk Okrug Control Commission can be found in *Gosudarstvennyi Arkhiv Minskoi Oblasti* (GAMO) fond 12-P (Minsk Okrug KPB), opis' 1, delo 458 (On the Opposition).

74. Questions for meeting at Minsk Tannery, undated, fall 1926, GAMO 12-P, op. 1, d. 164–166.

75. Closed meeting of the KPB of the glassmaking factory *Proletarii*, October 10, 1926, GAMO f. 12-P, op. 1, d. 458, l. 32 ob.

76. GAMO, 12-P, op. 1, d. 458, l. 258.

77. The shoemakers were hardly alone in this respect. On the contrary, the workers in most of the meetings on the Opposition raised an array of interesting issues surrounding questions of the relations between wages, prices, and currency reform, all of which suggest that they took these concerns quite seriously and did not have a unified, facile "class" line. See, for example, the debate on wages and currency reform that erupted during the party meeting on the Opposition in the glassmaking factory *"Proletarii"* on October 10, 1926. Like the boot makers, the glazers raised issues concerning the extent to which increased nominal wages would lead to a decline in real wages and purchasing power. See GAMO f. 12-P, op. 1, d. 458, ll. 32 ob.–34 ob.

78. GAMO f. 12-P. op. 1, d. 458, l. 259.

79. Report of meeting on Opposition at Minsk Shoemakers Workshop, August 1926, GAMO f. 12-P, op. 1, d. 458, ll. 259–260.

80. See the October 27, 1926, instructions from Sovnarkom BSSR on the increase of pay among industrial workers in V. N. Zhigalova et al., *Industrializatsiia Belorusskoi SSR*, 34–35.

81. The wage increases of October 1926 exacerbated divisions between lower-skilled and lower-paid workers and skilled labor, engendering dynamics similar to those outlined in Hiroaki Kuromiya, "The Crisis of Proletarian Identity in the Soviet Factory, 1928–29," *Slavic Review* 44, no. 2 (April 1984): 280–297.

82. Murphy, *Revolution and Counterrevolution*, 164–177.

83. The rhetorical attack was frequently associated with a defense of the mythical poor peasant, which followed the script of the Opposition being written in Moscow. See GAMO f. 12-P, op. 1, d. 458, ll. 265, 274.

84. NARB 15-P, op. 4, d. 254, l. 3.

85. NARB f. 15-P, op. 4, d. 254, l. 10.

86. According to the report, only 4 komsomol members out of 189 voted against resolutions favoring the expulsion of Trotsky and Zinoviev from the party. An additional twenty-nine, however, abstained from the vote. Ibid., 11–12.

87. NARB f. 15-P, op. 4, d. 254, l. 14.

88. NARB f. 15-P, op. 4, d. 254, l. 13.

89. NARB f. 15-P, op. 4, d. 254, l. 14.

90. Davies, *The Soviet Economy in Turmoil*, 11.

91. This, at least, is the argument Carr and Davies put forward. However, party utterances on this subject in Minsk seem to suggest that the question was never quite resolved.

92. Report from the okrug committee to the Central Committee on the Opposition in Vitebsk, November 1927, NARB f. 4-P, op. 5, d. 655, ll. 52–54.

93. Ibid., 187. Several other workers made similar comments concerning the need to work far more than eight hours to fulfill the norms of the eight-hour day. NARB f. 4-P, op. 5, d. 655, ll. 52–54.

94. NARB f. 4-P, op. 5, d. 656, l. 120.

95. NARB f. 15-P, op. 4, d. 254, ll. 25–28.

96. NARB f. 15-P, op. 4, d. 254, ll. 94–96.

97. The fascinating report from Gomel highlights similar opposition from workers in a wide variety of petty production enterprises and workshops. See NARB f. 4-P, op. 5, d. 656, ll. 118–125.

98. On Luddites and early artisanal rebels, see Thompson, *The Making of the English Working Class*, (New York: Vintage, 1966). While mechanization undoubtedly played a critical role in galvanizing workshop opposition, working-class opposition among English handworkers, quasi-artisans, and petty producers became radicalized long before the intervention of the machine, a fact stressed by Thompson. As Georges Lefebvre and Albert Soboul documented, the sansculottes in the French Revolution emerged from similar ranks, mobilized not by the machines per se, but by the unleashing of the unfettered market in bread and grain. See Georges Lefebvre, *The Coming of the French Revolution* (Princeton: Princeton University Press, 1986), and Albert Soboul, *The Sans-Culottes* (Princeton: Princeton University Press, 1980).

99. While this proved to be the general trend, it was not an absolute rule. In certain regions and industries, policy makers recognized the heavy burden on workers that accompanied the intensification or expansion of industrial production. See, for example, the debate concerning a proposal to increase wages for workers displaced by the mechanization of the matchstick industry in Gomel, in NARB f. 4-P, op. 3, d. 29, l. 721.

100. OKK report to the TSKK on conditions at Bobrshvei, undated, mid-1928, NARB f. 15-P, op. 4, d. 254, ll. 91–93. The report noted that pay levels in the Bobrshvei ranged from fifty to one hundred rubles a month. The report, however, gives no indication of where the Oppositionists fell along this wage continuum. Workers at the bottom of the stated scale would actually have ranked among the worst-paid laborers in the republic. Likewise, it does not consider the fact that inflationary pressures had begun eating away at wages, no matter how purportedly generous. See NARB f. 15-P, op. 4, d. 254, l. 91.

101. All three were subsequently expelled from the party for oppositional work. See NARB f. 15-P, op. 4, d. 254, l. 92.

102. Ibid.

103. NARB f. 15-P, op. 4, d. 254, l. 92.

104. Ibid.

105. Opposition to this resolution was likewise pronounced among the shoemakers. Thirteen of the twenty-three party cell members either voted against the resolution or refused to vote. See NARB f. 15-P, op. 4, d. 254, l. 95.

106. Kazimirovskii subsequently sent a letter to the Bobruisk City Committee (*Gorkom*) requesting reinstatement to the party. In his letter, he denounced the "factioneers" and "Trotskyite-Menshevik Opposition," and acknowledged the role that his actions played in weakening the party. There is no indication of whether Kazimirovskii was readmitted, although it seems highly doubtful. NARB f. 4-P, op. 5, d. 656, l. 94.

107. NARB f. 15-P, op. 4, d. 254, l. 92.

108. Ibid.

109. NARB f. 15-P, op. 4, d. 254, l. 13.

110. In Vitebsk, for example, the party conducted antioppositional meetings in more than thirty different local cells on November 9 and 10. See NARB f. 4-P, op. 5, d. 656, l. 30. Twenty-eight such meetings took place in Minsk at roughly the same time. See GAMO f. 12-P, op. 1, d. 458, l. 300.

111. The exhaustive results of the votes on the resolutions, as well as supporting documentation of active Opposition cells, can be found in NARB f. 4-P, op. 5, d. 656.

112. The numbers of total party members on October 1, 1928, are taken from N. Vlasenko, *Bor'ba kompartii Belorussii za postroenie ekonomicheskogo fundamenta sotsializma* (Minsk: Belarus', 1970), 37. It is clear, however, that not all party cells and party members took part in the votes. For example, Vlasenko noted that 4,679 people took part in votes on the resolutions in Vitebsk (with sixteen voting for the Opposition). Ibid., 27. Petrikov places the number of those voting in Minsk and Borisov *combined* at 4,124. See P. T. Petrikov, ed., *Istoriia rabochego klassa Belorusskoi SSR*, tom 2 (Minsk: Nauka i tekhnika, 1985), 378. The latter numbers were about one-half the total party membership in Minsk alone. A similar case probably existed in Vitebsk. It seems probable that the resolutions were voted on only in the "problematic" industries.

113. NARB f. 4-P, op. 5, d. 656, l. 166.

114. NARB f. 4-P, op. 5, d. 656, l. 167.

115. NARB f. 15-P, op. 4, d. 254, l. 29.

116. To begin with, there are two separate lists in the archive. One includes eighty-five purported sympathizers who abstained from the vote on whether or not to exclude Trotsky and Zinoviev (NARB f. 4-P, o. 5, d. 656, ll. 21–23). The other includes sixty-nine members who voted against exclusion (NARB f. 4-P, op. 5, d. 656, ll. 40–42). Taking both groups as sympathizers, the number in Minsk alone would be 155 Oppositionists.

117. NARB f. 15-P, op. 4, d. 254, ll. 26–27.

118. NARB f. 15-P, op. 4, d. 254, l. 3.

119. NARB f. 4-P, op. 5, d. 656, ll. 47–48.

120. As with all of the lists of Oppositionists, there tends to be a high degree of overlap in Vitebsk between those who voted against the expulsion of the Opposition and those who voted against the thesis on work in the countryside. NARB f. 15-P, op. 4, d. 254, l. 96.

121. NARB f. 4-P, op. 5, d. 656, l. 119.

122. NARB f. 15-P, op. 4, d. 254, l. 14.

123. NARB f. 4-P, op. 5, d. 656, l. 4–6, 13–14.

124. NARB f. 4-P, op. 5, d. 656, ll. 21–23; NARB f. f-P, op. 5, d. 656, ll. 40–42.

125. NARB f. 4-P, op. 5, d. 656, ll. 60–62.

126. Once again, the numbers are extremely difficult to determine due to spotty records. In one report of forty-one identified party members who either voted against the expulsion or abstained in the Bobruisk Okrug, forty were Jewish (NARB f. 4-P, op. 5, d. 656, ll. 60–60 ob.). However, additional reports, presumably from earlier votes, list far more Oppositionists (NARB f. 4-P, op. 5, d. 656, ll. 62–64).

127. For a list of the excluded, see NARB f. 4-P, op. 5, d. 656, l. 30. In total, among the excluded were twenty-three Jews, six Belorussians, four Russians, one Pole, and three workers "without state nationality." See NARB f. 4-P, op. 5, d. 656, l. 167.

128. NARB f. 4-P, op. 5, d. 655, l. 64.

129. GAMO f. 12-P, op. 1, d. 737, l. 29.

130. GAMO f. 12-P, op. 1, d. 737, l. 729.

131. Nor were they unprecedented. For an illuminating example of the persistently ambiguous line between acceptable discourse and antisemitic agitation, see Robert Weinberg, "Demonizing Judaism in the Soviet Union During the 1920s," *Slavic Review* 67, no. 1 (Spring 2008): 120–153.

132. This tendency culminated in a high-profile, sensationalized case of antisemitic violence at the Oktiabr' glassworks in the Bobruisk Okrug. For the procurator's report, see NARB f. 188, d. 1, l. 1777. The rising tide of antisemitism across the Soviet Union was likewise analyzed by the prominent Bolshevik theorist and economist Yuri Larin. Yuri Larin, *Evrei i antisemitizm v SSSR* (Moscow: Gos. izdat, 1929). On antisemitism in Belorussia during the period, see chapter 6.

133. NARB f. 15-P, op. 4, d. 254, l. 249.

134. NARB f. 15-P, op. 4, d. 253, l. 98.

135. For one report on the "problem" of Bundist vestiges in the party, see NARB f. 4-P, op. 5, d. 409, ll. 1–6. Also see chapter 5.

136. Ibid.

137. NARB f. 15-P, op. 4, d. 254, l. 188.

138. NARB f. 15-P, op.4, d. 254, l. 94.

139. NARB f. 4-P, op. 5, d. 656, l. 30.

140. Unfortunately, records do not include data concerning the ages of oppositional voters.

141. NARB f. 4-P, op. 5, d. 656, ll. 21–23, 40–42.

142. NARB f. 4-P, op. 5, d. 656, ll. 60–60 ob.

143. NARB f. 4-P, op. 5, d. 656, l. 120.

144. Ibid.

145. GAMO 12-P, op. 1, d. 458, l. 140.

146. Ibid.

147. See, most notably, Thompson, *The Making of the English Working Class*; Joan Scott, *The Glass-workers of Carmaux: French Craftsmen and Political Action in a Nineteenth-Century City* (Cambridge, MA: Harvard University Press, 1974); and William H. Sewell, *Work and Revolution: The Language of Labor from the Old Regime to 1848* (Cambridge: Cambridge University Press, 1980).

148. Halfin, *Intimate Enemies*.

7. Antisemitism and the Stalin Revolution

1. "Mezhdu dvukh sten," *Rabochii*, November 13, 1928. The party organ *Zviazda*, as well as the komsomol newspaper *Chirvonaia Zmena*, also covered events closely. For the extensive reports compiled by the procurator's office, see *Natsional'nyi Akrkhiv Respubliki Belarus'* (NARB) fond 188 (State Procurator), opis' 1, delo 1777.

2. In addition to coverage in the Belorussian press, the incident at the Oktiabr' Factory was followed closely by *Pravda*, *Komsomol'skaia Pravda*, and *Der Emes*, the main party organs in Moscow. Coverage also appeared in the Western press, including the Jewish Telegraphic Agency and the *New York Times*. See, for example, Walter Duranty, "Anti-Semite Trial Opens in Minsk," *New York Times*, January 10, 1929.

3. Sheila Fitzpatrick, *The Cultural Front: Power and Culture in Revolutionary Russia* (Ithaca, NY: Cornell University Press, 1992).

4. On the contradictory, gendered dynamics of political rhetoric of the Stalin Revolution, see Wendy Goldman, *Women at the Gates: Gender and Industry in Stalin's Russia* (Cambridge: Cambridge University Press, 2002), and Victoria Bonnell, *Iconography of Power: Soviet Political Posters Under Lenin and Stalin* (Berkeley: University of California Press, 1997), especially chapters 2 and 3.

5. On the return to revolutionary-era rhetoric during the Cultural Revolution, see Fitzpatrick, "Cultural Revolution as Class War," in Fitzpatrick, *The Cultural Front*.

6. The rhetorical process of constructing enemies linguistically has been stressed in Stephen Kotkin, *Magnetic Mountain: Stalinism as a Civilization* (Berkeley: University of California Press, 1995), and Igal Halfin, *Intimate Enemies: Demonizing the Bolshevik Opposition* (Pittsburg: University of Pittsburgh Press, 2007).

7. Kotkin, *Magnetic Mountain*, Chapter 5.

8. Sarah Davies, "'Us Against Them': Social Identity in Soviet Russia, 1934–1941," in Sheila Fitzpatrick, ed., *Stalinism: New Directions* (London: Routledge, 2000).

9. On interwar antisemitism, see Ezra Mendelsohn, *The Jews of East Central Europe Between the World Wars* (Bloomington: Indiana University Press, 1987), and Howard Sachar, *Dreamland: Europeans and Jews in the Aftermath of the Great War* (New York: Vintage Books, 2003). Both serve as useful correctives to the dubious recent attempt by Robert Wistrich to locate the origins of antisemitism solely in the history of the left. See Robert Wistrich, *A Lethal Obsession: Anti-Semitism from Antiquity to the Global Jihad* (New York: Random House, 2010).

10. The concept of "redemptive antisemitism," which posited that the national body remained locked in a Manichean struggle against existential evil in the form of the Jew that could only be won through the total annihilation of the enemy, is borrowed from Saul Friedlander, *Nazi Germany and the Jews: Volume 1: The Years of Persecution, 1933–1939* (New York: Harper, 1998), 87–90.

11. My reading of antisemitism as both a form of racial thought reconstituted in particular moments and a modality in which political economy experienced is indebted to Thomas C. Holt, *The Problem of Race in the 21st Century* (Cambridge, MA: Harvard University Press, 2000), and Stuart Hall, "Race, Articulation, and Societies Structured in Dominance," in *Sociological Theories: Race and Colonialism* (Paris: UNESCO, 1980). I am indebted to Brendam McGeever for suggesting the relevance of Hall's theoretical approach to this study. My understanding of the relationship between economic crisis and the particular racial configuration of antisemitism has been greatly informed by theoretical approaches of the Frankfurt School and their successors, most notably Max Horkheimer's 1938 essay "The Jews and Europe," republished in Stephen Eric Bronner and Douglas Kellner, *Critical Theory and Society: A Reader* (New York: Routledge, 1989), and Moishe Postone, "Anti-Semitism and National Socialism: Notes on the German Reaction to 'Holocaust,'" *New German Critique*, no. 19, Special Issue 1: Germans and Jews (Winter 1980), 97–115.

12. As Sarah Davies has demonstrated, this dichotomy of power and powerlessness would only deepen over the ensuing decade. See Davies, "'Us Against them.'"

13. In the case of *Hehalutz*, which was shut down in 1927, their permitted activities were quite real, as Jonathan Dekl-Chen has demonstrated. See Jonathan L. Dekel-Chen, *Farming the Red Land: Jewish Agricultural Colonization and Local Soviet Power, 1924–1941* (New Haven: Yale University Press, 2005).

14. Z. Gitelman, *Jewish Nationality and Soviet Politics: The Jewish Sections of the CPSU, 1917–1930* (Princeton: Princeton University Press, 1972), 473.

15. Local reports from the mid-1920s reported unemployment rates of up to 70 percent in many small shtetls in the region. NARB f. 4-P, op. 10 (Evsektsiia), d. 18, l. 125.

16. On the pogroms in Bobruisk and the region, see NARB f. 684, op. 1, d. 7, ll. 1–4, 145–145 ob., 159–159 ob., 258–260 ob.; on Polish-Jewish tensions, see NARB f. 4-P, op. 5, d. 484, l. 132, 134.

17. Perhaps most shockingly, the shtetl Zhlobin and the surrounding region was the site of a series of mysterious murders of several Jewish families in 1925, which the GPU blamed on underground counterrevolutionary Zionist groups who allegedly carried out the murders to punish families that joined local soviet agricultural cooperatives. On the murders, see Bobruisk Evburo, Protocol 21, April 29, 1925, NARB f. 4-P, op. 10, d. 18, l. 50.

18. Given the absence of full names in party reports, it is impossible to state with absolute certainty that the Comrade Pam who served as evburo secretary in Bobruisk at the time of the Oktiabr' affair was the same Leizer Isaakovich Pam encountered as a young man in chapter 1. However, based on his party review of 1924, during which time he worked in the Slutsk uezd administration, his later work in the evsektsiia and in the editorial office of daily newspaper *Oktyabr,* and the uncommon Jewish surname, they are almost certainly one and the same. For Leizer Pam's 1924 Party review, see NARB f. 15-P, o. 4, d. 125, l. 50.

19. Protocol 8, Bobruisk Evburo, March 10, 1928, and Pam's ensuing report on anti-Passover campaigns, GAMO f. 340-P (Bobruisk Okrug KPB), op. 1, d. 41, ll. 19–20; also see the September 1927 plan for antireligious campaigns in the Bobruisk Okrug, GAMO f. 340-P, op. 1, d. 41, ll. 55.

20. Protocol 17, Bobruisk Evburo, November 12, 1927, GAMO f. 340-P, op. 1, d. 41, ll. 27–28.

21. Resolutions sent by the Bobruisk Evburo to the okrug committee, November 27, 1927, GAMO f. 340-P, op. 1, d. 41, ll. 63–65.

22. The Bobruisk evburo generally dealt with the question of antisemitism only in the context of the countryside and villages. Characteristically, a evburo report concerning a January 1928 conference of Jewish teachers in Bobruisk focused exclusively on the question of antisemitism in the shtetl. GAMO f. 340-P, op. 1, d. 41, l. 11.

23. Pam's report, "Po obsledovaniiu raboty sredi evreiskikh trudiashchikhsia mass v Bobruis-kom Okruge," was originally presented before a conference of evsektsii party workers in Minsk and taken up for consideration in the Evsektsii Central Bureau meeting in Minsk on October 3, 1928. For the full report, see GAMO f. 4-P, op. 10, d. 110, ll. 56–66 ob.

24. NARB f. 4-P, op. 10, d. 110, ll. 57 ob.-60. Pam's emphasis on intensified differentiation and class conflict at the end of the 1920s reflected the broad discourse concerning social relations in the countryside characteristic of the Stalin Revolution. For the classic treatment of this question, see Moshe Lewin, *Russian Peasants and Soviet Power: A Study of Collectivization* (New York: W. W. Norton, 1968), esp. 41–80.

25. NARB f. 4-P, op. 10, d. 110, l. 61 ob.

26. NARB 4-P, op. 10, d. 110, l. 71 ob.

27. NARB f. 4-P, op. 10, d. 110, ll. 92–93.

28. NARB f. 4-P, op. 10, d. 110, ll.17 ob-18 ob.

29. NARB f. 4-P, op. 10, d. 100, l. 66 ob.

30. In fact, Comrade Pam's report left out warnings from the local Svisloch evsektsii that insisted that "the phenomena of antisemitism and chauvinism have still not been overcome at the Oktiabr' factory; they only hide deeper, breaking out from time to time." NARB f. 4-P, op. 10, d. 110, l. 18.

31. NARB f. 188, op. 1, d. 1777, l. 137.

32. NARB f. 265 (Trade Unions), op. 1, d. 2485, l. 50.

33. NARB f. 188, op. 1, d. 1777.

34. NARB f. 4-P, op. 3 (Executive Committee), d. 31, l. 77.

35. "Bandity-antisemity s 'Oktiabria' dolzhny derzhat otvet!," *Rabochii*, November 15, 1928, in NARB 188, op. 1, d. 1777, 117.

36. "Proletarskaia obshchestvennost' vozmushchena prestupleniem na 'Oktiabre'" *Rabochii*, November 16, 1928, in NARB 188, op. 1, d. 1777.

37. Protocol 10, General Meeting of the Minsk Metal Trust, November 19, 1928, in NARB f. 188, op. 1, d. 1777, l. 153.

38. Protocol 65, Bureau of the Bobruisk Okrug Committee, November 23, 1928, in NARB f. 4-P, op. 3, d. 31, l. 85.

39. A copy of the proclamation can be found in NARB 265, op. 1, d. 2485, l. 305.

40. The practices of "unmasking" class enemies constituted a primary rhetorical trope of the Sta-lin Revolution, as Sheila Fitzpatrick brilliantly illustrated in Sheila Fitzpatrick, *Tear off the Masks!: Identity and Imposture in Twentieth-Century Russia* (Princeton, NJ: Princeton University Press, 2005). As Fitzpatrick notes repeatedly throughout this work, and, indeed, her entire body of work, the language of politics at the local level was frequently conducted within languages of overt or coded antisemitism.

41. NARB f. 4-P, op. 3, d. 31, l. 85.

42. NARB f. 4-P, op. 3, d. 31, ll. 86–87.

43. NARB f. 265, op. 1, d. 2485, l. 51. Comrade Pam's report from September 1928 claimed that Jewish workers constituted 27 percent of the labor force in the factory. See NARB f. 4-P, op. 10, d. 110, l. 63 ob.

44. NARB f. 265, op. 1, d. 2485, l. 52.

45. NARB f. 4-P, op. 3, d. 31, ll. 80–81.

46. Central Bureau KP(b)B Protocol No. 55, November 27, 1928, in NARB f. 4-P, op. 3, d. 31, ll. 98–101.

47. Central Bureau KP(b)B Protocol No. 59, December 12, 1928, in NARB f. 4-P, op. 3, d. 31, l. 185.

48. Article 107-b, which punished counterrevolution, would become a catchall charge during the terror. NARB f. 188, op. 1, d. 1777, ll. 259–265.

49. NARB f. 188, op. 1, d. 1777, ll. 139–145.

50. Critical analyses of antisemitism, by contrast, recognize that while individual antisemites may exist in any given moment, antisemitism as a movement is always, fundamentally, a social phenomenon. While this literature is too vast to fully address here, works that have proven particularly important for this study (in addition to above-cited works) include Hannah Arendt, *The Origins of Totalitarianism* (San Diego: Harcourt, 1973); Max Horkheimer and Theodor W. Adorno, *Dialectic of Enlightenment* (New York: Continuum, 1999); and Shulamit Volkov, "Antisemitism as a Cultural Code: Reflections on the History and Historiography of Antisemitism in Imperial Germany," in *Leo Baeck Yearbook XXIII* (1978), 25–46.

51. A party investigation found the allegations ungrounded and blamed the attempted boycott on the children of priests and former tsarist officials. The investigation did, however, report numerous instances of mutual hostility between Jewish and Belorussian children. NARB f. 63-P (Komsomol), op. 2, d. 255, ll. 19–21.

52. NARB f. 63-P, op. 2, d. 287, ll. 111–112.

53. Several members of the group were finally arrested after engaging in a drunken melee with police. Officials initially denied that a riot had taken place and suppressed an article concerning the riot in *Komsomol'skaia Pravda* (Moscow); they eventually allowed the report to be published, in August. NARB 63-P, op. 2, d. 287, ll. 155–159. See "Antisemity v partii i komsomole," *Komsomol'skaia Pravda*, August 18, 1928.

54. NARB f. 63-P, op. 2, d. 449, ll. 46–48.

55. A translation of the letter, from April 30, 1928, can be found in NARB f. 63-P, op. 2, D. 467, ll. 130.

56. Reports from factory cell investigations, upon which this chapter draws extensively, are compiled in NARB f. 265, op. 1, d. 2485 (on Antisemitism).

57. "Bulletin from the Central Bureau of the *Evsektsii* of the Central Committee of the All-Russian Communist Party," February 1, 1927, in NARB 63-P, op. 2, d. 365, l. 9.

58. "Anti-Semitic Agitation Growing Among Soviet Students, Paper States," *Jewish Telegraphic Agency*, March 26, 1928. All references to the JTA have been acquired through the online archive at http://www.jta.org/jta-archive/archive-page. Where possible, I have corroborated cited sources; however, the JTA reported publishing dates are not always accurate.

59. "Anti-Semitism in Moscow Theaters Becomes Prominent Issue in Moscow Press," JTA, April 8, 1928. *Komsomol'skaia Pravda* and *Vechernaia Gazeta* published frequent updates on the story over the ensuing weeks, which included a scathing attack on Golanova by M. Talnikov, "Teatral'naia golgofa," *Komsomol'skaia Pravda*, April 8, 1928. The party eventually stepped in to stop the attack on Golovanov, who went unpunished.

60. "Moscow Hears of Anti-Jewish Acts in Several Russian Centers," JTA, December 4, 1928, and "Bor'ba s antisemitizmom v shkole," *Pravda*, December 4, 1928.

61. "Soviet Russian Press Reports Anti-Jewish Pogrom in Russian Town," JTA, December 10, 1928. Again, officials initially denied reports of a pogrom, before eventually acknowledging the events.

62. "Don Miners Tried For Anti-Semitic Actions," JTA, February 20, 1929.

63. "Young Communist Worker Kills Jewish Worker With an Axe Because He Was a Jew," JTA, February 20, 1929. According to the JTA story, the Russian worker, Trofimov, acknowledged upon his arrest that he killed Bolsheminikov "Because I am a Russian and he is a Jew," a claim he affirmed again during his trial. Nevertheless, Trofimov received only a five-year sentence. Two of the witnesses were also sentenced for failing to intervene. Also see "Gnusnoe ubiistvo komsomol'tsa," *Komsomol'skaia Pravda*, June 17, 1928, and coverage on the ensuing days.

64. "Sentence Soviet Official for Blood Libel," JTA, July 14, 1929. The official who made the accusation was arrested and sentenced to two months compulsory labor.

65. "Anti-Semitic Terrorism on the Increase in Soviet Russia," JTA, July 16, 1926. Following the riots, which left Jewish houses vandalized, OGPU agents arrested a number of the rioters.

66. The most alarming of which took place in Klynets, near Zhitomir, where pogromists drove out all nine Jewish families from an agricultural settlement, murdering one Jewish woman, Zlata Bychowski. Authorities arrested and executed the leader of the pogrom, and sentenced two others to prison terms of six to eight years. "Leader of Pogrom on Jewish Settlers Gets Death Sentence," *JTA*, October 13, 1929.

67. "Proposed Numerus Clausus for Jewish Students," *JTA*, October 22, 1929, based upon a report from the Moscow newspaper *Trud*.

68. "Aged Women Dying from Anti-Semitic Attack," *JTA*, October 24, 1929. According to the report, the two elderly women—the only Jews living in the village—were attacked in their house by the gang of peasant women, tortured, and tied to the fireplace, after which the attackers set fire to the house. Authorities reportedly arrested the attackers.

69. "Sentence 8 for Persecuting Jewish Workers in Soviet Factory," *JTA*, October 27, 1929.

70. Em. Iaroslavskii, "Protiv antisemitizma," *Pravda*, November 27, 1927.

71. Iurii Larin, *Evrei i antisemitism v SSSR* (Moscow: Gos. izdat., 1929), esp. 19, 23–24. Larin was one of the few leading Jewish Bolsheviks who demonstrated a persistent interest in Jewish questions. The son of a Hebrew writer and Zionist (and the father-in-law of Nikolai Bukharin), Larin emerged as a defender of Jewish minority rights in Ukraine and a strong proponent of Jewish colonization in the Crimea. On his activism in Ukraine, see Terry Martin, *The Affirmative Action Empire: Nations and Nationalism in the Soviet Union, 1923–1939* (Ithaca, NY: Cornell University Press, 2001), 48–50. On his promotion of Jewish colonization, see Jonathan Dekl-Chen, *Farming the Red Land: Jewish Agricultural Colonization and Local Soviet Power, 1924–1941* (New Haven: Yale University Press, 2005), 17–19 and 46–47.

72. Mikhail Gorev, *Protiv antisemitov: ocherki i zarisovski* (Moskva: Gos. izdat., 1928). For a discussion of Gorev's text, see also Jakob Lestschinsky, *Dos sovetishe Yidntum: zayn fargangenheyt un kegnvart* (New York: Yidisher Kemfer, 1941), 259–263.

73. Leon Trotsky, "Thermidor and Anti-Semitism," *The New International* 7, no. 4 (May 1941).

74. The persistence of underlying religious impulses could be seen most clearly in the alarming resurgence of blood libels, or accusations that Jews used Christian blood in the baking of Passover matzo. Elissa Bemporad, "Empowerment, Defiance, and Demise: Jews and the Blood Libel Specter Under Stalinism," *Jewish History* 26, no. 3–4 (December 2012): 343–361.

75. The tendency to locate the roots of the antisemitic upsurge exclusively in local conditions is reflected, as well, in Arkady Zel'tser's otherwise excellent study of Jews in the Vitebsk Okrug. Zel'tser attributed the upsurge to many of the above-identified factors, as well as the general process of "modernization." While undoubtedly true and consistent with the analysis here, the emphasis on domestic factors cannot explain why Soviet antisemitism followed contemporaneous patterns across Europe. See Arkadii Zel'tser, *Evrei sovetskoii provintsii: Vitebsk i mestechki, 1917–1941* (Moscow: Rosspen, 2006), 202–228.

76. Transcript of Lenin's speech against antisemitism, in Hyman Lumer, ed., *Lenin on the Jewish Question* (New York: International Publishers, 1974), 135.

77. To underscore the point, the original reads "chtoby otvlech' vzopry nastoiashchego vraga trudiashchikhsia—*ot kapitala* (https://www.marxists.org/russkij/lenin/works/2.htm#topp).

78. On the 1926–1928 period, stressing the relationship between the turn to the planned economy and the global economic crisis of the period, see Andrew Sloin and Oscar Sanchez-Sibony, "Economy and Power in the Soviet Union, 1917–1939," and Oscar Sanchez-Sibony, "Depression Stalinism: The Great Break Reconsidered," *Kritika: Explorations in Russian and Eurasian History* 15, no. 1 (Winter 2014). The critical importance of the global crisis for understanding the advent of Stalinism is also stressed in Michael Reiman, *The Birth of Stalinism: The USSR on the Eve of the "Second Revolution"* (Bloomington: Indiana University Press, 1987). For an analysis of the specific Jewish context, see Lestschinsky, *Dos Sovetishe Yidntum*, 128–149. For a critique of this position, stressing the end of the NEP and the turn to the planned economy as the intended action of Stalin's

indomitable ideological will, see Stephen Kotkin, *Stalin: Volume 1: Paradoxes of Power* (New York: Penguin Press, 2014), coda.

79. NARB f. 265, op. 1, d. 2485, l. 225.

80. NARB f. 265, op. 1, d. 2485, l. 238 ob.

81. NARB f. 265, op. 1, d. 2485, l. 225–226.

82. NARB f. 265, op. 1, d. 2485, l. 226.

83. NARB f. 265, op. 1, d. 2485, ll. 227–228.

84. NARB f. 265, op. 1, d. 2485, l. 228.

85. NARB f. 265, op. 1, d. 2485, l. 234–235.

86. Undated report on factory conditions at the Dvina factory, likely from early 1929, NARB f. 265, op. 1, d. 2485, ll. 234–238 ob. An accompanying January 1929 report by the Textile Workers Trade Union into the conditions of workers in the factory's mechanical section complained of similar reductions of wages in violation of collectively bargained contracts and systematic pressures to intensify labor. See NARB f. 265, op. 1, d. 2458, ll. 223–223 ob.

87. NARB f. 265, op. 1, d. 2485, l. 229.

88. This argument has been made most forcefully in Victoria Bonnell, *Iconography of Power: Soviet Posters Under Lenin and Stalin* (Berkeley: University of California Press, 1997), 103–105.

89. NARB f. 265, op. 1, d. 2485, l. 291.

90. To site one example, a composite report of episodes of intranational disturbances from the last months of 1928 reported fourteen episodes of antisemitic incidents, against one episode of Jewish chauvinism. NARB f. 265, op. 1, d. 2485, l. 291–293.

91. The reports compiled by the Soviet of Trade Unions in NARB f. 265, op. 1, d. 2485, while extensive, are by no means complete; the bulk of the extant materials are from the Bobruisk, Gomel, and Vitebsk regions. Many reports appear in fragmentary form, some are missing pages, and many reports do not provide sufficient information to locate factories precisely.

92. The union voted to exclude Bazhichko from its ranks. NARB f. 265, op. d. 2485, l. 292 ob.

93. NARB f. 264, op. 1, d. 2485, l. 292.

94. NARB f. 265, op. 1, d. 2483, ll. 43–44.

95. NARB f. 265, op. 1, d. 2485, 291 ob.–292.

96. Report on antisemitism in the second brickmaking factory, Bobruisk, NARB f. 265, op. 1, d. 2483, ll. 254–256.

97. The exact location of the factory is not given in the report, and the TorgStroi (Contract Builders) name was common across the republic. Nevertheless, the fact that the document was grouped together in the archive with other reports from Bobruisk proper suggests that it was located in the city. For the report on the mass meeting in the factory, see NARB f. 265, op. 1, d. 2485, ll. 282–283.

98. Kutsenko's bizarre comment was likely rooted in the folk tale of the Jewish queen Susanna, who supposedly ruled Austria with her husband, Abraham, 869 years after the Deluge. While a completely fantastical history lesson, Kutsenko's knowledge of this story offers a fascinating reminder of the persistence of folk beliefs about Jews active among workers only recently removed from villages.

99. The union ordered the immediate expulsion of both workers for six months. NARB f. 265, op. 1, d. 2485, l. 293.

100. NARB f. 265, op. 1, d. 2485, l. 33.

101. NARB f. 265, op. 1, d. 2485, l. 13–13 ob.

102. NARB f. 265, op. 1, d. 2485, l. 12.

103. Despite insisting that the attack was motivated by national animosity, reports provide no details concerning the nationality of any of the actors. The fact of Badanin's Jewishness was asserted only implicitly. At one point, a worker referred to Badanin and Tabenko, collectively, as Jews, but all other indications suggest Tabenko was not Jewish. Moreover, had both assailants been Jews, the episode would invariably have been explicitly labeled as an episode of Jewish chauvinism, which it was not.

104. NARB f. 265, op. 1, d. 2485, l. 35
105. NARB f. 265, op. 1, d. 2485, l. 37.
106. NARB f. 265, op. 1, d. 2485, l. 41.
107. Ibid.
108. NARB f. 265, op. 1, d. 2485, l. 41.
109. NARB f. 265, op. 1, d. 2485, l. 38.
110. NARB f. 265, op. 1, d. 2485, l. 35.
111. Horkheimer, "The Jews and Europe," 83.
112. "The German workers possessed the qualifications to rearrange the world. They were defeated." Ibid.
113. Ibid., 87.
114. Ibid., 91.
115. Ibid., 90.
116. This fact was not lost on Horkheimer, who drew direct parallels between Nazi and Stalinist authoritarianism, particularly in his 1940 essay "The Authoritarian State," reprinted in Arrato and Gebhardt, eds., *The Essential Frankfurt School Reader*.
117. Yosef Yerushalmi, "Servants of Kings and Not Servants of Servants: Some Aspects of the Political History of the Jews," in David N. Meyers and Alexander Kaye, eds., *The Faith of Fallen Jews: Yosef Yerushalmi and the Writing of Jewish History* (Waltham, MA: Brandeis University Press, 2013).
118. Yiddish culture as institutions limped on into the thirties before being closed in the mid- to late 1930s. Confessional Yiddish and Jewish literature was likewise run over, as the sad fates of Moishe Kulbak, Isaac Babel, and scores of other Jewish writers demonstrate.

Conclusion

1. Sheila Fitzpatrick, ed., *Cultural Revolution in Russia, 1928–1931* (Bloomington: Indiana University Press, 1978), and Sheila Fitzpatrick, *The Cultural Front: Power and Culture in Revolutionary Russia* (Ithaca, NY: Cornell University, 1992).
2. The transition from Bolshevik identities of revolutionary collectivism and Soviet identities of cultivated individuality in the sphere of nationality mirrored the broader social transition stressed in Anna Krylova, "Soviet Modernities: Stephen Kotkin and the Bolshevik Predicament," *Contemporary European History* 23, no. 2 (May 2014): 167–192.
3. For the record of the party purge of Ignatovskii, see NARB 15-P, O. 5, D. 103.
4. T. S. Prot'ko, *Stanovlenie sovietskoi totalitarnoi sistemy v Belarusi, 1917–1941 g.g.* (Minsk, Tesei, 2002), 659.
5. For the fates of these individuals, as well as a much broader list of the fates of leading figures in Belorussia, including Belorussian and non-Belorussian activists (but, unsurprisingly, few Jewish actors), see the very impressive and useful appendix to Prot'ko, *Stanovlenie sovietskoi totalitarnoi sistemy v Belarus.*
6. For the fates of these individuals, see G. G. Branover et al., eds., *Rossiskaia Evreiskaia entsiklopediia*, tt. 1–3 (Moscow: Epos, 1994).
7. It is also, however, almost certainly the case that Jewish party members fared better than nonparty inhabitants of those regions occupied during the Second World War, insofar as many were evacuated at the outset of the German invasion of White Russia.
8. Zvi Gitelman, *Jewish Nationality and Soviet Politics: The Jewish Sections of the CPSU, 1917–1930* (Princeton: Princeton University Press, 1972).
9. In a similar fashion, I agree with the assessment of Arkadii Zel'tser, who followed Gitelman in stressing the importance of this structural change. However, as with the ensuing critique of Gitelman, I disagree with Zel'tser's single-minded emphasis on top-down statist intentionality

as an explanatory model. Arkadii Zel'tser, *Evrei sovetskoi provintsii: Vitebsk i mestechki, 1917–1941* (Moscow: Rosspen, 2006).

10. "Articulaton," as used here and by Hall, not in the sense of "utterance," but in the sense of joining up, as with the anatomical articulation of joints. The use of this term, for Hall, is to underscore that while a basic relationship exists between social organization and the realm of ideas, including constructed conceptions of difference and race, the former cannot be reduced to the latter, and vice versa. Stuart Hall, "Race, Articulation, and Societies Structured in Dominance," in *Sociological Theories: Race and Colonialism* (Paris: UNESCO, 1980), especially 322–325.

11. Eric Weitz, "Racial Politics Without the Concept of Race: Reevaluating Soviet Ethnic and National Purges," in *Slavic Review* 61, no. 1 (Spring 2002), 3.

SELECTED BIBLIOGRAPHY

Archival Collections

Natsional'nyi Akrkhiv Respubliki Belarus' (NARB), Minsk

Fond 5	Minsk Military Soviet
Fond 4-P	Central Committee of the Communist Party of Belorussia (TsK KPB)
Fond 6	Central Executive Committee BSSR (TsIK BSSR)
Fond 7	Soviet of People's Commissars of the BSSR (Sovnarkom BSSR)
Fond 15-P	Central Control Commission of the KPB (TsKK)
Fond 34	People's Commissariat of Internal Affairs (NKVD BSSR)
Fond 42	People's Commisariat of Enlightenment of BSSR (Narkompros BSSR)
Fond 60-P	Institute for the History of the Party and the October Revolution
Fond 63-P	Central Committee of the Komsomol of Belorussia
Fond 188	Supreme Court BSSR
Fond 189	Higher Court BSSR
Fond 192	Special Office of the People's Court of the Extraordinary Commission (Cheka) of the BSSR
Fond 265	Central Soviet of the Trade Unions of the BSSR (Sovprofbel)
Fond 325	Council of People's Ministers of the Belorussian National Republic
Fond 684	The Belorussian Commission of the Jewish Public Committee for Aid to Pogrom Victims
Fond 782	People's Commissariat for Nationalities BSSR (Narkomnats BSSR)

Gosudarstvennyi Arkhiv Minskoi Oblasti (GAMO), Minsk

Fond 11-P	Minsk Uezd Committee of the KPB
Fond 12-P	Minsk Okrug Committee, KPB
Fond 37-P	Minsk City-Raion Committee, KPB
Fond 146	Minsk Concentration Camp
Fond 340-P	Slutsk and Bobruisk Raion and Okrug Committees, KPB

Fond 412   Minsk People's Court, 2nd District
Fond 413   Minsk People's Court, 3rd District
Fond 414   Minsk People's Court, 4th District
Fond 421-P   Borisov Uezd Committee, KPB
Fond 424-P   Borisov Raion Committee, KPB
Fond 517-P   Borisov Okrug Committee, KPB
Fond 4704-P   Minsk Uezd commission for 1921 Party Purge

Newspapers and Journals, Belorussia

Belaruskaia Veska
Chyrvonaia Zmena
Der Shtern (Minsk and Vilna)
Der Veker
Di Royte Nodl
Krigerisher Apikoyres
Oktyabr
Rabochii
Royte Bleter
Savetskaia Belarus'
Shtern (Minsk)
Shriftn
Tsaytshift
Zvezda/Zviazda

Primary Sources and Document Collections

Agursky, S. 1925. *Der yidisher arbeter in der komunistisher bavegung, 1917–1921*. Minsk: Vaysruslendisher melukhe farlag.
———. 1931. *Di revolutsyonere bavegung in vaysrusland, 1863–1917*. Moscow: Tsentrfarlag, vaysrusishe opteyl.
———. 1928. *Di yidishe komisaryatn un di yidishe komunistishe sektsyes (protokaln, rezolutsyes, un dokumentn [1918–1921])*. Minsk: Vaysruslendishn melukhe farlag.
Akademiia nauk BSSR. 1933. *Di oysgabe fun institut far Yidisher proletarisher kulur*. Minsk: Vaysrusishe visnshaft-akademye.
Altshuler, M. 1929. *Antireligyezer lernbukh*. Moscow: Tsentraler felker farlag fun F.S.S.R.
Aronson, G. 1944. *Di yidishe problem in sovet-rusland*. New York: Veker.
Azarov, A. I., E. P. Luk'ianov, and V. N. Zhigalov, eds. 1955. *Revoliutsionnoe dvizhenie v Belorussii, 1905–1907 gg.: dokumenty i materialy*. Minsk: Izd-vo Akademii nauk BSSR.
Besnasik, K., M. Erik, and Y. Rubin. 1930. *Antireligyezer literarisher leyenbukh*. Moscow, Kharkov, Minsk: Tsentraler felker farlag fn F.S.S.R.
Blekhman, Leyb. 1959. *Bleter fun mayn yugnt: zikhroynes fun a Bundist*. New York: Farlag Unzer Tsayt.
Brovikov, V. I., ed. 1983. *Kommunisticheskaia partiia Belorussii v rezoliutsiiakh i resheniiakh s'ezdov i plenumov TsK*, 2 vols. Minsk: Belarus'.
Bukhbinder, N. 1919. *Di oktyabr-revolutsye un di yidishe arbets-masn*. Petersburg: Komunist.
———. 1922. "Evreiskoe rabochee dvizhenie v Minske, 1895–1903 gg." *Krasnaia Letopis'*, no. 5.

———. 1925. "Istoria evreiskogo rabochego dvizheniia v rossii po neizdannym arkhivnym materialam." Leningrad: Akademicheskoe izd-vo.

1930. *Di Rabonim in dinst fun finants-kapital.* Moscow, Kharkov, Minsk: Tsentraler felker farlag fun F.S.S.R.

Dimanshtein, Sh. 1929. *Di revolutsyonere bavegung tsvishn di yidishe masn in der revolutsie fun 1905-tn yor.* Moscow: Tsentrfarlag.

Dimanshtein, Sh., ed. 1930. *Revoliutsyonnoe dvizhenie sredi evreev.* Moscow: Tsentrfarlag.

———. 1935. *Yidn in F.S.S.R., Zamlbukh.* Moscow: Farlag Emes.

Dubnova-Erlikh, S. 1937. *Garber-Bund un Bershter Bund: Bletlekh geshikhte fun der yidisher arbeter-bavegung.* Warsaw: Kultur-Lige.

Dunets, Kh. 1932. *In kampf af tsvey frontn: kegn rekht un "linke" opneyg un natsional-oportunizm in der ekonomisher arbet tsvishn di yidishe arbetndike.* Minsk: Vaysrusishe visnshaft-akademye.

———. 1932. *Kegn sotsyal-fashistishn Bund, kegn idealizatsye fun bundizm.* Minsk: Melukhe farlag.

Erik, M. 1934. *Etyudn tsu der geshikhte fun der haskole, 1789–1881.* Minsk: Melukhe-farlag.

Gimpelson, Ia. I., and L. M. Bramson, eds. 1914–1915. *Zakony o evreiakh.* St. Petersburg: T-va iurisprudentsiia.

Gorev, M. 1928. *Protiv antisemitov: ocherki i zarisovski.* Moskva: Gos. izdat.

Kantor, Ya. 1934. *Natsional'noe stroitel'stvo sredi evreev v SSSR.* Moscow: Vlast' sovetov.

Kirzhnits, A. 1928. *Di yidishe prese in ratnfarband, 1917–1929.* Minsk: Gosizdat.

Knorin, V. 1927. *1917 yor in vaysrusland un afn mayrev-front.* Minsk: Tsentrfarlag fun vaysrusland.

———. 1934. *Zametki k istorii diktatury proletariata v Belorussii.* Minsk: Part. izd.- vo.

Krutalevich, V. A., G. I. Litvinova, and V. A. Il'icheva. 1961. *Revoliutsionnye komitety BSSR (Noiabr' 1918 g.-Iiul' 1920 g.) sbornik dokumentov i materialov.* Minsk: Akademii nauk.

Larin, Iu. 1929. *Evrei i antisemitism v SSSR.* Moscow: Gos-izdat.

Lenin, V. 1952. *Sochineniia.* Moscow: Gos. izdat.

———. 1992. *The State and Revolution.* Translated and edited by R. Service. London: Penguin.

Levin, Y. 1924. *Fun yene yorn: Kleyne-Bund.* Gomel: Beltrespetshat.

Lestschinsky, Y. 1934. *Der idisher ekonomisher khurbn nokh der velt-milkhome in mizrekh un tsentral-eyrope.* Wilno: Zaklady Graficzne inz. G. Kleckina.

———. 1941. *Dos sovetishe Yidntum: zayn fargangenheyt un kegnvart.* New York: Yidisher Kemfer.

Leytskover, Kh. 1931. *Kegn religye, kegn peysakh.* Moscow, Kharkov, Minsk: Tsentraler farlage far di felker fun F.S.S.R.

Lumer, H. ed. 1974. *Lenin on the Jewish Question.* New York: International Publishers.

Luxemburg, R. 1961. *The Russian Revolution and Lenin or Marxism?* Ann Arbor: Ann Arbor Paperbacks.

Miliakova, L. B., ed., 2007. *Kniga pogromov: pogromy na Ukraine, v Belorussii i evropeiskoi chasti Rossii v period grazhdanskoi voiny, 1918–1922: sbornik dokumentov.* Moscow: Rosspen.

Nikolski, N. 1925. *Yidishe yomtoyvim: zeyer oyfkum un antviklung.* Minsk: Vaysruslender melukhe farlag.

Orshanski, B. 1931. *Di Yidishe literatur in Vaysrusland nokh der revolutsye: pruvn fun an oysforshung.* Minsk: Tsentraler felker-farlag F.S.S.R.

Preobrazhensky, E. 1965. *The New Economics.* Translated by B. Pearce. Oxford: Clarendon.

Rafes, M. 1929. *Kapitlen geshikhte fun "Bund."* Kiev: Kultur-Lige.

———. 1923. *Ocherki po istorii <<Bunda>>* Moscow: Moskovskii rabochii.

Rayner, O. T., 1925. *The Criminal Code of the Russian Socialist Federative Soviet Republic.* London.

Savitsky, E., ed. 1997. *Bund v Belarusi. 1897–1921: dokumenty i materialy.* Minsk: BelNIIDAD.

Solskii, V. 2004. *1917 god v zapadnoi oblasti i na zapadnom fronte.* Minsk: Tesei.

Sosis, Y. 1929. *Di geshikhte fun di yidishe gezelshaftlikhe shtremungen in rusland in XIX yorhundert.* Minsk: Vaysrusisher melukhe farlag.

Stalin, J. 1946. *Sochineniia.* Moscow. Gos. izdat.

Tsherikover, E. 1965. *Di Ukrayner pogromen in yor 1919.* New York: YIVO.

Trotsky, L. 1930. *My Life.* New York: Scribner and Sons.

———. 1924–1927. *Sochineniia.* Moscow: Gos. izdat.

———. 1969. *Stalin.* London: Panther.

———. 1937. *The Revolution Betrayed.* New York: Doubleday.

———. 1943. *The New Course*, ed. Max Shachtman. New York: International Publishers.

———. 1941. "Thermidor and Anti-Semitism," *The New International* 7: 5, 91–94.

Yarmolinsky, A. 1928. *The Jews and Other Minor Nationalities Under the Soviets.* New York: Vanguard.

Yaroslavski, Y. 1930. *Vegn di tsiln un metodn fun antireligyezer propagande: fortrog afn alfarbandishn tsuzamenfor fun apikorsim-farband.* Minsk: Tsentraler felker-farband fun F.S.S.R.

Secondary Sources

Abezgauz, Z. E. 1977. *Rabochii klass Belorussii v nachale XX v.* Minsk: Nauka i tekhnika,

Abramsky, Ch. 1982. "The Rise and Fall of Soviet Yiddish Literature." *Soviet Jewish Affairs* 12, no. 3:35–44.

Alexopoulos, G. 2003. *Stalin's Outcasts: Aliens, Citizens, and the Soviet State, 1926–1936.* Ithaca, NY: Cornell University Press.

Allen, R. C. 2003. *Farm to Factory: A Reinterpretation of the Soviet Industrial Revolution.* Princeton: Princeton University Press.

Altshuler, M. 1981. *Ha-yevsektsiya bi-vrit ha-mo'atsot: beyn komunizm ve leumiyut.* Tel Aviv: Sifriyat po'alim.

———. 1998. *Soviet Jewry on the Eve of the Holocaust.* Jerusalem: Yad Vashem,

———. 1969. "The Attitude of the Communist Party of Russia to Jewish National Survival, 1918–1930." *YIVO Annual of Jewish Social Science* XIV : 68–86.

Anderson, B. 1983. *Imagined Communities: Reflections on the Origin and Spread of Nationalism.* London: Verso.

Arato, A., and E. Gebhardt, eds. 1982. *The Essential Frankfurt School Reader.* New York: Continuum.

Arendt, H. 1973. *The Origins of Totalitarianism.* San Diego: Harcourt Books.

Arkhipov, V. A., and L. F. 1978. Morozov. *Bor'ba protiv kapitalisticheskikh elementov v promyshlennosti i torgovle, 20-e nachalo 30-x godov.* Moscow: Mysl'.

Arnold, A. 1937. *Banks, Credit, and Money in Soviet Russia.* New York: Columbia University Press.

Aronson, G., S. Dubnov-Erlich, I. S. Hertz, E. Novogrodski, H. S. Kazdan, and W. Sherer, eds. 1966. *Di geshikhte fun Bund, 5 vols.* New York: Unzer Tsayt.

Auslander, L. 2002. "'Jewish Taste?' Jews and the Aesthetics of Everyday Life in Paris and Berlin, 1920–1942." In *Histories of Leisure*, edited by R. Koshar. Oxford: Berg.

Avrich, P. 1978. *The Russian Anarchists*. New York: W. W. Norton.

Avrutin, E. 2010. *Jews and the Imperial State: Identification Politics in Tsarist Russia*. Ithaca, NY: Cornell University Press.

Azorov, A. U. 1955. *Revolutsionnoe dvizhenie v belorussii, 1907–1917*. Minsk: Akademie nauk BSSR.

Bailes, K. 1978. *Technology and Society Under Lenin and Stalin: Origins of the Soviet Technical Intelligentsia*. Princeton: Princeton University Press.

———. 1977. "Alexei Gatev and the Soviet Controversy Over Taylorism." *Soviet Studies* 29, no. 3:373–394.

Balibar, E., and I. Wallerstein. 1991. *Race, Nation, Class: Ambiguous Identities*. London: Verso.

Ball, A. 1988. *Russia's Last Capitalists: The Nepmen, 1921–1929*. Berkeley: University of California Press.

Bandera, V. N. 1963. "The New Economic Policy (NEP) as Economic System." *Journal of Political Economy* 71, no. 3:265–279.

Baron, S. 1976. *The Russian Jew Under Tsars and Soviets*. New York: Macmillan.

Bartal, I. 2005. *The Jews of Eastern Europe, 1772–1881*. Translated by Chaya Naor. Philadelphia: University of Pennsylvania Press.

Beizer, M. 1999. "Antisemitism in Petrograd/Leningrad, 1917–1930." *East European Jewish Affairs* 29, no. 1–2:5–28.

Behrens, J. C. 2009. "Back from the USSR: The Anti-Comintern's Publications on Soviet Russia and Nazi Germany (1935–1941)," *Kritika: Explorations in Russian and Eurasian History* 10, no. 3:527–556.

Bemporad, E. 2013. *Becoming Soviet Jews: The Bolshevik Experiment in Minsk*. Bloomington: Indiana University Press.

Bergson, A. 1961. *The Real National Income of Soviet Russia Since 1928*. Cambridge, MA: Harvard University Press.

Berlanstein, L., ed. 1993. *Rethinking Labor History: Essays on Discourse and Class Analysis*. Urbana: University of Illinois Press.

Bettelheim, C. 1978. *Class Struggle in the USSR: Second Period, 1923–1930*. Translated by Brian Pearce. New York and London: Monthly Review.

Bich, M. O. 1983. *Rabochee dvizhenie v Belorussii v 1861–1904 gg*. Minsk: Nauka i tekhnika.

Bonnell, V. E. 1997. *Iconography of Power: Soviet Political Posters Under Lenin and Stalin*. Berkeley: University of California Press.

———. 1983. *Roots of Rebellion: Workers' Politics and Organizations in St. Petersburg and Moscow, 1900–1914*. Berkeley: University of California Press.

Bonnett, A. 2002. "Communists Like Us: Ethnicized Modernity and the Idea of 'the West' in the Soviet Union," *Ethnicities* 2, no. 4:436–467.

Brinton, C. 1965. *Anatomy of Revolution*. New York: Vintage.

Brym, R. 1978. *The Jewish Intelligentsia and Russian Marxism: A Sociological Study of Intellectual Radicalism and Ideological Divergence*. London: Macmillan.

Budai, G. B., and N. S. Orekho, eds. 1970. *Khronika vazhneishikh sobytii istorii kommunisticheskoi partii Belorussii*. 2 vols. Minsk: Belarus'.

Budnitskii, O. V. 2005. *Rossiiskie evrei mezhdu krasnymi i belymi (1917–1920)*. Moscow: Rosspen.

Burbank, J. 1986. *Intelligentsia and Revolution: Russian Views of Bolshevism, 1917–1922*. Oxford: Oxford University Press.

Buslov, K., ed. 1958. *Iz istorii bor'by za rasprostranenie marksizma v Belorussii (1893–1917 gg.)*. Minsk: Akademii nauk BSSR.

Carr, E. H. 1950–1953. *The Bolshevik Revolution 1917–1923*. 3 vols. New York: Macmillan.

———. 1958–1964. *Socialism in One Country, 1924–1926, 3 vols*. London: Macmillan.

———. 1954. *The Interregnum, 1923–1924*. New York: Macmillan.

Carr, E. H., and R. W. Davies. 1969–1978. *Foundations of a Planned Economy, 1926–1929*. 3 vols. London: Macmillan.

Chapman, J. 1963. *Real Wages in Soviet Russia Since 1928*. Cambridge, MA: Harvard University Press.

Chase, W. J. 1990. *Workers, Society, and the Soviet State: Labor and Life in Moscow, 1918–1929*. Urbana: University of Illinois Press.

Clark, K. 1998. *Petersburg: Crucible of Cultural Revolution*. Cambridge, MA: Harvard University Press.

Cohen, S. F. 1973. *Bukharin and the Bolshevik Revolution: A Political Biography*. New York: A. A. Knopf.

Daniels, R. 2007. *The Rise and Fall of Communism in Russia*. New Haven: Yale University Press.

———. 1991. *Trotsky, Stalin, and Socialism*. Boulder, CO: Westerview.

Daniels, R. 1980. *The Conscience of the Revolution: Communist Opposition in Soviet Russia*. Cambridge, MA: Harvard University Press.

David-Fox, M. 2015. *Crossing Borders: Modernity, Ideology, and Culture in Russia and the Soviet Union*. Pittsburgh: University of Pittsburgh Press.

———. 1999. "What is Cultural Revolution?" *Russian Review* 58, no 2:181–201.

Davies, N. 1972. *White Eagle, Red Star: The Polish-Soviet War, 1919–1920*. New York: St. Martin's.

Davies, R. W. 1989. *The Soviet Economy in Turmoil, 1929–1930*. Cambridge, MA: Harvard University Press.

Day, R. B. 1973. *Leon Trotsky and the Politics of Economic Isolation*. Cambridge: Cambridge University Press.

———. 1975. "Preobrazhensky and the Theory of the Transition Period." *Soviet Studies* 2, no. 2:196–219.

Dekel-Chen, J. 2005. *Farming the Red Land: Jewish Agricultural Colonization and Local Soviet Power, 1924–1941*. New Haven: Yale University Press.

Dekel-Chen, J., D. Gaunt, and N. Meir. 2010. *Anti-Jewish Violence: Rethinking the Pogrom in East European History*. Bloomington: Indiana University Press.

Deutscher, I. 1968. *The Non-Jewish Jew and Other Essays*. London: Oxford University Press.

———. 2003. *The Prophet Unarmed, 1921–1929*. London: Verso.

———. 1967. *The Unfinished Revolution: Russia, 1917–1967*. London: Oxford University Press.

Dmitrenko, V. P. 1971. *Torgovaia politika sovetskogo gosudarstva posle perekhoda k nepu, 1921–1941*. Moscow: Nauka.

Dobb, M. 1953. *Soviet Economic Development Since 1917*. London: Routledge & Kegan Paul Ltd.

Dohan, M. 1976. "The Economic Origins of Soviet Autarky, 1927/28–1934." *Slavic Review* 35, no. 4:603–635.

Dubnow, S. 1946. *History of the Jews in Russia and Poland from the Earliest Times Until the Present Day*, 3 vols. Translated by I. Friedlander. Philadelphia: Jewish Publications Society.

Dunker, A., ed. 1937. *Nationalism and the Class Struggle: A Marxian Approach to the Jewish Problem, Selected Writings of Ber Borochov*. New York: Young Poale Zion Alliance of America.

Durkheim, E. 1984. *The Division of Labor in Society*. New York: Free Press.

Erlich, A. 1960. *The Soviet Industrialization Debate, 1924–1928*. Cambridge, MA: Harvard University Press.

Estraikh, G. 1994. "Evreiskie sektsie kompartii. Po materialam byvshego tsentral'nogo partarkhiva." *Vestnik Evreiskogo Universiteta v Moskve* 6, no. 2:35–44.

———. 2000. "From Yehupets Jargonists to Kiev Modernists: The Rise of a Yiddish Literary Centre, 1880s–1914." *East European Jewish Affairs* 30, no. 1:17–38.

———. 2005. *In Harness: Yiddish Writers' Romance with Communism*. Syracuse: Syracuse University Press.

———. 1999. *Soviet Yiddish: Language Planning and Linguistic Development*. Oxford: Clarendon.

Fainsod, M. 1963. *How Russia is Ruled*. Cambridge, MA: Harvard University Press.

———. 1958. *Smolensk Under Soviet Rule*. Cambridge: Cambridge University Press.

Ferro, M. 1985. *The Bolshevik Revolution: A Social History of the Russian Revolution*. Translated by N. Stone. London: Routledge and Keegan Paul.

———. 1972. *The Russian Revolution of February 1917*. Translated by J. L. Richards. Engelwood Cliffs, NJ: Prentice Hall.

Filtzer, D. 1986. *Soviet Workers and Stalinist Industrialization: The Formation of Modern Soviet Productive Relations, 1928–1941*. New York: M. E. Sharpe.

Fishman, D. 1995. *Russia's First Modern Jews: The Jews of Shklov*. New York: New York University Press.

Fitzpatrick, S. 1986. "After NEP: The Fate of NEP Entrepreneurs, Small Traders, and Artisans in the 'Socialist Russia' of the 1930s." *Russian History/Histoire Russe* 13:187–234.

———. 1993. "Ascribing Class: The Construction of Social Identity in Soviet Russia." *Journal of Modern History*, no. 65.

———. 1979. *Education and Social Mobility in the Soviet Union, 1921–1934*. Cambridge: Cambridge University Press.

———. 2000. *Everyday Stalinism: Ordinary Life in Extraordinary Times: Soviet Russia in the 1930s*. New York: Oxford University Press.

———. 1970. *The Commissariat of Enlightenment: Soviet Organization of Education and the Arts under Lunacharsky, October 1917–1921*. Cambridge: Cambridge University Press.

———. 1992. *The Cultural Front: Power and Culture in Revolutionary Russia*. Ithaca, NY: Cornell University.

———. 2008. *The Russian Revolution*. Oxford: Oxford University Press.

———. 2002. "The World of Ostap Bender: Soviet Confidence Men in the Stalin Period." *Slavic Review* 61, no. 3:535–557.

Fitzpatrick, S., ed. 1978. *Cultural Revolution in Russia, 1928–1931*. Bloomington: Indiana University Press.

———. 2000. *Stalinism: New Directions*. London: Routledge.

Fitzpatrick, S., A. Rabinowitch, and R. Stites, eds. 1991. *Russia in the Era of NEP: Explorations in Society and Culture*. Bloomington: Indiana University Press.

Frankel, J. 1981. *Prophecy and Politics: Socialism, Nationalism, and the Russian Jews, 1862–1917*. Cambridge: Cambridge University Press.

Frumkin, J., G. Aronson, A. Goldenweiser, and J. Lewitan. 1969. *Russian Jewry (1917–1967)*. New York: Thomas Yasseloff.

Garvy, G. 1977. *Money, Financial Flows, and Credit in the Soviet Union*. Cambridge, MA: Ballinger.

Geertz, C. 1973. *The Interpretation of Cultures: Selected Essays*. New York: Basic.

Gellner, E. 1983. *Nations and Nationalism*. Ithaca, NY: Cornell University Press.

Gerasimova, I. 1998. "Evreiskoe obrazovanie v Belarusi v 20–30 gg. XX v." *Evrei Belarusi: istoria i kul'tura* II: 58–75.

———. 1996. "K istorii evreiskogo otdela Instituta belorusskoi kul'tury (Inbelkulta) i evreiskogo sektora Belorusskoi Akademii nauk v 20–30-x. godakh." *Vestnik evreiskogo universiteta v Moskve* 12, no. 2:144–167.

Gershenkron, A. 1962. *Economic Backwardness in Historical Perspective*. Cambridge, MA: Harvard University Press.

Gessen, Iu. 1993. *Istoriia evreiskogo naroda v Rossii, 2 vols*. Reprint, Moscow: Evreiskii Universitet v Moskve.

Getty, J. A., and R. T. Manning, ed. 1993. *Stalinist Terror: New Perspectives*. Cambridge: Cambridge University Press.

Getzler, I. 1967. *Martov: A Political Biography of a Russian Social Democrat*. Cambridge: Cambridge University Press.

Gitelman, Z. 1972. *Jewish Nationality and Soviet Politics: The Jewish Sections of the CPSU, 1917–1930*. Princeton: Princeton University Press.

———. 2001. *A Century of Ambivalence: The Jews of Russia and the Soviet Union, 1881 to the Present*. 2nd ed. Bloomington: Indiana University Press.

Gitelman, Z., and Y. Roi. 2007. *Revolution, Repression, and Revival: The Soviet Jewish Experience*. Lanham, MD: Rowman and Littlefield.

Glasser, A. 2012. *Jews and Ukrainians in Russia's Literary Borderlands: From the Shtetl Fair to the Petersburg Bookshop*. Evanston, IL: Northwestern University Press.

Gleason, A., P. Kenez, and R. Stites, eds., 1989. *Bolshevik Culture: Experiment and Order in the Russian Revolution*. Bloomington: Indiana University Press.

Goland, Y. 1994. "Currency Regulation in the NEP Period." *Europe-Asia Studies* 46, no. 8:1251–1296.

Goldman, W. 2002. *Women at the Gates: Gender and Industry in Stalin's Russia*. Cambridge: Cambridge University Press.

Golubovicha, V. I., ed. 2005. *Ekonomicheskaia istoriia Belarusi*. Minsk: Ekoperspektiva.

Gorsuch, A. E. 2000. *Youth in Revolutionary Russia: Enthusiasts, Bohemians, Delinquents*. Bloomington: Indiana University Press.

Gross, J. 2002. *Neighbors: The Destruction of the Jewish Community of Jedwabne*. New York: Penguin.

Haberer, E. 1995. *Jews and Revolution in Nineteenth-Century Russia*. Cambridge: Cambridge University Press.

Haimson, L. 1955. *The Russian Marxists and the Origins of Bolshevism*. Boston: Beacon.

Halfin, I. 2000. *From Darkness to Light: Class, Consciousness, and Salvation in Revolutionary Russia*. Pittsburgh: University of Pittsburgh Press.

———. 2007. *Intimate Enemies: Demonizing the Bolshevik Opposition, 1918–1928*. Pittsburgh: University of Pittsburgh Press.

Hall, S. 1980. "Race, Articulation, and Societies Structured in Dominance." In *Sociological Theories: Race and Colonialism*. Paris: UNESCO.

Harshav, B. 1993. *Language in Time of Revolution*. Stanford, CA: Stanford University Press.

Harvey, D. 2006. *The Limits to Capital*. London: Verso.

Heberer, E. 1995. *Jews and Revolution in Nineteenth-Century Russia*. Cambridge: Cambridge University Press.

Hellie, R. 2005. "The Structure of Russian Imperial History." *History and Theory* 44:88–112.

Hessler, J. *A Social History of Soviet Trade: Trade Policy, Retail Practices, and Consumption, 1917–1953.* Princeton: Princeton University Press, 2004.

Hincks, D. 1992. "Support for the Opposition in Moscow in the Party Discussion of 1923–1924." *Soviet Studies* 44, no. 1:137–151.

Hirsch, F. 2005. *Empire of Nations: Ethnographic Knowledge and the Making of the Soviet Union.* Ithaca, NY: Cornell University Press.

———. 2002. "Race Without the Practice of Racial Politics." *Slavic Review* 61, no. 1:30–43.

Hobsbawm, E. 1990. *Nations and Nationalism: Programme, Myth, Reality.* Cambridge: Cambridge University Press.

Hobsbawm, E. J. and J. W. Scott. 1980. "Political Shoemakers." *Past and Present* 89, no. 1: 86–114.

Hoffman, D. L. 2003. *Stalinist Values: The Cultural Norms of Soviet Modernity, 1917–1941.* Ithaca, NY: Cornell University Press.

Holt, T. C. 2000. *The Problem of Race in the 21st Century.* Cambridge, MA: Harvard University Press.

Holzman, F. D. 1960. "Soviet Inflationary Pressures, 1928–1957: Causes and Cures." *The Quarterly Journal of Economics* 74, no. 2:167–188.

Horkheimer, M. 1989. "Europe and the Jews." In *Critical Theory and Society: A Reader*, edited by D. Kellner and S. Bronner. New York: Routledge.

Horkheimer, M., and T. Adorno. 1999. *Dialectic of Enlightenment.* New York: Continuum.

Hundert, G. 2004. *Jews in Poland-Lithuania in the Eighteenth Century: A Genealogy of Modernity.* Berkeley: University of California Press.

Ignatenko, I. M. 1977. *Istoriia Belorusskoi SSR.* Minsk: Nauka i tekhnika.

Ivanov, V. I. 1971. *Ocherk byta promyshlennykh rabochikh dorevoliutsionnoi Belorussii.* Minsk: Nauka i tekhnika.

Johnson, S., and P. Temin. 1993. "The Macroeconomics of NEP," *The Economic History Review* 46, no. 4:750–767.

Kahan, A. 1986. *Essays in Jewish Social and Economic History.* Edited by Roger Weiss. Chicago: University of Chicago Press.

Karapavin, M. I. 2003. *> v zhizni sovetskogo obshchestva (Oktiabr' 1917-go–nachalo 1930-x godov).* Volgograd: Peremena.

Kasarov, G. G. and N. S. Stashkevich. 1993. *Oktiabr' 1917 i sud'by politicheskoi oppozitsii*, 3 vols. Gomel: Belorusskoe agentstvo nauchno-tekhnicheskoi i delovoi informatsii.

Katsenel'son, L. A., and D. G. Gintsburg, eds. 1991. *Evreiskaia entsiklopediia.* Moscow: Terra.

Kindleberger, C. B. 1986. *The World in Depression, 1929–1939.* Berkeley: University of California Press.

Klier, J. 2005. *Imperial Russia's Jewish Question, 1855–1881.* Cambridge: Cambridge University Press.

———. 2011. *Russia Gathers Her Jews: The Origins of the "Jewish Question" in Russia, 1772–1825.* DeKalb: Northern Illinois University.

Klier, J., and S. Lambroza, eds. 1992. *Pogroms: Anti-Jewish Violence in Modern Russian History.* Cambridge: Cambridge University Press.

Kochan, L., ed. 1978. *The Jews in Soviet Russia Since 1917.* New York: Oxford University Press.

Koenker, D. 1996. "Factory Tales: Narratives of Industrial Relations in the Transition to Nep." *Russian Review* 55, no. 3:384–411.

———. 1981. *Moscow Workers and the 1917 Revolution.* Princeton: Princeton University Press.

———. 2005. *Republic of Labor: Russian Printers and Soviet Socialism, 1918–1930.* Ithaca, NY: Cornell University Press.

Koenker, D., W. Rosenberg, and R. Suny, eds. 1989. *Party, State, and Society in the Russian Civil War: Explorations in Social History*. Bloomington: Indiana University Press.

Kovkel', I. I, and E. S. Iarmusik. 2003. *Istoriia Belarusi s drevneishikh vremei do nashego vremeni*. Minsk: Aversev.

Kotkin, S. 1995. *Magnetic Mountain: Stalinism as a Civilization*. Berkeley: University of California Press.

———. 2001. "Modern Times: The Soviet Union and the Interwar Conjuncture." *Kritika* 2, no. 1:111–164.

———. 2014. *Stalin: Paradoxes of Power*, Vol. 1. New York: Penguin.

Kron, Ts. M. 1926. *Chastnaia torgovlia v SSSR*. Moscow: Trud i kniga.

Krylova, A. 2014. "Soviet Modernities: Stephen Kotkin and the Bolshevik Predicament." *Contemporary European History* 23, no. 2:167–192.

———. 2000. "The Tenacious Liberal Subject in Soviet Studies" *Kritika: Explorations in Russian and Eurasian History* 1, no. 1:119–146.

Kuromiya, H. 1990. *Stalin's Industrial Revolution: Politics and Workers, 1928–1932*. Cambridge: Cambridge University Press.

———. 1984. "The Crisis of Proletarian Identity in the Soviet Factory, 1928–29" *Slavic Review* 44, no. 2:280–297.

Kusnaeva, S. A. 1998. *Evreiskie obshchiny Belarusi v kontse XVIII–nachale XX veka*. Minsk: RIP Petit.

Lederhendler, E. 1989. *The Road to Modern Jewish Politics: Political Tradition and Political Reconstruction in the Jewish Community of Tsarist Russia*. New York: Oxford University Press.

Le Foll, Claire. 2008. "The 'Belorussianisation' of the Jewish Population during the Interwar Period: Discourses and Achievements in Political and Cultural Spheres." *East European Jewish Affairs* 38, no. 1:65–88.

———. 2012. "The Institute for Belarusian Culture: The Constitution of Belarusian and Jewish Studies in the BSSR between Soviet and Non-Soviet Science (1922–1928)." *Ab Imperio* 4:245–274.

Lefebvre, G. 1986. *The Coming of the French Revolution*. Princeton: Princeton University Press.

Lemon, A. 2002. "Without a 'Concept?' Race as Discursive Practice" *Slavic Review* 61, no. 1:54–61.

Levin, N. 1988. *The Jews in the Soviet Union Since 1917: Paradox of Survival*, 2 vols. London: I. B. Tauris.

Lewin, M. 1968. *Russian Peasants and Soviet Power: A Study of Collectivization*. New York: W.W. Norton.

———. 1985. *The Making of the Soviet System: Essays in the Social History of Interwar Russia*. New York: Pantheon.

Loeffler, M. 2011. "Producers and Parasites: The Critique of Finance in Germany and Britain, 1873–1944." PhD dissertation, University of Chicago.

Lohr, E. 2012. *Russian Citizenship from Empire to Soviet Union*. Cambridge, MA: Harvard University Press.

Low, A. 1990. *Soviet Jewry and Soviet Policy*. New York: East European Monographs.

Lukacs, G. 1971. *History and Class Consciousness: Studies in Marxist Dialectics*. Translated by Robert Livingstone. Cambridge, MA: MIT Press.

Malinin, S. M., and K. I. Shabuninia, eds. 1969. *Ekonomicheskaia istoriia BSSR*. Minsk: Vysheishaia shkola.

Mally, L. 1990. *Culture of the Future: The Prolekult Movement in Revolutionary Russia*. Berkeley: University of California Press.

Marcus, H. 1969. *Soviet Marxism: A Critical Analysis*. New York: Columbia University Press.

Markiianov, B. 1961. *Bor'ba kommunisticheskoi partii Belorussii za ukreplenie edinstva svoikh riadov v 1921–1925*. Minsk: Izdatel'stvo ministerstva vysshego, srednego, spetsial'nogo i professional'nogo obrazovaniia BSSR.

Markiianov, B. 1970. *Ukreplenie edinstva riadov kommunisticheskoi partii Belorussii (1921–1937 gg.)*. Minsk: Belarus'.

Martin, T. 2001. *The Affirmative Action Empire: Nations and Nationalism in the Soviet Union, 1923–1939*. Ithaca, NY: Cornell University Press.

Martinkevich, F. S., and V. I. Dritsa, eds. 1973. *Razvitie ekonomiki Belorussii v 1921–1927 gg.* Minsk: Nauka i tekhnika.

Martinkevich, F. S., ed.1967. *Ekonomika sovetskoi Belorussii, 1917–1967*. Minsk: Nauka i tekhnika.

Marx, K. 1977. *Capital, Vol. 1*. New York: Vintage.

McGeever, B. F. 2015. "The Bolshevik Confrontation with Antisemitism in the Russian Revolution, 1917–1919." PhD dissertation, University of Glasgow.

Medvedev, R. 1989. *Let History Judge: The Origins and Consequences of Stalinism*. New York: Columbia University Press.

Meier, C. 1970. "Between Taylorism and Technocracy: European Ideologies and the Vision of Industrial Productivity in the 1920s." *Journal of Contemporary History* 5, no. 2:27–61.

Mendelsohn, E. 1970. *Class Struggle in the Pale: The Formative Years of the Jewish Workers' Movement in Tsarist Russia*. Cambridge: Cambridge University Press.

Mendelsohn, E., ed. 1997. *Essential Papers on the Jews and the Left*. New York: New York University Press.

Mendes-Flohr, P. 1991. *Divided Passions: Jewish Intellectuals and the Experience of Modernity*. Detroit: Wayne State University Press.

Michlic, J. 2007. "The Soviet Occupation of Poland, 1939–1941, and the Stereotype of the Anti-Polish and Pro-Soviet Jew." *Jewish Social Studies* 13, no. 3:135–176.

Morozov, L. F. 1960. *Reshaiushchii etap bor'by s nepmanskoi burzhuaziei: iz likvidatsii kapitalisticheskikh elementov goroda*. Moscow. Akad. ob. nauk pri TsK KPSS.

Moss, K. 2009. *Jewish Renaissance in the Russian Revolution*. Cambridge, MA: Harvard University Press.

Murphy, K. 2005. *Revolution and Counter-Revolution: Class Struggle in a Moscow Metal Factory*. New York: Bergham.

Nathans, B. 2002. *Beyond the Pale: The Jewish Encounter with Late Imperial Russia*. Berkeley: University of California Press.

Nedava, J. 1972. *Trotsky and the Jews*. Philadelphia: Jewish Publication Society.

Nove, A. 1992. *An Economic History of the USSR, 1917–1991*. New York: Penguin.

O'Keefe, B. 2013. *New Soviet Gypsies: Nationality, Performance, and Selfhood in the Early Soviet Union*. Toronto: University of Toronto Press.

Paniutich, V. P. 1969. *Iz istorii formirovaniia proletariata Belorussii, 1861–1914 gg*. Minsk: Nauka i tekhnika.

Peled, Y. 1989. *Class and Ethnicity in the Pale: The Political Economy of Jewish Workers' Nationalism in Late Imperial Russia*. New York: St. Martin's.

Penslar, D. 2001. *Shylock's Children: Economics and Jewish Identity in Modern Europe*. Berkeley: University of California Press.

Peris, D. 1998. *Storming the Heavens: The Soviet League of the Militant Godless.* Ithaca. NY: Cornell University Press.

Petrikov, P.T., ed. 1985. *Istoriia rabochego klassa Belorusskoi SSR, tom 2.* Minsk: Nauka i tekhnika.

Petrovsky-Shtern, Y. ed., 2014. *Jews and Ukrainians: Polin,* Volume 26. Oxford: Littman Library.

———. 2014. *The Golden Age Shtetl: A New History of Jewish Life in Eastern Europe.* Princeton: Princeton University Press.

Pinkus, B. 1988. *The Jews of the Soviet Union: The History of a National Minority.* Cambridge: Cambridge University Press.

———. 1971. "Yiddish Language Courts and Nationalities Policy in the Soviet Union." *Soviet Jewish Affairs,* no. 2:41–61.

Pipes, R. 1997. *The Formation of the Soviet Union: Communism and Nationalism.* Cambridge, MA: Harvard University Press.

Polanyi, K. 2001. *The Great Transformation: The Political and Economic Origins of Our Time.* Boston: Beacon.

Polesskaia, L. P. 2004. *Vospominanie o gorode: istoriia Minsk v fotografiiakh iz kollektsii Vasiliia Kaledy.* Minsk: Chetyre Chetverti.

Postone, M. 1980. "Anti-Semitism and National Socialism: Notes on the German Reaction to 'Holocaust.'" *New German Critique,* no. 19, Special Issue 1: Germans and Jews: 97–115.

———. 1993. *Time, Labor, and Social Domination: A Reinterpretation of Marx's Critical Theory.* Cambridge: Cambridge University Press.

Prot'ko, T. S. 2002. *Stanovlenie sovetskoi totalitarnoi sistemy v Belarusi (1917–1941 gg.).* Minsk: Tesei.

Pultzer, P. 1964. *The Rise of Political Anti-Semitism in Germany and Austria.* Cambridge, MA: Harvard University Press.

Rabinowitch, A. 2004. *The Bolsheviks Come to Power: The Revolution of 1917 in Petrograd.* Chicago: Haymarket.

———. 2008. *The Bolsheviks in Power: The First Year of Soviet Rule in Petrograd.* Bloomington: Indiana University Press.

Rabinovitch, S. 2014. *Jewish Rights and National Rights: Nationalism and Autonomy in Late Imperial and Revolutionary Russia.* Stanford, CA: Stanford University Press.

Radkey, O. 1977. *Russia Goes to the Polls: The Election to the All-Russian Constituent Assembly.* Ithaca, NY: Cornell University Press.

Raisin, J. 1913. *The Haskalah Movement in Russia.* Philadelphia: Jewish Publication Society of America.

Ree, L. 2007. "Heroes and Merchants: Stalin's Understandings of National Character." *Kritika: Explorations in Russian and Eurasian History* 8, no. 1:41–65.

Reiman, M. 1987. *The Birth of Stalinism: The USSR on the Eve of the "Second Revolution."* Bloomington: Indiana University Press.

Riga, L. 2008. "The Ethnic Roots of Class Universalism: Rethinking the 'Russian' Revolutionary Elite." *American Journal of Sociology* 114, no. 3:649–705.

Rogger, H. 1986. *Jewish Policies and Right-Wing Politics in Imperial Russia.* Berkeley: University of California Press.

Rosenberg, W. 1990. *Bolshevik Visions. First Phase of the Cultural Revolution in Soviet Russia,* 2 *vols.* Ann Arbor: University of Michigan Press.

Rossman, J. J. 2005. *Worker Resistance under Stalin: Class and Revolution on the Shop Floor.* Cambridge, MA: Harvard University Press.

Rubinstein, J., and V. P. Naumov, eds., 2001. *Stalin's Secret Pogrom: The Postwar Inquisition of the Jewish Anti-Fascist Committee*. New Haven: Yale University Press.

Rudé, G. 1972. *The Crowd in the French Revolution*. London: Oxford University Press.

Sachar, H. 2003. *Dreamland: Europeans and Jews in the Aftermath of the Great War*. New York: Vintage.

Sanchez-Sinbony, O. 2014. "Depression Stalinism: The Great Break Reconsidered." *Kritika: Explorations in Russian and Eurasian History* 15, no. 1:23–49.

Savitsky, E. 1998. "Sotsial'no-ekonomicheskoe polozhenie Belorusskikh evreev v kontse XIX–nachale XX vv." *Evrei Belarusi, istoria i kul'tura* II: 18–29.

Schneiderman, J. 1976. *Sergei Zubatov and Revolutionary Marxism: The Struggle for the Working Class in Tsarist Russia*. Ithaca, NY: Cornell University Press.

Schwarz, S. 1951. *Labor in the Soviet Union*. New York: Praeger.

———. 1951. *The Jews in the Soviet Union*. Syracuse: Syracuse University Press.

Scott, J. W. 1974. *The Glassworkers of Carmaux: French Craftsmen and Political Action in a Nineteenth-Century City*. Cambridge, MA: Harvard University Press.

Sewell, W. H. *Work and Revolution in France: The Language of Labor from the Old Regime to 1848*. Cambridge: Cambridge University Press, 1980.

Shapiro, L. *Russian Studies*. New York: Penguin, 1988.

Shkliar, M. E. 1960. *Bor'ba kompartii Belorussii za ukreplenie soyuza rabochego klassa i trudiashchegosia krest'ianstva v vosstanovitel'nyi period (1921–1925 gg.)*. : Gosizdat BSSR.

Shlapentokh, D. 1997. *The French Revolution and the Russian Anti-Democratic Tradition*. New Brunswick, NJ: Transaction Publishers.

Shneer, D. 2004. *Yiddish and the Creation of Soviet Jewish Culture, 1918–1930*. Cambridge: Cambridge University Press.

Shternshis, A. 2006. *Soviet and Kosher: Jewish Popular Culture in the Soviet Union, 1923–1939*. Bloomington: Indiana University Press.

Siegelbaum, L. H. 1992. *Soviet State and Society between Revolutions, 1918–1929*. Cambridge: Cambridge University Press.

———. 2006. "The Late Romance of the Soviet Worker in Western Historiography." *International Review of Social History* 51, part 3:463–481.

Siegelbaum, L. H., and R. Suny, eds. 1994. *Making Workers Soviet: Power, Class, and Identity*. Ithaca, NY: Cornell University Press.

Sinkoff, N. 2004. *Out of the Shtetl: Making Jews Modern in the Polish Borderlands*. Providence, RI: Brown Judaic Studies.

Slezkine, Y. 2004. *The Jewish Century*. Princeton: Princeton University Press.

———. 1994. "The USSR as a Communal Apartment, or How a Socialist State Promoted Ethnic Particularism." *Slavic Review* 53, no. 2.

Slobin, M., ed. 1982. *Old Jewish Folk Music: The Collections and Writings of Moshe Beregovski*. Philadelphia: University of Pennsylvania Press.

Sloin, A., and O. Sanchez-Sibony. 2014. "Economy and Power in the Soviet Union, 1917–1939." *Kritika: Explorations in Russian and Eurasian History* 15, no. 1:7–22.

Smilovitsky, L. 1999. *Evrei v Belorussii: iz nashei obshchei istorii 1905–1953*. Minsk: Arti-Feks.

———. 1997. "Sovetskaia evreiskaia shkola v Belorussii v 1920–1930-x godakh." *Vestnik evreiskogo universiteta v Moskve* 1, no. 14.

Smith, A. 1976. *An Inquiry into the Nature and Causes of the Wealth of Nations*. Chicago: University of Chicago Press.

———. 1988. *The Ethnic Origins of Nations*. Malden, MA: Blackwell.

Smith, S. A. 1983. *Red Petrograd: Revolution in the Factories: 1917–1918*. Cambridge: Cambridge University Press.

Snyder, T. 2010. *Bloodlands: Europe between Hitler and Stalin*. New York: Basic.

———. 2003. *The Reconstruction of Nations: Poland, Ukraine, Lithuania, Belarus, 1569–1999*. New Haven: Yale University Press.

Soboul, A. 1980. *The Sans-Culottes*. Princeton: Princeton University Press.

Sorkin, D. 1999. *The Transformation of German Jewry, 1780–1840*. Detroit: Wayne State University Press.

Steinberg, M. 2002. *Proletarian Imagination: Self, Modernity, and the Sacred in Russia, 1910–1925*. Ithaca, NY: Cornell University Press.

Stites, R. 1989. *Revolutionary Dreams: Utopian Vision and Experimental Life in the Russian Revolution*. Oxford: Oxford University Press.

Suny, R. 1993. *The Revenge of the Past: Nationalism, Revolution, and the Collapse of the Soviet Union*. Stanford: Stanford University Press.

———. 1972. *The Baku Commune, 1917–1918: Class and Nationality in the Russian Revolution*. Princeton: Princeton University Press.

Suny, R., and T. Martin. 2001. *A State of Nations: Empire and Nation-Making in the Era of Lenin and Stalin*. Oxford: Oxford University Press.

Tanny, J. 2011. *City of Rogues and Schnorrers: Russia's Jews and the Myth of Old Odessa*. Bloomington: Indiana University Press.

Thompson, E. P. 1966. *The Making of the English Working Class*. New York: Vintage.

Timasheff, N. 1946. *The Great Retreat: The Growth and Decline of Communism in Russia*. New York: E. P. Dutton and Company.

Tobias, H. 1966. "Primordial Ties and Political Process in Pre-Revolutionary Russia: The Case of the Jewish Bund." *Comparative Studies in Society and History* 8, no. 3:331–360.

———. 1972. *The Jewish Bund in Russia: From Its Origins to 1905*. Stanford: Stanford University Press.

Traverso, E. 1994. *The Marxists and the Jewish Question*. Translated by Bernard Gibbons. Atlantic Highland, NJ: Humanities Press.

Trifonov, I. Ia. 1969. *Klassy i klassovaia bor'ba v SSSR v nachale nepa, 1921–25*. Leningrad: Izd.-vo Leningradskogo Universiteta.

———. 1960. *Ocherki istorii klassovoi bor'by v SSSR v godu nepa, 1921–1937 gg*. Moscow: Gos. izdat. polit. lit-ry.

Tucker, R. 1990. *Stalin in Power: The Revolution from Above, 1928–1941*. New York: Norton.

Tucker, R., ed. 1978. *The Marx-Engels Reader*. New York: Norton.

Ulam, A. 1973. *Stalin: The Man and His Era*. New York: Viking.

Urban, P. 1959. "The Belorussian Soviet Socialist Republic: A Brief Historical Overview." *The Belorussian Review* 7:3–22.

Vakar, N. 1956. *Belorussia: The Making of a Nation, a Case Study*. Cambridge, MA: Harvard University Press.

Veidlinger, J. 2000. *The Moscow State Yiddish Theater: Jewish Culture on the Soviet Stage*. Bloomington: Indiana University Press.

Vlasenko, N. 1970. *Bor'ba kompartii Belorussii za postroenie ekonomicheskogo fundamenta sotsializma*. Minsk: Belarus'.

Volokhovich, L. I. 1962. *Partiinoe stroitel'stvo v Belorussii v pervye gody nepa (1921–1924 gg.)*. Minsk: Izadatel'stvo Ministerstva vysshego srednego spetsial'nogo i professional'nogo obrazovaniia BSSR.

Volkov, S. 1978. "Antisemitism as a Cultural Code: Reflections on the History and Historiography of Antisemitism in Imperial Germany." *Leo Baeck Yearbook XXIII*: 25–46.

Ward, C. 1990. *Russia's Cotton Workers and the New Economic Policy*. Cambridge: Cambridge University Press.

Weber, M. 1946. *Essays in Sociology*. New York: Oxford University Press.

Weinberg, R. 2008. "Demonizing Judaism in the Soviet Union During the 1920s." *Slavic Review 67*, no. 1:120–153.

———. 1998. *Stalin's Forgotten Zion: Birobidzhan and the Making of a Soviet Jewish Homeland: An Illustrated History, 1928–1996*. Berkeley: University of California Press.

———. 1993. *The Revolution of 1905 in Odessa: Blood on the Steps*. Bloomington: Indiana University Press.

Weiner, A. 2002. "Nothing but Certainty." *Slavic Review 61*, no. 1:44–53.

Weitz, E. 2002. "Racial Politics Without the Concept of Race: Reevaluating Soviet Ethnic and National Purges." *Slavic Review 61*, no. 1:1–29.

Wistrich, R. 2010. *A Lethal Obsession: Anti-Semitism from Antiquity to the Global Jihad*. New York: Random House.

———. 1976. *Revolutionary Jews from Marx to Trotsky*. New York: Barnes and Noble.

Wynn, C. 1992. *Workers, Strikes, and Pogroms: The Donbass-Dnepr Bend in Late Imperial Russia, 1870–1905*. Princeton: Princeton University Press.

Yalen, D. 2007. "Documenting the New Red Kasrilevke: Shtetl Ethnography as Revolutionary Narrative." *East European Jewish Affairs 37*, no. 3:353–375.

———. 2007. "On the Social-Economic Front: The Polemics of Shtetl Research During the Stalin Revolution." *Science in Context 20*, no, 2:239–301.

Yatskevich, I. 1998. "Bund i natsional'nyi vopros v 1908–1910 gg." *Evrei Belarusi, istoria i Kul'tura* II: 49–57.

Yodfat, A. 1971. "The Closure of Synagogues in the Soviet Union." *Soviet Jewish Affairs 3*, no. 1:49–57.

Young, G. 1997. *Power and the Sacred in Revolutionary Russia: Religious Activists in the Village*. University Park: Pennsylvania State University Press.

Zakharov, N. 2015. *Race and Racism in Russia*. London: Palgrave Macmillan.

Zasinets, G. 2001. "Evreiskoe sovetskoe obrazovanie na Gomel'shchine v 20-x godakh XX veka." *Evrei Belarusi: istoriia i kul'tura VI*.

Zavaleev, N. E. 1967. *Rabochii klass Belorussii v bor'be za sotsializm*. Minsk: Nauka i tekhnika.

Zel'tser, A. 1998. "Belorusizatsiia 1920-x gg.: dostizheniia I neudachi." *Evrei Belarusi: istoriia i kul'tura, III–IV*.

———. 2006. *Evrei sovetskoi provintsii: Vitebsk i mestechki, 1917–1941*. Moscow: Rosspen.

Zhigalova, V. N., ed. 1975. *Industrializatsiia Belorusskoi SSR (1926–1941 gg.) sbornik dokumentov i materialiov*. Minsk: Belarus'.

Zipperstein, Steven J. 1999. *Imagining Russian Jewry: Memory, History, Identity*. Seattle: University of Washington Press.

———. 1986. *The Jews of Odessa: A Cultural History, 1794–1881*. Stanford: Stanford University Press.

INDEX

Adamovich, Aleksandr Fomich, 155, 239
Adler shoe factory, 94, 96
affirmative action, 4, 14, 152-56, 168, 172, 177
Agitprop (Agitation and Propaganda), 147, 173, 191, 239
agricultural settlements, 85, 212, 213
Agudas Yisroel, 26
Agursky, Samuil, 38, 40, 84, 101, 113, 184, 240
Aksel'rod, Pavel, 22, 25
Alexander I, 123
Al'tman (Borisov evsektsii), 109
American Relief Agency, 184
Anarchism, 28, 32, 38, 40, 47, 92, 247
antireligious campaigns, 128-33, 136, 143, 153, 155, 212
Antisemitism, 3, 6, 13; anti-antisemitism campaigns, 15, 150, 202, 209, 216-17, 226-34, 236, 238; Bolshevik interpretations of, 11, 61, 150, 216, 219, 220-21, 224-25, 232; and capitalist crisis, 6, 15, 17-18, 153, 210-11, 219-21, 235; Jewish chauvinism, 168, 171, 174, 223, 225-26, 233; Soviet economic crisis and 18, 172-73, 211, 213, 221, 224, 234, 242-45; in Stalin Revolution, 17-18, 182, 212, 221, 224-25, 234, 235-36, 237, 240, 241-45; Trotskyism and, 17, 182, 202, 204-205, 207, 210, 219, 224, 227, 230, 236, 242, 243-44; among workers, 171-72, 205, 209, 211, 213-24, 226-34, 235, 244
arendators, 92, 97, 99

artel' (worker cooperative), 57, 101, 103-104, 106, 144, 213, 221
artisans, 2, 22, 23-24, 28, 51, 246; defined, 86-87; Bolshevik policies, 85, 108, 110, 123, 137; political deviation, 166, 173, 196
As'man, Hinda, 70-71
As'man, Mera, 70-71
austerity, 186, 198, 224, 236
Austro-Marxists, 61, 151
Avrutin (Narpit), 172

Badanin, Aron, 231-34
Bakunin, Mikhail, 61
Balitskii, Anton Vasil'evich, 155, 239
Balkov'skii, Bernard Emmanuilovich, 35
Baranov (glassmaker), 169
Barshai, Dreiza Leibova, 209, 214-15, 217, 225, 229, 231, 233, 235
Bauer, Otto, 151
Bazhichko, Alesia Bazileva, 226
Beilin, Abram Grigor'evich, 38, 87, 148, 150, 161, 163; biography, 120-21, 137-46; purged, 155, 240
Belinski (cultural activist), 125-26
Belkozha (Belorussian Leather Administration), 97, 195
Belorussian Socialist Revolutionary party (BSR), 162
Belorussian State University (BGU), 162, 184, 191

Belorussianization, 153-55, 157-61, 176, 244; opposition to, 168, 170-72, 203
Bende, Robert Martsevich, 164
Berenshtein (criminal investigator), 70
Bereznitski, Pinkhes, 94
Bernshtein (youth activist), 136
Bernshteyn, Moishe, 78
Bernshteyn, Sakhne, 78
Berson, Stanislav, 21, 62
Birger, Vol'f, 75
black market, 104, 105
Bobrshvei (Bobruisk sewing factory), 197-99
Bobruisk, 2, 35, 131, 136, 252; antisemitism, 209, 212-15, 226-29; Bund in, 8, 9, 29, 31-32, 40, 203; kustari, 96, 105-106, 110; Trotsky-ists in, 181, 182, 193, 196-99, 200-204, po-groms, 33
Bobruisk Okrug Committee KPB, 215-16
Bogin (brickmaker), 228
Bogutsky, Vatslav, 159
Bolshevik (tannery), 190, 194-95, 199
Bolshevik Revolution of 1917, 1-2, 21-23, 61, 241; anticapitalist, 92, 220-21; commemo-rated, 101, 129-30, 136, 198, 229; Jewish par-ticipation, 31, 35, 50, 83-84, 138, 198; Jewish Revolution and, 2, 4-6, 10-11, 18, 118-121, 126, 241, 246-47
Bontshe Shvayg, 117-20, 146
Borisov, 109, 125, 171, 193, 215, 226, 252; Bund, 35, 40; industry, 96-97, 98-99, 106, 190
Borochov, Ber, 9, 28, 83
Botvinik, M. (shoemaker), 129-30
Bravyi, Aron Moisevich, 74
Breinzen (printer), 229
brick makers, 37, 144, 227-29
bristle makers, 95, 182, 190
builders (construction), 27, 129, 194, 250, 251
Bukharin, Nikolai Ivanovich, 108, 140, 150, 176, 195; Right Opposition, 145, 187, 202
Bulak-Balakhovich, Stanislav, 33
Bund (General League of Jewish Working-men in Lithuania, Poland, and Russia), 5, 8-10, 61, 66, 139, 165-66, 184; in Bolshevik Revolution 6, 30-31, 34-35, 84; in KPB, 28-49, 83, 93-95, 109, 124, 133-34, 137-38, 144-45, 148-49; Opposition, 191, 197-99, 201, 203-206; purged from KPB, 162-64, 201, 203, 240; Yugend Bund, 37, 48

Bundism (deviation), 13, 17, 61, 108, 242, 243-45; defined, 148; anti-Bundism campaign, 121, 139, 145, 148-151, 158-59, 162-77, 184, 238; Trotsky Opposition, 199, 203-205, 212, 226, 227
Butman, Arthur, 94
Bykhovskii (woodworker), 196

Capital, 6, 83, 86-87, 124, 141, 181, 195-96, 201, 206, 220-221, 242; antisemitism and, 6, 11, 61, 152, 219-20; capitalism; 2, 22, 60-61, 124, 132, 141, 211, 221, 242; fixed, 187-88, 189, 224; international, 15, 18, 132, 173, 181, 187-88, 195, 224; NEP, 86-87, 100, 107, 173; merchant, 80, 82, 84, 141; postcapitalism, 1, 5, 18, 107, 141, 219, 242; print, 32
carpenters, 29, 43, 120, 136, 138-39, 182
Central Bank (Gosbank), 57
Central Committee of the Communist Party of Belorussia (TsK KPB), 30, 125; against antisemitism, 216-17; Bund and, 30, 34, 38, 39, 54, 147-48, 170, 172; Jewish affairs, 26, 30, 34-36; nationality policy, 159, 160, 161, 170, 175; NEP, 62, 68, 92, 109, 140, 150, 160, 189; against Opposition, 191, 196, 198; 36, 40, 62, 68, 92
Central Committee of the Communist Party (Moscow), 92, 148, 155, 176, 186, 189, 198, 216
Central Control Commission (TsKK): of KPB 144-46, 161-62, 164, 184, 191, 193, 194-95, 197, 200; Moscow TsKK, 155; Okrug Control Commissions (OKK), 184, 191, 198-99, 202, 203-204
Central Soviet of Trade Unions (Sovprofbel), 27, 39, 88, 98, 109, 161, 250, 251
Cheka, 30, 41, 56, 98-99, 121, 138-39; anti-speculation, 56, 57-58, 62, 65-66, 68, 71, 74-77, 91
Cherviakov, Aleksandr, 146, 159, 160, 240
Cherven, 101, 129
chervonets, 68, 73, 76, 77-78, 104, 106, 185-86, 192
Choral Synagogue (Minsk), 129, 131
Chyrvonaia Zmena, 217
clericalism, 121, 122, 123, 130, 153, 184, 233; Beilin on, 139, 140-42, 143
Comintern, 39
Commissariat for Jewish Affairs (Moscow), 83

Il'ich (glassmaking factory), 226
Independent Jewish labor movement, 8
Inflation: in 1918-21, 62-63, 66-67, 73-74; counterinflation, 106, 174-75; hyperinflation of 1923, 58, 68, 77-78, 80; 104-105, 210; NEP, 99, 150, 174-75; NEP crisis and cryptoinflation, 142, 183, 185-86, 188, 194, 216, 221, 243; wage, 103, 183, 186, 188, 189, 192
internationalism, 16, 134, 135, 150
Iskra, 25, 49, 138
Ivanov, Ivan Aleksandrovich, 160

Jacobins (French Revolution), 60-61
Jewish Communist Party (EKP), 30-31, 84
Jewish emancipation, 1-2, 13, 18, 84, 119, 122-24, 244, 246
Jewish Enlightenment. *See Haskalah*
Jewish Party School (evpartshkola), 41-51
Jewish question, 3, 6, 11-13, 61, 112, 145; nationality policy and, 150-56, 158, 177
Jewish Revolution, 2, 4-6, 11, 59, 118, 120-22; end of, 138, 146, 234, 240, 245
Jewish Socialist Workers Party (SERP), 26, 34

Kabailo (Narkomzem), 169
Kadets. *See* Constitutional Democrats
Kagan (youth activist), 135-36
Kalmanovich, Moisei, 64, 240
Kamenev, Lev Borisovich, 181-82, 191, 193, 202
Kanchik (youth activist), 136
Kantsler (leatherworker), 165
Kaplan, Isaac Borisovich, 74
Kaplan, Kalman Zalmanovich, 201
Karonin (Oktiabr' factory administrator), 215
Karpeshin, Anton Stepanovich, 92
Kastovich (evpartshkola), 45
Kats, Nakhim-Leib, 95, 98
Katsenbogen, Lyubvi, 75
Katsilevich (Mogilev city party administration), 167-68
Katsman, Elka, 46-47
Katsman, Musia, 48-49
Kazhdan (evpartshkola), 44, 48
Kazhdan, Mordukh Nakhimov, 35
Kazimirovskii, S. G. (Oppositionist), 198, 201
Keller (Narpit), 168
Keynesianism, 187

Khaikin, Zalman, 65, 66, 67
Khoban'ko (brickmaker), 227
Khodosh, Shepshel Shepshelevich, 39, 159, 240
Khokhlov (brickmaker), 228
khozraschet (economic accountability), 92-93, 103
Khrapunova (linen factory worker), 222
Kiev, 65, 201
Kitaichik, Gdalii, 197
Klal yisroel bloc, 25-26, 84
Klionskii (anti-Bundism activist), 168-69
Klionskii (shoemaker), 192
Knorin, Vil'gel'm Georgievich, 39, 92, 159, 239
Koidanov, 63, 78, 79, 141
Kolas, Yakob, 155, 239
Komsomol, 34, 45, 132, 136-37, 163, 166, 194; antisemitism, 209, 214, 215, 216, 218, 219, 223, 226, 231, 233
Komsomol'skaia Pravda, 217-18, 219
Korenizatsiia (indigenization), 14, 154, 155, 156, 176
Kornilov, Lavr Georgievich, 25
Kostiuk (printer), 229-30
Kozerski, Vladislav, 78
Krasnaia Berezina (matchstick factory), 190
Krasnapelski, Adam, 79-80, 81
Krasnoselski, Abrahm, 130
Krasnyi Metallist (machine plant), 190
Kremer (leatherworker), 165-66
Kren' (glassmaker), 231
Krinitskii, Aleksandr Ivanovich, 147, 159, 173, 239
Krol (criminal investigator), 70
Kronstadt Rebellion, 68, 91, 163
Krytski, Rygor, 230
Kuksin (Trotskyist), 201
kulaks (rich peasants), 66, 102, 140, 141, 142; in Stalin Revolution, 194, 207, 209, 210, 224, 231
Kurnovskaia (glassmaker), 169
kustari (cottage producers), 23, 24, 51, 85-86, 106-107, 139-44, 213; Bundism, 166, 173; defined, 86-87, 103; deproletarianized labor, 89, 93-94, 98, 100, 111-13; industrialization, 147, 149-50; in Opposition, 194, 199, 203, 204; societies (obshchestva), 87 101-103, 108, 111; unionized labor against, 95-96, 99,

105-106, 227; workshops, 89, 97, 100-101, 103; Zionism among, 108-11, 213. *See also* Evsektsii, labor, and individual industries

Kutsenko (brickmaker), 228

labor (concept), 1-2, 5-6 11, 21-22, 83-85, 99-100, 112-13, 122, 188-89, 236; alienated, 6, 242-43; Bolshevik conceptions of, 5-6, 85-87, 91, 236; citizenship and, 2, 21, 38, 45, 84, 93; in Haskalah, 123-24, 145; market, 97, 99, 100, 105-109; Jews and, 12, 58, 81-86, 87-91, 109-111, 189, 190; proletarian, 47, 58, 84-89, 93-94, 98; undifferentiated, 111, 206-207, 236; wage labor, 5, 23 86-87, 100, 103, 107, 242-43. *See also* Kustari, productivization

Lander, Karl, 159

Larin, Iurii, 219

League of the Militant Godless, 143

leatherworkers, 5, 24, 28, 86, 89, 94-95, 118, 225; Bund, 29, 38, 149, 165-66, 172; kustari, 100-101, 105-106, 144; Opposition, 182, 189, 195, 199, 206; speculation, 71, 97; trade union, 27, 88, 95-97, 99, 105-106, 161, 175, 225, 250, 251; rationalization of, 97-100, 189, 190, 193, 195, 196

Left Opposition, 184-85, 187

Lekert, Hirsh, 29, 190

Leonov (Union of Soviet Workers), 56

Lenin, Vladimir Ilyich, 9, 21, 22, 23, 25, 34, 138, 193; on antisemitism and nationality, 11, 61, 152, 154, 220, 232; on Bund, 28; death of, 80, 134; on NEP, 68, 91, 92, on labor and capital, 86-87, 102, 220-21; on speculation and money, 61, 74

Lenin Club. *See* Grosser Club

Lenin Communist University, 215

Lenin Levy of 1924, 134-35, 161, 162, 165

Leningrad, 184

LesBel (Belorussian lumber trust), 194

Levin (evpartshkola), 47

Levin (Trotskyist shoemaker), 201

Levin (watchmaker, speculator), 76

Levin, Kh. (speculator), 66

Levin, L. (speculator), 66

Levin, Yankel, 26-27, 40, 125, 133, 159, 240; removed as evsektsiia head, 137-38, 148

Levit (Minshvei), 105

Liady, 141

Liebknecht, Karl, 32

Likhavidov (linen factory worker), 222-23, 224

Lilienthal, Max, 125

Liozno, 101

Lipets, Mordukh Zokorov, 24-25, 28

lishentsy, 161, 234

Litvinov, Max, 124

Livit (Mozyr evsektsii), 109

Livshits, D. (speculator), 66

Luk'ianchik (Narkomzem), 170

Luxemburg, Rosa, 22, 32

L'vov (Lemberg) (Ukraine), 33

L'vovich, El'ia Abramovich, 197, 198, 201

L'vovski (Moscow evsektsiia), 102

Maevskii (Narkomzem), 169-70

Maisel' (Narpit), 166, 167

Marchlewski, Julian Baltazar, 36

Margolin, Aron Isaakov, 215, 233-34

Mariasin (kustar' union), 144

Margolis, Khaiia, 71-72

Martov, Iulii Osipovich, 9, 22, 25

Marx, Karl, 22, 23-24, 47, 61, 120; on labor and capital, 83, 86, 107, 195-96, 242

Marxism: Bolshevik conceptions, 1, 22-23, 84, 217, 234, 240, 242; Bolshevik culture, 122, 123, 124, 125, 132; Bolshevik economic interpretations, 32, 61, 80, 86, 107-108, 112, 221; Nationality, 14, 61, 151, 156-58; RSDWP, 25, 28; non-Bolshevik interpretations, 9, 28, 32, 22

matchstick makers, 29, 33, 88; factories, 23, 88, 190, 230

mechanization, 22, 88, 103, 106, 187, 189-90

Meleshevich (brickmaker), 228-29

Melikhovitskaia, Rebekka Simkhovna, 133

Mendele Moykher-Sforim, 125

Mendelssohn, Moses, 122

Mensheviks, 8, 22, 25, 26, 29, 61; in Communist Party, 32, 46-47, 193, 219; Menshevism (deviation), 102, 108; 148, 166, 184

Merezhin, Avrom, 102

metalworkers, 25, 27, 43, 89, 118, 144, 189; antisemitism, 215, trade union, 166, 167, 250, 251; Opposition among, 193, 202

Metprom (metal factory), 190, 196, 202

Miasnikov, Aleksandr Fedorovich, 159

Miller (leather worker), 96

milliners, 29, 32, 182

Minsk 2, 7, 12-13, 24, 87, 107, 160, 252; antisemitism in, 202, 229, industries in, 94, 95, 96, 97, 98, 99, 103, 105, 168, 170, 190; KPB members in, 24-25, 34, 37, 38, 40-41, 41-49, 55-56, 121, 133, 138-39, 147; KPB composition in 26-27, 33, 162, 163; Opposition in, 181, 182, 184, 189, 190-92, 193, 195, 199, 200, 201, 203-204, 205-206; prerevolutionary politics in, 8, 9, 10, 25-26, 28-29; in Revolution and Civil War, 10, 21, 23, 29-31, 33-36, 62-63, 65-66; under Soviets, 24, 38, 50, 57-59, 66-67, 69, 74, 75, 79-81, 128, 129-31, 153; working class in, 87-88, 93, 98, 100, 101, 103-104, 109, 167, 215, 250, 251

Minsk Bootmakers Workshop, 167, 200

Minsk City Soviet, 25, 133

Minsk Military Soviet (*Minvoensovet*), 21, 62

Minsk Okrug Committee KPB, 136, 170, 200

Minsk Palace of Culture, 129

Minsk Railroad Factory, 170

Minsk Shoemaking Factory, 192, 205

Minsk Soviet of Workers and Red Army Deputies, 31

Minshvei (Minsk sewing factory), 105, 106

Mitnagdim, 7

Mogilev, 7, 23, 24, 87, 101, 136, 138, 168, 252; antisemitism in, 218, 219; KPB administration, 166, 167, 171, 199

Monchazh (evpartshkola), 46, 48

monetary reform. *See* chervonets

monopoly, 57, 68, 140; on grain, 64-67; on staple goods and alcohol, 71, 72-73; on precious metals, 76; on leather, 89, 97

Moscow, 7, 83, 94, 218; economic relations with, 103, 104, 105; as imperial metropole, 4, 7, 138, 158, 172, 177; Opposition in, 184, 193

Movshovich (evpartshkola), 45-46

Mozyr, 40, 109, 218, 252; economy, 96, 98, 100; pogroms, 33-34

Mstislav, 121, 138, 148

Naiman (leatherworker), 225

Narodniki (Populists), 22, 25, 28, 61, 135

Nationality policy, 3-4, 14-18, 61, 151-59, 168, 176-77, 239; intranationalism, 3, 10, 38, 241; Jews, 135, 148-49, 150-51, 168-71, 211, 240

nationalization of industry, 89, 92, 95-96, 99, 242

Needleworkers, 5, 37, 47, 79-80, 95; Bund, 29, 167-68; cultural work among, 130, 136; NEP, 93, 105, trade union; 27, 88, 105, 161, 166-67, 175, 250, 251; in Opposition, 189, 193, 197-98, 203

Nemiga (market district of Minsk), 66, 78, 80-81, 190

Nevel', 138, 152

New Economic Policy (NEP), 5, 14, 17, 57-59, 67-69, 87, 91, 106-107, 139-45, 219, 243-44; culture and, 80-81, 120, 121, 137; crisis of (1926-1928), 138, 142-44, 150, 158, 173-75, 176-77, 185; market, 68-69, 71, 77-78, 86, 103, 105; labor and production, 86-89, 92-94, 95-97, 99, 100-101, 113, 124, 184, 221; tax in kind, 68, 91-92, 97; political deviation in, 108-11, 141, 161-63; Stalin Revolution ends, 221, 231-32, 234, 239

Nicholas II, 9

Nikolai ruble, 73, 74, 75-76, 104

Nitsievskaia, Tatiana Alekseevna, 214

Nodel', Vul'f Abramovich, 109, 133

Novitskii (Mogilev city party administration), 166

Novogrudskii (antireligious activist), 129

Notkin, Nota, 123

October Revolution. *See* Bolshevik Revolution of 1917

Odessa, 7, 130, 133

Oliker, Ber Leibov, 34

Ol'shenbaum (evpartshkola), 45

Okrug Control Commissions. *See* Central Control Commission of the KPB

Oktiabr' (glassmaking factory), 209, 214-218, 222, 225, 227-34

Oktyabr, 38, 149, 216, 240

Oran, 56

Orlov (glassmaker), 232

Orsha, 171, 225

Orshanskii, Boris Mikhailovich, 38, 133, 163, 240

Osherovich, Il'ia Peretsevich, 38, 109, 124, 133, 159, 163, 240; haskole, 121-22

Osherovich, Sh., 41, 44, 46, 47, 48

Osip, Makei, 78

overaccumulation, 103-107, 187

Pale of Settlement, 2, 7-9, 33, 57, 94, 95, 117, 143, 149

Pam, Leizer Isaakovich, 43-44, 212-14

Parichi, 213

Paris Commune, 130

Partitions of Poland, 7

Party Review of 1924-1925, 17, 134, 138, 161-65, 184

peasantry, 8, 28; in Bolshevik thought, 22-23; Bundism, 148, 149, 170; hoarding, 63-65, 142; Jews and, 108, 172, 213, 219, 220, 228; in KPB, 134, 162; NEP, 68, 87, 91, 103, 107-108, 140, 143, 149, 174; Stalin Revolution, 187-88, 194

Peigin (Minshvei), 106

People's Courts, 57, 70, 71, 77

Peretz, Hersh, 123

Peretz, I. L., 117-18

Perstin (woodworker), 196

Petrikov, 141

Petrograd, 10, 23, 25, 29, 138

Petrovskii (glassmaker), 232

Petrushkevich (glassmaker), 232

piecework, 93, 98, 100

Piłsudski, Józef Klemens, 10

Pioneer youth movement, 136, 169, 209, 218

Planned economy, 17, 58, 107, 143, 186, 188, 211, 221, 242

Plekhanov, Georgii Valentinovich, 25, 28

Poalei Tsion, 8, 9, 26, 28, 31; in KPB, 30, 34, 40, 42, 43, 108, 134; suppressed, 155, 162, 185, 201, 212

pogroms, 3, 7, 8; Civil War, 10, 33-34, 36, 65, 212; under Soviets, 218, 219, 227

Poland, 7, 56, 76, 153, 210. See Polish-Soviet War

Polish Socialist Party (PPS), 26, 30, 36, 62

Polish-Soviet War (1918-1921), 23, 33-37 66, 84, 160

Political-Enlightenment Work, 90, 135

Polotsk, 7, 139

Polovinkov (woodworker), 196

Poltava, 130, 218

Posner, Jacob, 123-24

Pozniak, Leiba, 75

Preobrazhensky, Evgenii Alekseevich, 62, 73-74, 187-88

price controls, 62-63, 186

primitive socialist accumulation, 187-88

printers, 46, 171, 229, 250, 251

private traders, 58, 62, 68; kustari and, 87, 99, 102, 109; crisis of NEP, 140, 142, 194; liquidated, 143, 221

productivization: of Jews, 84-85, 86, 90-91, 94, 99-107, 111-13, 144-45; Stalin Revolution, 183, 188-90, 194, 196-97, 199, 206-208, 224, 236, 243

Profintern (garment factory), 190

Proletarianization. See labor

Proletarii (glassmaking factory), 168, 171, 192

Proudhon, Pierre-Joseph, 61

Pskov, 218

Purges, 3, 17; 1921 party purge, 24, 32, 34, 37, 40-51; 1929–1930, 140-46, 155-56, 239-40. See also Party Review of 1924–1925

Rabinovitch (builder), 173-74

Rabochii, 209, 215

race, 6, 82; antisemitism as, 210-12, 217, 226, 229, 230, 244-45; defined, 14-18; race-blind justice, 59, 61; Trotskyism and, 183, 205, 207. See also antisemitism

Raichuk, El'ia El'iashev, 95, 96-97, 103-104, 159

Rakhazel'skii (antireligious activist), 131-33

Rakovshchik, Iakov Zendelev, 71

Rashon (evpartshkola), 35, 48, 49

rationalization of industry. See economic rationalization

rationing, 89, 96, 175, 186

Rechitsa, 130, 200

Red Army, 5, 10, 43, 62, 66, 164; Civil War, 55-56, 84, 121, 220; after demobilization, 93, 103; Jews in, 31, 34-37, 48, 55-56, 57, 74, 75, 79, 198; Conquest of Belorussia, 21, 29, 33, 50; workshops for, 41, 89, 96

Revolution of 1905, 9-10, 25, 29, 49, 121, 138

Revolutionary Committees (revkoms), 36, 62, 138

Riga, 94

Rives (Narpit), 173

Rivo, Tsalia, 77

Rodzinskii (shoemaker), 99, 104

Rogachev, 135-36

Romashev, Nikolai, 75

Rosenberg (leatherworker), 165, 172

Rubenchik (shoemaker), 104
Rubinchik, Mota Tsalev, 215
Rudna (Russia), 218
Russian Civil War, 3, 10, 11, 23, 34, 55-56, 210, 241; as model for Great Break, 143, 175, 185, 221, 238; society during, 24, 59, 89, 95, 96, 121, 160. *See also* Pogroms, Red Army
Russian Social Democratic Workers Party (RSDWP), 8, 9, 28-29

St. Petersburg, 7, 94
Sadkovskii (metalworker), 167
Savchuk (brickmaker), 228
Savel'eva, Sofiia, 77
Savetskaia Belarus', 217
Scissors Crisis, 78-79, 104-107, 108, 174
schools and education, 10, 11, 12, 106, 119, 150, 209, 212, 245; Belorussian, 154, 170; Soviet Yiddish, 124-28, 135-37, 141, 142, 148, 152-53, 167-68; party, 40-51, 128. *See also* heder
seamstresses, 29, 32, 38; in KPB, 43, 45, 46, 47, 51, 133, 163; in Opposition, 182, 201
S'egnikov, Mikhail Aleksandrovich, 74
Sergeenko (matchstick maker), 230
Sewing Production Administration (Shveiprom), 105
Shafer (shoemaker), 192, 205
Shapiro, Iakov, 69
Shapiro, Mordukh, 75
Sharai (tanner), 225
Shatsk, 136, 141
Shavel, 94
Shelkov (brickmaker), 228
Shevelevich (brickmaker), 227-28
Shevkuna (Bolshevik activist), 63, 65
Shimeliovich, Iulius Abramovich, 83-84, 113
Shislevich, 94
Shneider (shoemaker), 192
shoemakers, 5, 24, 51, 93, 94-95, 215, 246; in Bund, 29, 38, 95, 163, 166; cultural activism, 126, 129; in KPB, 31, 32, 35, 41, 43; kustari, 95-97, 100, 101, 110, 213; in Opposition, 182, 192, 196, 197, 200, 201, 203, 204, 205-206; workshops, 98, 103-104, 105
shortages, 62, 99, 103, 175, 186, 243; crisis of NEP, 194, 213, 219, 221, 224; grain, 60, 63, 194; labor, 90, 163; leather, 97, 99

Shpeer (builders union), 226
Shteinklaper (evpartshkola), 45, 48
shtetl, 2, 8, 23, 24, 26, 78-79, 184, 213-14, 232-33; "Face to shtetl," 108, 132-37; kustari, 87, 100, 101, 107-10, 137, 144; Zionism, 109-11, 140-42; 232-33. *See also* individual shtetlekh by name
Shul'man, Il'ia, 74
Shul'man, Mariia, 74
Sirmanom (glassmaker), 226
Slutsk, 35, 40, 96, 130, 252
Smith, Adam, 60, 61
Smilovich, 136
Smolensk, 23, 138, 218
smuggling, 9, 71-72, 76, 107
smychka, 23, 103, 140, 142, 174
Sobol (glassmaker), 231-32
Socialist Revolutionary Party (SR), 26, 29, 31
Sovnarkom (Soviet of People's Commissars), 70, 159, 160, 189, 192, 239
Sovznak (currency), 57, 73, 77-78, 104
Spartak Workers' Club, 128-29
speculation, 36, 55-57, 58-59, 62-63, 104, 243; Bolshevik attacks against, 36, 63, 64-67, 70, 78, 91, 142-43; gold and money, 73-82; historical precedents, 60-61; Jews identified with, 67, 76-77, 79-82, 84-85, 91, 111, 232; NEP trade and, 68, 69-70, 70-73, 77-79; 91, 100; pogroms and, 65
Stalin (machine factory), 226
Stalin, Joseph Vissarionovich, 3, 151, 156, 157, 173, 188, 219; bloc, 174, 176, 181, 187, 188, 192, 202, 206
Stalin Revolution, 4, 13, 14, 17, 138, 207, 220-221, 230-245; antisemitism and, 172, 209-11, 212, 220, 224, 231-37; gender, 210, 225, industrialization, 150, 187-88, 206-208, 216, 224; Jewish life, 143-45, 156, 206
Stepanova (linen factory worker), 222, 223
strikes, 28, 49, 96, 98, 108, 184, 196, 206
Sukenik (evpartshkola), 44
Supreme Soviet of People's Economy (VSNKh), 92, 106, 166, 188, 205
Sverdlov, G., 30-31
Svisloch (shtetl), 171, 209, 213-14, 215, 216, 217, 227, 231, 234

Tabenko, 230-34

tailism, 148, 169

tailors, 24, 29, 51, 70, 118, 126; in KPB, 32, 38, 41, 43, 46, 92; kustari, 93, 100, 110; in Opposition, 182, 201, 206, 246

tanners. *See* leatherworkers

Tambov Rebellion, 68

taxation, 68, 91-92, 97, 101-102, 143, 171; evasion, 78, 72-73; kustari, 108, 109, 140; Stalin Revolution, 143, 221

Teklin (needleworker), 167

Timofeev (Narkomzem), 169

tobacco workers, 24, 28, 88, 95; in KPB, 33, 38, 43, 44

Tochilin, Aleksei Artemov, 214-15, 217

TorgStroi brick factory, 227-29

trade unions, 5, 23, 27, 28, 47; in antisemitism campaign, 218, 222, 227, 228; Jewish membership, 86, 88, 93, 161, 175, 203, 250, 251; kustari, 100, 101, 109; as schools of Communism, 102, 124, 125, 209; under Soviets, 95-99, 103-104, 118, 158, 185

Trotsky, Lev Davidovich, 9, 22, 34, 81, 104, 184, 187, 191; on antisemitism, 219; expulsion from party, 181-82, 195, 199, 201; on industry and labor, 185, 188, 189; Opposition, 193-94, 198; United Opposition, 182, 189, 190, 191, 192, 193, 200, 202, 204, 205, 206

Trotskyism, 13, 17, 181-85, 190, 196-207, 212, 224, 226, 230; antisemitism and, 181-83, 236, 238, 239, 243-44

Trudy, 230

Tsarenok (anti-Bundism activist), 168-69

Tsel'man, P. P., 159

Tshernov, Aron, 78

Tsirkin (Linen factory worker), 222-23

Tsygel'nitskii (evpartshkola), 46, 47

Tuliakov, Ivan Panfilov, 214, 217

Turnel'taub (professor), 202

Turov, 33, 131-33

Unemployment and layoffs, 28, 210, 212, 214, 235; NEP, 78, 93, 95, 99-100, 106, 111, 222; among kustari, 103, 105-106, 107, 137, 144, 147; Opposition, 191, 192, 194; Stalin Revolution, 175, 187, 189, 191; 195, 196

United Opposition. *See* Trotsky

Unzer Kultur, 121-22

Vikhman (student Oppositionist), 197

Vainer, Iosif Abramovich, 68, 92

Vainshtein, Aron Isaakovich (Rakhmiel), 39, 133, 240

Vaitsok (Narkompros), 168

Varlet, Jean, 60

Vezuvii (matchstick factory), 190, 230

Vilna, 7, 84, 138; Bund in, 8, 28, 29, 133; Polish-Soviet War, 30, 34, 67, 84

Vilenstovich, Pavel Grigor'evich, 191, 203

Vitebsk, 2, 7, 23, 128, 138-39, 252; antisemitism, 170, 218, 221-24; Bund in, 8, 9, 29, 165; industry, 106, 190, Jewish workers, 23, 24, 87, 93, 100; Opposition in, 181, 182, 190, 193, 196, 199, 201, 202, 204

Voitsekovskii, A., 36

Volabrinskii (bootmaker), 167-68

Vol'fson (evpartshkola), 43, 46

Volkov, Fedor Tikhonovich, 194-95, 196, 201

Vosk, Bronia Natanovna, 37-38

wages: inflation and, 105, 174, 183, 194; NEP, 98, 100, 103, 117, 147, 150; Opposition, 191-96, 207; Stalin Revolution, 188-89, 216, 222, 223, 224

Warsaw, 7, 25, 28, 37, 44, 94; Red Army offensive against 1920, 35, 36

War Communism, 58, 62-68, 71, 73-74, 89-90, 91, 96, 221

White-collar workers (sluzhashchii), 2, 147, 171; Jewish, 26, 42, 43, 51, 100, 182, 201, 226

woodworkers, 27, 32, 38, 95, 148, 206; trade union, 41, 88, 194, 250, 251

World War I, 10, 58, 73, 136, 152, 241; individuals during, 25, 43, 55, 56, 138

World War II, 6, 187, 235, 240

Workers' Opposition, 47, 95, 185

workshops, 4, 23, 41, 89, 93, 213, 221, 242; Bundism in, 149, 184; kustar', 87, 96-100, 103-104, 105-106; illegal, 57. *See also* specific industries

Yanka Kupala, 155, 239

Yiddish, 9-12, 38, 237, 245; cultural production, 64, 67, 75, 80-81, 116-18; on cultural front, 119-25, 133-34, 135-38, 139, 156; newspapers, 31, 38, 63, 67, 69, 78-82, 104, 149, 218, 240; language policy, 153, 154, 167-69, 171; schools, 126-28, 136, 167; in workers institutions, 44, 105, 167, 175, 203, 214